REAL WORLD PAGEMAKER 4

THE BANTAM ITC SERIES

REAL WORLD PAGEMAKER 4

Industrial Strength Techniques

Windows Edition

JESSE BERST

STEPHEN ROTH

OLAV MARTIN KVERN

SCOTT DUNN

BANTAM BOOKS
NEW YORK • TORONTO • LONDON • SYDNEY • AUCKLAND

REAL WORLD PAGEMAKER 4:
INDUSTRIAL STRENGTH TECHNIQUES
WINDOWS EDITION

A Bantam Book/June 1991

All rights reserved
Copyright © 1991 by Stephen Roth, Jesse Berst,
Olav Martin Kvern, and Scott Crandell Dunn.
Cover art © Gary Kelley.
Interior design by Nancy Sugihara

Throughout the book, the trade names and trademarks of
some companies and products have been used, and no
such uses are intended to convey endorsement of or other
affiliations with the book or software.
No part of this book may be reproduced or transmitted
in any form or by any means, electronic or mechanical,
including photocopying, recording, or by any information
storage and retrieval system, without permission in
writing from the publisher.

For information address: Bantam Books.

ISBN 0-553-35264-4

Published simultaneously in the United States and Canada

Bantam Books are published by Bantam Books, a
division of Bantam Doubleday Dell Publishing
Group, Inc. Its trademark consisting of the words
"Bantam Books" and the portrayal of a rooster, is
Registered in U.S. Patent and Trademark Office and
in other countries. Marca Registrada, Bantam Books,
666 Fifth Avenue, New York, New York 10103

PRINTED IN THE UNITED STATES OF AMERICA

0 9 8 7 6 5 4 3 2 1

FOREWORD

Pharaohs and Thunder Lizards

By Daniel Brogan
Editor-in-Chief
Personal Publishing

Be forewarned: This is not a book that's going to sit on your shelf looking impressive. It's going to spend its days open on your desk, always within easy reach. Before long, its pages are going to be dog-eared from use, the binding will crack from repeated openings, and a tribe of paper clips and Post-It notes will invade its chapters, serving as guides to your favorite tricks.

Because this isn't a book like all those other computer books you've seen. After all, how many computer books promise to make you into a "a raging, inexorable thunder lizard of a page maker?" In fact, it's not a computer book at all. It's a *publishing* book—a distinction that's crucial to the success it achieves. What you're about to learn in the pages ahead isn't the mechanics of running a piece of software. You'll be making pages.

But *Real World PageMaker 4* has more to recommend it than simply the right attitude. Steve Roth, Jesse Berst, Ole Kvern, and Scott Dunn bring to the table more combined PageMaker experience than you're likely to find anywhere else, in print or out.

Steve was my predecessor as editor at *Personal Publishing*. He's knowledgeable, tough, and the straightest shooter in town (sometimes too straight: I'm still taking heat for the time Steve referred—in print—to a major software vendor's pride and joy as "dog meat").

Ole is senior documentation designer at Aldus. But don't let that prissy title fool you. At Aldus, Ole is the Pharaoh of PageMaker—the guy the tech-support team turns to when everyone else is stumped.

Jesse Berst and Scott Dunn are Windows impressarios extraordinaire, and longtime PageMaker masters. Jesse has authored over a dozen books on desktop publishing, and his newsletter, *Windows Watcher*, is the authoritative word on Windows and the companies that make Windows move. Scott was producing a monthly magazine from the moment he got his hands on PageMaker's first beta (never mind how he got a copy). Jesse and Scott are the Windows PageMaker gurus that everyone should have around the office.

Together, they form a remarkable team: the tough outsider, the savvy insider, and the guys in the know. And they're funny to boot.

So remember: If you just want something that will look impressive on your shelf, maybe you should try one of those other books. Or better yet, buy another copy of *Real World PageMaker*. These guys won't mind a bit.

PREFACE

About 97,515 Words Ago...

"So what should we do?"

"Let's write a PageMaker book."

"Is there anything new to say about PageMaker?"

"Oh . . . I guess not."

When we first discussed writing a PageMaker book, we decided that there just wasn't enough material that hadn't been covered elsewhere. About a week later, we thought again, and we'd been thinking the same thing: that the PageMaker techniques we routinely used and talked about weren't covered in the manuals, and weren't covered in any of the books on the market.

We finally realized that like the authors of every other PageMaker book to date, we had been seduced by PageMaker's fluid interface—by its reach-out-and-touch-it, warm-and-fuzzy look and feel. Even though we use dozens of tricky techniques in PageMaker day in and day out, we'd been lulled into complacency, fooled into thinking that there wasn't much to say beyond the standard PageMaker book's waltz through the menus.

We'd also started to believe something we'd heard—from the advertisements of PageMaker's competitors, from software reviewers for magazines, and even from Aldus: that PageMaker is easy to learn, has an elegant user interface, and excels at producing a wide variety of documents, but just isn't as powerful as the competition. Just isn't suited for high-end users. Or just isn't good enough for professional typographers.

Going Deep

We wrote this book because we wanted to show that PageMaker is not only easy to learn and use, but is also deep and powerful. PageMaker's user interface itself empowers users by being elegant, pleasant, and operating in an intuitively obvious fashion. Like Windows, there's far more to PageMaker than its surface. There's a diabolically powerful engine inside for laying out pages, newsletters, magazines, books, and encyclopedias.

So we thought some more. We started building lists of the devious techniques that we use. We searched back issues of all the magazines, scoured the online services, went through all the other PageMaker books, talked to every PageMaker aficionado we know (and we know lots), and came up with enough material to convince us that we really had a book.

That exercise convinced us of something else, as well: PageMaker users really need this book. Unlike the plethora of excellent, in-depth, tip-laden books on Ventura Publisher, PageMaker books are almost all of the how-to-design-your-newsletter variety. There is no compendium of the techniques that hundreds of thousands of PageMaker users have developed over the last five years. And no book really dives into PageMaker's hidden depths—things like precise positioning, paragraph rules, and making PageMaker work with your Windows setup.

In fact, not one of the books we looked at explains satisfactorily how PageMaker handles leading—an important topic, to say the least. There are huge, gaping holes in the material available on using PageMaker, patched only sporadically by tip-and-tricks and how-to columns in various magazines. The tips in this book go a long way, we hope, toward filling those holes.

PREFACE **ix**

PageMaker and the Real World

We didn't want to just put together a list of tips, though. If you're coming to visit us once, we're happy to tell you to turn left at the second tree and right at the fire hydrant (the press-this-key approach to computer books). If you're living in the neighborhood, though, you'd better get a map and learn your way around. We wanted to create the definitive roadmap and explanation of how PageMaker works—how it "thinks" about pages—and how you can best work within its metaphors.

Finally—and perhaps this is the most important—we wanted to make clear throughout the book that PageMaker doesn't exist in a vacuum. There are hundreds of things that affect you when you're building PageMaker pages—from the way you've got your Windows system set up, to the printing method you're using, to your colleague across the office who yells out "Hey, Harry! I've got an update of that sidebar!" and tosses you a disk. All the PageMaker expertise in the world means nothing if it's not informed by knowledge of the whole publishing process, and how to make that process smooth and seamless.

Because we want you to understand PageMaker's role in the publishing process, you'll find some lengthy conceptual discussions here—discussions of how PageMaker works, how Windows works, how publishing works, and how they all work together in the real world. The idea is to develop your own PageMaker expertise—building the comprehensive body of knowledge that becomes so ingrained that it looks and feels like intuition.

On Becoming a Monster

Intuition is often the subconscious product of bitter experience. We have developed our intuitive approaches to PageMaker through intensive use of the product (expletives deleted). We've been through the tight deadlines, the pages that, for some reason, refused to print, and the files that wouldn't open. We've produced piles of published pages several stories tall (including hundreds of pages using prerelease versions of PageMaker 4—not a pretty sight).

Along the way, we've been able to pass on our experience to dozens of others, creating new monster PageMaker users—sometimes in less than a week. Now, with this book, we want to do the same for you. We want to make you to PageMaker what Godzilla was to Tokyo—a raging, inexorable thunder lizard of a page maker, letting nothing stand in your way.

About this Book

We've tried to address many different types of PageMaker users in this book—from newcomers with strong backgrounds in typography and design, to long-time PageMaker pros who still probably don't know all the tricks hidden away in the program, to beginners who want to get started on the right foot—using the program the way the pros do.

This book is for PageMaker users who want to use the program right—the way it was designed to work—and for those who want to make it do double back flips. Unfortunately, those two goals are not always compatible.

PageMaker's design encourages a certain working style, and it's nice to you when you adopt that style. Pages come together smoothly, and page elements act the way they're supposed to act. Wherever possible, we espouse methods that work well within PageMaker's metaphors and that PageMaker can handle with ease. These techniques are much preferable to fighting the program, trying to do things in ways that confuse or enrage PageMaker.

At the same time, we often need to do things that PageMaker wasn't designed to do. You'll find a number of tips and tricks herein that make Aldus engineers blanch. Some of those techniques are not elegant, and a few are downright hacks ("greasy," our tech reviewer said). They essentially solve problems by fooling PageMaker into doing things it doesn't really know how to do.

Just because some of our techniques seem complicated, though, that doesn't necessarily mean they're not proper ways to use PageMaker. If you take the time to work through them, and get a feel for how they operate within PageMaker's working style, you'll go a long way toward developing your own relationship with PageMaker, and learning your own ways of cajoling it into amazing and previously untried machinations.

Organization

The organization of this book is simple—just like most of the chapter titles. We begin with the basics—building your system and whipping PageMaker into line—then move on to the main subject areas—words, pictures, printing, color, and using PageMaker in a workgroup. Here's a rundown of the chapters.

Chapter 1: What's New in PageMaker 4. The latest release of PageMaker adds dozens of new features, and new ways to use existing features. This chapter is written mainly for PageMaker 3 users who are moving up to version 4 and want a quick overview of the new features. If you want to go deeper, we've included page references for each feature, directing you to lengthier discussions in later chapters.

Chapter 2: Building a PageMaker System. There's a lot more to using PageMaker than just using PageMaker. From your Windows system to fonts, graphics programs, and utilities, there are dozens of little tools that comprise a complete PageMaker system. This chapter talks about putting all those pieces together into a working package, and describes our favorite tools and utilities.

Chapter 3: Making PageMaker Mind. This chapter explains how PageMaker works, and how you can best work with it. It covers the pasteboard, the Toolbox, selecting, moving, and sizing page elements, and modifying PageMaker to work the way you do.

Chapter 4: Words. Words are the basic building blocks of most PageMaker publications. This chapter covers stories, text blocks, paragraph and character formatting, style sheets, text editing tools, and text import filters, with a dose of special type effects for emphasis.

Chapter 5: Pictures. Words alone can make for dull publications. This chapter talks about creating graphics in PageMaker, bringing them in from other programs, and working your will on them no matter where they come from. It covers the various graphics formats you can import, and how to size them, crop them, and control their appearance.

Chapter 6: Printing. When you come right down to it, printing is what PageMaker is all about. This chapter covers all the options in the Print dialog box, and the seemingly endless series of dialog boxes that emanate from it.

Chapter 7: Color. You can get color out of PageMaker in several ways—by printing on a color printer, producing spot color overlays, or running PageMaker PostScript through a process separation program. This chapter explains the best ways to specify color in PageMaker, and the best ways to produce and reproduce that color.

Chapter 8: Workgroup Publishing. Using PageMaker proficiently is one thing. Using it proficiently with two, five, or fifty other people is something else again. This chapter discusses PageMaker's place in the workgroup environment, and focuses on PageMaker's new tools for keeping track of source files.

Chapter 9: How We Made this Book. We used many, if not most, of the techniques discussed in this book in making the book itself. This chapter details the production process for *Real World PageMaker 4*, including a fully-documented style sheet.

Appendix: Resources. The appendix lists all the products mentioned in the book, and provides addresses and phone numbers for the companies from which they are available.

Finding What You Need

We've tried to organize the book so you can get at the information in several ways. You can read the book from beginning to end, of course (being the authors, we highly recommend this method). For the less hardy (or foolhardy), we've divided the chapters with heads hanging in the margins. You can scan through those heads, or look through the table of contents that follows this preface. All the first- and second-level heads are included there along with the chapter heads, so you can jump right to the topic that interests you.

We've also encapsulated all of our favorite techniques in tips—easily recognizable, because they start with the word "Tip." There's a list of tips following the table of contents. Finally, if you just have one question about using PageMaker, or are trying to remember where you saw something, you can resort to the index in the back of the book.

If we get enough requests, in the next edition we're going to use an *Information Anxiety*-style table of contents (we call it that because it's been made popular by Richard Saul Wurman's book by that name), with little write-ups of each chapter right there in the contents. We decided against using one in this book because Steve thinks they promote information anxiety rather than assuaging it. Ole disagrees. Send your ballot now.

Conventions

We wanted this book to be as immediately accessible and intuitively obvious as PageMaker, so we've avoided clogging it up with lots of little icons and typographic cues that nobody can understand without an explanation. We did face the difficulty of identifying items in PageMaker, however—dialog boxes, menus and menu items, options, commands, etc. To make it easy, we've established one simple convention: if we identify an item when we name it (the Preferences *dialog box*, the Snap to rulers *option*, 400% *page view*), we simply leave it at that. If we don't identify the item, we put quotes around it (with "Snap to rulers" on, zoom to "400%," select "Image control"). The only exceptions are standard Windows commands (Save, New, Open, etc.), which don't need quotation marks. It's so simple that you probably didn't even need to read this section.

Disclaimer

Kids! Don't try this at home! Some of the techniques described in this book are truly industrial strength, and like the person pouring molten metal at the steel mill, you should either know what you're doing, or be prepared to accept the consequences of your actions before you attempt them. Here are several rules to keep in mind when you're using *Real World PageMaker 4*.

Always work on copies of files, never on the originals. If you don't keep a backup file, how will you be able to retrace your steps when something goes wrong?

Don't call Aldus technical support if something you read in this book doesn't work. They're the best in the business, but they're not responsible for what we've written, and shouldn't be expected to support it. Instead, write to us c/o Bantam Computer Books, and we'll try to put changes and fixes in future editions (we're expecting the 23rd edition to be published sometime in 2027). We want to provide you the most powerful set of PageMaker tools, but we assume you will use them responsibly, and at your own risk.

Think of others. If you modify your defaults, your dictionary, or your tracking tables, remember to protect other users on your network or your service bureau by making sure your modified files aren't used inadvertently by others. Few things can cause more trouble for your publishing cohorts than a font file that you've changed without telling anyone and without saving it under another name.

Acknowledgments

We hate to end on such an admonitory note, so we'll resort to thanks and congratulations. Congratulations to everyone at Aldus for delivering a great product in spite of incredible pressures, and thanks in particular to Ben Rotholz, jwhiting, John "that's almost certainly a bug" Nelson, Mitch "Deep Page" Boss, Doug Stuart, Matt Crosby, Tim Roth, Robin Briggs, Ann Sauer, Sheri Hargus, Eric McCashey, Laura Urban Perry, Harry C. Edwards, Stacy "those keys are fixed now, really!" Robinson, and to John V. and Patricia Callander Hedtke. Very special thanks to Jan C. Wright and Tracy Tobin, the other surviving members of the original Documentation Graphics team, and to Dave Fogelsong, Joe Friend, Jeff Harmon, Alan Wagner, Reuben Lam, Jeff Rowley, Diane Catt, Janet Williams, Conrad Chavez, Maire Masco, Pam Trebon, and Beth Norton of Aldus Technical Support. Our deep and abiding thanks to the founding members of Aldus—Paul Brainerd, Jeremy Jaech, Mark Sundstrom, Mike Templeman, and Dave Walter—for creating PageMaker and thereby empowering designers, illustrators, writers, and editors everywhere.

Thanks also go to Mike Roney, one of the few computer book editors who deserves the title (he's even on MCI Mail); Kenzi Sugihara, for publishing thoroughbred books; Louise Domenitz at Bitstream for providing us with this great version of the Garamond family; Chris Dickman for his help with Chapter 5; Don Sellers for his attention to detail and keen editorial insights; Pike Place Brewery for the "river of beer"; Chuck Cantellay and the whole staff of Seattle ImageSetting for helping us nurse the book out of the Lino; Leslie Simons, for her charm and wit; and Susie Hammond for her sharp eye and warm heart. We owe so many people so many favors that we've probably missed a few. If you're among them, thanks. We couldn't have done it without you.

Steve Roth
Jesse Berst
Ole Kvern
Scott Dunn

Overview

CHAPTER 1
What's New in PageMaker 4 1

CHAPTER 2
Building a PageMaker System 13

CHAPTER 3
Making PageMaker Mind 61

CHAPTER 4
Words 103

CHAPTER 5
Pictures 259

CHAPTER 6
Printing 311

CHAPTER 7
Color 375

CHAPTER 8
Workgroup Publishing 393

CHAPTER 9
How We Made This Book 411

APPENDIX A
Resources 421

Contents

FOREWORD

Pharaohs and Thunder Lizards v

PREFACE

About 97,515 Words Ago… vii

CHAPTER 1

What's New in PageMaker 4 1

    Words 1
        Story Editor 1
        Text Block Tools 2
        Text Place Filters 3
        Character Formatting 4
        Paragraph Formatting 5

    Pictures 7
        Inline Graphics 7
        Wrapping Around Master Items 8
        Color 8

Books 8
- *Table of Contents 9*
- *Indexing 9*

General Features 9
- *Paste 9*
- *Links 10*
- *Page Numbering 10*
- *Help 10*
- *Table Editor 11*

Going to Pages 11

CHAPTER 2

Building a PageMaker System 13

Windows and the PC 14
- *PageMaker 4 and Windows 15*

Of Fonts and Faces 17
- *Rasters of the Universe 17*
- *The Bottom Outline 18*
- *Screen Fonts 19*
- *Printer Fonts 21*
- *A Word about TrueType 21*

These Are a Few of Our Favorite Things 21

Printing and Type Tools 22
- *Adobe Type Manager 22*
- *FaceLift 25*
- *SuperPrint 26*

Art and Design Tools 28
- *Scrapbook+ 28*
- *Screen Captures Part One: The Cheap Way 30*
- *Screen Captures Part Two: The Right Way 32*
- *The Graphics Link Plus 33*
- *ExpressPage 34*

File Tools 36
- *File Manager 36*
- *Command Post 38*
- *Prompt 39*
- *File Organizer 41*

General Utilities 42
Sysedit 42
Macro Makers 43
Recorder 44
Recorder Run 48
BatchWorks 51
Launch 53
RunProg 55
Anything You Can Do Icon Do Better 56
hDC First Apps 57
Dinger 60

Living With Your System 60

CHAPTER 3

Making PageMaker Mind 61

Rules to Live By 61

Getting Ready 63
Turning On 65
Changing PageMaker's Defaults 66

The Publication Window 68

The Toolbox 70

Getting from Place to Place 72
Zooming 72
Turning Pages 74

Working with Pages 76
Working with Master Pages 77
Displaying Master Items 77
Adding Page Numbers 77
Adding and Deleting Pages 79

Selecting Objects 79

Moving Objects 82
Moving Groups of Objects 83
Constraining Movement 83

Rulers, Ruler Guides, and Measuring 84
Rulers 85
Ruler Guides 85
Measurement Increments 86
Snap to Guides and Snap to Rulers 88

Using Paste 90
- *Power Paste* 90

Using the Place Command 92
- *Installing Import and Export Filters* 92
- *Place Guns* 93
- *Using Replace* 95

PageMaker 4's Book Command 95

Saving Your Work 98

Other People's Pages 100

PageMaker Help 101

CHAPTER 4

Words 103

PageMaker, Text, and Type 103
- *Taking Measure* 104
- *What's an Em?* 105

Stories and Text Blocks 106
- *Column Guides* 113

Creating Text Blocks 116
- *Vanishing Text Blocks* 119
- *Replacing Text* 120
- *Moving and Resizing Text Blocks* 120
- *Rotating Text Blocks* 122

Inside Text Blocks 122
- *Moving Through and Selecting Text* 122

Formatting Text 124
- *Paragraphs and Characters* 125

Vertical Spacing 126
- *Leading* 126
- *PageMaker Leading* 127
- *Space Before and Space After* 128
- *Leading Methods* 129
- *Leading Grids* 131
- *Custom Rulers and Leading Grids* 132
- *Dealing with Anomalies* 133
- *Understanding Align to Grid* 136
- *Custom Vertical Rulers* 138

Horizontal Spacing and Alignment 139
   Working with Tabs 142
   Tab Selection 142
   Take Me to Your (Tab) Leader 148
   Using Table Editor 151
   That Pesky Spacing Dialog Box 155
   Tracking 157
   Paragraph Rules 159
   Playing for Keeps 164
   Column and Page Breaks 167

Character Formatting 168
   Type Specs 168
   Keyboard Shortcuts for Character Formatting 169
   Set Width 169
   Fun with Type options 169
   Kerning Text 173
   Kerning in PageMaker 4 175
   Fractions and Drop Caps 176

Working with Styles 184
   The Hard Way 184
   Styles, Tags, and Codes 185
   Local Formatting 186
   Using the Styles Palette 189
   Based on and Next style 191

Editing Text 198
   Using Special Characters 198

The Story Editor 202
   Finding and Changing Text 205
   Checking Spelling 208
   Adding to the Dictionary 210
   PageMaker's Dictionaries 212

Hyphenation in PageMaker 213
   Hyphenation Methods 214
   Hyphenation Control 215
   In the Hyphenation Zone 216
   Dictionary Hyphenation 218

Book Tools 219
   Let's TOC 220
   Generating an Index 221
   Creating Index Entries 222
   Formatting the Index 225

Index Levels 227
Sort Entries 228
See and See also 228
Index Ranges 230

Importing Text 231
Text import options 231

Working with text filters 232
Importing from Word and WinWord 232
Word's Own Import Dialog Box 233
Importing Text from WordPerfect 238
Importing ASCII Text 240
Importing Rich Text Format Files 241
The PageMaker Story Filter 244

Importing Database Files 246
Importing dBase Files 246
DataShaper 248
PageAhead 249
Importing Spreadsheets 251

The Time and Date Filter 253

Getting Text Out of PageMaker 255

Fixing Bad RIX 257

CHAPTER 5

Pictures 259

Graphics in PageMaker 260
Working with Layers 260

PageMaker's Drawing Tools 262
Lines and Fills 262
Precise Line Positioning 264
Constraining LBOs 266

Pasting Graphics From the Clipboard 267

Placing Graphics 267
Bitmaps and Objects 268
File Types 268
Formats and Filters 269
Bitmapped Graphics 269
Object-oriented Graphics 270
Creating EPS Graphics with PageMaker 274

Back to Placing 278
Replacing Graphics 280

Working with Bitmaps 282
Image Control 282
Displaying Bitmapped Graphics 285
Resizing Placed Graphics 286
Magic Stretch 287

Cropping Placed Graphics 289

Inline Graphics 292
Selecting and Modifying Inline Graphics 293
Horizontal Positioning for Inline Graphics 295
Leading for Inline Graphics 297

Using Text Wrap 302
Wrapping Around Master Items 308

Getting Graphic 310

CHAPTER 6

Printing 311

Setting the Target Printer 312

PageMaker and Printer Fonts 314
A WIN.INI Primer 315
Resident Fonts 317
Adding and Removing Soft Fonts 319
Copying Soft Fonts between Ports 321
Soft Fonts: Automatic/Temporary Downloading 323
Soft Fonts: Manual/Semipermanent Downloading 325
Soft Fonts: Manual/Permanent Downloading 330
Soft Fonts: The Rasterizer Option 331
The Blight of the Bloated WIN.INI 331

The Micrografx PostScript Driver 333

The Print Dialog Box 335

Setup 346

The PostScript Printer Dialog Box 349
PostScript Options 350

PCL/Hewlett-Packard LaserJet Dialog Box 353

Printing PostScript to Disk 355

Prism: PostScript Without Pain 358
   Mirror and Negative 359
   Rotate Pages 359
   Scaling 360
   Halftone Screens 360

Handy PostScript Programs 363

Changing PageMaker's PostScript 364
   PostScript Dictionaries 365
   Making a Copy of Win33Dict 365
   Outline text 366

Printing Problems 369

CHAPTER 7

Color 375

Color Printing Techniques 376
   Color Models 377
   Overlays and Separations 378

Defining Colors 378

Applying Colors and Fills 380
   The Color Paper 382

Color Specs and Color Correspondence 383
   Color Printer Output 384
   Spot Color Output 384
   Four-Color Printing 386

Overprinting, Knockouts, and Traps 387
   Getting Trapped 389

CHAPTER 8

Workgroup Publishing 393

What You're Trying to Achieve 393

What You're Trying to Avoid 394
   The Fascist Approach Versus the Laissez-Faire Ideal 395

Link, Link info, and Link options 396

Live Files and Dead Files 402
   File Transfer Methods 406

Dealing with Text Files 407
Using Export with Links 408

Dealing with Graphic Files 409

If at First... 409

CHAPTER 9

How We Made This Book 411

Design 411

Fonts 412

Styles 412

Table of Contents 419

Index 420

Imagesetting 420

APPENDIX

Resources 421

Tips

Building a PageMaker System 13

Thanks for the Memory 16
Keep an Even Hand 16
Enhanced Ain't Necessarily So 16
Use a Font Rasterizer 20
Mix and Match 20
Remove then Delete 20
Maximizing ATM's Screen Font Powers 23
The Plus Pack Pressure Ploy 24
But the Fonts I've Installed are Printing as Courier! 24
The Old Switcheroo 27
Who's Zooming Whom 30
Edit First, then Crop 31
The Wonderful World of Monochrome 31
Keep It Handy 36
Recorder Does Windows 37
Loading Your Macros Automatically 45
Masterful Methods for Multiple Macro Mavens 46
The Autoexecuting Macro 47
Use Keystrokes Your Keyboard Doesn't Have 49
Use Key Words, Not Keystrokes 49
Managing Icon Macros 50
Punch In and Out with BatchWorks 52
The Launch-RecRun-Recorder Triple Play 53
Launch does BatchWorks 54
Use RunProg to launch apps from File Manager 56

Making PageMaker Mind 61

Changing PageMaker's Startup Directory 65
Remapping PageMaker's Keyboard Shortcuts with Windows Recorder 67
Close All Dialog Boxes 68
Constraining Tools 70
Selecting Tools with Function Keys 71
Toggling the Pointer Tool 72
Use the Grabber Hand 72
Fit in World 74

Saving Time on a Two-Sided Document 75
Changing to fit in Window View as You Change Pages 75
Changing Page View for All Pages 75
Viewing Your Pages One After Another 75
Adding Pages with a Loaded Gun 79
Selecting the Unselectable 82
Selecting Through Layers 82
Moving Before Constraining Movement 83
Positioning Identical Objects Directly on Top of Each Other 84
Use Custom for Vertical Rulers 85
Copying Master Guides 86
Graphic Design's Native Measurement System 87
To Enter Values in Inches When the Default is Set to Picas 87
Typing Picas and Points 87
Don't Cancel that Place 89
An Odd Thing About Snap to Guides 89
Evenly Spaced Objects 89
Copying Master Items 92
Placing from Right to Left and Bottom to Top 95
Cancelling a Place 95
Quick-Copying Your Book List to Every Chapter 97
Continuous Page Numbering 97
Overriding Continuous Page Numbering 98
Forcing PageMaker to renumber the publications in your book list 98
Make Mini Book Lists for Sections of a Book 98
Recovering from Crashes 99
Skip the RAM Disk 99
Mini-Revert 100
Using Save as to Compress Your file 100
Make All Saves Save As 100
Meet Your Makers 101

Words 103

Deleting Threaded Text Blocks 108
Moving Items from Page to Page 109
Careful Method for Combining Unlinked Text Blocks 109
Alternative Rather Dashing Method for Combining Text Blocks 110
Emergency Method for Combining Unthreaded Text Blocks 111
Yet another way to combine stories 112
Using More Column Guide than You Have Columns 113
Using Odd Numbers of Columns for Asymmetrical Layouts 113
Creating Different Margins on Facing Pages 114
Finding the Horizontal Center of a Column 114
Finding the Horizontal Center of a Column (Alternate Method) 115
Small Text Blocks 117
Text Import Filters 118
Text Blocks that Don't Vanish 119
Resizing with Multiple Objects Selected 121
Move and Select 124

Select All 124
Select a Paragraph or a Word 124
Use the Text Tool 125
Selecting Paragraphs and Characters 126
Use Space Before and After Instead of Carriage Returns 128
Retaining Space Before 128
Designing for Leading Grids 133
More Type than Leading 133
Multiple Styles for Multiple-line Heads 135
Bullet List Leading 135
Placing Illustrations 139
Keyboard Shortcuts for Type Alignment 139
Use the New-line Character 141
Aligning Tabs Quickly 143
Use the New-line Character Within Tabular Matter 143
Use a Tab for Hanging Indents 144
Shift-Dragging the Indent Marker 146
Decimal/Right Aligning Numbered Lists 146
Flush Right/Flush Left 147
Aligning Financial Tabular Matter 148
Changing The Font of Tab Leader Characters 149
Make These Tabs Like Those 149
Changing Borders 151
Two Fonts in a Single Cell 153
Export Columnar Text from Table Editor 154
Zooming in Table Editor 154
New Lines in Table Editor 155
See Loose and Tight Lines 156
Slaves to Fashion 163
Orphan Killer 165
Setting Widow/Orphan Controls 166
Keeping Heads with Text 166
Use Column break before for Heads in a Companion Column 167
PageMaker 3 Tip: Forcing Column Breaks 167
Faking "Paragraph break after" 167
Type Within Type 171
More Snazzy Type 172
Kerning Whole Words 176
Lose that Kerning 176
Creating Drop Caps as Graphics 177
The Old, Slow Method of Creating Drop Caps 178
The New, Nifty Way to Create Drop Caps 179
Fraction-making Macros 182
Automate Character Styles with Change 186
Retaining Local Formatting While Changing Styles 187
Getting Rid of Local Formatting 188
Use Keyboard Shortcuts to Apply Styles 189
Use Recorder to Apply Styles 190
Creating Styles by Example 190
Easy Way to Edit Styles 190

Easy Way to Base One Style on Another 192
Merging Two Styles 192
Copy Styles Between Documents for Formatting Consistency 195
Build Specialized Style Sheets 195
Export Styles for Use in Word 196
Printing Your Styles 196
Exporting Styles to Word for Windows 197
Use FirstApps for Quick Access to Foreign Characters 202
Use Recorder for Quick Access to Foreign Characters 202
Delete Next Character Right 205
Reverting all Change Attributes to Any 206
Special Characters Used in the Find and Change Dialog Boxes 207
Using Searches to Enter Index Topics 208
Adding Without Replacing 211
Removing Words 211
Wraparound Spell Checking 211
Check Selected Word 212
Swapping User Dictionaries 212
Using Multiple Language Dictionaries 213
Keeping Words from Breaking 218
Keeping Words Together 218
Keeping Compound Words from Breaking 219
Other Nonbreaking Characters 219
Where You Can Put Your Table of Contents 221
The Fast Way to Build a Topic List 223
Multiple Topics for a Single Range 224
Super-Quick Index Entries 224
Quick Index Entries for Names 224
Instant Capitalization 225
Viewing Your Index Entries 226
Word's Margins and PageMaker's Paragraph Indents 237
Applying Interesting Formatting to Database Fields 247
Importing Date Fields 248
Value Formats 251
Tab stops in the XLS and WKS styles 252
Move Spreadsheets Through the Table Editor 252
Placing a Time/Date Stamp as an Inline Graphic 255
Exporting All Stories 255
Text and Tags 255
Recompose World 256

Pictures 259

White-out Boxes 261
Bringing Multiple Objects to Front 261
Selecting Different Layers 261
Use Recorder to Select Lines and Fills 263
Custom Gray Fills 263
Positioning Thick Diagonal Lines 265
Sizing LBOs Proportionally 266
When You Can't See a File You Know Is There 269

Don't Name Your EPS Files—Yet 275
Creating Your Own EPS Graphics 277
Extracting EPS Files 277
Extending your Range of Fills with EPS Graphics 280
Replacing LBOs with EPS Shades 281
Replacing Paint-type Graphics 282
Image Control Settings for Gray-scale Images 283
Improving Bitmapped Clip Art 283
Making Bitmaps Negative 284
Switching to High Resolution 285
The Vanishing Point 286
Resizing Graphics to a Mathematical Proportion of their Original Size 286
Use the Right Target Printer 289
Changing Target Printers 289
Cropping a Placed Graphic Proportionally 290
Cut, Don't Crop 292
Colorizing Placed Graphics 292
Redraw Your Screen 293
Make Graphics Inline to Center Them 295
Incredible Horizontal Positioning Accuracy with Inline Graphics 296
Precise Repeating Graphics 297
Using Autoleading with Inline Graphics 299
Slugs the size of graphics 300
Boxed Paragraphs 301
Hanging Inline Graphics in the Companion Column 302
A Graphic's Wrap Boundaries Can be Anywhere 305
Delaying Text Reflow When Adjusting Wraps 305
Angled Margins 305
Inside-out Text Wrap 306

Printing 311

Back Up That File 314
Rereading WIN.INI 317
Reorganizing WIN.INI 317
Adding Font Metrics for Resident Fonts 318
Don't Mix Font Metric Files 319
Removing Fonts with ATM 319
Download the Most Frequently Used Typefaces 326
Download Selected Fonts on Startup 327
Multiple Batch Files for Customized Downloading 327
Speeding Up Font-Downloading Batch Files 328
Batch Files for Customized Downloading 329
Downloading Selected Fonts on Startup 329
Dig Out Those Adobe Floppies 334
Skip the Font Print Out 335
Voodoo Page Ranges 336
Fitting Tabloids on Letter and Legal Paper 337
Improving Output Resolution 337
Have the Printer Overexpose to Smooth out Jaggies 337
Chill Out Those Pages Before Printing Side Two 338

Printing Outside the Page Area 340
Hang Rotated Items off the Sides of Pages 342
Double Your Pages, Double Your Funds 343
Another Way to Get Double Pages 344
Use "Extra" Sizes for Imagesetters 347
Multiple Copies for Duplication Fanatics 348
Download the Header Semipermanently for Faster Printing 352
Install Your Printer Twice 356
Selective Downloading of Typefaces to PostScript Files 356
Scaling to Match True Printer's Points 360
Defaults Faults 361
What You Ask for Ain't What You Get 362
If a TIFF Image Prints as a Low-resolution Bitmap 372
Forever and a Day 372
Nested EPS Files 372

Color 375

Additional Color Printing Options 376
The Fast Way to Define Colors 378
The Fast Way to Redefine Colors 379
Taking Advantage of Being Unable to Apply Color to Text Blocks 380
Spot Color Tints for Type 381
Gray Type 381
PageMaker-drawn Graphics Print on the Wrong Overlay 382
To See What it Will Look Like on Colored Paper 383
Easier-to-Read Composites 384
Use Process Separation for Spot Color Printing 385
Use PMS Color Names and Numbers 385
Working with Spot Colors on a Monochrome Display 385
To Replace Every Instance of One Color with a Different Color 386
Blacks that are Really Black 387
Knockouts of EPS Graphics 388
Trapping LBOs 390
Overprinting Thin Lines 390
Traps for Process Colors 391

Workgroup Publishing 393

Use WinWord's Compare Versions 400
Using Link info as Replace 401
Link Placeholders for Automatic Replacement 402
Use Naming System for Source Files 403
Name Publication Files with Version Numbers 405
Name Publication Files with Dates 405
If You've Already Placed It 406

CHAPTER 1

What's New in PageMaker 4

If you want to find out quickly what's new in PageMaker 4, this chapter is for you. It's also a good pathway into the book as a whole. We've divided the new features into four categories—words, pictures, books, and general features—and each feature discussion ends with a page reference telling you where to look for more details.

Words

Most of the changes in PageMaker 4 are in the areas of text and type. This latest version removes almost every limitation that typophiles railed against in earlier versions, and adds a nice complement of word-processing tools.

Story Editor Triple-clicking on a text block in PageMaker launches the Story Editor, and a whole new view of the story appears—the story view. Story view provides a robust text-editing environment, unencumbered by how the copy fits into your layout. You can just scroll through the story and edit it, without PageMaker having to recompose the story with every keystroke. You can see local style changes such as bold and italic in story view, and the style bar on the left shows you what style is applied to each paragraph. See page 202.

In addition to a better environment for text editing, the Story Editor also adds searching, replacing, and spell checking.

Find and change. The Find and Change functions in PageMaker 4 are very similar to search and replace in Word or Word for Windows, but they go much further. You can use special codes to find and change all of PageMaker's special characters, for instance—thin spaces, discretionary hyphens, etc. You can also search for certain formatting attributes—paragraph style, font, size, and type style—and change them to other attributes.

You can even combine character- and attribute-based changes, to change the formatting for any occurrence of "PageMaker," for example, to 16-point Brush Script. PageMaker will do any of this finding or changing throughout the publication, the story, or the selected range of text. See page 205.

Spell checking. The other major feature of the Story Editor is spell checking. It uses the same dictionaries as the hyphenation routines, so you can fine-tune both at once. See page 208.

Text Block Tools

PageMaker 4 has two new features for working with text blocks. You can now rotate text blocks, and the improved icons on the top and bottom windowshade handles give you a better idea of how selected blocks are threaded to other blocks.

Text rotation. You can rotate text blocks in 90-degree increments, as long as they're not threaded to other text blocks, and as long as all the text in that story has been placed. See page 122.

Windowshade icons. PageMaker 3 showed a + sign in a windowshade handle if the text continued (whether that continued text had been placed or not), a blank handle at the beginning of a story, and a

sign at the end. In PageMaker 4, you get a little more information, and the conventions have changed a bit. A blank windowshade handle means there's no more text preceding or following that text block, so they only appear at the beginning and end of stories. A + sign means that there's more placed text preceding or following the text block—it's threaded to another text block. A down arrow (the "overset indicator") in a bottom windowshade handle means there's more text in the story that hasn't been placed yet. See page 106.

Text Place Filters
The filters that PageMaker uses to place various kinds of text files are much improved in this version, and there are more of them (hold down Ctrl and select "About PageMaker" from the Help menu to get a list of your installed text filters). They're also easier to install. If you didn't get all the ones you needed when you installed PageMaker, you can add more with the Aldus Setup utility that is added to Program Manager when you install PageMaker.

WordPerfect. Where previous versions of PageMaker only imported the most rudimentary of formatting from WordPerfect (like bold, italic, and the like), the WordPerfect filter in PageMaker 4 imports just about all WordPerfect's formatting—up to and including styles and style sheets. See page 238.

Microsoft Word. PageMaker features import filters for both Microsoft Word (for DOS) and Word for Windows. The Word for Windows filter lets you control a number of aspects of the file as it's placed—how PageMaker handles page breaks, for example, and table of contents and index entries. It also imports WinWord's footnote references correctly. See page 232.

Rich Text Format. With the new RTF filter, you can import and export files in this extremely robust (though somewhat clunky) ASCII text format. Everything that you can specify in a Microsoft Word document can be coded in ASCII using RTF , including styles, local formatting, and graphics. See page 241.

Lotus 1-2-3, Excel, and dBase. When you choose to place a file from Lotus 1-2-3, Excel, or dBase, you get a dialog box that lets you control several aspects of how the file is imported. You can control the order that fields are imported from dBase, the styles that are applied, and how PageMaker should align imported values, among other things. You can also import an Excel range as a graphic, and when you Ctrl-double click on that graphic, PageMaker launches Excel so you can edit the spreadsheet and update the page. See page 246.

Time and date stamping. Place the file TYMDAT.FLT that's in your PageMaker directory, and you'll be able to place the time and date that the publication was printed into your publication. You can import the time and date in a variety of formats. See page 253.

Character Formatting

A good portion of the typographic improvements in PageMaker 4 relate to character formatting. You can specify a wider range of type sizes and leading with better accuracy than in PageMaker 3; adjust the width of characters, expanding and condensing the type; adjust the size and position of super- and subscripts, and the size of small caps; and kern more accurately, using a more flexible and powerful approach than that in PageMaker 3.

Type sizes. You can now specify type from 4 to 650 points in increments of a tenth of a point. See page 168.

Leading. The finest leading increment PageMaker 3 could handle was half a point. In PageMaker 4, you can specify leading in increments of a tenth of a point, from 1 to 1300 points. See page 126.

Set width. You can now condense and expand type horizontally in 1 percent increments, from 5 to 250 percent. See page 168.

Type options. The new Type options dialog box lets you adjust the size and position of subscripts and superscripts, and the size of small caps. While it seems mundane, it allows for some amazing type effects that formerly required careful manual positioning. See page 169.

Manual kerning accuracy and approach. PageMaker 3 applied manual kerning by inserting invisible "kerning" characters between letter pairs, but PageMaker 4 makes manual kerning a character attribute; kerning values apply to the space following a character. Kerning accuracy has been improved to increments of one hundredth of an em. Manual kerning is now cumulative with automatic kerning; PageMaker 4 adds the manual kerning to the automatic kerning. See page 174.

Range Kerning. You can select a range of text in PageMaker 4 and apply kerning to all the character pairs in that text. See page 174.

Tracking. There are five different tracking levels that apply to selected ranges of text. This automatically sets type looser or tighter depending on the size of the type. Tracking tables are supplied for the PostScript "plus" set of typefaces and a few others. See page 157.

Paragraph Formatting

There are probably more changes in paragraph formatting than in any other portion of PageMaker 4. You can specify automatic rules above and below paragraphs; control letter and word-spacing parameters on a paragraph level (rather than PageMaker 3's story level); force-justify a paragraph; control hyphenation more comprehensively; control tabs more conveniently and accurately; insert a new-line character that doesn't begin a new paragraph; align paragraphs to a baseline grid; control widows and orphans; keep paragraphs together; specify page and column breaks before paragraphs; and ask PageMaker to highlight lines that break your spacing and/or keep-together rules.

Paragraph rules. If you want a paragraph to have a rule above or below, PageMaker will do it for you automatically, so the rule moves with the paragraph. You have control over the thickness, position, and color of the lines. See page 159.

Word and letter spacing. Word- and letter-spacing controls now work on the paragraph level, so you can fine-tune these adjustments for different types of paragraphs. Subheads can have different settings from body copy, for instance. See page 155.

Force justification. The Force justify alignment option justifies the last line of a paragraph (including one-line paragraphs) to the width of the text block. See page 140.

Next style. With this new feature, you can set up your styles to automatically change to another style when you press Enter. This is handy, for instance, if you know that para1 style always follows a level3 style. If you're doing most of your text entry in PageMaker, this is a great enhancement. See page 191.

Hyphenation controls. You can now limit the number of consecutive hyphens, set hyphenation to manual, dictionary, or algorithmic (or any combination of those three methods), and use multiple hyphenation dictionaries in a publication. See page 213.

Tab handling. When you call up the Indents/tabs dialog box, it aligns the ruler zero point to the left edge of the text block (if the left edge is visible in the window), making it much easier to align tabs visually. You can select a tab in the Indents/tabs dialog box and specify a new position, alignment, or leader character instead of removing the tab and adding a new one, and you can type numeric values for tab positions, in addition to moving tabs with the mouse. PageMaker now aligns decimal-tabbed figures properly, even when some of the figures are enclosed in parentheses. See page 142.

New line. Pressing Shift-Enter inserts a new-line character, just like in Word and Word for Windows. This lets you break a line without creating a new paragraph with all its attendant attributes (first-line indent, space before, paragraph rule, etc.), and break justified paragraphs without forcing the line flush left. See page 141.

Align to grid. The Align to grid option (for some reason it's hidden in the Paragraph rule options dialog box) forces the succeeding paragraph to align to a leading grid that you specify, measured from the top of the text block. See page 136.

Widow and orphan control. You can specify the minimum number of lines in a paragraph that PageMaker should keep together at the tops and bottoms of columns. See page 164.

Keeps and breaks. The Keep lines together and Keep with next *n* lines options let you keep a paragraph together on a page, or keep it together with a given number of lines in the ensuing paragraph. See page 164.

Show Loose/tight lines and "Keeps" violations. These options (in the Preferences dialog box) ask PageMaker to highlight on screen any violations of the rules you've set up for word and letter spacing, and for keeping paragraphs together. See page 156.

Pictures

There are only two changes to graphics handling in PageMaker 4, but they are perhaps the most significant new features. You can insert graphics into text, and wrap text around items from the master pages. In addition, PageMaker 4 includes a number of new features for handling color.

Inline Graphics

In addition to the stand-alone, independent graphics that PageMaker has always offered, you can now insert a graphic within text, so it moves as the text reflows. Inline graphics act just like characters in the text (with some exceptions), so you can use them for special characters or for larger graphics that constitute paragraphs in their own right. See page 292.

Wrapping Around Master Items

When you apply text wrap to items on the master page, text adheres to that wrap on every page that has master items displayed. This lets you customize your text flow behavior, for example to exclude certain page areas such as companion columns or header regions. This feature is especially useful for autoflowing larger documents. See page 308.

Color

PageMaker 4's color handling features are significantly improved over previous versions. Here's a summary of some of these features.

Larger palette of colors. You can define up to 32,767 colors in PageMaker 4.

Printing to color PostScript printers. You can print color pages on color PostScript printers such as the QMS ColorScript.

Place color images. PageMaker 4 can place and print color files in BMP, PCX, and TIFF formats.

Pantone colors. You can choose colors from a palette of PMS (Pantone Matching System) colors.

Besides these features, PageMaker 4 also adds the ability to print selected spot color overlays.

Books

You can create publications up to 999 pages in length in PageMaker 4, though with the new Book tools, you won't need or want to. In the Book publication list dialog box, you set up a list of PageMaker pubs that make up your book, in the order you want them to appear. This allows automatic page numbering from chapter to chapter. You can also print all of the publications in the Book list, and generate tables of contents and indices for the book.

Table of Contents

There's a new paragraph attribute check box in PageMaker 4, "Include in table of contents." You generally check this for chapter heads, and perhaps first- and second-level heads. When your book is finished, PageMaker builds a table of contents. It creates a new story, compiling all the paragraphs for which "Include in table of contents" is selected, and inserts the page number for each. It either loads a text place gun containing this new story or replaces a previously created table-of-contents story. PageMaker builds new styles and applies them to the different table-of-contents levels as it builds the story, so you can adjust the styles and format the table of contents quickly. See page 220.

Indexing

Long-document users, rejoice: PageMaker 4's indexing tools are the best we've ever seen. You still need to do all of the thinking—because that's the way indexing works—but PageMaker does all of the tedious bookkeeping: tracking page numbers (including ranges of pages), and keeping an eye on cross-references. See page 221.

General Features

PageMaker 4 sports a number of general improvements, not least of which is an increase in speed over PageMaker 3. Pages draw faster, text recomposes faster, and, through the Story Editor, text entry speed has increased by an order of magnitude. Besides performance improvements, PageMaker 4 offers a new and powerful Paste technique; keeps track of the source files you've used to create your publication through the Links command; adds new options for numbering pages; and adds a context-sensitive online help system. The Table Editor application, included in the PageMaker 4 package, creates simple tables.

Paste

It doesn't seem like there's much you can do with the Windows Paste command, but PageMaker 4 does a lot. If you simply copy and paste an item, PageMaker either pastes the copy on top of the original with a slight offset, or it pastes it in the middle of the screen. If you press Ctrl-Shift-P, you invoke PageMaker 4's "power paste" feature.

When you power paste, PageMaker pastes the item at exactly the same position on the page as it was cut or copied from—even if you've changed pages, publications, or page view (as long as part—more than about 10 percent—of that position is still visible). That's handy, but it gets better. If you power paste an item, move it a given distance, then power paste again, the new copy is offset by that same distance. With power paste, step-and-repeat duplication is a breeze. See page 90.

Links

The Links command on the File menu is one of the most important new features in PageMaker 4. Using "Links," you can keep track of the files you've placed in your publication, see whether a file has been modified since you placed it, choose whether to include a copy of the file in your publication, set the file to replace automatically if the source file has been modified, and locate files in a workgroup publishing environment. If you've ever had problems with revision control, the Links command is for you. See page 396.

Page Numbering

PageMaker 4 will number pages alphabetically (upper- or lowercase), with Roman numerals (upper- or lowercase), and with good old Arabic numerals. PageMaker's Book command also permits automatic consecutive numbering across publications. If your page numbers are broken out by chapter (1–15, 4–23, etc.), you can designate a page-number prefix for PageMaker to insert when creating tables of contents and indices. See page 77.

Help

PageMaker 4's online help is context-sensitive. If you want information on the Export command, for example, you can invoke Help by pressing Shift-F1, then choosing the command from the menu using the ? cursor. The Help window will appear with information on the Export command. You can also choose "Help" from the Windows menu to get a listing of Help topics. See page 101.

Table Editor

The PageMaker 4 package includes an application for creating and editing tables called Table Editor (pretty catchy, eh?). If you need to create simple, black-and-white tables, Table Editor could be for you. Table Editor can export its tables as tab-delimited text or as Windows metafile-type graphics for placement in a PageMaker publication. See page 151.

Going to Pages

PageMaker was already a big program and you can see it has gotten even bigger. We're going to leave it for a moment though. In the next chapter we'll discuss building a Windows system that provides the foundation for working with PageMaker, and all the tools that go into such a system.

CHAPTER 2

Building a PageMaker System

If you're building a house, you don't set the walls down on mud. You build forms, position steel rods for reinforcement, and pour cement for the foundation. Your computer system should provide the same kind of solid foundation for PageMaker. If your system configuration, device drivers, or memory-resident utilities conflict with Windows, PageMaker, or each other, you'll have a hard time building solid publications. There are several things you'll want to take care of before you ever double-click the PageMaker icon. The first part of this chapter discusses ways to configure and supercharge both your computer and the Windows environment to work with PageMaker.

Page-building, just like house-building, requires the proper tools. PageMaker doesn't exist in a vacuum, after all. You can build pages with PageMaker and nothing else, but most people use PageMaker with a whole suite of programs. To begin with, you need a word processor; we use both Microsoft Word for DOS and Word for Windows. You probably also need a drawing program; Corel Draw (Corel Systems) and Micrografx Designer (Micrografx, Inc.) are top notch in this department. There are numerous gray-scale bitmap-editing programs available, but if you want a Windows-specific program in this area, look into Image-In (Image-In Inc.) or Publisher's Paintbrush

(ZSoft). Finally, you'll probably want any of a dozen little utilities.

In the second part of this chapter we discuss our favorite tools and utilities, trying hard to limit our discussion to those that really do relate to PageMaker. If you want to know more about word processors, drawing, and painting programs, refer to the reviews and articles you'll find in general PC and desktop publishing magazines (such as *PC Magazine* and *Personal Publishing*).

Before we get to the tools themselves, though, let's discuss Windows and the PC—the foundation on which your PageMaker publishing edifice is built.

Windows and the PC

For the first several years of its existence on the IBM PC and compatibles, PageMaker ran only under a much maligned, kludgy-looking graphical environment known as Windows. In those days, the only time most people used Windows was when they had to—to work with PageMaker or some other Windows-based program.

Then, in May of 1990, everything changed. Windows 3.0 took the world by storm. In the months that followed its long-awaited release, Windows 3.0 won over millions of adherents, mostly because it was faster, prettier, and easier to use than Windows 2.0, but also because of its memory management, multitasking, and network support.

We've had people tell us that they'd never understood PageMaker's page-layout metaphor before they saw it running under Windows 3.0. Windows 2.0 was so slow that PageMaker's greatest strengths—fluidity of movement and hands-on action—never quite worked. The "hands-off" approach of other (non-Windows) applications seemed to make more sense. Because of Windows 3.0's performance improvements, PageMaker finally runs the way it should.

Though Windows has improved the ease of use of our computers, you'll be better equipped to cope with the unexpected if you have a basic understanding of the DOS system underlying Windows. Find yourself a good book. One of the best books on DOS is *Running MS-DOS* (Microsoft Press).

There are now Windows wizards, just as there were DOS wizards. There may be some basic human craving for technical expertise, for knowing more than the next person. We don't know. We do know that, if you have some question about your Windows system, and can't find the answer in this book, you should ask your local Windows guru (everyone needs a guru).

It's also a good idea to study up on Windows. For basic information about Windows, consult the *Windows Companion* (Microsoft Press) or *Windows Power Tools* (Bantam Books). If you own a 386 and aspire to computerized greatness, check out *Fully Powered Windows* (Brady Books). For a friendly collection of power techniques, look for *101 Windows Tips* (Peachpit Press). (Okay, Jesse and Scott had a hand in writing this last one. But that doesn't affect our unbiased, objective assessment of its quality.)

PageMaker 4 and Windows

Although Windows 3.0 does run (barely) on the 8088 and 8086 microprocessor chips that were found in early IBM PCs, PageMaker does not. The minimum configuration recommended by Aldus is 1MB of RAM and a 20MB hard disk in a 286-based computer.

As with most "minimums" in life, this configuration doesn't really make sense for any but the desktop dabbler. Even Aldus's preferred configuration (386-based machine, 40MB hard drive, and 2MB of RAM) is, in our opinion, skimpy. You probably already have a computer, but if you are in the market for a new one, by all means go for a 386 with a hefty hard drive. (And RAM, RAM, RAM.) With the additional RAM, you can run Windows in enhanced mode.

Enhanced mode enables Windows' virtual memory powers, which means that Windows treats your hard disk as extra memory if/when it runs out of RAM. This means that the amount of RAM your applications think is available is limited only by the amount of free space on your hard disk. Using the hard disk as a RAM substitute is slow, though, so there's still no excuse for skimping on RAM.

If you buy a new machine, consider retiring your old computer to the role of a file server for your network (see "File Transfer Methods" in Chapter 8, *Workgroup Publishing*). Or connect it to a modem and use it as a bulletin board. Or use it as a spare machine for word processing. There is still life in the older machines.

▼ Tip: Thanks for the Memory

If you're like most people reading this book, you want to know how to make PageMaker howl on the system you now have. Given that, we have one recommendation regardless of whether you have a 286 or a 386: Buy more memory. Not long ago the official Microsoft/IBM party line was that Windows was for 2MB machines and OS/2 was for machines with 4MB or more. Folks, it just ain't so. Frankly, we wouldn't bother to run Windows without at least 4MB. Half the power of Windows is being able to multitask programs and transfer data between them. The less memory you have, the fewer Windows benefits you can take advantage of. Adding RAM is the cheapest—and most powerful—hardware tip we can give you.

▼ Tip: Keep an Even Hand

If you're upgrading your computer's memory, stick to an even number of megabytes (2, 4, 6, 8, etc.). Apparently, Windows 3.0 memory manager does some kind of interleaving and gets lost if you've got an odd number of megabytes installed. Users with odd numbers of memory megabytes report error messages and other problems. We know it sounds weird, but we don't make this stuff up. (Not this time, anyway.)

▼ Tip: Enhanced Ain't Necessarily So

Don't be fooled by the terms "enhanced mode" and "standard mode." Although Windows automatically starts up in enhanced mode on 386 computers with at least 2MB of RAM, that doesn't necessarily mean it's superior to standard mode. If you need to multitask DOS (i.e., non-Windows) applications while using PageMaker, then enhanced mode is definitely for you. But if you use Windows applications exclusively and spend most of your time in PageMaker, then stick to standard mode. In these circumstances, standard mode is 5 to 20 percent faster. To force Windows to start in standard mode, just type *win/s* at the DOS prompt.

Of Fonts and Faces

Take a deep breath. Even before Windows, font facts were difficult enough to keep straight. Now, with new font products for Windows appearing almost weekly, complications multiply. For every rule you make, there's an exception.

If you are to become formidable fondler of fonts, you need to understand some basic distinctions: *outline* versus *bitmap* and *screen* versus *printer* fonts. If you already have a grasp of these terms, you can skip this section. Otherwise, read on.

Rasters of the Universe

Bitmapped or *raster* fonts are made up of patterns of pixels like the pictures you make in Windows Paintbrush. Bitmapped fonts are usually the screen fonts you see on your monitor, though there are bitmapped fonts for printing, as well. Sometimes, the bitmapped font you see on your screen is exactly what you'll see when you print; sometimes your printer uses another, higher-resolution font instead (Figure 2-1).

Figure 2-1
What you see and what you get

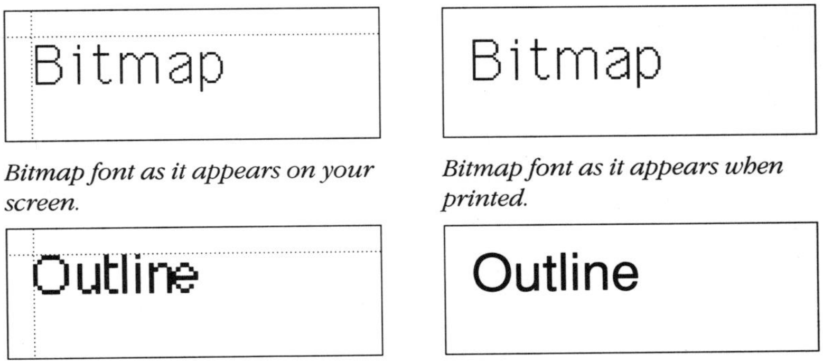

Bitmap	Bitmap
Bitmap font as it appears on your screen.	*Bitmap font as it appears when printed.*
Outline	Outline
Outline font as it appears on your screen.	*Outline font as it appears when printed.*

Because bitmapped fonts are built around a specific matrix of pixels, your output device (printer or screen) needs bitmaps for each point size you intend to use (which can take up disk space). For example, Windows comes with a number of screen fonts: Tms Rmn, Helv, Courier, and Symbol. These fonts are only available in fixed sizes: 8, 10, 12 14, 18, and 24. If you choose a different size in your application, Windows scales the bitmap, which usually means that the characters look jagged and ugly on your screen. This happens because Windows is squashing or stretching the matrix of pixels which makes up the characters (Figure 2-2).

Figure 2-2
What happens when you scale bitmapped fonts

 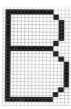 

A character from a bitmap font at its original size.

When you scale the character, Windows has to remap the character to a new matrix of pixels.

You can't have fractional pixels, so Windows guesses about the shape of the character, resulting in distortion.

The Bottom Outline

Outline fonts are mathematical descriptions that tell your output device (screen or printer) how to construct individual characters. The same description can produce type of almost any size. For this reason, outline fonts are often called *scalable* fonts.

Because outline fonts don't have to contain a pixel-by-pixel rendition of each character, they take up less space (both on your hard disk and in your printer's memory) than their more literal-minded cousins, the bitmapped fonts.

Windows comes with a sampling of outline fonts for your screen: Modern, Roman, and Script. Scalable though they are, these particular fonts are incredibly ugly and stick-like. Viewing them leaves the distinct impression that Microsoft is part of a conspiracy to discredit scalable fonts. Fortunately, not all outline fonts are so devoid of typographic charm.

Screen Fonts

In addition to scalable and bitmapped, fonts also fall into the categories of screen and printer. Screen fonts are the characters you see on your monitor. They're just a way to give you an on-screen approximation of what you'll see on paper when you print. Good screen fonts can save you time and trouble because you can see what you're doing on-screen before you print.

Screen font files can be recognized by their file extension .FON. To see what screen fonts you have installed on your system, double-click the Fonts icon in the Windows Control Panel. A listing of installed fonts appears.

This part of the Control Panel is widely misunderstood and only marginally useful. To begin with, the Fonts panel governs *only* screen fonts (so don't come around here to manage your printer fonts). You use the Add button to install FON files (though, generally, font manufacturers include an installation program for their screen fonts that does this work for you). The Remove button does not delete these FON files from your disk, but only turns them off, so Windows doesn't use them.

In addition to ready-made FON files from commercial font vendors, you can also create bitmapped screen fonts by using one of the popular font-generating utilities on the market today, such as Adobe's Font Foundry, Bitstream's Fontware, Hewlett-Packard/Agfa Compugraphic's Type Director, and ZSoft's SoftType.

The best way to get screen fonts is to use a *rasterizer*. A rasterizer uses scalable font information to size type to the desired size on the fly, then rasterizes it (makes it into a bitmap image) for screen display or printer output. Bitstream Facelift and Adobe Type Manager (ATM)—which may or may not have been included in your PageMaker package, depending on when you bought PageMaker—are examples of font rasterizers. Rasterizers build bitmapped screen fonts as you need them, and can build them in any size you want.

Because rasterizers use scalable outlines instead of FON files, you won't see any difference in Control Panel's Fonts section. In fact, if you're using a rasterizer, you can ignore the Fonts panel altogether.

▼ *Tip: Use a Font Rasterizer*

Get a font rasterizer and fonts of the type it supports and use them. If you got ATM with your PageMaker package, install it and use it. If you didn't, you should strongly consider buying a copy. Bitstream FaceLift is constantly improving, and might have caught up with ATM by the time you read this book, so do compare the two packages before you buy. This is one of the biggest tips in this book, and we're going to assume that you've installed and are using a font rasterizer for the rest of the book.

▼ *Tip: Mix and Match*

Because they have to make size calculations each time a font is placed, specified, or scrolled onto your screen, rasterizers can slow down performance. If this is a problem for you, try using both pre-built bitmapped fonts as well as those generated by a rasterizer. For example, if you're using PostScript fonts, you could install the screen fonts you use most often—probably roman (i.e., not italic, not bold, not bold-italic) typefaces between 6 and 12 points. Then let ATM scale and create the rest—headlines, display type, and so on.

This should speed up screen redraw. But here's the trade-off: Each prebuilt screen font takes some memory (not to mention disk space). Therefore, you may need to experiment a little to find the best combination for your particular machine. If your font package doesn't have a screen font for a size you use often, you can use Adobe's Type Foundry to generate a screen font in the size you need.

▼ *Tip: Remove then Delete*

Maybe you've just installed ATM and you want to junk some of the screen font (FON) files you used before. The best way is to go *first* to Control Panel, double-click Fonts, select the screen font in question, and click the Remove button. *Then* go to File Manager (or whatever utility you prefer) and delete the FON files from your hard disk. If you remove but don't delete, those font files will take up disk space. On the other hand, if you delete the FON files without first removing them with Control Panel, the names will stay in the Fonts panel, and you may not be able to get rid of them.

Printer Fonts Like screen fonts, printers can also use either scalable outlines (in the case of PostScript printers and the Hewlett-Packard LaserJet III) or bitmapped fonts (in the case of most LaserJets and compatibles, and all dot-matrix printers). Printer fonts can also be divided into other categories, depending on whether the fonts are built into your printer (*resident*) or reside on your computer's hard drive (*downloadable*). Downloadable fonts are also called *soft fonts*. We won't take the space to discuss those here; you can find complete details on printer fonts and how to manage them in Chapter 6, *Printing*.

A Word about TrueType Just when you thought you'd settled on a particular font technology, Apple and Microsoft decide to throw a wrench in the works by bringing out a PostScript competitor called TrueImage with accompanying fonts called TrueType. Though much ado was made about these so-called Font Wars, there's little to worry about. That's because TrueImage functions as a superset of PostScript and works on your existing PostScript printer (or HP printer with Adobe PostScript cartridge). Moreover, Microsoft plans to build TrueType rasterizing technology into Windows 3.1, in effect creating an ATM clone as part of the Windows environment.

These Are a Few of Our Favorite Things

As we said, you'll get the most out of PageMaker if you treat it as one instrument in your software ensemble. There are dozens of different tools out there that quickly become indispensable. What follows is a rundown of our favorites. We've divided these tools into categories—tools for type and printing, art, file management, and general utilities—but as is so often the case, the categories don't always fit perfectly. It's often difficult, for instance, to draw the line between type and printing. (Is a font downloader a font utility or a printer utility?) So if you don't find a given tool where you expect it to be, refer to the table of contents in the beginning of the book.

If you aren't interested right now in all the tools that surround PageMaker and make it really fly, you might want to just skim the rest of this chapter. It will give you an idea of some of the tools that we use all the time, and that we'll be referring to in other parts of the book. Then when you find an interesting program mentioned in one of the other chapters, you can come back here for a description. Manufacturers and products are listed in the appendix.

Printing and Type Tools

Type is the graphic medium we use to convey our text, our message. It is not the same as text, but it is not quite the same as art or illustration—but it can complement both. To ensure the highest quality possible for your publications, you need the proper tools for crafting, massaging, and reproducing your typography.

Adobe Type Manager

As we mentioned before, font rasterizers can give you smooth-looking characters on your screen. They'll also create smooth characters for printing, depending on the fonts and printer you're using. But which one is for you?

That depends on what system(s) and fonts you're using now. If you've got lots of Type 1 PostScript typefaces, then Adobe Type Manager (ATM) is for you. Type 1 fonts come from Adobe, Linotype, Agfa-Compugraphic, and Monotype, and other font vendors. Type 1 fonts usually have the file extension .PFB. Some non-Adobe PostScript fonts are Type 3. Type 3 fonts usually have the file extension .PFA. ATM can't read them, so you have to rely on fixed-size screen fonts for display. ATM is the choice for any desktop publishing group that wants cross-platform consistency: only ATM is available for the Mac, DOS, and OS/2.

Like its chief competitor, FaceLift, ATM gives you screen fonts that look smoother, closer to the way they'll appear when printed—even when you zoom in close. The screen display of kerning, for example, is far better with ATM than without (you can adjust kerning on screen, rather than having to print the page six or eight times before you get it right). Non-PostScript printers like LaserJets can use the characters ATM generates to print PostScript typefaces with good quality.

ATM is very simple to use. Just install it from the floppy using the Run command from File Manager or Program Manager. Once that's done, you can adjust ATM's settings by clicking the ATM Control Panel icon in Program Manager (Figure 2-3). You can adjust the size of ATM's font cache, but remember that the larger you make the font cache, the more RAM ATM uses; the smaller you make the font cache, the longer it takes ATM to display your fonts.

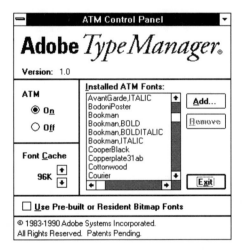

Figure 2-3
The ATM Control Panel

▼ *Tip: Maximizing ATM's Screen Font Powers*

PageMaker's Vector text above option (accessed through the Other button, Preferences dialog box, Edit menu) specifies the point at which PageMaker stops using available screen fonts and instead draws them. To give ATM the most breathing room to operate, you should set "Vector text above" to 600 pixels or more in the Screen font options dialog box, and set "Greek text below" to 6 pixels in the Preferences dialog box. ATM will only use its screen-font-generating powers on fonts that fall within this range. Be aware that whether a font falls between 6 and 600 pixels depends on the current page view.

▼ Tip: The Plus Pack Pressure Ploy

Because ATM generates screen fonts from soft (outline) font files, you won't see screen representations of typefaces built into your printer or PostScript printer cartridge unless you have those soft font files, as well. The exceptions are four faces each of New Times Roman, Gill Sans, Courier, and one Symbol face, all of which come with ATM. And you can't even use the old prebuilt screen fonts available free from CompuServe and nearly every service bureau; they don't work with most Windows 3.0 apps, including PageMaker. To get the standard 35 typefaces that come on many PostScript printers, you have to shell out $198 (almost twice the cost of ATM) to get Adobe Plus Pack, which includes the additional 22 faces not found in ATM.

If you're already hooked on ATM, you might find the Plus Pack worth the investment. However, if you're strapped for cash, try this: Find a service bureau that owns the Plus Pack and a copy of Adobe Font Foundry (which comes with all the latest Adobe fonts). See if they'll use Font Foundry to generate bitmapped screen fonts in the sizes you use most often. Okay, the fonts aren't scalable, but at least you'll have passable screen fonts. Moreover, it's legal and free (unless your service bureau chief is a greedy tightwad).

▼ Tip: But the Fonts I've Installed are Printing as Courier!

When you install your Type 1 PostScript fonts using ATM's control panel, the names and locations are written into your ATM.INI and WIN.INI files. This is a good thing. What's not so good is that they're entered into these files as resident, rather than as nonresident (i.e., downloadable) fonts. Everything works fine as long as the fonts are resident in the printer; but if you use a nonresident font, you'll get Courier (or your printer's default font) on your printed page.

To fix this problem, open your WIN.INI file with any ASCII text editor (Notepad or Sysedit, for example), and look for the section describing your printer. It'll look something like this (your printer port might differ).

[PostScript,LPT2]

Inside this section, you'll see a line describing each of your installed fonts. These entries tell Windows where to find the spacing information for each font. The entries follow this convention:

softfontX=drive:\path\fontname.pfm

For example:

softfont1=c:\psfonts\pfm\gn.pfm
softfont2=c:\psfonts\pfm\gnb.pfm
softfont3=c:\psfonts\pfm\gnbi.pfm
softfont4=c:\psfonts\pfm\gni.pfm

You need to add a path to these lines that will direct Windows to the downloadable font. To do this, you enter a comma, followed by the pathname for the downloadable font, like this:

softfontX=drive:\path\fontname.pfm,drive:\path\fontname.pfb

The example lines shown above would look like this:

softfont1=c:\psfonts\pfm\gn.pfm,c:\psfonts\gn.pfb
softfont2=c:\psfonts\pfm\gnb.pfm,c:\psfonts\gnb.pfb
softfont3=c:\psfonts\pfm\gnbi.pfm,c:\psfonts\gnbi.pfb
softfont4=c:\psfonts\pfm\gni.pfm,c:\psfonts\gni.pfb

Save the file, quit and restart Windows (or use the tip "Rereading WIN.INI in Chapter 6, *Pictures*), and try printing again. This time (unless you've made an error in the font name or path), your printer download and print your selected font. Instead of Courier. Yuck.

FaceLift FaceLift is our second choice for a font rasterizer. That's because it's intended to work with Bitstream Speedo fonts. If you have a bunch of Bitstream fonts purchased before the advent of the Speedo format, you're out of luck. (You can tell by the label on your floppies: Speedo fonts have a silver label and the Bitstream diamond logo.) If you have a PostScript printer, you can still use your PostScript fonts, even in combination with FaceLift—but only at the printer. FaceLift won't generate screen fonts for your PostScript fonts. To do that, you have to buy the Bitstream FaceLift Companion Pack for PostScript. For $179, this package provides Speedo outlines to match the 35 fonts found in many PostScript printers.

On the plus side, FaceLift lets you make bitmapped soft fonts that you can manually download to HP LaserJet printers for faster printing. In addition, FaceLift's font cache "remembers" the fonts you used last time and loads these into cache when you start up each day. And, in addition to the usual suspects (imitation Helvetica, Times, Symbol, and Courier fonts), FaceLift does include four display faces: Cooper Black, Formal Script, Park Avenue, and Brush Script.

We expect FaceLift to improve, and give ATM a run for its money. Or a run for your money.

SuperPrint

If your PageMaker publications include graphics and you do much or most of your printing on one of the Hewlett-Packard family of printers (or even a dot matrix printer), you definitely need to look into SuperPrint from Zenographics (Figure 2-4). SuperPrint is actually a whole collection of font and printing goodies—a replacement driver for your HP printer, a print spooler superior to Windows' Print Manager, a font rasterizer, and a handful of scalable typefaces.

SuperPrint actually rasterizes the pages of your publication, essentially treating each page (including text) as a graphic. This process has some interesting effects. First of all, it means you can't use downloaded or even internal printer fonts or font cartridges. And it means that pages with nothing but simple text (which otherwise print very quickly) take just as long to print as a page with complex graphics. In other words, using SuperPrint slows down printing of your single-font, text-only publications, but speeds up those with heavy-duty graphics. You can use SuperPrint to control the dithering of bitmapped graphics, which can result in higher quality output than you'd get with the drivers that come with Windows.

Figure 2-4
Zenographics' SuperPrint

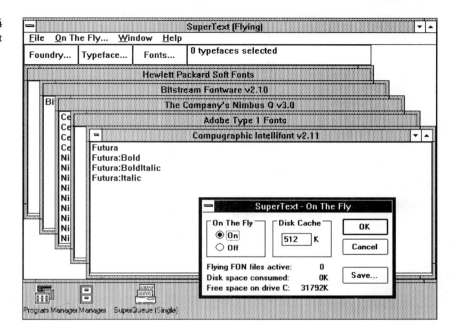

To help speed printing even more, SuperPrint includes a spooler called SuperQueue, which (with the exceptions noted above) returns you to PageMaker more quickly after you issue a Print command. You can also use SuperQueue to spool all your print files to a disk for later printing—at the end of the day, for example.

SuperPrint supports a wide range of font formats: PostScript Type 1, Bitstream Fontware, The Company's Nimbus Q (URW typefaces), and Compugraphic Intellifont. With SuperPrint, you can mix these font formats in a single publication or on a single page. And SuperPrint comes with a handful of typeface families: Futura (Compugraphic), Century Schoolbook (Nimbus Q), as well as the Helvetica, Times, and Courier clones. In effect, SuperPrint gives any HP printer the ability to use scalable outlines without cartridges or downloading.

▼ *Tip: The Old Switcheroo*

When you install the SuperPrint driver, don't remove your standard PCL driver that came with Windows. Leave both of them active so they show up in the lists in PageMaker's Target printer dialog box and the

Print dialog box. If your design calls for a relatively long publication with only one or two fonts and no graphics, assign the regular PCL driver as your target printer and make sure that driver is selected in the Printer list box when you print. If your design calls for multiple fonts and graphics or both, assign the SuperPrint driver as the target printer, and print your publication with that driver. This ensures the fastest printing for each type of publication.

Art and Design Tools

Without graphics, a publication is just words. While words are fine and good things, pictures add a needed spice to publications. With the growth of icon-based systems like Windows, we're looking forward to a return to hieroglyphic writing, which will heal the schism that has existed between words (left-brain) and pictures (right-brain) since the decline of ancient Egyptian civilization.

We use a number of art tools to prepare graphics for use in Page-Maker. Naturally, we use major graphics applications, including a drawing package and a gray-scale editor. But we also use lots of smaller applications for everything from file conversion to touching up screen shots. Despite some overlap, the tools covered in this section consist of our picks for three important categories: a graphics file manager (Scrapbook+), a screen-capture utility (Tiffany Plus), and a graphics format converter (The Graphics Link Plus). Naturally, there are a number of other worthwhile products in these categories, but we decided it would be fun just to talk about those with "plus" in their names. In addition, we'll talk about a new design tool, ExpressPage, not because it belongs here, but because we couldn't figure out where else to put it. For more on working with graphics in PageMaker, see Chapter 5, *Pictures*.

Scrapbook+

If you deal with illustrations or graphics files in any kind of quantity, Scrapbook+ quickly becomes an indispensable tool. Produced by Eikon Systems, Scrapbook+ lets you store all your graphics in one file where you can view, arrange, crop, export, and store them. You can either import all your images through the File menu or paste them in through Windows' Clipboard. Or you can use the Autopaste feature—which automatically imports anything that passes through the Clipboard. You can even select and quickly import a directory full of clip art files in a single operation.

Once inside, graphic images or text blocks form one "page" in a given Scrapbook+ file. You can view several pages at once in thumbnail format (with up to 48 on your screen at once) or zoom to full size and color. We prefer the combined Page & Thumbnail view, which shows the selected image in a large window with thumbnails of 8 other images underneath (Figure 2-5)

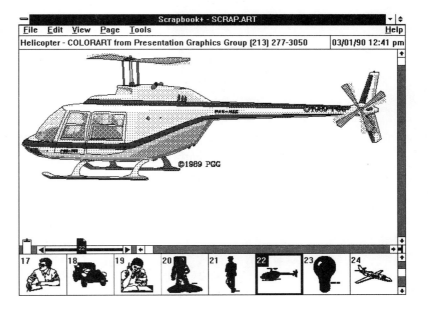

Figure 2-5
Scrapbook+

But Scrapbook+ doesn't make you scroll through every picture to find what you need. You can attach key words or descriptive phrases (up to 99 characters) and use these to conduct quick searches. At any time, you can add, delete, export, or copy images to the Clipboard. You can also merge other Scrapbook+ files, which can have a virtually unlimited number of pages.

Scrapbook+ supports a number of formats for bitmaps (BMP, PCX, MSP), encapsulated PostScript (EPS), PostScript, (PS), as well as TIFF and Windows metafiles (These file formats are discussed in Chapter 5, *Pictures*). It can also store text in ASCII or rich text format (RTF—discussed in Chapter 4, *Words*). It can do some limited conversion of these formats, but basically line art stays line art, text remains text, etc. (For a format converter, see our comments on The Graphics Link Plus later in this chapter.)

Scrapbook+ also features a screen-capture utility, but we prefer another product for that task. That's next.

Screen Captures Part One: The Cheap Way

Windows provides a way to take pictures of the Windows screen—just press the Print Screen key to capture the entire screen or Alt-Print Screen to capture only the active Window. The image is sent to the Clipboard, from which you can paste it directly into PageMaker or into Windows Paintbrush for retouching or storing in a couple of different formats: PCX (a popular format pioneered by ZSoft, who programmed Paintbrush for Microsoft) or BMP (Windows bitmap format).

This method, while undeniably cheap and easy, presents a number of limitations. First of all, if you need only a small section of a screen—a menu, for example—you'll have to edit the picture in Paintbrush. Second, you are forced to use either full-color formats or monochrome—no gray scale allowed. Still, for folks who only need an occasional screen shot, this may be the best way to go.

▼ *Tip: Who's Zooming Whom*

An oft-heard complaint about pasting full-screen captures in Paintbrush is its inability to include any pasted image that doesn't fit into its immediate window. In other words, if you just press Print Screen, open Paintbrush, and paste (Shift-Insert), everything looks fine—until you scroll around your picture and find that Paintbrush has lopped off the edges. Fortunately there is a solution:

1. Set up the screen the way you want and press Print Screen to make your screen capture.

2. Next, open Paintbrush and make sure your Paintbrush image area

is the right size—standard VGA resolution is 640 by 480 pixels. In Paintbrush, choose "Image Attributes" from the Options menu, select "pels" (for pixels) under the Units option, and enter the right numbers. Then select "New" from the File menu. Paintbrush opens a new file with the size you specified.

3. Choose "Zoom Out" from the View menu.
4. Choose Paste from the Edit menu or press Shift-Insert. (If you stored your screen shot in a Clipboard file, you can choose "Paste From" and enter the file name.)
5. To complete the paste, click somewhere outside the image, such as on some tool in the Toolbox.
6. Choose "Zoom In" from the View menu. You can now edit your picture and save it in the format you want.

▼ *Tip: Edit First, then Crop*

If you only want to use a portion of your screen in an illustration, you could just import the whole screen into PageMaker and use its cropping tool to focus on the parts you need. But this is wasteful: it creates graphic and PageMaker files that are unnecessarily large and take longer to print. To save on file size (and disk space), first paste your screen shot into Paintbrush as instructed above. Then use the Pick cutout tool to drag select the portion of the picture you want to place in PageMaker. From the Edit menu choose "Copy To" and enter a file name for your screen shot. If you want to change the file format, open it again in Paintbrush and click the Options button in the Save As dialog box. The result is a smaller picture file, smaller PageMaker file, and much faster printing.

▼ *Tip: The Wonderful World of Monochrome*

Unless you plan to print to a color laser printer or cope with one of the few color separation utilities available on the PC, chances are you'll want to save your screen captures in a black-and-white format. Pasting your screen shot into Paintbrush and saving as a monochrome bitmap (click "Options" in the Save As dialog box) will usually work fine. But you will only get black blacks and white whites—no shades of gray. Moreover, some fine colored lines (such as PageMaker's ruler guides) may disappear in the transition to a monochrome format.

To get better results, exit from Windows and enter *setup* at the DOS prompt while in the Windows directory. Under "Display" select a monochrome screen driver, such as the "VGA with monochrome display." After you have installed this driver, start Windows again and capture the screens you need. Your fine lines should now be visible, and you will also have dot patterns that simulate gray.

Screen Captures Part Two: The Right Way

To get true gray-scale screen shots, as well as control over the screen region you want to capture, Windows' built-in capture function just doesn't do the job. There are now a number of screen-capture utilities for Windows, some of them built into other graphic tools (such as Scrapbook+ and The Graphics Link Plus). Other excellent choices are DoDOT, from Halcyon Software (which also does graphics file conversions), and Collage, from Inner Media, Inc. We find that Tiffany Plus gives us the greatest control and creates the highest-quality images.

As its name implies, Tiffany Plus excels at producing TIFF (Tagged Image File Format) files. You can choose from monochrome, gray-scale, or color, with variations on each of these to support your hardware and output needs. For example, if you want gray-scale TIFF files, you can choose between 4 bits (16 gray levels) or 8 bits (256 gray levels). Even monochrome is not a single-choice option as it is in Paintbrush: You can set the threshold percentage (1 to 99%) to control the point at which bright colors become white or dim colors become black.

Tiffany Plus can also save screen captures to color or monochrome BMP or PCX files, as well as to monochrome MSP (the Microsoft Paint format).

Tiffany Plus is especially useful for the control it gives you over capturing a particular screen region. Menu options let you choose from among full screen, active window, a child or parent window of your choice (even if another window overlaps the window you want), active client area (captures an active window but not its frame or border), as well as menus with or without the attached menu bar (see Figure 2-6). You can also drag-select areas (our favorite) to capture by choosing "Box," or you can specify areas numerically (generally more trouble than it's worth).

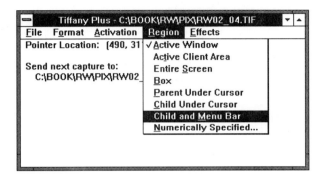

Figure 2-6
Tiffany Plus

If you'd rather just paste your screen shot into PageMaker, Tiffany can also send the image you want to the Clipboard. Or, if you'd prefer, Tiffany can send images directly to your printer.

The Graphics Link Plus

If your publications require importing graphics images from a variety of sources and in a number of different formats, you already know how useful a graphics file converter can be. While PageMaker can place a large number of graphics formats, chances are you still need to manipulate those images—convert color to gray scale or either of these to monochrome, for instance. If so, there are a number of programs to choose from.

Halcyon Software's DoDOT can convert files from and to PCX monochrome, gray-scale, 16 color, and 256 color; TIFF monochrome, gray scale, and color; GIF (CompuServe's Graphics Interchange Format); MacPaint; IMG (GEM's format, for those of you who don't remember what GEM was); CUT (Dr. Halo); and more.

DoDOT also handles the usual Windows formats, MSP, BMP, and CLP (Clipboard). DoDOT can convert files in the background while you're off doing something else, though there's a speed price to pay for doing so.

For more options and power than DoDOT can offer, check out The Graphics Link Plus (TGL Plus). Although not a Windows program, TGL Plus's features make it worth that inconvenience. Supported formats include most of those mentioned for DoDOT (but not CLP and BMP), as well as others.

Since many of your publications will probably be black and white, whether printed commercially or from laser copies, a good graphics conversion program must be able to *dither;* that is, convert gray-scale and color pictures to a pattern of dots for output on a monochrome printer. TGL Plus gives you 11 different dithering algorithms. Every graphic is different, so you may have to experiment a little to find the best option for your picture. But with this many choices, you're bound to get it right.

TGL Plus also comes with a batch of utilities, including keystroke-recording macros, a PCX-rotation function, a screen-capture utility for both DOS and Windows, and a way to convert ASCII (text only) files to PCX images using certain fonts.

ExpressPage

Tired of sketching out your design on paper only to have to reproduce all that work in PageMaker? Frustrated because you can't rotate text in one-degree increments or graphics at all? Annoyed because you can only see two pages at once? Then we have good news: ExpressPage from Carberry Technology (Figure 2-7). This Windows graphics design tool is especially designed for PageMaker users.

ExpressPage is like a sketch pad for designers in which you can quickly slap down blocks of greeked text, create headlines, paste in graphics, and sketch other graphic elements. Before you know it, you've created a rough sketch of your publication—except that you don't have to redo it in PageMaker. Check out some of these goodies:

High-powered views. For those big jobs, ExpressPage lets you see four pages at once, in any arrangement—great for designing a brochure with multiple folds. In addition, you can display thumbnails of your entire publication on screen.

Figure 2-7
ExpressPage

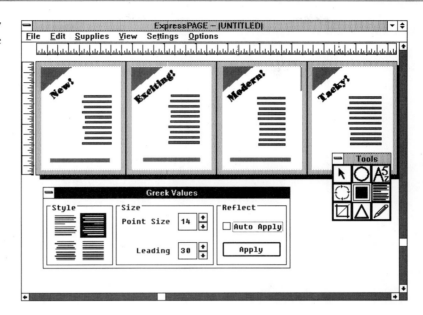

Text power. Express Page lets you treat your outline fonts like graphics—stretching and sizing them with handles and even rotating them in one-degree increments. Type in your headlines, then use the greeking tool for instant blocks of simulated text.

Added graphic oomph. ExpressPage goes beyond PageMaker's graphic powers, providing polygon and freehand drawing tools as well as gray-scale and color options with customizable palettes. You specify line weights up to 25 points in 1-point increments. You can import TIFF, PCX, and GIF formats and rotate these images in 90-degree increments. You can create a custom grid, visible or invisible, with an optional snap-to feature.

Sound too good to be true? It is. All of the above features would be great if ExpressPage could write them to a PageMaker file. It can't. Instead, you have to re-do your page setup in PageMaker, then place the file as a graphic and position ruler guides over the graphic. If you need a tool for creating comps quickly, and you don't mind having to do your work twice, you should look into ExpressPage.

File Tools

Since PageMaker's biggest job is bringing together many different types of files, we often find ourselves rooting around on disks and inside files trying to get them to act the way we want them to act. What kind of file manager suits you best depends as much on your individual style as on your budget. If you're a long-time DOS user, you may wish to stick to the utility you're already familiar with and run it in Windows using a PIF (see your Windows manual for more on PIFs). But made-for-Windows programs run faster and better under Windows, as you'd expect.

While a number of good shareware file management tools exist (Aporia is one of the best), we'll restrict our discussion to the major commercial alternatives for Windows file management.

File Manager

Your first and most obvious choice for file management is the tool that comes with Windows: File Manager (known affectionately as FileMan). Despite its lack of file viewers and failure to remember your arrangement of directory windows, FileMan handles most of the basics: drag-and-drop copy and move functions; file search, delete, and rename; disk formatting and copying; and more. The next upgrade of Windows promises major improvements in File Manager. Until then, you can either keep your old DOS file manager (the Jesse approach), jump ship and get a different package (the Steve and Ole approach), or come up with clever workarounds (the Scott approach).

▼ *Tip: Keep It Handy*

Unless you're really strapped for memory, keep your file utilities available on the desktop at all times. To automatically launch File Manager each time you start Windows, use a ASCII editor like Notepad or Sysedit to open WIN.INI and add FileMan's executable file name (WINFILE.EXE) to the load= line like this:

load=winfile.exe

Once that's done, FileMan runs minimized (appears as an icon) on your desktop the next time you start Windows. If you want FileMan to start with its window open, type *winfile.exe* on the run= line instead.

Finally, if you're the type who thinks icons are for sissies and would rather have FileMan replace Program Manager, ignore WIN.INI altogether and use your text editor to open SYSTEM.INI. There, search for the line that says Shell=progman.exe and change it so it reads:

Shell=winfile.exe

You can use some of these same techniques to start PageMaker automatically when you launch Windows. For more information, see Chapter 3, *Making PageMaker Mind*.

▼ *Tip: Recorder Does Windows*

Perhaps the most oft-voiced complaint about File Manager is that it doesn't remember its arrangement of tree and directory windows between sessions. We fully expect this problem to be solved when Windows 3.1 hits the streets. Until then, the Windows Recorder accessory can help you out. First, decide on the arrangement of windows in FileMan that suits you best. Then make a Recorder macro that duplicates that arrangement.

We prefer the arrangement shown in Figure 2-8. This lets us view the directory tree as well as the file lists of two subdirectories (any more than that gets crowded, unless you have a high-res monitor). The narrow tree window and wide directory windows let us see all the details we need about our files (size, last modification date, etc.), which we set with the Other command from the View menu. We also keep the Replace on Open option checked (View menu) so that each time we double-click a directory in the tree, it replaces one of the open directory windows—saving us the pain of constantly moving or resizing the windows. In addition, our Recorder macro arranges the tree so that the directories we seldom use are collapsed, while those we use most often are expanded to show their subdirectories. And it all takes just seconds to set up each time we invoke our macro.

Figure 2-8
Windows' File Manager

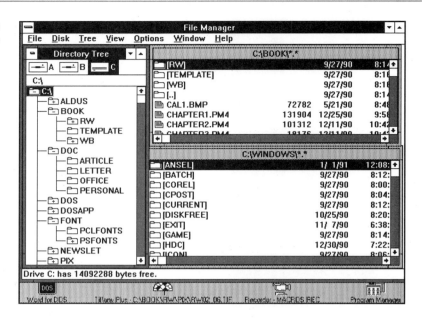

Command Post

Is File Manager too limited for your needs? Do icons disgust you? Do you want flexibility and the power to customize? Need a good text file viewer? Is cost a concern? If you answered yes to all or even most of these questions, you should consider Command Post from Wilson WindowWare. At $50, it's the cheapest of the commercial alternatives to File Manager, and pretty functional too. And looks? Well, you can't have everything (Figure 2-9).

Command Post eschews the drag-and-drop approach of other file tools. For all basic file and directory management chores, you must select one or more items from the file/directory list, then choose the appropriate menu command (and, in many cases, submit to the whims of a dialog box). To change drives, click the appropriate drive icon just below the menu bar. To open a directory, click its name; to move back in the path, click the appropriate portion of the path name next to the drive icons.

A tree diagram lets you save time moving through directories, but you cannot selectively collapse or expand the branches. The tree's only function is to let you change the file list in the main window.

Command Post also includes Browser, an ASCII and hex file viewer with a number of useful functions, including search and

Figure 2-9
Command Post

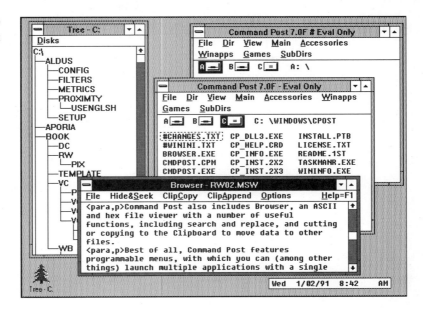

replace, and cutting or copying to the Clipboard to move data to other files or applications.

Best of all, Command Post features programmable menus, with which you can (among other things) launch multiple applications with a single command, add a prompt for the file name to load with PageMaker or other apps, or create custom dialog boxes that get input from the user. Command Post's manual includes a complete command reference for its programming language.

Command Post suffers from its inability to search for files by name or to search for text across files and directories. But its reasonable price, customizable menus, and file viewer make it worth looking into.

Prompt

If Command Post reviles the drag-and-drop approach, Prompt exemplifies it. Copying, moving, and deleting files is handled by moving icons (showing the number of selected files!) to other branches of its directory tree or to a trash can. Another icon lets you create new directories (Figure 2-10).

Prompt stands out from File Manager in a number of ways. Prompt can display multiple directory trees, for example, and automatically

Figure 2-10
Prompt

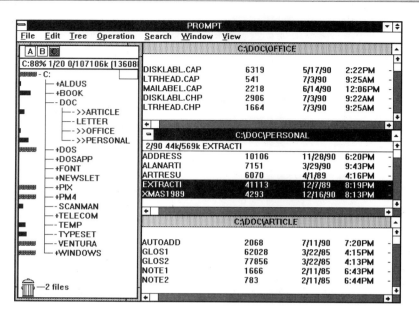

tiles its directory windows. At all times Prompt displays extremely useful information about your disks and files: percentage of disk used, total files in a selected directory, total size of a selected directory, and total number and size of selected files.

Prompt has the competition beat cold when it comes to file viewing. Shift-double click instantly opens a window into the file you need to see. The viewer supports a number of text formats (Lotus 1-2-3, Microsoft Excel, dBASE, Microsoft Word, Word Perfect, Windows Write). Even if your file format is not supported, you can still see an ASCII display of it. Unfortunately, the viewer lacks word wrap: you have to scroll horizontally for miles to read one paragraph.

When it comes to graphic viewing, Prompt goes way beyond Command Post's Browser. You can view graphics in such formats as : CGM, HPGL, PCX, DBF, TIFF, Micrografx DRW, and Lotus PIC. You can expect to be able to view more file formats (such as EPS or Corel CDR files, which aren't currently supported) in future upgrades.

Prompt hasn't forgotten your need to search for text strings across files—far from it. But they have decided to charge you an extra $145 for that ability in the form of Dragnet, a powerful disk-searching utility with dynamic links to Prompt. If your disk housekeeping is so bad that you need to conduct complex disk searches in background, consider shelling out for this product. Otherwise, stick to Prompt alone.

File Organizer

PubTech's File Organizer can best be described in one word: Macintosh. Like the Mac, folders representing directories hold icons representing files (Figure 2-11). Moving a file is as simple as dragging an icon to another folder or disk icon. (Copying files requires using the menu bar that is always at the top of your desktop.) Similarly, deleting means dragging to the trash icon; printing means dragging to a printer icon.

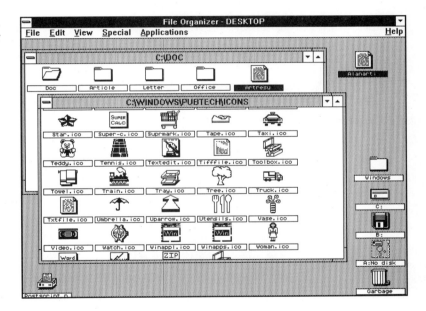

Figure 2-11
File Organizer

Like a real desk, files and folders remain on your desktop until removed. Unlike Windows, File Organizer doesn't require that applications be running to appear on the desktop. Consequently, a dozen apps and files can sit on your desktop without taking up any memory or system resources until you launch them. A menu option automatically replaces all or selected items in their original folders. Other utilities let you customize icons and store multiple arrangements of the desktop for different purposes or different users.

File Organizer lacks a useful display of disk statistics. The Get information command displays a list of each file's size, not the total of all selected files. The product also has no file viewers. As a workaround, you can append up to 128 characters of descriptive information about any icon. That's useful for document tracking, but no substitute for the ability to glance inside files.

Despite all the fun and functionality, File Organizer has problems in the speed and power department. It just takes more time and memory to draw all those icons on your screen the first time you open or scroll through a folder.

Finally, the very similarity to the Macintosh may not appeal to you. But if you run a desktop publishing office that mixes PCs and Macintoshes, File Organizer is a great way to reduce training and achieve a similar (if not identical) interface office-wide. Power users may want to look elsewhere.

General Utilities

There are a rapidly growing number of tools and utilities for Windows. Many of them have some relevance to PageMaker, however tangential. We've chosen to mention the ones we like and/or have been recommended to us by people we trust. This section could be a whole book in itself, but then we'd be writing *101 Windows Tips*, not *Real World PageMaker 4*. (Come to think of it, Scott and Jesse *are* writing *101 Windows Tips*. But that's for another publisher.)

One word of caution: Every little utility you have running on your desktop, from memory monitors to screen savers to macro files, consumes a small amount of your available RAM. If you're running PageMaker on a machine that is already starved for memory, you may want to forego the luxury of some of these items.

Sysedit   The Windows Notepad is great for editing your various .INI files, but Windows comes with something even better: Sysedit. Sysedit is a text editor that automatically opens four of the most important files on your system: WIN.INI, SYSTEM.INI, CONFIG.SYS, and AUTOEXEC.BAT. You'll find Sysedit in the system directory that's installed inside your Windows directory. Do yourself a favor and add the Sysedit icon to one of the Program Manager windows so that you can launch it from there. Anytime you need to work on a system file, just double-click Sysedit.

Macro Makers

Macros are sequences of commands and actions you string together and assign to a particular keystroke. If you want PageMaker to choose "Preferences" from the Edit menu, change your unit of measure to Inches in the Preferences dialog box, then close the dialog box, you can create a macro that does all of that. Then you can assign that macro to Ctrl-Shift-H. The next time you want to change your measurement system to inches, you can just press Ctrl-Shift-H. It's easier than choosing a menu item, making a change in a dialog box, and pressing Enter. Macros are shortcuts, just like the shortcuts software developers put into their applications; but they're *your* shortcuts that you've created for your specific tasks and ways of working.

There are a number of programs available for generating macros in Windows. (We'll discuss two of the most prominent below.) No matter which you use, the sequence is similar and the purpose the same: Let the macro do the work for you.

If the idea of creating macros is new to you, don't worry. There's nothing terribly technical about it. Just think of those tasks you do every day, over and over again, like selecting a certain font, leading, or point size for some piece of local formatting. Then try to duplicate that task in a macro recording.

Suppose, for example, you always add a Zapf Dingbats character to the end of stories in a newsletter, then change the point size of the character to 6 points. Here are the basic steps.

1. Place your cursor at the end of a story. Turn on the record mode of whatever product you're using. If your macro maker doesn't record keystrokes, you'll have to follow its special instructions—or switch to Windows Recorder.

2. In many macro programs, it's better to avoid trying to record mouse

movements. Therefore, use only keyboard commands as you change the font to Zapf Dingbats and the size to 6. Then type the character you normally use to mark the end of the story.

3. Stop the recording.

That's all there is to it! Some programs require you to name the macro in advance; some afterwards. Most will let you change the name, properties, or keyboard shortcut later. Now sit back and try it out. You'll probably want to press your shortcut key a few times, just to see the characters enter themselves, like magic, on your screen.

But wait a minute! Couldn't you add another keystroke that took you to the end of the story, then typed that string of characters? You bet. If your macro app allows nesting (like Recorder), you can make a new macro that moves the cursor to the end (Ctrl-A to select the story, followed by the Right Arrow key) and then invokes the previously built macro to create the character.

On the other hand, if your macro app allows editing (like Batch-Works), you can go into its text file and type in the new commands. If you don't know what they are, record them, find the new file, and copy the lines to the end of your first macro file. (For more on moving through text, see "Moving Through and Selecting Text" in Chapter 4, *Words*).

Most of our macros were built just like this: Create a very simple time saver. Then, as you use it over the course of hours, days, or months, you'll think of more and more ideas to expand your macros' power and efficiency. Before you know it, you've entered a whole new world as valuable for its fun and creativity as for the speed and efficiency it brings.

Recorder

Recorder is perhaps the most important time-saving Windows tool you own, and you shouldn't be caught without it. And you won't be, because it comes free inside each package of Windows. Your Windows documentation gives you the full scoop on creating macros, but let's review the essential steps:

1. Start PageMaker and set up a page arrangement and cursor position where you want your macro to begin. Make a backup copy of this publication first, in case something goes wrong.
2. Start Recorder and open the file where you want to store your macros. If you plan on having lots of macros for each of your Windows applications, you may want to start a new macro file just for PageMaker.
3. Choose "Record" from the Macro menu and adjust the dialog box settings to suit your needs. This is the place to assign the shortcut key sequence. As a general rule, choose "Ignore Mouse" from the Record Mouse list box. As an extra help, type some instructions in the Description text box. When you're finished, click Start. Recorder returns you to your PageMaker window.
4. Carefully perform the operation you want to record. Remember to use only keyboard commands (not the mouse) for actions you want to record. When you're done, press Ctrl-Break or click the flashing Recorder icon. When the Recorder dialog box appears, choose Save and click the Okay button. (You can also choose "Cancel" at this point if you made a mistake.) Finally, be sure to use Save or Save as from Recorder's File menu to save the entire macro file.
5. To play back your macros, Recorder must be active and have your macro file loaded. Your shortcut keys will then play back the keystrokes you recorded.

If you have problems with your macros, you may be trying to play them back in conditions that are too different from the setting in which you recorded them. For example, it's best to record and play macros with no menus showing or dialog boxes open. If you need to use dialog boxes in your macro, open them as part of the macro, not before you start recording.

▼ *Tip: Loading Your Macros Automatically*

Since the whole point of macros is to save time, who wants to have to start Windows, start the Recorder, load the macro file into Recorder, and only then start PageMaker? No way. A better route is to load your macros the same time you start Windows—just as we showed you earlier with File Manager. The only difference is that you add the name of your macro file (not Recorder's file name) to the load= line of WIN.INI For example, to automatically start both FileMan and your macro file, your load= line would read as follows.

load=winfile.exe macros.rec

MACROS.REC is your macro file's name. Don't use the run= line, or Recorder opens as an obtrusive window instead of an icon.

▼ Tip: Masterful Methods for Multiple Macro Mavens

If you use lots of different applications and Recorder macros for each, you can quickly run out of key-combinations to use for macros. The obvious solution is to keep multiple macro files. But how to switch among them? We don't have space to walk you through all your options, so we'll just give you some quick tips in telegraphic form. Your favorite Windows or DOS manual can help you with the details.

Multiple icons for intra-Windows switching. To switch quickly between different macro files within a single Windows session, you always take the obvious approach: use the Open command from Recorder's File menu. But a faster way (especially if you keep Program Manager open all the time) is to copy your Recorder icon several times. Then edit the Properties of each so that each icon loads a different macro file (Figure 2-12). Once done, you can load a new set of macros just by double-clicking on the appropriate icon in Program Manager. Instead of manually minimizing the Recorder window, choose Minimize on Use from the options menu. Recorder then shrinks to an icon the first time you invoke a macro.

Command line options for custom sessions. If you're likely to use the same macros throughout a Windows session, but different macros for each, try launching Recorder from the command line. Just

Figure 2-12
Launching Recorder files from multiple icons

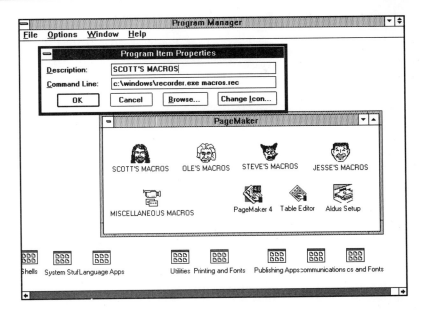

follow the win command with the name of the macro file you want to use that day. For example, typing *win macro_pm.rec* at the DOS prompt starts Windows and loads a macro file named MACRO PM.REC—a suitable name for your PageMaker macros. You could also store these commands and other command line options in a batch file. (See also the next tip below.)

Multiple WIN.INIs for the ultimate in custom sessions. If you really want to customize each Windows session, you won't be satisfied just to change the macro files. Instead, keep multiple copies of WIN.INI with custom run= and load= lines to launch the applications you want for each session. Then create a batch file for each WIN.INI file that copies the appropriate WIN.INI replacement over your existing WIN.INI This is great for workgroup situations where different users need Windows for different purposes.

▼ *Tip: The Autoexecuting Macro*

You can have one of your macros execute automatically each time you start Windows, thanks to an undocumented and little-understood "-h" parameter. To do this, don't load Recorder from the WIN.INI load= or run= lines as we suggested before. Instead, load it from the DOS prompt when you start Windows. Enter the line win recorder -h *keystroke filename*. To indicate the macro's assigned keyboard shortcut, use ^ to indicate Ctrl, + to indicate Shift, and % to indicate Alt. Here's an example.

win recorder -h ^F12 macros.rec

In the above example, our startup macro is assigned to Ctrl-F12 and is stored in MACROS.REC. We use it to arrange the icons on our desktop and set up File Manager's directory windows the way we like them.

Recorder Run

While Recorder is a wonderfully helpful Windows accessory, it does have some annoying limitations. One of these is its inability to store a single macro in an icon for quick execution. Recorder Run to the rescue! This simple shareware utility from e-Image of Edmonton, Alberta, Canada costs only 10 bucks. What's more, it takes up no RAM whatsoever (except for a second or two when you execute a macro).

Available from CompuServe and various electronic bulletin boards (or the address in the back of this book), Recorder Run (RecRun) lets you create a Program Item in Program Manager, and, on its Properties command line, specify a macro file and the name of the macro to execute. If you have an icon editor (like Icondraw, an inexpensive shareware app), you can create your own icon for each macro. Double-clicking on the icon executes the specified macro.

For example, here's Scott's favorite use of RecRun: Create a macro that launches File Manager and subsequently runs a previous macro for configuring File Manager's windows (see our tip under File Manager earlier in this chapter). Then store this macro in a Program Item that uses the File Manager icon. (Once it's working, you can delete the normal File Manager icon altogether.) The result is an icon that looks just like File Manager, but automatically configures FileMan's windows upon startup.

RecRun's big advantage to power users is that it lets you create a vast number of macros without using up a limited number of Ctrl, Alt, or Shift keystrokes for shortcuts (a practice that is likely to preempt keystrokes already used by PageMaker or other apps). Here are a couple of tips to help you exploit that feature.

▼ Tip: Use Keystrokes Your Keyboard Doesn't Have

Recorder's Properties dialog box gives you a pop-up list of possible keyboard shortcuts, including function keys from F1 to F16. Most of us only have twelve function keys, and a few of you old timers still use keyboards with only 10. With RecRun, you can put these unavailable keys to work. Just use Recorder to assign Ctrl-F16 or Alt-F15 (or whatever) to a macro you intend to invoke with RecRun. Then, in Program Manager, type this name into the command line of your macro's Program Item Properties—for example:

recrun.exe macros.rec ctrl+alt+F16

RecRun doesn't care that the keys aren't on your keyboard; it just looks for the first macro that exactly matches the listing in Recorder.

▼ Tip: Use Key Words, Not Keystrokes

Neither Recorder nor RecRun require you to use shortcut keys at all. To save on keystroke combinations, just leave blank the Shortcut Key section of Recorder's Macro Properties dialog box. Under Macro Name, type in a short but unique moniker for your macro. Then, in Program Manager, type that name into the command line of your macro's Program Item Properties—for example:

recrun.exe macros.exe AddPage

It's obvious from the macro's name that it adds a page to your publication. Besides saving on key combinations, this trick makes your icon's command line (Properties dialog box, File menu) a little more clear to others who need to figure out what all your icons are for.

▼ Tip: Managing Icon Macros

Since it's usually much quicker to hit a few keystrokes than go outside your window to click a macro icon, you'll generally want to limit RecRun to those macros that help manage your Windows system—launch apps, fiddle with File Manager, arrange icons or windows on your desktop, etc. Then devote your keyboard shortcuts to macros you'll use exclusively inside PageMaker.

If you still run out of keystrokes for macros, use an arrangement of icons and windows that will maximize your efficiency. For example, you could size your PageMaker window to fill the whole screen except for a strip along one edge. Then arrange Program Manager to peek through along that edge with your macro icons lined up in the visible area. (The mockup in Figure 2-13 shows one possibility.) This way, your icon macros function like an extra toolbox that you access whenever you need to. Naturally, you can toggle between this view

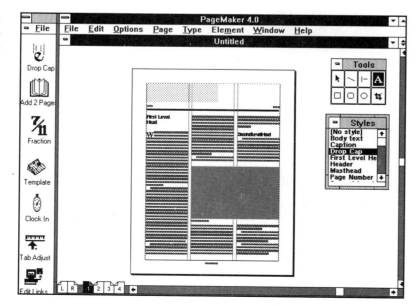

Figure 2-13
Using icons to launch macros

and a maximized (full-screen) PageMaker just by double-clicking on PageMaker's title bar.

BatchWorks

Even with RecRun, Recorder is a limited macro-making tool. Perhaps its biggest drawback is its refusal to let you edit the keystrokes you record. Ironically, Recorder was developed for Microsoft by Softbridge Microsystems Corporation, whose product Bridge lets you edit macros but not record keystrokes. Brilliant. Though Bridge offers powerful tools for programming, building dialog boxes, and implementing Dynamic Data Exchange, we suspect most users will be scared off by its $695 price tag.

Stepping into the void between "free" Recorder and pricey Bridge is BatchWorks from Publishing Technologies (the same folks who brought you File Organizer). With BatchWorks, you can create batch files and macros (basically the same thing) and launch them by double-clicking on an icon or file name (batches), or using a keyboard shortcut or custom menu option (macros). This last feature is very handy: you can have one set of macros appear on PageMaker's control menu, another set on Word for Windows' control menu, and so on. You can also have global menu macros which appear on the control menus of all applications.

Like Recorder, you can create macros by recording your keystrokes. But unlike this limited accessory, you can go back and edit these macros. That's because macros and batches are nothing but ASCII files that can be created and edited with any text editor like Notepad. BatchWorks' programming language lets you open and close applications, position windows, perform calculations, manipulate integers and text strings, receive information from the user, and even create custom dialog boxes with all the trimmings: radio buttons, check boxes, list boxes, and so on. It does not, however, support dynamic data exchange, arrays, or "while" loops. If you have any programming experience at all, you'll be creating miniature Windows programs in no time—and without any expensive software developer kit or compiler.

And what if you have no programming experience? Aye, there's the rub. The manual starts out nice and friendly, but then jumps into advanced level without much warning or guidance. But if you study the examples in the manual and on the disk, you'll eventually figure things out.

▼ Tip: Punch In and Out with BatchWorks

Among BatchWorks many useful commands is one called DateTime, which generates the current date and time in the format specified in the International section of Windows Control Panel. Used with Send-Key (a command that transmits keystrokes to the currently active window), you can keep track of how long you've been working on a PageMaker publication. This macro is only two lines long:

```
SendKey("This file was last modified on+; ")
SendKey(DateTime())
```

Here's how to use it:

1. Store the above lines in a text file with the BatchWorks macro extension, .PTM.
2. Following the instructions in the BatchWorks manual, assign the macro to PageMaker's control menu with a name like Punch In/Out. (You can also add a keyboard shortcut if you like.)
3. Open a PageMaker publication and create a text block somewhere off the page.
4. Go to the control menu and choose Punch In/Out.
5. Watch with glee as your macro types the message about the last modification date, along with the current date and time.

Now, every time you open or close the publication, place a text insertion point at the end of the text block with the date and time in it, and choose your menu command (or press its keyboard shortcut). BatchWorks enters a new date and time, and you'll be able to see how much time you've spent working on the publication. This is handy for keeping track of when a publication was last modified. If that was too easy for you, see how many other steps you can add to the macro to automate the process as much as possible.

If all you need is the date the publication was printed, use the Time/Date import filter, as described in Chapter 4, *Words*.

Launch

Launch is a very handy bit of shareware, written by David Stafford ($25 registration fee). You use Launch to create a custom pop-up menu when you click anyplace on your desktop. From that menu you can launch any application that runs under Windows. As with Program Manager, you can also specify a file to be loaded with the application you're launching. For example, Scott has WIN.INI as a Launch menu item—which really means that Notepad opens with WIN.INI ready to edit any time he needs to fiddle with a font or change a startup option.

Setting up is simple. Just edit the LAUNCH.INI text file that Launch creates, adding your own menu items and the name of the associated applications (example: PageMaker = pm4.exe). Then edit WIN.INI to start Launch from the run= line (as explained earlier in this chapter). The next time you start Windows, your menu system will be active.

Why Launch? Because working with PageMaker usually involves working with a whole suite of programs. Moving quickly between those programs makes for faster, easier page makeup. And once you start collecting software, shareware, freeware, elseware, and anyware, Program Manager can quickly become littered with icons. No matter how good your organization, it simply takes time to hunt through various program groups to find the right application icon—especially annoying if you only needed the app for a minute or two. Launch simplifies things by letting you put five or ten (or whatever) of your most-used apps at the touch of your mouse button. And the whole thing takes very little RAM to operate.

▼ *Tip: The Launch-RecRun-Recorder Triple Play*

Just as you can use RecRun to assign Recorder macros to icons, you can also use Launch to assign RecRun commands to your pop-up menu. When you edit your LAUNCH.INI file, just enter a RecRun command where you would normally type an application name—for example:

Add New Page= recrun.exe macros.rec AddPage

This Launch sequence runs a macro that adds pages to your publication. Your Launch menu has suddenly become twice as productive.

Now for the final touch. When you open and size your PageMaker window, be sure to leave a tiny sliver of space (or more) along one edge so your desktop can show through. Then, to use any of your Launch-RecRun-Recorder macros, you just move your cursor to the desktop space and click to bring up your Launch menu (Figure 2-14). It's like adding an entire extra menu to PageMaker, and it's completely customizable. Total cost of this macro recording, icon-creating, and menu-creating system: thirty-five dollars.

▼ *Tip: Launch does BatchWorks*

Anything that you can assign to a Program Manager icon (via the Command Line in the Properties dialog box) can also be assigned to

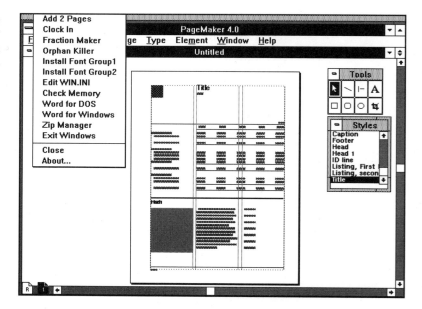

Figure 2-14
Combining Recorder macros with RecRun and Launch

Launch. That means your BatchWorks batch files can also be run from Launch if you don't want them to appear as macros on PageMaker's system menu. Just save your BatchWorks file with the .PTB (not .PTM) extension to indicate it's a batch file (not a macro). Assign the PTB file to your Launch menu with an appropriate name, reload Launch, and you're ready to go. Naturally, you'll need some portion of the desktop showing so you can bring up the Launch menu and run your batch.

RunProg

How much time do you spend arranging your program windows each time you start a work session? Some polite applications start their windows in the same size and position last used, but most, unfortunately, do not. You could solve this with hDC First Apps' Work Sets, but that might be overkill. For a cheaper solution, get RunProg.

RunProg is an affordable ($10 plus the cost of disks) bit of shareware that runs invisibly but enhances all your other programs. It lets you designate whether your applications should start up in normal, minimized, maximized, or custom size. If you choose the custom option, you can also designate exactly where on the desktop the window should appear. RunProg also lets you add these features to the programs you launch automatically when starting Windows (via the WIN.INI file).

In addition, RunProg lets you designate the startup directory for any given application. For example, if you start PageMaker from Program Manager, and then choose the Open command from the File menu, you'll see that you're in the PageMaker directory—not the directory where you keep your publications. RunProg fixes that so that the first directory you get in PageMaker is the one you want.

RunProg requires a few arcane parameters on an icon's Command Line in the Program Item Properties dialog box (choose "Properties" from Program Manager's File menu). If you don't use Program Manager, not to worry. RunProg also works with most menuing application launchers, like Launch.

▼ *Tip: Use RunProg to launch apps from File Manager*

But what if you don't usually launch PageMaker from Program Manager or Launch? What if you just double-click on a PM4 file in File Manager? No sweat. If your application is listed in the path command in your AUTOEXEC.BAT file (and PageMaker is), you can still use RunProg (version 1.5) to customize your startup window. For example, to use RunProg with a PageMaker file, select a PM4 file in a File Manager window. Next, choose Associate from File Manager's File menu. In the dialog box, type in the RunProg parameters as you would if you were working with a Program Manager icon. The only difference is you omit the information for a startup directory. Now click OK. The next time you double-click a PageMaker filename, PageMaker will open that document with the window sized and positioned at the coordinates you specified.

Anything You Can Do Icon Do Better

As you've already learned, you can store macros in Program Manager icons whether you use BatchWorks or Windows' own Recorder (with the help of RecRun). But having to use Windows' ugly default icons for your macros is not only an eyesore, it defeats the purpose of a graphical interface—to use graphics to communicate quickly and effectively.

For icons that really communicate the purpose of your programs, batches, and macros, you need a utility to create your own—or borrow them from existing files. One of the best is Icon Designer from hDC Computer Corporation (Figure 2-15). This program lets you store icons in clumps (several icons in one file). Icon Designer's strong point is its ability to import icons from virtually any file containing an icon. For example, if you want to touch up PageMaker's icon, you could import it from the PM4.EXE file and edit it as you please. Icon Designer includes over 100 sample icons to get you started. The utility is low on drawing tools; you have to do everything freehand.

Another offering in this area is Icondraw, a shareware program for painting your own icons. Like Icon Designer, Icondraw features a 16-color palette, but lacks import ability. You can, however, paste in

Figure 2-15
hDC Icon Designer

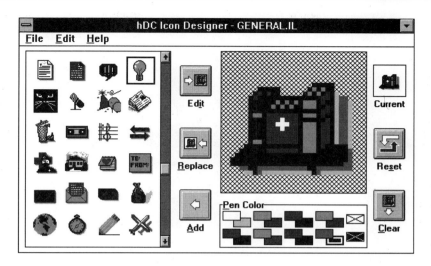

bitmaps from the Clipboard. Its strongest point is its drawing tools: freehand, straight line, and open and filled circles and rectangles.

To assign icons to program items, select the current icon in Program Manager and choose Properties from the File menu. Click the Change Icon button and type the name of the file containing your icon in the File Name text box. If your file contains more than one icon, click the View Next button until you see the icon you want. For more on items and properties, consult your *Microsoft Windows User's Guide*.

hDC First Apps

As its name suggests, FirstApps is a starter set of utilities (hDC calls them MicroApps) intended to meet the needs of a wide range of users (see Figure 2-16). Trying to please everybody may seem a fool's errand, but this package has garnered widespread appeal in a short period of time. Although few people are apt to want every utility in this package, we think you'll find enough goodies here to make it worth the $100 investment.

Tying these MicroApps together is the First Apps MicroApp Manager, which takes the place of your control menu on all your applications. This is handy if you're likely to need to jump into a MicroApp without leaving PageMaker or some other program. It can also be annoying—especially if you are already using BatchWorks: Your control menu can quickly become huge—bigger even than some

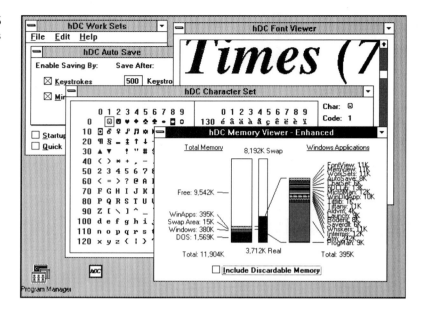

Figure 2-16
hDC First Apps

of the FirstApps windows themselves. Fortunately, MicroApp manager gives you the option of staying by itself on the desktop without affecting your control menus.

Either way, MicroApp Manager becomes the launch point for all the other MicroApps in this collection. Most of them appear in small, pop-up windows of fixed size. hDC plans to produce more MicroApps in the future. In the meantime, let's look at some of the ones we find most useful.

Auto Save. If you're the type who gets so involved in your pub that you forget to save once in a while, this MicroApp could rescue you. It automatically saves the file in the active window at an interval you specify. You can designate your interval in keystrokes, minutes, or both. You can also set it to prompt you before saving. This is handy if you're playing "what if" with your publication and want to be able to revert to the way things were before.

Character Set. This pop-up window displays the character sets for ANSI (American National Standards Institute) as used by Windows as well as the OEM (Original Equipment Manufacturer) set used by some

DOS applications. It is useful for finding, copying, and pasting unusual characters into your application, especially if your publication deals with foreign currency (¥, £) or languages (ç, ÿ). For most users, however, this MicroApp has little utility. What we'd really like to see is the character sets for Symbol or Zapf Dingbats. Oh well—maybe in their next upgrade.

Font Viewer. Unlike Windows Control Panel, this micro app lets you view printer fonts as well as screen fonts. Each size is displayed at actual size for bitmapped fonts or in a single size for scalable fonts. Note, however, that Font Viewer is just that—it doesn't give you any downloading or other font handling functions.

Memory Viewer. This window provides a graphic breakdown and list of everything currently occupying your computer's RAM (and virtual memory if you're operating in 386 enhanced mode). Unlike a number of shareware memory viewers, the hDC version doesn't just give a total of available RAM, but tells how much each application (including itself) is taking up. If your system is caught in a memory crunch, this can be a useful diagnostic tool. After consulting Memory Viewer, for example, you may discover ATM is a RAM hog and cut back on the size of its font cache. We like this MicroApp—now if only it also reported on disk space.

Work Sets. If you have enough RAM to run PageMaker and your supporting apps all at once, Work Sets is for you. By memorizing your screen, Work Sets lets you launch your favorite apps simultaneously with the windows arranged the way you like them. You can create different work sets for different work sessions or tasks. This is also handy for workgroup situations where different users want their own apps or arrangement of windows.

You get the picture: You could duplicate a lot of these functions with various shareware or commercial utilities. But if three or four of these utilities are just what you're looking for, then the MicroApp approach is certainly a quality product at a reasonable price.

Dinger

Strictly speaking, Dinger isn't a separate utility. It's a $19 shareware package consisting of three Word for Windows macros: QwikSymbol, Accenter, and Dinger itself. All three present characters not readily apparent from your keyboard. Just double-click on the character you want, and poof! The character appears in your document.

QwikSymbol brings up a dialog box of commonly used Zapf Dingbats (if you have that font) and Symbol characters, including the em dash, copyright symbol, and true typographic quotation marks.

Accenter presents a display of characters common to other languages, complete with diacritical marks. Accenter works with any font that supports the Windows ANSI character set—which is probably most of the fonts you use.

Dinger creates a table on your screen showing all the characters in a font you designate upon installation. It differs from QwikSymbol in presenting the entire character set for a given font. You can change the font displayed in the table while you watch. Or, for faster access, you can install multiple Dingers—one for each font you use.

The main disadvantage of Dinger is its speed. QwikSymbol and Accenter are brisk, but Dinger itself can be sluggish on any but the fastest computers. But if you consider the time you waste rummaging through reference cards or manuals to find the key that brings up your favorite Dingbat, Dinger probably ends up saving you time.

Living With Your System

Living with a system setup is sort of like living with a person. It takes a while to get used to their foibles and idiosyncrasies, and to adapt your patterns around those peculiarities. Sometimes you're furious at them, while at other times you can't imagine how you'd get by without them.

Happily, though, your computer system is not like a person in most other ways. It doesn't think, talk, or make noise during movies. It never gets mad at you (though sometimes it seems to), and it doesn't respond to flattery, bribery, or cajoling humor. When it does, we'll be able to stop writing books, and let the computer write them for us.

CHAPTER 3

Making PageMaker Mind

They say there's no such thing as a bad dog, only different dogs. You may not feel that way, but one thing is certain: everyone sets up and uses PageMaker differently. We all have our own ways of making PageMaker mind.

Your copy of PageMaker should heel, fetch, speak, and print to disk exactly as you think it should. Otherwise the darn thing just sits around eating disk space and scaring the neighbor's kids. Training your copy of PageMaker takes time and effort, but you'll end up with a version of PageMaker that'll bring your pipe, your slippers, and, we can only hope, your newspaper.

Rules to Live By

In this chapter we'll cover techniques that apply to working with PageMaker in general—from master pages to getting help. Some of the material covered here may seem elementary; we urge you to read it anyway. We're trying to communicate ways of thinking about the program that will help you solve your own PageMaker problems and develop your own PageMaker tips and tricks.

To begin with, there are several maxims we've developed during those brief periods when we weren't rushing to make deadlines. Follow them, and *you* won't have to rush to make deadlines.

Be lazy. Computers are supposed to take the drudgery out of life. If you find yourself doing the same thing over and over again, you can probably make the computer do it for you, so you can do something fun. Also, people tend to tire of doing the same thing over and over again, and make mistakes. Computers don't. Although automating processes seems time-consuming at first—it can be tough creating Recorder macros, for example—it's well worth doing for the time it'll save you in the future.

And if you're in a position to hire people, be smart: hire the lazy.

Keep it simple. We don't mean that you should keep the design of your publication simple, but that you should keep the PageMaker implementation of that design as simple as possible. Accomplish your design goals using the smallest number of PageMaker elements possible. Large numbers of text blocks, lines, stories, and boxes slow PageMaker to a crawl. Extraneous items placed on the pasteboard and text blocks that are too wide or full of extra carriage returns can also slow (or knock) you down. And besides, you don't want to have to remember what you did with all that stuff.

Keep it organized. Pick a system for producing a publication and stick to it. Set up a file naming system and subdirectories in some fashion that makes sense to you and then use them consistently. If you're working in a group, make sure everyone understands the file naming system and organization, keeps their files updated, and has and uses the same fonts. There are few experiences more painful in desktop publishing than taking the wrong version of your publication to an imagesetting service bureau, or taking the wrong versions of linked graphics files.

Make it repeatable. Approach each publication with the idea that you'll be revising it sometime in the future, even if you think you won't. If you've been lazy, kept the publication simple, and maintained your file organization, you'll have most of the work done the next time you open the file.

Use styles. Paragraph styles are the key to keeping your text formats repeatable, and they make experimenting easier and faster.

Avoid things you can't see. This is one rule that you'll want or need to break in some cases, but in general, don't put things on your pages that you can't see. You'll trip over them every time.

Experiment. We know it takes time to learn a new way of doing things, like using a new keyboard shortcut. Take the time. Try out new things. You won't remember them all, but some of them will stick, and you'll have a better, faster way of making PageMaker mind.

If it doesn't work, poke at it. It sounds dumb, but it's the most important rule. Try doing the same thing again; sometimes it'll work. If, for example, you're having trouble printing a page, try proof printing. If the page prints, you'll know something's wrong with the graphics. Just keep on poking at it until it works. And finally—we know this sounds absurd but it often works—try having someone else do the same thing.

Getting Ready

With those rules in mind, you still need to make sure you're set up before you ever get into PageMaker. Even if you weren't a Boy Scout (none of us was), always be prepared.

Is your system ready? Is your printer set up to print? Are the fonts you want to use downloaded? If your system isn't set up, go to the previous chapter, go directly to the previous chapter. There are few things more frustrating than reworking an entire publication because you've changed your system configuration. Do it now.

Have you designated your target printer? Ignore this step at your peril. *Before you begin your publication*, choose Target printer from the file menu and select the printer you will use for your *final* output (i.e., not intermediate proofs). Depending on your printer, you should also designate which font cartridges you'll be using. PageMaker optimizes your typography based on this printer designation.

If you lay out your publication with this setting on the wrong printer, you'll either have less-than-optimal output (the charl be off) or you'll have to let PageMaker recompose your publication for the new printer—a process that can result in different line breaks, columns too short or too long, and generally a lot of work to fix something that should have been right in the first place. Do it now, before you place a single file. For more information on setting up your printer, see Chapter 6, *Printing*.

Are the files you want to place in PageMaker really ready to place? You can save an enormous amount of time if your text and graphics files are in good shape before you bring them into Page-Maker. It's far better, for example, to have a piece of art that is exactly what you want than to place something in PageMaker and try to "fix it up" with PageMaker lines and boxes; getting the alignment right is tough.

It's also better to import a graphic that is exactly the portion of the image you want, rather than importing a graphic and cropping it. Make the changes with the graphic application you used to create the artwork whenever possible.

Similarly, if your text files are styled and/or tagged, you won't have to style (or format) each paragraph in PageMaker. Text files should have been proofed and corrected. Even with the Story Editor, it's still easier to make text changes in a word processor than in PageMaker. For more on preparing your files for PageMaker, check out Chapters 4, *Words*, and 5, *Pictures*.

Where are your hands? Most of the serious PageMaker users we've seen—even southpaws—keep their right hand on the mouse while their left hand hovers over the left end of the keyboard. You might find that another arrangement works better for you, but you should know that most of the keyboard combinations you'll want to use are found around the left end of the keyboard.

Of course, you can always use a macro maker to change PageMaker's keyboard shortcuts, so you can set up your PageMaker keyboard shortcuts to suit whatever personal, idiosyncratic, and sick preferences you might have (see Chapter 2, *Building a PageMaker System* for more information on macro-making utilities).

Turning On

Your Windows user's guide outlines a number of ways to launch applications, including PageMaker. For example, if PageMaker is the only Windows application you use, you might want to have it launch automatically when you start Windows. Follow these steps:

1. Use a text editor like Notepad or Sysedit to open your WIN.INI file.
2. Find the run= and load= lines near the top of the file.
3. If you want PageMaker to start as an open window, enter the name of its executable file on the run= line (for instance, run=pm4.exe). If you want PageMaker to load as an icon when you start Windows, add its filename to the load= line (for example, load=pm4.exe).

That's all there is to it. Of course, a thoroughly prepared user will also use these lines to launch macro files and other utilities at the same time. For more ideas on customizing startup options for different users and utilities, see Chapter 2, *Building a PageMaker System*.

▼ *Tip: Changing PageMaker's Startup Directory*

One annoying fact about life in Windows is that most Windows applications start in the directory where the program lies—not where you keep your documents (unless you keep them in the same place). That means you'll have to go clicking through directories in the Open publication dialog box every time you need to open a PageMaker file. Our preferred solution to this problem is a program called RunProg (discussed in Chapter 2, *Building a PageMaker System*), but if you can't find this piece of shareware, there's a way around this inconvenience. The only prerequisite is that PageMaker's executable file be in a directory specified in the path command of your AUTOEXEC.BAT file. No problem here; PageMaker's installation program normally adjusts the path command for you. So here's what you do:

1. Select PageMaker's icon in Windows Program Manager. Choose "Properties" from Program Manager's file menu to access the Program Item Properties dialog box.
2. In the Command Line text edit box, add the path of your desired startup directory before the PageMaker executable filename. For example, to start PageMaker in the \BOOK directory on your C: drive, your Command Line would read as follows.

c:\book\pm4.exe.

3. Click OK. An error message appears, stating that path you've specified is invalid. Click OK to clear the message. Your PageMaker icon will have changed to a generic computer-screen icon.
4. Select the icon and again choose Properties from the file menu. In the Program Item Properties dialog box, click Change Icon.
5. In the file Name text edit box, type the actual path where PageMaker resides—for example, c:\pm4\pm4.exe. Click OK, and OK again to close the dialog box. You'll receive another error message. But this time, your PageMaker icon should now look normal. Moreover, if you've done everything right, double-clicking the icon brings up PageMaker in the directory you specified.

Changing PageMaker's Defaults

Do you often find yourself choosing "Preferences" under the Edit menu so that you can change your unit of measurement to picas, rather than inches? Or having to change your paper size setting from "Letter" to a custom size you often use? Or setting the line width to "Hairline"? Let's fix that.

You can change almost all of PageMaker's default settings—page size, styles, units of measurement, paragraph specs, colors, typeface, point size, etc. This is a good thing, because the defaults that come with PageMaker are mostly useless.

With no document open, just go through and change the menus and dialog boxes to your preferred settings. Every change you make becomes the default for all future publications. To set defaults that apply to a single publication only, open the publication, select the pointer tool, and, with no text or graphic selected, change any settings you want.

For example, in the Preferences dialog box, we always change the default measurement to "Picas." Ole and Jesse set the ruler guides to "Back," so they can see things that are behind them. Steve and Scott prefer guides in front, and Ctrl-click to select objects that are behind the ruler guides. And you'd better get rid of those default styles (keep clicking "Remove" in the Define styles dialog box until you've eradicated them). They'll just confuse you later if you don't, because you're bound to have a different style named "Headline" that gets mixed up with the "Headline" in PageMaker's default styles list.

Changing PageMaker's defaults is one of the easiest and best ways to save yourself time. We'll explain our preferred defaults throughout the book; you'll have to decide whether your preferences are the same, or whether you want to be wrongheaded and recalcitrant.

▼ Tip: Remapping PageMaker's Keyboard Shortcuts with Windows Recorder

In Chapter 2 you learned how to use the Windows Recorder accessory to create macros with keyboard shortcuts. You can also use the same accessory to reassign PageMaker's existing shortcuts. Just start the recording, fill out the dialog box with the keyboard shortcut of your choice, perform the function you want, and save the macro. The shortcut will override PageMaker's use of the keys and perform only the new Recorder macro.

For example, suppose you like to leave the rulers showing most of the time, but you often need to turn "Snap to Rulers" on and off. The shortcut Ctrl-Shift-Y is too cumbersome for this frequent maneuver. Solution: Switch the shortcuts for displaying rulers (Ctrl-R) and Snap to Rulers (Ctrl-Shift-Y). Just make a Recorder macro for each, but swap their shortcut keys. (Or make a macro that turns both on at once, if that's your preference.) Naturally, the PageMaker menus will still show the old shortcuts, but your fingers will know what really works.

Scott's favorite key remap is to assign F12 (move to next page) to the Page Down key and F11 (move to previous page) to the Page Up key. It seems so obvious, it's hard to understand why Aldus didn't do it this way in the first place. Of course, the trade-off is you can no longer use those keys to scroll the screen up and down.

One caution: When recording a macro to replace keyboard shortcuts, don't use any keystrokes already assigned to another Recorder macro. If you do, your macro may merely nest another Recorder macro instead of executing the PageMaker shortcut you want. One way to avoid this is to use the Alt-key shortcuts to replace Ctrl-key combinations.

▼ *Tip: Close All Dialog Boxes*

When you're more than one dialog box deep, you can close all of the dialog boxes and apply any changes you've made by holding down Alt-Ctrl and pressing Enter (or clicking OK). PageMaker closes all of the dialog boxes and applies your changes. If you don't want to apply the changes you've made, hold down Alt-Ctrl and press Esc (or click Cancel). PageMaker closes the dialog boxes without applying the changes. This trick only applies to PageMaker-generated dialog boxes; it doesn't work with dialog boxes built into Windows (such as the many dialogs accessed through "Setup" in the Target printer dialog box).

The Publication Window

You've no doubt heard about Aldus marketing's oft-touted "pasteboard metaphor." It's good marketing malarkey, but it's also a good description of how PageMaker works. The Layout view is an electronic version of the good old pasteup board (Figure 3-1).

MAKING PAGEMAKER MIND   **69**

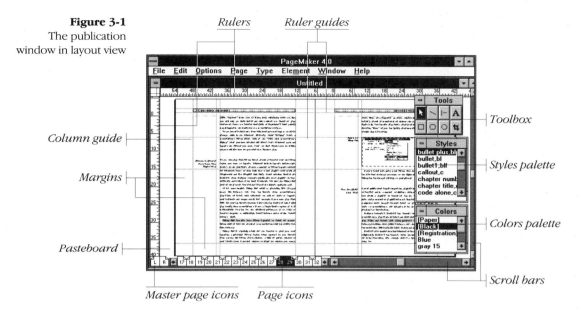

Figure 3-1
The publication window in layout view

Labels: Rulers, Ruler guides, Toolbox, Styles palette, Colors palette, Scroll bars, Page icons, Master page icons, Pasteboard, Margins, Column guide

In addition to layout view, PageMaker 4 offers a new view of your publication—the story view (Figure 3-2). The story view is for text editing, spell checking, indexing, using search and replace functions, and other text-specific tasks.

For more information on using story view, see "The Story Editor" in Chapter 4, *Words*.

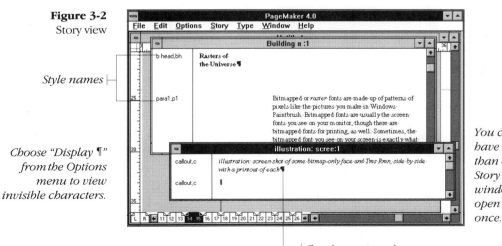

Figure 3-2
Story view

Style names

Choose "Display ¶" from the Options menu to view invisible characters.

Carriage return icon

You can have more than one Story editor window open at once.

These two views comprise PageMaker's "child windows"—smaller windows that you can resize, move, and shrink to an icon within PageMaker's main or "parent window." You can arrange these child windows any way that works for you, but the size of your screen imposes some limitations. A large monitor has the luxury of showing many windows at once. For most folks, however, we recommend keeping your layout view window maximized (the quickest way is to double click on the publication title bar). Then open story view windows in front of the layout window as you need them. You can leave these windows open all the time, toggling among them with Ctrl-E. (If you have more than one story view window open, place your cursor in the story you want to edit and then press Ctrl-E).

This can be a time saver as long as you have enough memory and don't leave too many windows open. However, having numerous windows open drains Windows' system sesources—creating a kind of memory bottleneck. If your system runs slow or you get out-of-memory messages, try leaving only your layout window open. Then open Story view windows as you need them and close each as soon as you're done.

The Toolbox

If the pasteboard is the palette on which you build your pages in PageMaker, the Toolbox is, well, your toolbox. It doesn't contain every tool you need (many of them are in menus and dialog boxes), but the basic tools are here for grabbing, moving, sizing, and drawing things (Figure 3-3). You want the Toolbox to be your friend. At Aldus, lines, circles, squares, and other graphics drawn in PageMaker are called *LBO*s (Lines, Boxes, and Ovals—pronounced "elbows").

▼ *Tip: Constraining Tools*

If you hold down Shift while using the Ellipse or either of the Rectangle tools, you'll draw perfect circles and squares. Hold down Shift while drawing lines with the Line tools, and you'll draw lines

MAKING PAGEMAKER MIND **71**

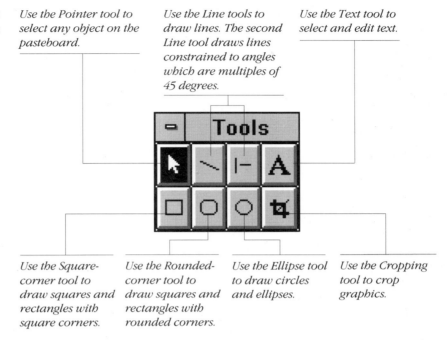

Figure 3-3 PageMaker's Toolbox

Use the Pointer tool to select any object on the pasteboard.

Use the Line tools to draw lines. The second Line tool draws lines constrained to angles which are multiples of 45 degrees.

Use the Text tool to select and edit text.

Use the Square-corner tool to draw squares and rectangles with square corners.

Use the Rounded-corner tool to draw squares and rectangles with rounded corners.

Use the Ellipse tool to draw circles and ellipses.

Use the Cropping tool to crop graphics.

constrained to 45-degree angles. If you're dragging things with the Pointer tool, holding down Shift limits the movement of those objects to 90-degree angles.

▼ *Tip: Selecting Tools with Function Keys*

You can select the tools in the Toolbox by pressing the Shift plus some function key as shown in Table 3-1.

Table 3-1 Shift-key tool selection shortcuts

Press	To select			
F9	▶	Shift-F2	╲	
Shift-F3	⊢	Shift-F4	A	
Shift-F5	□	Shift-F6	○	
Shift-F7	○	Shift-F8	⌐	

▼ *Tip: Toggling the Pointer Tool*

You can also switch to the Pointer tool—no matter what tool you're currently using—by pressing F9. Press it again to toggle back to the tool you were using.

Getting from Place to Place

The most obvious tools for getting around your publication—which you can think of either as moving your publication in the window or changing your window's view of the publication—are the scroll bars on the right and bottom of the publication window and the page icons at the lower-left.

Don't use them. It's just like driving—the tourists, the bewildered, and the damned clog the obvious routes, while the cabbies and old hands scream through the back streets, reaching their destinations faster and with fewer headaches.

▼ *Tip: Use the Grabber Hand*

A good way to make adjustments in your view of the publication—particularly after you've zoomed to a point—is to use the Grabber hand. Hold down Alt and drag. The cursor changes into the Grabber hand regardless of the tool you have selected, and your view of the publication moves in the direction you're dragging (Figure 3-4). Use the Grabber hand to push and pull the publication around in the publication window.

Zooming

The fastest way to get from point to point on a page is by zooming (why do you think they call it zooming?). Although you can zoom using the various commands in the Page menu, the best ways involve the right mouse button. If your mouse only has one button, you can also zoom by combining mouse clicks with the Ctrl, Alt, and Shift keys.

Figure 3-4
The Grabber hand

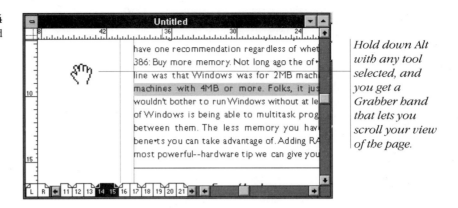

Hold down Alt with any tool selected, and you get a Grabber hand that lets you scroll your view of the page.

You just point to the place you want to zoom to, and with the appropriate key combination, click. See the key-click combinations in Table 3-2.

These shortcuts are generally better than pressing Ctrl-1 and Ctrl-2 (as shown on the Page menu) because the key-click combinations zoom in on the area you point at in the window, taking you right where you want to go. The keyboard menu shortcuts, on the other

Table 3-2 Key-click zoom combinations

Current View	Key-click Combination	Resulting View
Any view except actual size	Right mouse button Or: Ctrl-Alt-left mouse button	Actual size
Actual size	Right mouse button Or: Ctrl-Alt-left mouse button	Fit in window
Any view except 200%	Shift-right mouse button Or: Ctrl-Alt-Shift-left mouse button	200%
200%	Shift-right mouse button Or: Ctrl-Alt-Shift-left mouse button Or: Right mouse button	Actual size

hand, do one of three things depending on what you're doing when you invoke them.

- Take you to the center of the page (at whatever size you specify).
- Take you to the last view of the same magnification you used.
- Center any currently selected object (or the text cursor) in the window.

Mix and match the zooming techniques until you find combinations you like. We always use key-clicks to move to Actual and 200% views, and Ctrl-W to return to fit in window view from Actual size and 200% views.

▼ *Tip: Fit in World*

A great "hidden" page view is available: "fit in world." To see the entire pasteboard, hold down Shift and choose "fit in window" from the Page menu (or press Ctrl-Shift-W). Of course, on many monitors "fit in world" isn't very different from 25% view. But it's nice to know something no one else knows. (Actually, "fit in world" doesn't really make sense; this should be called "fit pasteboard in window," but we like "fit in world" because it imparts a sense of power.)

Turning Pages

The quickest way to get to the next page isn't clicking on the icon for the next page. Instead, press F12. To go to the previous page, press F11. If you hold either of these keys down (or hit them several times in a row), you'll jump several pages without stopping to display each one. So even if you're moving forward 10 pages, you may find it easier to press F12 ten times (or five times with a facing-pages layout). (Note: If you used a Recorder macro to assign these keys to Page Up and Page Down as we suggested earlier, this trick won't work. You still have to use F11 and F12 to jump across multiple pages.)

To move to other pages, use the Go to page dialog box. The shortcut is to press Ctrl-G (or Alt-P, G), type a page number, and press Enter to reach another page.

▼ Tip: Saving Time on a Two-Sided Document

To save yourself the trouble of constantly turning pages when working on a single-sheet, two-sided document, just insert a blank first page and select the Facing pages option in the Page setup dialog box. Then build the document on pages 2 and 3. This lets you see both sides of your document while you work. When you're finished, print only the second and third pages, or delete the empty first page.

▼ Tip: Changing to fit in Window View as You Change Pages

You can view turn to any page and view it at "fit in window"—regardless of its current page view setting—by holding down Shift as you click the page icon.

▼ Tip: Changing Page View for All Pages

To change the page view for every page in the document, hold down both Alt and Ctrl as you choose the page view from the Page menu. (As a convention, we normally write Ctrl before Alt in this book. However, this is one case where order makes a difference; you must either press both keys simultaneously or press and hold Alt, then Ctrl, then select the page view.)

▼ Tip: Viewing Your Pages One After Another

Can't remember what page you want to go to? Hold down Shift and choose "Go to page," and PageMaker jumps to the first page of the document and starts displaying pages (or spreads) one after another. When PageMaker gets to the end it goes back to the first page and starts over.

Click the mouse or press Esc to stop at any time. This is also a great way to review a document one last time before you print it or take it to a service bureau. You might want to change the page view for all pages to "fit in window" first (see the previous tip).

Working with Pages

The first step in building a publication is setting up the pages—setting margins and columns, building a grid, putting running items on master pages, and moving things between pages. To begin, define the size and orientation of the pages (42 picas wide by 57 picas tall, for example), and the shape of the *live area* within the page. The live area is the part of the page within which the bulk of your publication will fall. It is established by the margins that you define in the Page setup dialog box. Running heads and page numbers, and perhaps some special graphic elements, will lie outside the live area, but PageMaker works best if your body copy, captions, and illustrations fall inside it (Figure 3-5).

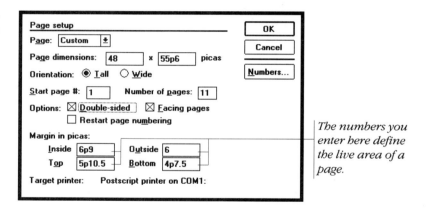

Figure 3-5
Page setup

The numbers you enter here define the live area of a page.

You can set up multiple columns within the live area, using "Column guides" on the Options menu. When you click-place text, it automatically fills these columns. If you do not define columns, PageMaker defaults to one column, with column guides running down the outside of the live area. Remember: column guides and margins are different. You can move column guides with the mouse.

Complex publications may require some thought in defining the live area (what elements should and shouldn't fall inside the margins?), but for most pubs it's straightforward. Body copy—the stuff that's different on every page—is inside the margins, running elements are outside.

Working with Master Pages

Use PageMaker's master pages for items (such as headers, footers, and page numbers) and guides (ruler guides and column guides) that repeat on most pages of your publication. There are no hard-and-fast rules for what goes on the master pages and what doesn't; the only rule is to set things up to save as much time as possible.

A new feature in PageMaker 4 is the ability to automatically wrap text around master items. This lets you customize text flow in some interesting ways. For more on using this very useful new feature, see "Wrapping Around Master Items" in Chapter 5, *Pictures*.

Displaying Master Items

If you do not want to display the elements from the master pages on a given page or spread, turn off the Display master items option on the Page menu rather than covering the elements over with no-line, white-filled boxes. This is a habit that seems to be left over from earlier versions of PageMaker. Every time we've used the "cover it up" technique, we've tripped over it when the time came to reuse the file. And every time we've tripped over it in someone else's files, we've made nasty comments about their ancestors' relations with herbivores.

If you want some items from the master pages but not others, turn off "Display master items" and copy the items you want from the master pages to the current page. (Use the power paste technique described in "Using Paste," later in this chapter. If you're copying page numbers, use the page number token (Ctrl-Shift-3 with the text tool) rather than typing in the number of the page. You never know when you'll be adding or deleting pages before the current page.

Adding Page Numbers

You determine the starting page number for your publication by entering it in the Start page # text edit box in the Page setup dialog box. You can return to this dialog box and change the page number at any time.

PageMaker 4 adds new page numbering features through the Page numbering dialog box, which you reach by pressing the Numbers button in the Page setup dialog box. In the Page numbering dialog box, as shown in Figure 3-6, you can specify Roman numerals (in both upper- and lowercase), alphabetic (also in upper- and lowercase), and standard Arabic numerals. Roman numeral page numbers revert to Arabic numeral page numbers above IMMMM (3999), and alphabetic page numbers revert to Arabic above ZZ (52). Feel constrained? If you have a use for Roman numeral or alphabetic page numbers above those limits, please let us know and we'll develop some kind of workaround.

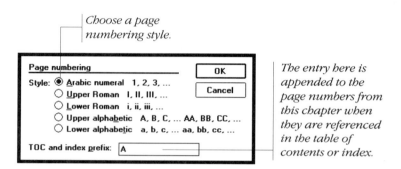

Figure 3-6
Page numbering dialog box

If you number sections of a document separately rather than continuously (e.g., 1-23, 5-18, A-33), you can enter a page number prefix in the TOC and index prefix text edit box. PageMaker inserts that prefix prior to page numbers from this pub when creating tables of contents and indices.

You enter a page number marker in a text block by pressing Ctrl-Shift-3. You can type anything you like before or after the page number marker (in this book, for example, the running heads for the left pages would be entered by pressing Ctrl-Shift-3, Tab, and then typing "Real World PageMaker 4"). When you enter a page number marker on the master pages, the marker displays as "RM" if you're on the right master page, or "LM" if you're on the left master page. Otherwise, in layout view, the marker displays the current page number. If you're in the story view, the page number marker displays as an icon.

You can enter a page number marker on any page, anywhere on the page, and you can always override the page number on the master pages for specific pages by turning off the Display master items option on the Page menu, just as you can with all other master items.

If your publication is part of a book, you can choose to tie the publication's page numbering to its position in the book using the page numbering options in the Page setup dialog box. For more information on book page numbering, see the tip "Continuous Page Numbering," later in this chapter.

Adding and Deleting Pages

Adding and deleting pages is pretty straightforward. Just do it (it's on the Page menu). If you're using irregular columns and facing pages, though, be prepared to have weird things happen if you add or delete an odd number of pages.

▼ *Tip: Adding Pages with a Loaded Gun*

You can add pages when you have a loaded place gun. We're always clicking the bottom windowshade handle of a text block to get a loaded text gun, then realizing that we need a new page to place the text. Just go up to the menu and add pages.

When you delete pages, make sure that you've rolled up or pulled off the page any text blocks you don't want to lose when you delete the page. Threaded text blocks (see "Stories and Text Blocks" in Chapter 4, *Words*) on preceding and succeeding pages remain threaded to each other, but you lose the text on the deleted page.

Selecting Objects

The standard technique for doing things in Windows applications is to select something, then act on the selection. There are several ways to select things (text, text blocks, and graphics) with PageMaker, and the better you are at selecting the faster you can work your will on those selections (Figure 3-7).

You can use "Select all" (Ctrl-A) with the Pointer tool to select all the objects, including text blocks as objects, on the current page (or facing pages). This is a great way to see "invisible" things that can trip you up,

Figure 3-7
Selecting things

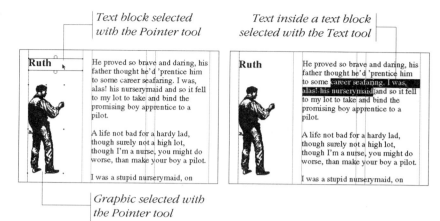

Text block selected with the Pointer tool

Text inside a text block selected with the Text tool

Graphic selected with the Pointer tool

like graphics that have been set to the color Paper, reversed type, and lines that have been reversed or set to a line width of None.

Similarly, with the text cursor placed in a story, you can select all of the text in the story (including parts of the story that aren't placed yet) by pressing Ctrl-A. This is a good way to see whether the story actually is threaded into that mysterious text block you can't figure out (Figure 3-8). There'll be more about text selection shortcuts in Chapter 4, *Words*.

Figure 3-8
Finding the thread

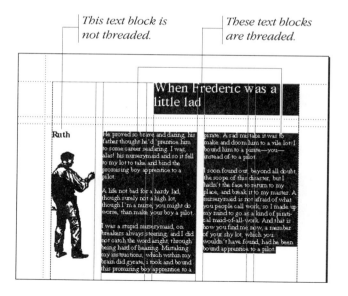

This text block is not threaded.

These text blocks are threaded.

You can select several objects by holding down the Shift key while clicking on them with the Pointer tool (Figure 3-9). If you select an object you didn't want to select, just click on it again while holding down the Shift key to deselect the object.

Figure 3-9
Selecting a series of objects

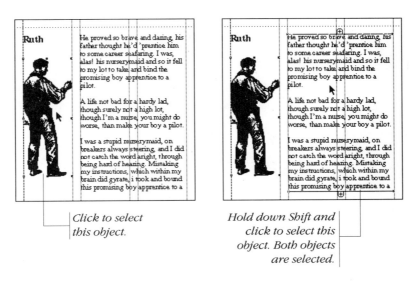

Click to select this object.

Hold down Shift and click to select this object. Both objects are selected.

You can also select several items by dragging a selection marquee over them with the Pointer tool (Figure 3-10).

Figure 3-10
Dragging out a selection marquee

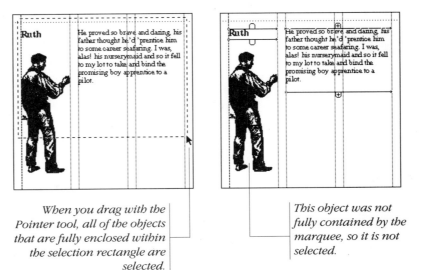

When you drag with the Pointer tool, all of the objects that are fully enclosed within the selection rectangle are selected.

This object was not fully contained by the marquee, so it is not selected.

Obviously, you can use combinations of these selection techniques to select exactly the objects you want. To select all of the objects on a page but one, press Ctrl-A for "Select all," then deselect the object you don't want by holding down Shift and clicking on it.

▼ Tip: Selecting the Unselectable

You can see the items on the page but can't select them. Ever been there? Check the master pages. People sometimes accidentally compose whole pages on the master pages. We know this never happens to you, but we see it all the time, even in pubs created by experienced users.

▼ Tip: Selecting Through Layers

If you have several objects on top of each other, you can select specific layers by holding down the Ctrl key and clicking on the objects. The first click selects the object on top of the stack, the second selects the next object down, and so on. Use "Send to back" (Ctrl-B) and "Bring to front" (Ctrl-F) in conjunction with this technique to change the stacking order of the objects or to bring an object out of the stack (Figure 3-11).

Figure 3-11
Selecting through layers

Ctrl-click to select the object in front. The text block is selected.

Ctrl-click again to select the object behind it. The gray box is selected.

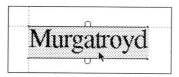 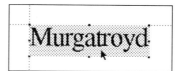

Moving Objects

Once you've selected the objects (graphics or text blocks) that you want to act on, it's time to act. Moving is the simplest action, but PageMaker has some nifty ways of moving things that you can take advantage of if you know about them.

If you grab an item and move it quickly, PageMaker displays only a box showing the outline of the object. This is preferable if you just want to align the object to a ruler guide or to the ruler tick marks. It's fast, and the object doesn't clutter up your view.

If you wait a moment before moving the item, PageMaker displays the item itself so you can move that. This is handy if you want to align the graphic or text to some other graphic or text—as with dropped initial capitals that you want in perfect relationship to their surrounding text, or graphics that you want to position perfectly.

Moving Groups of Objects

Once you've selected a group of items, you can move them as a group. Place the Pointer tool over one of the selected items, press the mouse button, and drag the selected objects to where you want them.

The only trick to this is that you have to pick the point at which you grab the objects fairly carefully, or you may end up sizing graphics or pulling windowshade handles when what you really wanted to do was move things. We usually aim for the middle of a graphic or text block—areas with few windowshade handles or selection handles nearby.

This points out another feature that you may find useful—you can size graphics and text blocks within a group of objects that are multiselected. Just size the objects as you normally would, and you still have your multiselected group of objects (Figure 3-12).

Constraining Movement

You can limit the movement of objects to vertical or horizontal by pressing the Shift key before you drag the objects. This comes in handy when you're aligning objects, or want a horizontal or vertical line to stay that way as you move one end. It's also great when you're duplicating an object repeatedly for placement across or down a page.

▼ *Tip: Moving Before Constraining Movement*

You can press the Shift key to constrain movement at any time while you're dragging an item. So you can move it to a given point, then press Shift to constrain its movement to straight up and down.

Figure 3-12
Sizing selected objects

Even though several objects are selected, you can size individual objects within the group. Try this technique for top-aligning text blocks.

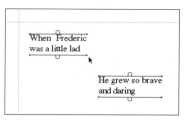

Select two text blocks.

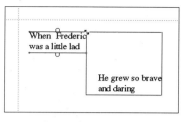

Drag the top windowshade handle of the lower text block up as shown.

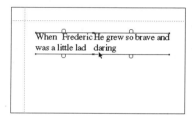

The tops of the text blocks align.

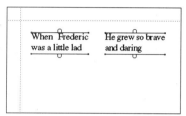

Adjust the horizontal position of the blocks.

▼ *Tip: Positioning Identical Objects Directly on Top of Each Other*

To place identical objects exactly on top of each other, position one object, then drag the other one over the top of it until both objects disappear. Even better, copy the item and use "power paste" (Ctrl-Shift-P, discussed in "Using Paste," below) to duplicate the item directly on top of itself.

What use is this? It's especially useful when you want a PageMaker-created box to have a fill of a different color from the border (a red fill and a green border, for example). It's also great for precisely controlling how objects overprint and/or knock out when you're printing spot color overlays. See the color pages in this book for an explanation of the benefits of selectively knocking out items.

Rulers, Ruler Guides, and Measuring

PageMaker's rulers and ruler guides are two of the keys to using the product well. They provide real positioning accuracy and speed when you're moving objects. The rulers run along the top and left sides of the publication window.

Rulers

To begin with, turn the rulers on. Ctrl-R (or Alt-O, R) displays (or hides) the rulers. The only time to turn these off is when you want to get an overall look at a page (though you're generally better off printing the page if that's what you want). You can adjust the increments of the vertical and horizontal rulers independently from the Preferences dialog box.

▼ *Tip: Use Custom for Vertical Rulers*

If you set the vertical ruler increment to equal your body copy leading (in the Preferences dialog box), you can measure in lines of type, which is more than handy for many situations. For more on using custom-increment vertical rulers and leading grids, see "Leading Grids" in Chapter 4, *Words*.

As you move the Pointer tool in the publication window, notice how marks in the rulers (shadow cursors) show its position. When you drag an object, the shadow cursors try to show its left, right, top, and bottom edges, but their accuracy depends on the type of object you're dragging. With text blocks, TIFFs, and LBOs, the shadow cursors represent the object's position fairly well, but EPS graphics seem to throw them off (mainly because the screen representations of EPS graphics often have a small amount of space around them; the rulers continue to measure the size of the object by its selection handles, but the image is actually smaller than that area).

Ruler Guides

You can drag guides out of the rulers onto the page to function much like blue lines on grid paper in traditional pasteup. Ctrl-J (or Alt-O, G) displays (or hides) the ruler guides. You can use either rulers or ruler guides or both to get things exactly where you want them. To position a ruler guide, move the cursor over one of the rulers and drag the new ruler guide onto the page. If no ruler guide appears, you've exceeded PageMaker's limit of 40 ruler guides. (Either that, or you never turned on "Guides" to begin with.) Drag some ruler guides off the page and try positioning the new ruler guide again.

Not only do pages snap together quickly using the rulers and ruler guides, but you can attain positioning accuracy of a quarter point. So much for the misguided idea that PageMaker doesn't provide accuracy. To get that quarter-point accuracy, though, you'll need to zoom in to the 400% view (Ctrl-4). In 400% view, each pixel is equal to a quarter point (Figure 3-13).

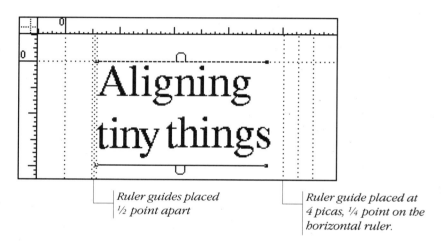

Figure 3-13
Ruler guides at 400% view

At 400%, each pixel on the screen equals a quarter point.

Ruler guides placed ½ point apart

Ruler guide placed at 4 picas, ¼ point on the horizontal ruler.

▼ Tip: Copying Master Guides

If you've run out of ruler guides (that is, you've used more than 40 guides on a spread), select "Copy master guides" on the Page menu to clean up the page (assuming that you've used fewer than 40 guides on the master pages).

Measurement Increments

You change PageMaker's measurement increments via the Preferences dialog box (Figure 3-14). You can set the vertical and horizontal ruler increments independently, and you can set the vertical ruler to any custom measurement you want.

Figure 3-14
Changing measurement
increments

These change the default measurement increment for dialog boxes, and for the vertical and horizontal rulers.

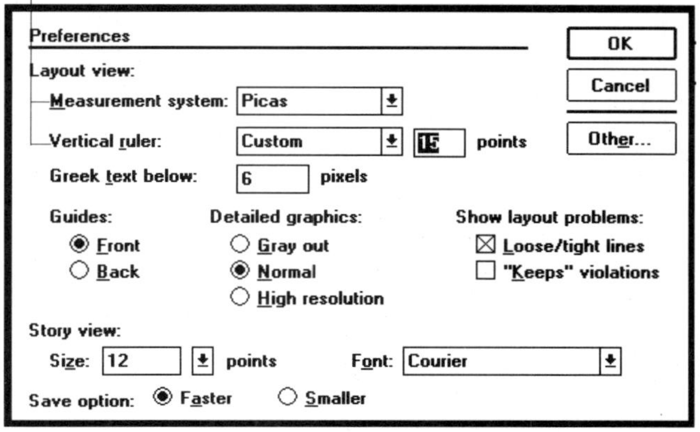

```
Preferences                                              OK
Layout view:
  Measurement system: [Picas      ▼]                    Cancel
  Vertical ruler:     [Custom     ▼] [16] points       Other...
  Greek text below:   [6] pixels
  Guides:         Detailed graphics:    Show layout problems:
   ◉ Front        ○ Gray out            ☒ Loose/tight lines
   ○ Back         ◉ Normal              ☐ "Keeps" violations
                  ○ High resolution
Story view:
  Size: [12] ▼ points    Font: [Courier        ▼]
  Save option: ◉ Faster    ○ Smaller
```

▼ Tip: Graphic Design's Native Measurement System

Use picas and points, not inches, for your measurement system, because type, the backbone of your page designs, is measured in picas and points. Basing your measurement system on the type gives your page designs an underlying order that leads the reader's eye through the page, and makes your page-makeup task easier and more consistent.

▼ Tip: To Enter Values in Inches When the Default is Set to Picas

You can override the publication's default measurement system (which you specified in the Preferences dialog box) by typing the following characters after the value you type in PageMaker's dialog boxes (see Table 3-3).

▼ Tip: Typing Picas and Points

Now that you're sold on picas and points, you should know that you can type them like this in most dialog boxes: 1p3 (that comes

Table 3-3 Overriding the Default Unit of Measurement

To enter the value as	Type (immediately after the number)
inches	i
millimeters	m
picas	p
ciceros	c

to 15 points—1p3 means 1 pica + 3 points, or 12 points + 3 points = 15 points), 4p6 (that's 54 points), or 0p23 (that's 23 points).

Usually, you'll want to position the zero point at the upper-left corner of the image area (the live area inside the margins) so that you can use the vertical ruler to get everything aligned, but you'll often want to move the zero point when you want to measure from one point to another (measuring the width of a graphic, for instance, as in Figure 3-15).

You can lock the zero point in a particular position by choosing "Zero lock" on the Options menu.

Figure 3-15
Measuring with the zero point

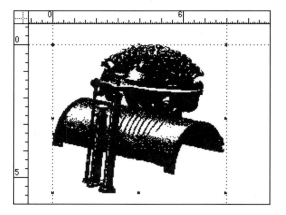

If you set the zero point to the upper-left corner of an object, it's easy to measure the object's height and width.

Snap to Guides and Snap to Rulers

With rulers turned on and some guides dragged out, you can align objects perfectly using "Snap to guides" and "Snap to rulers" from the Options menu. As an object gets close to a guide or ruler increment with these options turned on, the object is pulled over or up or down to align with it. Toggle the snap options on and off from the Options menu (Ctrl-Shift-Y for ruler snap and Ctrl-U for guides snap). You can toggle them with any tool selected. At large magnifications (200%, 400%), you can snap to individual pixels on the rulers.

▼ Tip: Don't Cancel that Place

We often load a place gun and then find we need to toggle snap options on or off to place the text or graphic properly. You can turn the Snap to guides and Snap to rulers options on and off even when you have a loaded place gun, using either the menu options or the keyboard shortcuts.

▼ Tip: An Odd Thing About Snap to Guides

When you are working with "Snap to guides" on, graphics snap directly to ruler guides on their upper-left, yet snap one pixel inside ruler guides on their lower-right. We have no idea why. The graphics print in proper position at the proper size, even if they appear to be one pixel off on the screen.

▼ Tip: Evenly Spaced Objects

If you want several lines or objects equally spaced over some set distance (for instance four lines dividing an 11-pica distance), you can save yourself the arithmetic (see Figure 3-16).

1. Create a "ladder" of evenly spaced lines using a draw program.
2. Place the ladder on your page, and size it to fit the area you want to divide.
3. Align ruler guides with the lines in the ladder. Remove the ladder.
4. Turn on "Snap to guides" (if it's not on already), and place, paste, or draw your graphics, aligning them with the ruler guides.

Figure 3-16
Dividing space equally

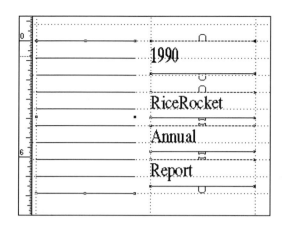

Resize the "ladder" graphic to subdivide any area.

Drag ruler guides to align with the ladder rungs.

Align objects to the ruler guides.

Using Paste

Usually, there's no need to document how the Paste command works in a Windows program. You just press Shift-Insert, and whatever's on the Clipboard is pasted to the center of your screen. For some reason, Aldus also provides about ten zillion other keyboard shortcuts for this function: Insert alone works fine, as does Ctrl-V (a holdover from the Macintosh). And that doesn't even count using the menu and its shortcut (Alt-E, P).

But that's not all. PageMaker 4 gives you a lot more control than these shortcuts. If the original position of the object you cut or copied is still visible on the screen, the normal paste command (Shift-Insert or any of the other techniques mentioned above) places the object slightly offset from the point it was cut or copied from. If the original position is not visible, the object lands in the center of the screen.

Power Paste

However, another paste option, Ctrl-Shift-P, places the object into exactly the position it was cut or copied from (you can also hold down Ctrl and Shift while choosing Place). If the position you cut/copied from is not visible in the publication window, the contents of the Clipboard are pasted to the center of your screen, just as with a normal paste. Aldus calls this "power paste," and you'll soon see why. Figure 3-17 shows how the two different pasting methods work.

Figure 3-17
Normal paste and power paste

Copy an object and paste normally, and it pastes into the middle or the screen (or offset slightly from the original object).

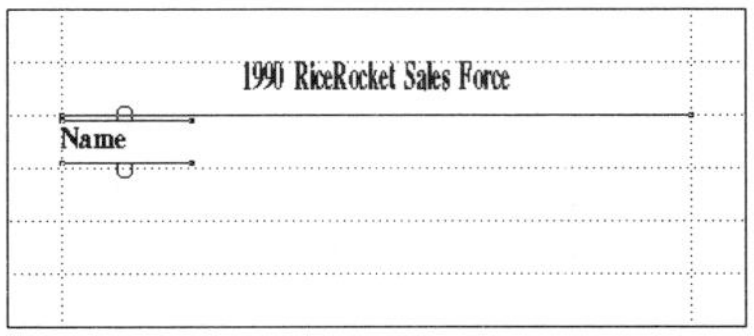

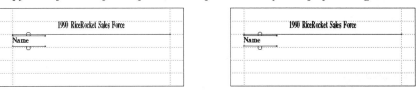

Copy... 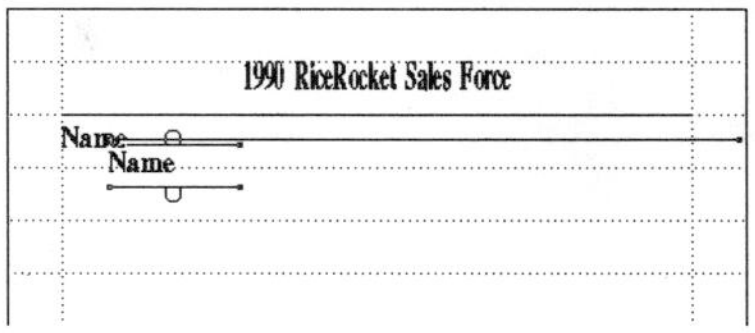   *...and paste.*

Copy an object and power-paste, and it pastes directly on top of the original.

Copy...   *...and power-paste.*

You can even turn pages and paste to the same location on a different page—even if you open a different publication.

And there's more. If you copy an item, power-paste the copy on top (Ctrl-Shift-P), drag the copy a given distance, and power paste again, the third copy is pasted that same distance from the second copy (see Figure 3-18).

Figure 3-18
Step-and-repeat duplication with power paste

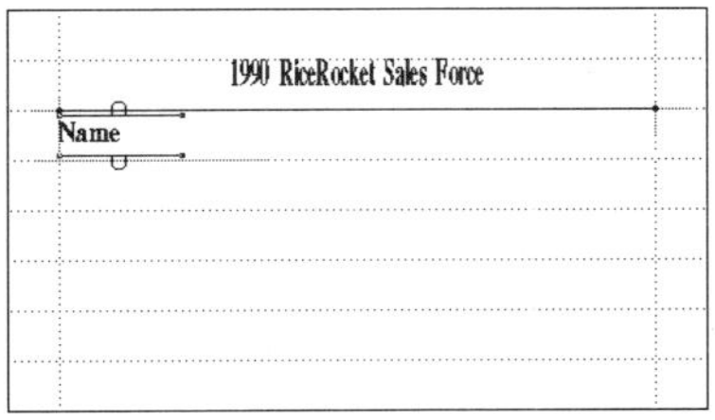

Select an object, copy it, and power-paste the copy directly on top.

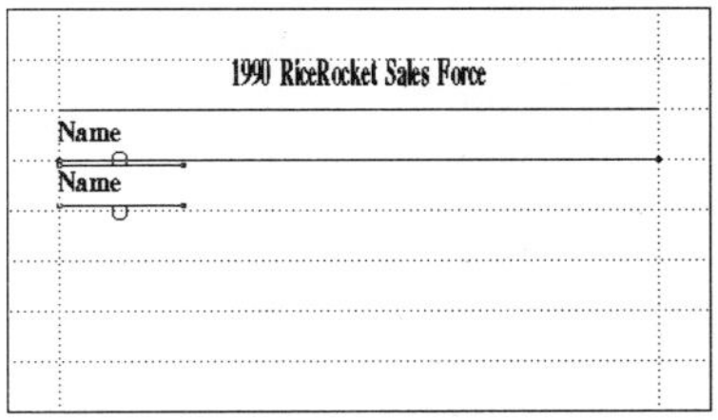

Then move the copy.

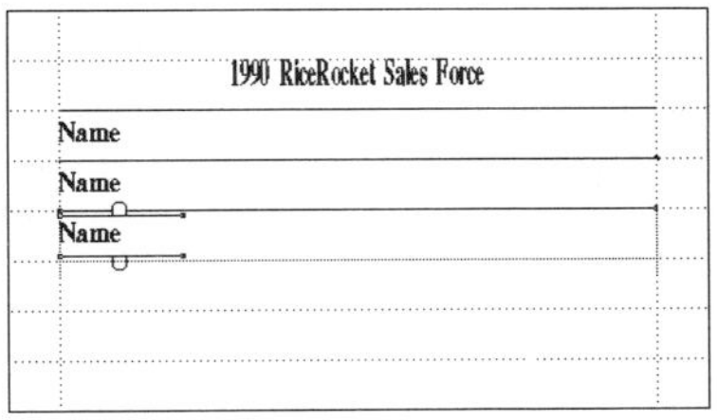

Power-paste again, and a third copy is pasted the same distance from the second object as the second object is from the first.

▼ *Tip: Copying Master Items*

When you want some master items on a page but not all, use the following technique.

1. Change to fit in window page view.
2. Turn off "Display master items" on the Page menu.
3. Go to the master page, select and copy the items you want.
4. Go back to the page you were working on (F11 is the easy way), and power paste the items (Ctrl-Shift-P).

The master items will land perfectly on your page. If you want most of the master items, it's generally easiest to select all the master items (Ctrl-A), copy and power paste them, and delete the ones you don't need.

Using the Place Command

Desktop publishing is all about bringing together material from many different sources, so PageMaker's Place command (as a pro, you'll use Ctrl-D) is probably its most important command. You use "Place" to import text and graphics files into PageMaker. The Place dialog box displays only files types that PageMaker can import—with extensions .TXT, .PIC, .PCX, .TIF, .MSP, .PNT, .EPS, .IMA, PTL, .WMF, and so on.

If the file you want to place doesn't show up in the Place file dialog box, odds are that it's a type of file that PageMaker doesn't know how to place. See the tip "When You Can't See a file You Know is There" in Chapter 5, *Pictures*.

Installing Import and Export Filters

If you don't have the proper filter for a given file type installed, you can't place that file type. When you installed PageMaker, you had the option to install some or all of its many filters for importing a variety of text and graphic file formats. If you didn't install all the filters at that time and later decide you want more (or if Aldus releases some new ones), don't worry. You can use Aldus Setup to install them.

Double-click on the Aldus Setup icon in Program Manager. You'll be asked for a CTL file; choose PM412.CTL (the numbers in your filename may differ) from the ALDUS\USENGLISH\SETUP directory. You are presented with the Aldus Setup main window, which provides you with options for installing additional filters, templates, font metric files, or the PageMaker tutorial.

Select "Filters" and click the Setup button. The Select filters dialog box shows you the filters you have already installed (on the right), as well as a list of all available filters (on the left). From the left side, select the filters you want (or click the Select all button) and click OK. You will be prompted to insert a PageMaker disk in your floppy drive. Insert the proper disk and click OK.

Place Guns

When you choose a file from the Place dialog box, the cursor changes into a loaded place gun (they're not particularly warlike at Aldus, but that's what they call it—probably because it describes it so well). The place guns look different depending on what type of file you have loaded (Table 3-4).

Once you've got a loaded place gun, you can either click to simply place the file, or drag a selection rectangle that defines the area in

Table 3-4 Place guns

Icon	Place Method and file Type
	Manual flow text gun
	Automatic text gun
	Semi-automatic text gun
	Paint-type gun
	Draw-type gun
	EPS gun
	Bitmap or TIFF gun

which the file is placed. The results vary depending on whether you're placing text or a graphic (Figure 3-19).

With graphics, if you simply click (fire) the place gun, the graphic lands on the page at its original size, with the upper-left corner at the point you clicked. If you drag out a place rectangle, the graphic fills that rectangle. It ignores proper height/width proportions, though, and will probably distort the graphic. You can restore the graphic's proportions by Shift-sizing it using a corner handle.

Figure 3-19
Firing place guns

Click-placed text fills the column.

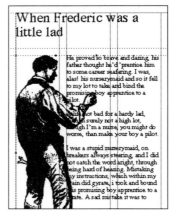

Click-placed graphics place at original size.

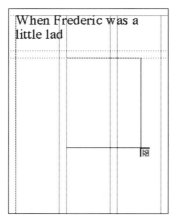

Define an area for placed text by dragging the place gun.

Placed text fills the area you defined.

With text, dragging a rectangle while placing is a great way to define columns for the text to occupy—especially if you have guides set up with snaps turned on.

▼ Tip: Placing from Right to Left and Bottom to Top

Note that you can drag the place rectangle for text or graphics in any direction. The graphics don't come in reversed or upside down, and the text doesn't come in in reverse order, as you might think. It's funny how often we get stuck thinking we have to drag from the upper-left to the lower-right, when dragging from the lower-right to the upper-left works equally well.

▼ Tip: Cancelling a Place

If you decide you don't want to place a file that's loaded in the place gun, you can cancel by clicking on any tool in the Toolbox, or by pressing F9.

Using Replace

If you've selected a graphic or have a text cursor placed in a story when you choose Place, the Place dialog box offers you options for replacing the selected text or graphic. You can use graphics or text blocks as placeholders, then replace them with the material you want to use. You can build placeholders into a publication template and replace them with the final words or pictures when they're ready, or (this is where it's really useful) replace existing stories and graphics with their latest versions. For more on replacing, see Chapters 4, *Words*, 5, *Pictures*, and 8, *Workgroup Publishing*.

PageMaker 4's Book Command

Yes, it's true PageMaker 4 can handle a publication that's up to 999 pages long in a single pub file. But that doesn't mean you should create pubs that big. Long publication files get huge, slow, and unwieldy. And if the file goes south on you and you haven't backed up recently, you lose work. You'll find long documents to be much more manageable if you break them up into chunks—usually chapters—and build each chapter in its own publication file.

The only real problem arises when you want to print all the chapters in a row, or use PageMaker 4's new indexing and table of contents features to compile those elements from the whole book. How does PageMaker know which files are included in book, and what order they're in? That's where the new Book feature comes in. It lets you build a list of pub files in their proper order. After you choose "Book" from the file menu, the Book publication list dialog box appears (Figure 3-20).

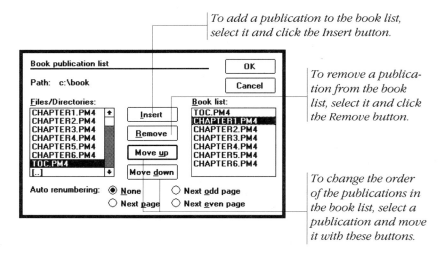

Figure 3-20
Book publication list dialog box

To add a publication to the book list, select it and click the Insert button.

To remove a publication from the book list, select it and click the Remove button.

To change the order of the publications in the book list, select a publication and move it with these buttons.

If you need to print a draft copy of the entire book, open any publication containing a book list and choose "Print entire book" in the Print dialog box.

If PageMaker can't find a publication in the book list when you use any of the Book-related commands (printing, table of contents or index generation), it displays the find pub dialog box so that you can locate the missing publication. Simply navigate through your files and directories until you find it.

Where's the best place to keep a book list? If you're not planning to index your book, we think the best place to keep the book list for a multipublication book is in a separate publication containing just the table of contents and index for the book. That way, you don't have to worry about which file contains your book list. Even if your book list contains only one publication, you should consider creating a separate publication for the index and table of contents so that you won't have to make room for those elements in your publication.

▼ Tip: Quick-Copying Your Book List to Every Chapter

On the other hand, if you think you might do an index for your book or magazine, it's very helpful to have your book list in every publication. In fact, that's the only way you can import index topics from other publications in the list—an important tool for keeping your index entries consistent.

Fortunately, there's an easy way to copy your book list to every pub in your book. First create the book list the way you want it in one of your publications (say, your table of contents or index pub). Then click OK. Now choose the Book command from the file menu again, this time holding down the Ctrl key.

PageMaker copies the book list to all the other publications on that list. One note: This gimmick won't work if you try to do it inside an untitled publication.

▼ Tip: Continuous Page Numbering

In some ways, PageMaker 4 for the PC exceeds its Macintosh counterpart, and this is one of them: The Book publication list dialog box provides for consecutive page numbering across several publications, based on their order of appearance in the book list.

For simple consecutive page numbering, click the Next Page button. To make all chapters begin on the right hand page, choose "Next odd page"; to make all chapters begin on the left, choose "Next even page." To make these last two options work, PageMaker automatically inserts a blank page where necessary at the end of a publication—a real headache saver. Naturally, the None option numbers each publication independently, just as they normally do when they're not part of a book. The Macintosh version caught up with this feature with the release of Macintosh PageMaker 4.01.

▼ Tip: Overriding Continuous Page Numbering

If you want some of the chapters in a book to be numbered independently, open those pubs, and in the Page setup dialog box, click "Restart page numbering" and type the starting page number in the Start Page # text edit box.

▼ Tip: Forcing PageMaker to Renumber the Publications in Your Book List

Sometimes, you need to force PageMaker to update all of the pages in your book. To do this, choose one of the operations that makes PageMaker look at all of the publications in the book list, like "Show index," "Create index," or "Create TOC."

▼ Tip: Make Mini Book Lists for Sections of a Book

Note that because you can include a publication in any number of book lists, you could easily generate separate tables of contents for individual publications and groups of publications by simply creating a master publication for that section of your book. Suppose you have several chapters making up part 1 of a book, for instance, and you need an index or table of contents for just that part. Simply call up your "Part 1 book list" pub, and build the table of contents.

Saving Your Work

While PageMaker crashes infrequently these days, computers do crash. Building and city power fluctuates or fails altogether, your PC dies, and you start to sweat. Hours of your work might be lost.

You've heard it before and we'll say it again: save often (Ctrl-S is all it takes). To be really safe, save under a different file name every so often

often, so you have the old version as back-up if your current version is lost somehow. Steve uses version numbers for his pub files—1A, 1E, 2, etc. That way he knows which is the latest version, and which to go back to if necessary.

PageMaker does a very good job of saving your file for you as you work on it—saving, in fact, every time you add or remove pages, print, switch between layout and story view, use the Clipboard, or change page setup (these saves are called "mini-saves"). So in theory you'll never lose more than two pages worth of work.

▼ Tip: Recovering from Crashes

When you reopen a pub after a crash, you should find that all of the work done before the last time you turned pages has been saved. If not, or if you were working on an untitled file, you'll find a temporary version of the file stored in your root directory. The temporary files begin with the characters ~PM and have the extension .TMP. For example, your file may be named ~PM40AOD.TMP. Open the file, save and name it, and get back to work.

▼ Tip: Skip the RAM Disk

A number of books about Windows, including the *Microsoft Windows User's Guide* that comes with Windows, recommend creating a RAM disk with a TEMP subdirectory and having your applications store their temp files there. This is supposed to enhance your application's speed, but with PageMaker it makes things more risky, since a RAM disk vanishes whenever the power goes off. Obviously, if you want to use PageMaker's temp files as an emergency back-up, you should avoid the RAM disk strategy.

PageMaker always stores a copy of the last-saved version of your file in the publication, so you can always use "Revert" on the file menu to go back to the earlier version if you've made changes you don't want to keep. This means that you can experiment as much as you want—as long as you don't save—and still return to your starting point.

▼ Tip: Mini-Revert

An even more powerful way to undo your last several changes is to hold down the Shift key when you choose Revert from the file menu. We call this a "mini-revert" because it only reverts your file back to the last mini-saved version of your publication, instead of the last time you actually used the Save command.

▼ Tip: Using Save as to Compress Your file

PageMaker files tend to grow as you work with them because PageMaker is saving the last-saved version of the file, the current mini-saved version of the file, as well as currently active information that doesn't fit in available memory.

To compress your file so it takes up less disk space, choose Save as from the file menu, then just click OK or press Enter to save under the same file name. Click Yes when you're prompted "Replace existing *filename?*" PageMaker saves the current version of the file and deletes the internal back-up version, compressing the file.

▼ Tip: Make All Saves Save As

To make all of your save commands (including Ctrl-S) have the compressing power of Save As, choose "Preferences" from the Edit menu. Under Save options, click "Smaller." This takes a bit longer, but it saves the most compact version of the file to your disk each time you save.

Other People's Pages

A lot of times you end up working on PageMaker pubs that other people have created. The first thing to do when you're given someone else's publication to work on is to look at each page or spread with all items selected. Select the Pointer tool and choose "Select all" from the Edit menu (Ctrl-A).

Notice where each text block falls, and be on the lookout for reversed type or white boxes or lines. Watch for text blocks that have been rolled up but are still full of copy. Try to understand why your predecessors did what they did, based on the evidence on the pages. We call this "PageMaker archaeology," and it's saved us enormous amounts of time.

PageMaker Help

PageMaker 4 has a built-in, context-sensitive help system. To use help, press Shift-F1. The cursor turns into a question mark. Point at the menu or menu item you're curious about and click. The Windows help window appears full of information on the selected command. Alternatively, you can press F1 or choose "Help," from the Windows menu to go to the main listing of help topics.

If you're really at a loss, check out the Troubleshooting help topic. It encapsulates the first several questions that you would be asked by an Aldus tech support rep if you called Aldus. These questions lead you through a process of elimination that goes a long way toward pinpointing your difficulties.

▼ *Tip: Meet Your Makers*

Hold down Shift as you select "About PageMaker," and you'll see a list of the software engineers who created PageMaker 4.

CHAPTER 4

Words

Words are the backbone of PageMaker publications. Though we suppose there are people who use PageMaker for drawing pictures, we feel pretty confident in saying that words are central to most publications. If you know how type works, how PageMaker handles type, and the difference between text and type, you'll be a long way down the road toward mastering PageMaker.

PageMaker, Text, and Type

PageMaker has been characterized as a good, serviceable product hampered by a lack of usable text editing or fine typesetting controls. PageMaker 4 goes a considerable distance toward correcting this perception, adding a complete word-processing environment—the Story Editor—and beefed-up typographics.

The Story Editor has basic word-processing tools, improves text-editing speed considerably, and adds some really slick search-and-replace functions. PageMaker 4 also adds spell-checking and index and table of contents generation to its list of publishing tools.

On the formatting side, PageMaker 4 adds the ability to specify type and leading in tenths of a point, and increases the maximum point size to 650 points. It brings word- and letter-spacing control (that pesky Spacing attributes dialog box) down to the paragraph level (from story-level), and adds type expansion and condensation (horizontal scaling). Kerning accuracy has been improved to a hundredth of an em; you can now apply kerning changes to a selected range of text, and tracking has been added.

In this chapter we're going to start with the big picture—stories and text blocks—and work our way down through paragraphs and characters. Then we'll talk about using styles to automate your formatting, and finally move on to text editing—including the Story Editor and text tools like spell-checking, indexing, searching, and replacing. Finally, we'll talk about placing formatted text from word processors, databases, and spreadsheets. In the course of the chapter, we'll also cover some special situations that lots of people have trouble with, like drop caps and fractions.

We've had a hard time making distinctions between type and graphics in many parts of this book. Is a piece of type placed from a draw program a graphic? It acts just like a graphic, after all—you can crop it, resize it, and apply text wrap to it (but you can't rotate it). And are paragraph rules actually type? You can't select them with the Pointer tool, resize them, crop them, or apply text wrap to them. Where should we draw the lines (so to speak)?

We've tried to group items functionally—by the way you act on them in PageMaker. If a piece of text acts like a graphic, we talk about it in the chapter on graphics. Of course, we've broken this rule all over the place. That's what makes life so much fun.

Taking Measure

During the 1970s, Ole worked as a graphic designer, specifying type and sending copy to typesetting shops where someone like Scott, a typesetter back then, would set it. Somehow it never seemed to come back quite the way he thought it should. He blamed the typesetters for misunderstanding his specifications, though he had a sneaking suspicion that something else was wrong. (Scott could have told him, but he didn't know Ole. And nobody listens to typesetters anyway.)

One day, quite out of the blue, the manager of a typesetting shop asked Ole if he'd like to learn to set type. Ole jumped at the chance, and, for the next year, he set type for many of the best graphic designers in Seattle using a Compugraphic 7500 EditWriter.

Ole learned, to his horror, that not only had his type specifications been bad, but that very few graphic designers wrote good type specs. He found himself explaining, over and over, that leading was a vertical, rather than a horizontal, measurement.

What's an Em?

Understanding what units of measure to use for different situations is one key to using PageMaker effectively. We generally recommend that you use picas and points, but there are exceptions, primarily when you need to work with relative units—ems and ens—rather than absolute units. You already know what inches are, but ems and ens manage to confuse most of the people most of the time. If you've got a handle on these, feel free to skip the next two paragraphs.

You have to understand ems and ens if you want to use PageMaker's horizontal spacing controls and special characters. So here it is right up front. Ems and ens are *relative* units of horizontal measure—relative to the type size—unlike inches, millimeters, picas, and points, which are absolute.

An em is as wide as the type size—10 points wide with 10-point type, 24 points wide with 24-point type. Ens are half as wide as ems. So if you type an em space with 10-point type, you'll get a 10-point-wide space. Change the type size to 24 points, and the width of the space changes to 24 points. It doesn't matter what typeface you're using.

Relative units of measure are especially useful for specifying horizontal measurements within text, such as kerning (see "Kerning Text" later in this chapter). Since kerning is specified in fractions of an em (a relative unit), if you change the type size, the kerning changes appropriately. You'll see ems and ens used throughout this chapter (and throughout PageMaker).

Stories and Text Blocks

In the legend of Theseus and the Minotaur, King Minos' daughter Ariadne gives Theseus a ball of thread to trail behind him as he explores the Labyrinth. The idea is that he can follow the trail of thread to find his way out—and, she hopes, into her arms. Remember this tale—and the idea of following a thread—when you're working with text in PageMaker.

An important concept to understand in PageMaker is that of threaded text—text that proceeds through a maze of text blocks (if you meet a guy with a bull's head, call us). Threaded text—usually one placed file—is called a story. A story may consist of one text block all by itself, or it may be made up of many threaded blocks scattered throughout a pub (see Figure 4-1).

Figure 4-1
Text blocks, stories, and windowshade handles

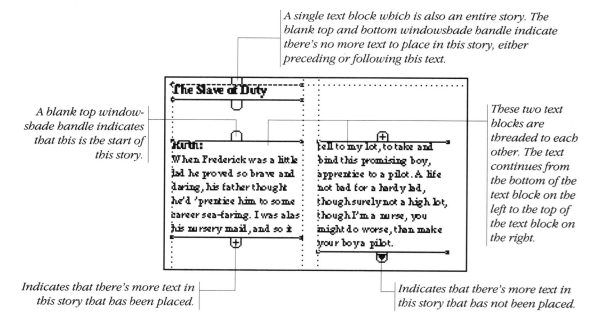

A story may even include text that hasn't been placed yet. It's still threaded with the rest of the story, but isn't on a page yet. You can tell if a text block is threaded to any other text blocks by the symbols that appear in the block's windowshade handles.

Suppose you have two threaded text blocks, with the text from the first block flowing into the next one. If you move the bottom windowshade handle of the first text block up, the text you displace flows into the second one (Figure 4-2).

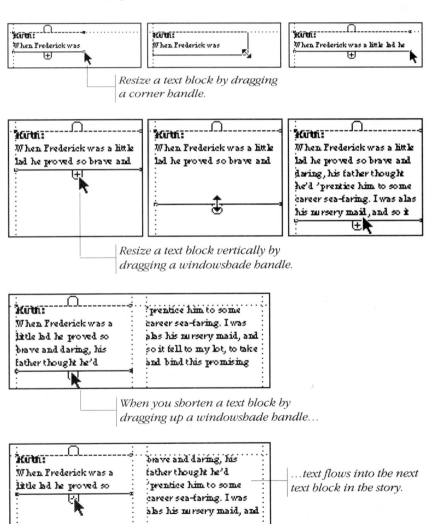

Figure 4-2
Resizing text blocks

Resize a text block by dragging a corner handle.

Resize a text block vertically by dragging a windowshade handle.

When you shorten a text block by dragging up a windowshade handle...

...text flows into the next text block in the story.

You can also interpolate another text block between two threaded blocks. With the pointer tool, select the first block and click on its bottom windowshade handle (it will have a + in it); you'll get a loaded text place gun. Click or drag out a new text block, and the new block fills with text sucked back from the succeeding text block (Figure 4-3).

Figure 4-3
Adding a text block between two text blocks

Click on the bottom windowshade handle.

The cursor turns into a loaded text place gun. Drag-place a new text block.

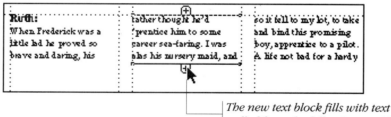

The new text block fills with text pulled from the following text blocks.

▼ **Tip: Deleting Threaded Text Blocks**

If you delete a text block that's part of a threaded story, the thread still flows from the preceding to the succeeding text block. You just lose the text in the block you've deleted. The same is true when you delete pages that have threaded text blocks on them.

▼ Tip: Moving Items from Page to Page

If you cut items to the Clipboard, text blocks within the cut group remain threaded to each other, but lose their threads to other text blocks. If you drag the text blocks to the pasteboard, change pages, then drag them onto the new page, text blocks will retain any existing links to other text blocks in the publication.

You can combine unthreaded text blocks into a threaded story using any of several methods described in the following tips.

▼ Tip: Careful Method for Combining Unlinked Text Blocks

When you have several unlinked text blocks that you want to combine into one story, and you have the time to do it right (if you're impatient or desperate, see the techniques below), use the Text tool to cut and paste the text between stories (Figure 4-4).

Figure 4-4
Threading stories
(safe method)

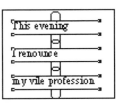

Three unlinked stories

Select all of the text in a story and copy it to the Clipboard.

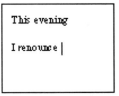

Place an insertion point in the preceding story...

...and paste the text. The two text blocks are now linked.

Repeat this process for all of the text blocks you want to link.

The stories are now one linked story.

1. Place the text insertion point in one of the stories.
2. Choose "Select all" from the Edit menu, or press Ctrl-A.
3. Copy (or cut) the text to the Clipboard.
4. Place the text insertion point in the next story at the point you want the text on the Clipboard to enter the thread of the story (generally at the start or end of the story).
5. Paste in the text from the Clipboard (Shift-Insert).
6. Repeat steps 1 through 5 until you've threaded all the text you want.

▼ *Tip: Alternative Rather Dashing Method for Combining Text Blocks*

When you have several text blocks you want to combine and you want to do it the cool way, the hip way, the way they do it downtown, use a combination of the Pointer tool and the Text tool to cut and paste the type between text blocks (Figure 4-5).

Figure 4-5
Threading stories
(dashing method)

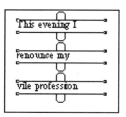

Three unthreaded stories

Select a text block with the Pointer tool and copy it to the Clipboard.

Place an insertion point in the preceding story and paste.

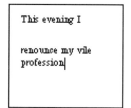

The text blocks are now threaded together.

Repeat the process.

All three text stories are threaded together.

1. Select a text block with the Pointer tool.
2. Choose Copy from the Edit menu, or press Ctrl-Insert (or, if you're in a swashbuckling mood, choose Cut or press Shift-Delete).
3. Place the text insertion point in the target story at the point you want the text on the Clipboard to enter the thread of the story (generally at the start or end of the story).
4. Choose Paste from the Edit menu, or press Shift-Insert.
5. Repeat steps 1 through 4 until you've linked up all the text you want.

▼ *Tip: Emergency Method for Combining Unthreaded Text Blocks*

When you have several unthreaded text blocks that you want to combine into one story, and you're desperate enough to try something that has some rough spots, try this (Figure 4-6).

1. Put the text blocks in order. Select the story you want to appear last in your new story and send it to the back (Ctrl-B). Then select the next to the last story and send it to the back. Continue until you've sent the story you want to appear first to the back.

Figure 4-6
Threading stories
(emergency method)

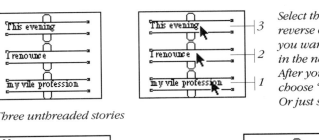

Three unthreaded stories

Select the stories in the reverse order in which you want them to appear in the new, linked story. After you select each one, choose "Send to back." Or just stack them up.

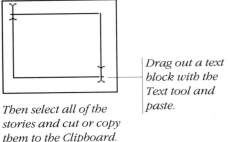

Then select all of the stories and cut or copy them to the Clipboard.

Drag out a text block with the Text tool and paste.

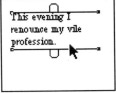

The stories are now threaded. The story that was in back comes in first.

2. Select all the stories with the Pointer tool.

3. Copy or cut the stories to the Clipboard (Ctrl-Insert or Shift-Delete).

4. Select the Text tool, click or drag and insertion point where you want the combined stories to go, and choose Paste from the Edit menu (Shift-Insert).

The text block that was in the back comes in first, and the text block in front comes in last. The combined stories flow into the column you've defined for them. You will sometimes need to add or remove carriage returns where the previously uncombined stories meet. Nevertheless, this is the quickest way to join text blocks into a single, threaded story.

▼ Tip: Yet another way to combine stories

As if the previous methods weren't enough, there's still another way to combine text blocks: use the Story filter (see "The PageMaker Story Filter," later in this chapter).

1. Close the publication containing the stories you want to combine.

2. Create a new publication.

3. Press Ctrl-D. The Place file dialog box appears.

4. Select the original publication in the Place file dialog box and press Enter. The Place PageMaker stories dialog box appears. Select the stories you want to merge and press Enter. Place the merged stories as one story.

5. Close the new publication, saving your changes as you go.

6. Open the original publication and press Ctrl-D to display the Place file dialog box.

7. Locate and select the publication containing the merged stories (the one you created in the previous step) and press Enter. The Place PageMaker stories dialog box appears.

8. Select the merged story (it should be the only story in the publication) and press Enter. PageMaker displays a loaded text gun.

9. Flow the merged stories into your publication and delete the original text blocks.

Column Guides

Many people are confused about the relationship between PageMaker's column guides and text blocks. It's actually quite simple: the column guides are exactly that—guides—that make it easy to create text blocks in the sizes and shapes you want. It's important to remember that you can make the text blocks any width or height you want—regardless of the position of the column guides.

Use the Column guides dialog box to set up the number of columns you want, turn on "Snap to guides" under the Options menu, then use one of the techniques below for creating text blocks that snap to those column guides.

▼ Tip: Using More Column Guide than You Have Columns

If you're working with a two- or three-column design, you don't necessarily have to set up two or three columns. It's often useful to set up four columns for a design that features two columns of text, or six columns for a three-column design. Using more column guides than you have columns makes it easy for you to place illustrations, pull-quotes, or other items at half- or quarter-column intervals. Swiss grids make for very flexible designs. When you're flowing the text into a columnar grid you've created using this method, you'll have to drag-place the text. Otherwise, you'll end up flowing text into half- or quarter-columns. (See "Creating Text Blocks" later in this chapter.)

▼ Tip: Using Odd Numbers of Columns for Asymmetrical Layouts

If you are working with a page design that features two main columns of text and a narrow side (or "companion" column)—also known as "Swiss grids"—try using a five-column layout as shown in Figure 4-7.

Figure 4-7
Swiss grid

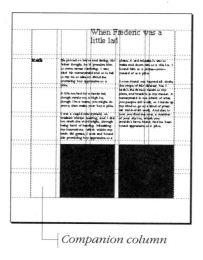 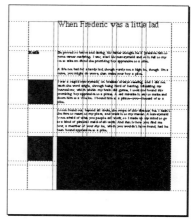

Companion column

Swiss grids are very versatile design tools.

▼ Tip: Creating Different Margins on Facing Pages

Everyone tends to think of column guides for one-column layouts as automatically starting at the edges of the live area, but you can drag the column guides anywhere you want. Suppose you need a double-sided, facing-pages design, but also need an irregular inside measure.

Simple. Set the inside margin to zero in the Page setup dialog box, then drag the inside column guide to the position needed for each page (Figure 4-8). Text flow, including autoflow, respects the column guides, not the margin guides, so text will autoflow into different-sized columns on each page.

▼ Tip: Finding the Horizontal Center of a Column

Here's a way (Figure 4-9) to find the middle of a column with an odd, difficult-to-divide measure. (Otherwise, you'd be able to determine the center of the column by measuring on the rulers, right?)

1. Draw a rectangle (LBO) that is as wide as the column.
2. Place a vertical ruler guide over one of the horizontally centered selection handles. You'll need to do this at 200% or 400% view. The vertical ruler guides mark the center of each column .

Figure 4-8
Column guide being moved independently

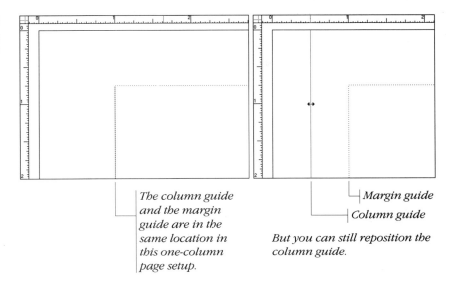

The column guide and the margin guide are in the same location in this one-column page setup.

Margin guide
Column guide

But you can still reposition the column guide.

Figure 4-9
Determining the center of the column using an LBO

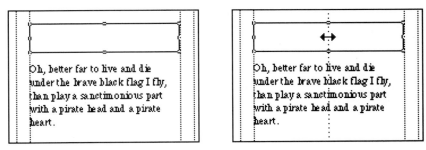

Draw a box across the width of the column.

Drag out a vertical ruler guide so that it precisely bisects the center of the selection handles.

▼ Tip: Finding the Horizontal Center of a Column (Alternate Method)

Here's another method for finding the center of a column.

1. Drag out a text block across the column.
2. Press Ctrl-C for centered text. Make sure that the left, right, and first-line indents for the paragraph are set to zero. A text insertion point appears at the center of the column.

3. Though the insertion point is flashing, you should be able to drag a vertical ruler guide over from the vertical ruler so that it lines up with the insertion point. (You can slow down the blinking from the Desktop icon in the Windows Control Panel.) Since the insertion point is at the center of the column, you've just placed a vertical ruler guide at the center of the column (Figure 4-10).

Figure 4-10
Determining the center of the column using a text block

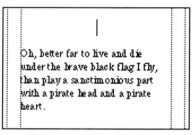

Create a text block that is the width of the column, change the paragraph's alignment to "Center" and make sure that it has no indents.

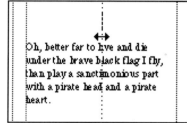

Drag out a vertical ruler guide so that it precisely aligns with the text insertion point.

Creating Text Blocks

People often get confused in PageMaker by the width of text blocks. They don't know why they ended up with a text block of a certain width, or what to do about it once it's there. Let's simplify things: There are four basic ways to create text blocks, with just a variation or two here and there.

Either you create a text block and type, or you create a text block with a loaded place gun. In either of those cases, you can either click-create, or drag-create the text block.

Click-creating. The first method of creating a text block is clicking the Text tool anywhere in the layout window, and typing. It's that simple.

- If you click within column guides and start typing, you'll get a text block as wide as those guides (unless there's another text block or a graphic with a text wrap applied inside the column, in which case you'll get a text block that's as wide as the column, minus the width of the object's intrusion into the column).

- Click on the pasteboard and type, and you'll get a text block as wide as your page margins (defined in the Page setup dialog box), with the following exception.

- Click on the pasteboard to the left of the page, and you'll get a text block that runs from where you clicked to the left edge of the page (unless that distance is greater than the width of the page margins).

Try these three techniques and select each text block with the Pointer tool to see what you've got. Figure 4-11 shows the PageMaker pasteboard (to obtain this view hold down Shift and select "Fit in window"), with several text blocks generated by clicking in various places and then typing text.

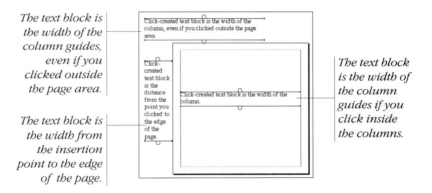

Figure 4-11 Click-creating text blocks

The text block is the width of the column guides, even if you clicked outside the page area.

The text block is the width from the insertion point to the edge of the page.

The text block is the width of the column guides if you click inside the columns.

▼ *Tip: Small Text Blocks*

If you want a very narrow text block, for example to contain a single character like a drop cap, click the Text tool on the pasteboard close to the left side of the page, and type the character. Or just drag-create a narrow text block, as described below.

Drag-creating. The second method of creating a text block is basically the same, but instead of just clicking with the Text tool, you hold down the mouse button and drag out a rectangle (Figure 4-12). You won't actually get a rectangular text block (PageMaker doesn't work with "text frames" the way other programs do), but you will get a text block as wide as you dragged. Start typing and you'll see the text

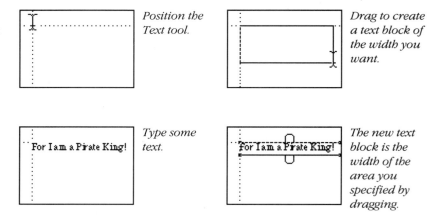

Figure 4-12
Drag-creating a text block

wrap at the end of the line. Or type a couple of characters and then select the block with the Pointer tool to see its width.

This is actually the best method for creating small text blocks, or any text block that's not column-width—drag it out to the width you want. Ole habitually drag-creates every text block—it's easier to control where the top of the text block falls that way.

Place-creating. The third and fourth methods of creating text blocks are basically the same as the first two, but you use a loaded text gun. (You can load the text gun by placing a text file, or by clicking on the + in a windowshade handle.) The only difference from the techniques we outlined above is that when you click-place text, the block flows down until it hits something that stops it (like the bottom of a column or the bottom of the pasteboard). If you drag-place a text file, it actually fills the rectangular area you define. The column widths that result are the same as when creating text blocks from scratch.

▼ *Tip: Text Import Filters*

PageMaker comes with several *text import filters*—external files that it uses to place different types of text files. There are filters for Microsoft Word, Microsoft Works, MultiMate, Office Writer, PC Write, Windows Write, WordPerfect, XyWrite, Word for Windows, and WordStar, as well as dBase and Lotus 1-2-3, among others. To see what text filters you have installed, hold down Ctrl while selecting "About PageMaker" from the Help menu.

To learn more about PageMaker's text filters, see "Importing Text" later in this chapter.

Vanishing Text Blocks

PageMaker doesn't bother with empty text blocks, so if you create a text block, don't type anything, and then click somewhere else, the first text block you "created" simply vanishes. This also happens if you delete all of the type inside a text block, or close up a text block completely, displacing all the text into the following linked blocks.

This was not true in early versions, as any PageMaker veteran will tell you. Pubs from those days always ended up with dangerous phantom text blocks floating around on the page, ready to trip you up or crash the program at the slightest opportunity.

Ole once received a set of files from a very well-known, well-respected desktop publishing design and production agency. He needed to complete their work (they were months late and thousands of dollars over budget) and take the book to press. When he opened the files, he found amazing things: drop shadows that had been created using six boxes, rather than two, for example; and the rolled-up windowshades of stories that had been placed several times—increasing the size of the files by several hundred kilobytes. Many of the pages wouldn't print.

Included in the publication (with its windowshade handles rolled up) was an agency internal memo that was very critical—to the point of being very insulting—of their client. Because he understood well the particular pressures of desktop publishing projects, Ole deleted the offensive memo without bringing it to the client's attention. You cannot always count on such discretion, however, so try not to leave anything in a file calling your client/boss/whatever a "#!@&head" or "bimbo."

▼ *Tip: Text Blocks that Don't Vanish*

In the interest of completeness, we point out that there are a couple of cases where empty text blocks don't vanish.

- If all of the text is forced out of a text block by a graphic's wrap boundary.
- If text is forced out of a text block due to the Page break or Column break before options in the Paragraph specifications dialog box.

PageMaker remembers the size and shape of these text blocks, and fills them with text if the graphic is moved or the break options are changed. This can come as quite a surprise, which is why we class autowrap as one of those things that can be invisible and trip you up.

Replacing Text

If you have a story selected with either the Pointer tool or the Text tool when you choose "Place," you can replace the entire story with the file. If you have a section of text selected, you can replace that selection with the file. If you have your cursor in the middle of a story, you can insert the file into the story at the text cursor's position. PageMaker flows the new text through the story, jumping from text block to text block.

Theoretically. Replacing selected text and Inserting text options work quite well. But the one that everyone needs is "Replacing entire story." That option doesn't work very well. If you have a very (very!) simple publication—with one text block per page—"Replacing entire story" works as advertised. If your file is more complex, you can expect "Replacing entire story" to flow the text through about the first page or two. Plan to reflow the story for the rest of the file, even if the new file has exactly the same number of lines as the file it's replacing.

If you've clicked a text insertion point on the page or in a text block and choose a graphic file in the Place dialog box, PageMaker 4 presents you with a new option, "As inline graphic," which places the graphic file into the current story at the insertion point as an inline graphic (Figure 4-13). For more on working with inline graphics, see "Inline Graphics" in Chapter 5, *Pictures*.

Moving and Resizing Text Blocks

Once you've got a text block on a page, you can move it around by grabbing it with the Pointer tool and dragging. If you drag quickly, you'll see a rectangle representing the size and shape of the text block;

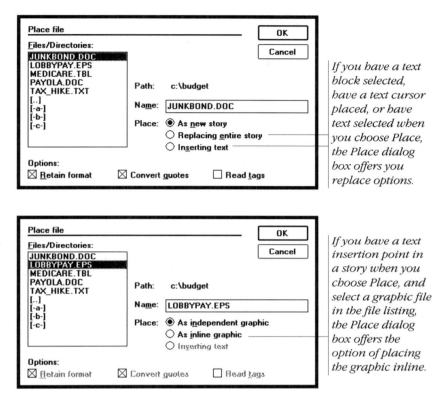

Figure 4-13
Replace options in the Place dialog box

If you have a text block selected, have a text cursor placed, or have text selected when you choose Place, the Place dialog box offers you replace options.

If you have a text insertion point in a story when you choose Place, and select a graphic file in the file listing, the Place dialog box offers the option of placing the graphic inline.

if you drag slowly, you'll see the text inside the text block. Or you can reshape the text block, reflowing the text inside it. You can't create irregularly-shaped text blocks (we'll show you how to fake it later on), but you can create any rectangular shape you want.

To resize a text block in any direction, grab any corner handle with the Pointer tool and drag. You can constrain the motion of the corner handles to horizontal by holding down Shift. To resize a text block vertically, drag the top or bottom windowshade handles up or down.

▼ Tip: Resizing with Multiple Objects Selected

You can resize text blocks (or graphics for that matter) even when you have several other page elements selected. Just grab a corner handle or windowshade handle and resize as you normally would. This is especially useful when you're working with automatic text wraps, because you can see the wrap boundaries of the selected graphic and resize the text block at the same time.

Rotating Text Blocks

Using PageMaker 4, you can rotate unthreaded text blocks in 90-degree increments. The rotated type is treated as a graphic (sort of) and cannot be edited with the Text tool—though you can edit it with the Story Editor (triple-click on the rotated text, or select it and press Ctrl-E). It's not like other graphics, because you can't size it, crop it, apply a text wrap to it, or make it an inline graphic. Still, it moves like a graphic, not a text block. To get it to act like a text block again, rotate it back to horizontal (the first icon in the Text rotation dialog box), where you will once again be able to edit it.

If you've been trying to rotate a selected text block and the Text rotation command remains grayed out on the Element menu, make sure of the following.

- All of the text in the story has been placed.
- The text block is not threaded to any other text block.
- You have no more than one text block selected.
- The text block does not contain any inline graphics.
- The story is not open in the Story Editor.

Rotated text printed to non-PostScript printers will be printed using rotated screen bitmaps (yuck), though the bitmaps do benefit from the smoothing presence of Adobe Type Manager, if it's installed.

Inside Text Blocks

Once you've clicked an insertion point in a text block, you're ready to enter and edit text. PageMaker has lots of techniques for getting around in, selecting, and entering text, with or without the mouse.

Moving Through and Selecting Text

There are many different ways to move through and select text in PageMaker, besides using the mouse. It's pretty obvious that the arrow keys will move you right a character, left a character, up a line, and down a line, but by pressing Ctrl as you press the arrow keys, you can move one paragraph at a time. Press Ctrl-Up arrow to move to the start of the current paragraph (or the start of the previous paragraph if the cursor is already at a paragraph start), and press Ctrl-Down arrow to move to the next paragraph. Ctrl-Left arrow and Ctrl-Right arrow take you one word left or right.

You can use your cursor keys or numeric keypad to really move around on pages (Figure 4-14). Some of these keyboard shortcuts resemble those in Microsoft Word.

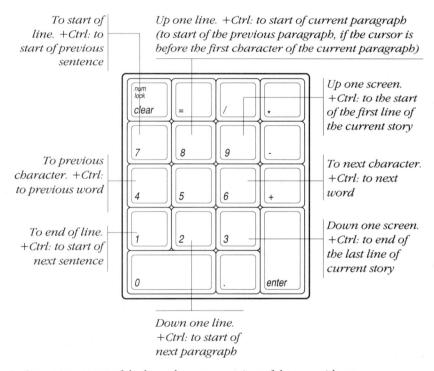

Figure 4-14
Using the numeric keypad to move the text cursor

In Story view, some of the keys change your view of the text without moving the cursor:

9	Up one screen without moving the insertion point
3	Down one screen without moving the insertion point
Ctrl-9	To top of story, without moving the insertion
Ctrl-3	To end of story, without moving the insertion point

Pressing Shift before you press any of these keys, still does extend the selection in the direction you're moving.

In addition, the Home, End, Page Up, and Page Down keys take you to the start of the current story, to the end of the current story, up a screen, and down a screen, respectively, as you'd expect. They're a little harder to hit, though.

▼ Tip: Move and Select

Remember that you can turn any keyboard movement of the text cursor into a selection by pressing Shift as you move the cursor. Shift-Right arrow, for instance, selects the character to the right.

▼ Tip: Select All

With the Text tool, click an insertion point in a text block. Then use "Select all" on the Edit menu (Ctrl-A) to select all of the text in the story—even text that's in PageMaker's netherland and hasn't been threaded into text blocks yet.

▼ Tip: Select a Paragraph or a Word

Triple-click with the Text tool to select a paragraph. This is the fastest way to delete a paragraph—triple-click and hit Backspace or Delete.

Double-click to select a word (including the space after the word). Note that if you type over the word you've selected, you have to type a space after it so it doesn't run right into the next word.

In spite of all of these cool ways to select text, never forget that you can select text by simply clicking a text insertion point and dragging the cursor with the mouse. Sometimes it's the best way.

Formatting Text

Moving around in text blocks and selecting text is all very well and good, but it's about time we got to the thing everyone buys PageMaker for: formatting text. We'll start with a few definitions, then get into PageMaker's leading methods, leading grids, and character formatting.

▼ *Tip: Use the Text Tool*

You cannot apply any text formatting—paragraph or character—by selecting a text block with the Pointer tool. You have to select the paragraph or characters with the Text tool. We know you already know this, it's just that we recently watched a person getting really frustrated trying to center a text block that was selected with the Pointer tool. To format text, use the Text tool.

Paragraphs and Characters

One of the first things to understand about PageMaker is the difference between character and paragraph formatting. There are two completely separate menu items and dialog boxes for these two functions, but people still seem to get them confused—possibly because styles apply to paragraphs, but contain character formatting information.

Press Ctrl-T, and the Type specifications dialog box appears (see Figure 4-15).

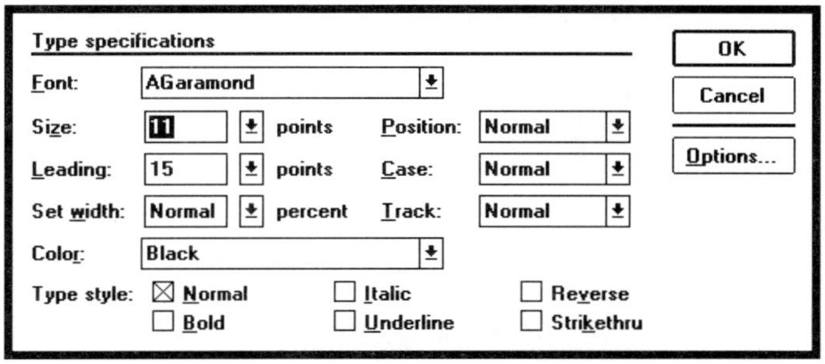

Figure 4-15
Type specifications dialog box

Character formatting controls the font, size, style, and all the stuff within a line of text. Paragraph formatting controls the left, right, and first-line indents, the space before and after the paragraph, automatic rules before and after—anything that affects the paragraph as a whole.

Ctrl-M gives you the Paragraph specifications dialog box (Figure 4-16). A paragraph might be a single line, or even a single character—as long as it ends with a hard return (what you get when you press Enter).

Figure 4-16
Paragraph specifications dialog box

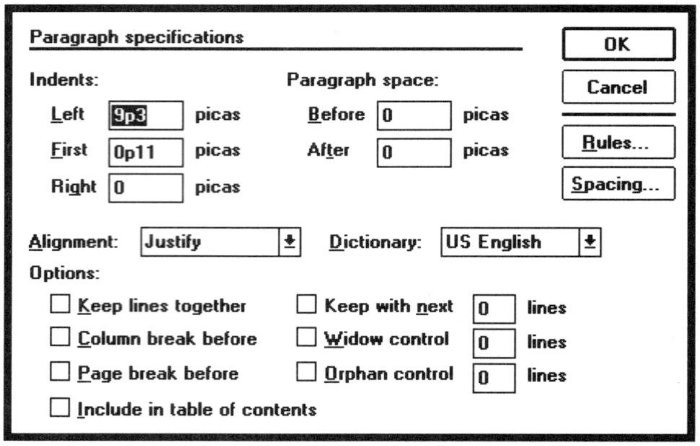

Paragraph specifications			OK
Indents:		Paragraph space:	Cancel
Left 9p3 picas		Before 0 picas	
First 0p11 picas		After 0 picas	Rules...
Right 0 picas			Spacing...
Alignment: Justify		Dictionary: US English	
Options:			
☐ Keep lines together		☐ Keep with next 0 lines	
☐ Column break before		☐ Widow control 0 lines	
☐ Page break before		☐ Orphan control 0 lines	
☐ Include in table of contents			

▼ *Tip: Selecting Paragraphs and Characters*

You don't have to select all of the text in a paragraph (by drag-selecting or triple-clicking) to apply paragraph formatting to it. Just use the Text tool to click an insertion point in the paragraph, or swipe over some part of the paragraph, and you can change its indents, space before, space after, rules, justification, or any other paragraph-level control. As long as your selection is touching the paragraph, you can apply paragraph formatting to it.

You can apply character formatting to all the characters in a paragraph, on the other hand, by selecting them all with a quick triple-click using the Text tool.

Vertical Spacing

In this section, we'll talk about leading—the vertical distance between the baselines of type—and setting vertical space around paragraphs.

Leading

There is one hazy area in the paragraph/character distinction, and unfortunately it's one of the most important specifications: leading. Leading in PageMaker can apply to any character, so two characters right next to each other might have totally different leading values. The larger value dominates, displacing the preceding and succeeding lines.

Steve and Jesse think it's stupid that PageMaker has the leading control in the Type specifications dialog box, because leading is a paragraph-level control. They think it's better the way it works in WinWord—with type size in the Character dialog box and leading in the Paragraph dialog box.

Ole and Scott disagree. They think that leading is a character-level attribute, and that you always think "10 on 12," and shouldn't have to open another dialog box to spec your leading. Luckily (we guess), you can have it both ways—Steve and Jesse's way in WinWord, and Ole and Scott's way in PageMaker. If there's enough demand, we'll establish a call-in hotline to debate the issue.

PageMaker Leading

If you're new to type, you need to understand leading. If you're not new to type, you still need to understand leading according to Page-Maker. Traditional typographers and typesetters might have some trouble understanding PageMaker's two leading methods, Top of caps and Proportional, as neither one provides the true, baseline-to-baseline leading that they're used to. Whatever your background, unless you know how PageMaker thinks about leading, you won't really know what's going on with your type.

PageMaker uses the metaphor of the slug—a line of type as cast in hot metal, encompassing the space above and below the characters. To see PageMaker's slugs, select a piece of text with the Text tool (Figure 4-17). The area that turns black is the slug. Paragraph slugs (seen by selecting the entire paragraph) show the paragraph's line slugs, plus the paragraph's Space after setting, plus any Space before setting for the following paragraph.

Think of a text block as a stack of slugs filling a hole.

Aldus probably chose to use slugs as the metaphor for lines of type because slugs are never far from the minds of anyone living in the Pacific Northwest. Large, 5- to 7-inch banana slugs—some with racing stripes—can be found hanging from the doorknobs of most houses on most of our rainy, cold, dark mornings. You wouldn't want to live here unless you really liked slugs. We live in Seattle because we like slugs. Steve is also partial to mildew.

Figure 4-17
Text slugs

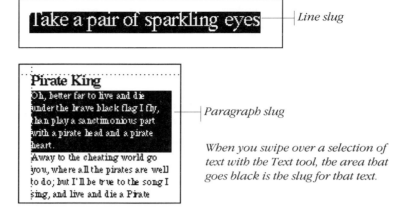

When you swipe over a selection of text with the Text tool, the area that goes black is the slug for that text.

Space Before and Space After

There are two other paragraph-level controls that work very closely with leading—"Space before" and "Space after" (in the Paragraph specifications dialog box). Oddly, any added space before a paragraph appears as part of the slug of the paragraph above. This is the one area where the metaphor of the slug in PageMaker sort of breaks down.

▼ *Tip: Use Space Before and After Instead of Carriage Returns*

If you specify space before a paragraph, PageMaker ignores it if that paragraph lands at the top of a text block. Specify space after, and PageMaker ignores it if the paragraph lands at the bottom of a text block. This is much nicer than putting extra carriage returns between paragraphs; they're always getting in your way at one column break or another. It works especially well if you automate it with style sheets.

▼ *Tip: Retaining Space Before*

PageMaker deletes any space above a paragraph if that paragraph falls at the top of a text block. This is generally a good thing, but sometimes you want to keep that space. To retain space before a paragraph even when it falls at the top of a text block, add a paragraph rule above the paragraph, set its Line Style to "None," and adjust its space above baseline in the Paragraph rule options dialog box. To retain a Space before setting for a paragraph that has a paragraph rule above, create a spacer paragraph above it that has a Keep with next setting that glues it to the following paragraph.

Leading Methods

What is this Leading method button in the Spacing attributes dialog box? Proportional? Top of caps? Which should you use?

It's simple. Use the proportional leading method. If you use "Top of caps," you won't be able to tell where the baseline of the type falls in the slug. Even worse, PageMaker distorts the slug based on the height of the largest character in the line (Figure 4-18). If you use the Top of caps leading method, PageMaker sets the distance between the top of the slug and the baseline to the height of the tallest font ascent encountered within the line. This is not necessarily the same as the height of the tallest character in the line: a lowercase character from a large font can have a larger font ascent than an uppercase character from a smaller font. This can throw everything off.

And nothing is more obvious, and looks less professional, than uneven leading within a paragraph.

And what about this Auto setting in the Leading pop-up list in the Type specifications dialog box (or on the Leading submenu)? Does choosing "Auto" ensure good leading every time?

It's simple. Use "fixed" leading, specifying the leading you want. If you use "Auto," PageMaker distorts the slug based on the height of the

Figure 4-18
Top of caps versus Proportional leading methods

If you use the Top of caps leading method, PageMaker distorts leading based on the height of the largest character in the line.

If you use the Proportional leading method, PageMaker uses the leading you specified, regardless of the characters in the line.

Top of Caps leading method

Proportional leading method

Oh, better far to live and die under the brave black flag I fly, than play a sanctimonious part with a pirate head and a pirate heart.

Oh, better far to live and die under the brave black flag I fly, than play a sanctimonious part with a pirate head and a pirate heart.

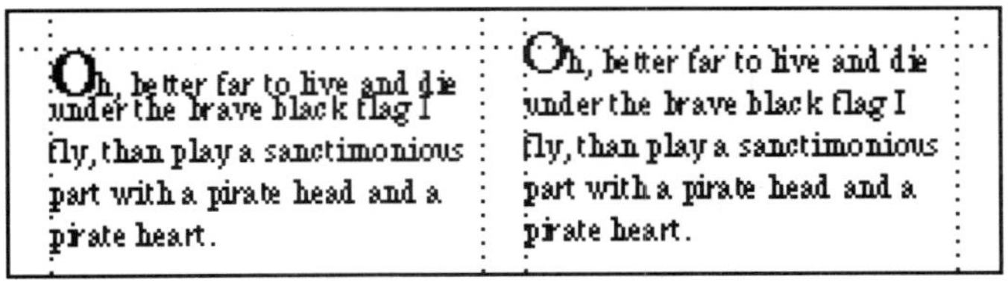

largest character in the line. *Don't use "Auto,"* because the leading of your lines should have nothing to do with what characters or fonts they contain. Autoleading is intended to protect the innocent; Aldus doesn't want naive users calling to complain that their type is colliding. If your type overprints on the line above, you've done something wrong (like specifying 36-point type on an 18-point lead). Fix it. You know more about what you want than PageMaker does. Furthermore, there are lots of times when you need to set 36-point type on an 18-point lead (Figure 4-19).

Figure 4-19
Fixed leading versus autoleading

If you use autoleading, Page-Maker distorts leading based on the height of the largest point-size character in the line.

If you specify a fixed amount of leading, PageMaker uses the leading you specified, regardless of the characters in the line.

Oh, better far to live and die under the brave black flag I fly, than play a sanctimonious

Oh, better far to live and die under the brave black flag I fly, than play a sanctimonious

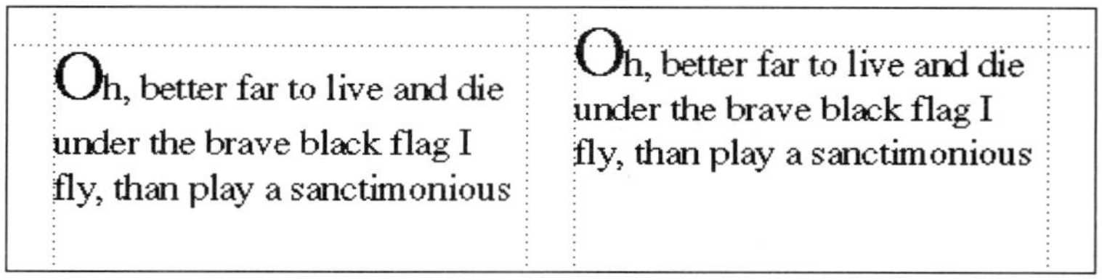

Auto leading (10 point type with a large initial cap)

Fixed leading (10-point type with a 12-point lead with a large initial cap)

Autoleading and top of caps leading are intended for "general business users" who don't want to worry about getting the leading right. The result is type that doesn't collide, doesn't require much thought, and doesn't look professional.

We think that even if you can't consciously perceive a difference between these leading methods, you still *feel* a difference that translates into an impression of a publication's quality—or lack of quality. More significantly, as far as this book is concerned, it's easier to work with type when you know where the baseline of each line of type will fall.

If you use the proportional leading method and fixed leading, the baseline of your copy always falls two-thirds of the way from the top of the slug (and the slug is equal to the leading setting), regardless of the height of the characters in the line (Figure 4-20). This way you at least know what's happening, which is not the case with top of caps and autoleading. The effect with proportional, fixed leading is very similar to—but not, unfortunately, exactly the same as—baseline-to-baseline leading. You *can*, at least, always determine where the baseline will fall, which is more than we can say for "Top of caps."

Figure 4-20
Baseline with proportional leading

With proportional leading, the baseline of the type falls two-thirds the way down from the top of the slug.

Since PageMaker breaks the leading up, two-thirds above the baseline and one third below, it's easy to figure the results when you add leading. If you go from 10/12 to 10/24, for instance (adding 12 points of leading), you'll get 8 additional points at the top of the slug (above the baseline), and 4 at the bottom. Add 36 points of leading, and you get 24 above, 12 below. Therefore, the distance from the baseline of one line to the baseline of the line below is equal to ⅓ of the lead of the line above, plus ⅔ of the lead of the line below. To use a different leading for a single line in a paragraph, make sure you've selected the entire line.

Leading Grids

This is not a book on design, and we're not going to try and tell you how to design a newsletter, like most of the other PageMaker books do. There is one area, though, where your design interacts very closely with the way you use PageMaker—leading grids. PageMaker offers several tools that support leading grid-based design, and that let you build tight, consistent pages very quickly.

The trick here is to set up your design with all vertical measurements based on the leading of your body copy. If your leading is 13 points, you design the whole page so elements work in 13-point increments. Your captions will line up with the body copy, as will your graphics, and when you get to the bottom of the page, you'll find the baselines all nicely aligned. When you're setting up your top and bottom margins, set them so that the height of the live area is an integral multiple of your base leading, and you'll see the bottom of the slug of the last line of text land perfectly on the bottom margin—very pretty.

Custom Rulers and Leading Grids

One of PageMaker's best features is the ability to set custom increments for the vertical ruler. If you're using 15-point leading for your body copy, for instance, you can set the vertical ruler to 15-point increments (from the Preferences dialog box), turn on "Snap to Rulers" on the Options menu, and everything—text blocks, graphics, captions, etc.—will line up on the 15-point grid.

At Fit in world and Fit in window page views, you'll see vertical ruler increments exactly as you specified in the Preferences dialog box. At the other page views, however, you'll see that the major increments have been divided into thirds. If that sounds familiar, it should. The baseline of type set with the proportional leading method falls two-thirds of the way down the slug. You can align baselines perfectly using the minor tick marks on the vertical ruler. PageMaker's proportional leading method and custom vertical ruler were made for each other—literally.

If you set up your design and your master pages with a leading grid and custom vertical rulers, you can make incredibly tight pages very quickly. And we guarantee that you'll start producing better-looking pages. Remember—when deadlines loom, consistency and accuracy make your life less—not more—difficult. If you set up your styles and leading grid properly, pages seem to fly together of their own accord. You'll also avoid one of the hallmarks of amateur design, "leading creep" (Figure 4-21). Like mildew, once it starts, it's almost impossible to get rid of.

Figure 4-21
Leading creep

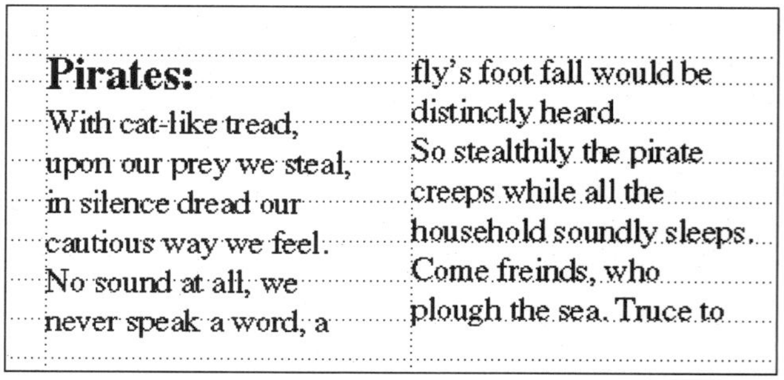

> **Pirates:**
> With cat-like tread, upon our prey we steal, in silence dread our cautious way we feel. No sound at all, we never speak a word, a fly's foot fall would be distinctly heard. So stealthily the pirate creeps while all the household soundly sleeps. Come freinds, who plough the sea. Truce to

When the baselines of two adjacent columns don't align, you've got leading creep.

▼ Tip: Designing for Leading Grids

To design a publication using a leading grid, follow these steps.

1. Decide on a leading grid size—the leading for your body copy (for example, 12 points).
2. Decide how many lines you want on a page.

You can either decide on your margin measurements and choose the number of lines that's closest to the measurements you want, or you can choose a number of lines and pick the margin measurements that seem appropriate—whichever seems most natural to you.

Dealing with Anomalies

Not every paragraph in your publication will have the same leading, of course. The goal is to design elements so that the space they take up equals some integral multiple of your body copy leading. Try this:

Body copy   12/15
Subheads   14/15, 15 points before (30 points total)
Main heads 24/24, 6 points before (30 points total)

It looks tight and professional. Lines in adjacent columns line up, and the last line of a column always aligns with its neighbor. The main heads aren't specced 24/30, because that would put 2 points of extra space below (one-third of the six extra points), and 4 above. We wanted all 6 points above.

A leading grid has limitations, of course. If you're working with a 15-point grid, for instance, you may have to set your subheads 16 on 30 to keep things aligned, which may be more space than you want. It gets even trickier to set up styles for two- or three-line subheads.

▼ Tip: More Type than Leading

If you want subheads of a slightly larger type size than your body-copy leading, *and* stay on the leading grid, *without* going to double leading.

It's a puzzle. If you're using a 14-point leading grid, try making your subheads 18 on 14, with 14 points of paragraph space above.

The top windowshade of this text block in Figure 4-22 shows how the 18-point type exceeds the 14-point leading. The line isn't there on the printed page, though, so it's much less obvious to the eye. Notice also how PageMaker ignores the Space before value when the paragraph is at the top of the column. If you want to maintain a certain amount of space before the paragraph even if the paragraph falls at the top of a text block, see the tip "Retaining Space Before" earlier in this chapter.

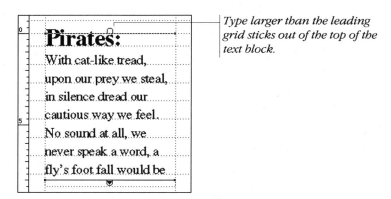

Figure 4-22
Type larger than the leading grid

Type larger than the leading grid sticks out of the top of the text block.

With this technique you'll have a top-of-page subhead every so often that hangs a point or two above the live area, but we think that looks better (it's less noticeable) than most of your pages running ragged bottom because your subheads have knocked you off the leading grid. Many subheads will only be a point or two larger than the body copy.

This last tip is a good example of how you can break design rules and get away with it—how you have to sometimes. Not every line on the page has to land on the 15-point grid. Pullquotes, for instance, often work better if they're off the leading grid, because they stand out better from the surrounding text. The idea, though, is to have everything line up, especially at the bottom, without having to jimmy it around.

▼ Tip: Multiple Styles for Multiple-line Heads

If your subheads sometimes run one line, sometimes two, sometimes three, then a single style doesn't cut it if you want to stay on the leading grid. Set up multiple styles with different space before, space after, and leading values. You'll need a style for the one-line subhead, two for the two-liner, and three for the three-liner—six total. You might also need to correct for those situations where the subhead's at the top of the column and there's no space before.

This is a mind bender to figure out sometimes, but it's just a matter of adding and subtracting until it looks right and the numbers add up. Then build the styles and lock them up someplace. Note that you could also solve this problem using the Align to grid option in the Paragraph rule options dialog box (discussed in "Understanding Align to Grid" later in this chapter).

▼ Tip: Bullet List Leading

With bulleted and numbered lists, you often want half a line or so of extra leading between the items in the list. You can spec a half-line space after for each bullet (7 points with 14-point leading), but that only works when you have an even number of bullet items. With an odd number, you'll end up half a line off your grid. You also have to consider space before and after the first and last bullet items—you'll usually want it set off a bit from the surrounding copy. And don't forget the list heading, if you use one.

Table 4-1 shows some sample styles that handle bullets with 14-point leading.

This setup shown in the table means you have to count the items in the list and format accordingly, and it also means you're a little inconsistent in the space before and after bullet lists. But it keeps you on the leading grid, and people probably won't notice the 3.5-point difference between pages. As they say in the auto body business, you can't see both sides at once.

Note that you could also apply the Align to grid option in the Paragraph rule options dialog box to the last paragraph to accomplish

Table 4-1. Bullet styles for a leading grid

	Leading	*Space Before*	*Space After*
List with odd number of bullets			
First bullet	14	7	7
Normal bullets	14	0	7
Last bullet	14	0	7
List with even number of bullets			
First bullet	14	10.5	7
Normal Bullets	14	0	7
Last bullet	14	0	10.5

a similar effect (see below)—though you can end up with different amounts of space above and below the list.

Understanding Align to Grid

The methods above work very well, but there are a couple of other techniques for automating your design and layout work. PageMaker 4 adds a very powerful Align to grid feature for working with leading grids. Because it's a late-breaking feature (this happens in software development), it's hidden away in the Paragraph rule options dialog box (Figure 4-23; it's about a mile deep in dialog boxes). You can use "Align to grid" even if the paragraph has no paragraph rules.

The other tricky thing about the Align to grid option is its name, which doesn't really describe its function. Think of it as "Align top of next paragraph slug to grid." It's a better description of how the option works (Figure 4-24).

When the Align to grid option is turned on for a paragraph, Page-Maker calculates where the top of the next paragraph falls relative to a leading grid measured down from the top of the current text block. PageMaker includes any Space after setting for the current paragraph in this calculation, and considers the top of the next paragraph to start at the top of that paragraph's Space before setting (if one is present). It's very easy for a Space before setting to throw a paragraph—and possibly succeeding paragraphs—off the leading grid, so be careful

Figure 4-23
Rule options dialog box

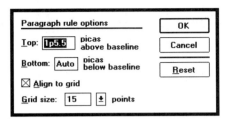

The Align to grid option works even if paragraph rules are turned off. It should be called "Align top of next paragraph slug to grid."

Figure 4-24
Align to grid option

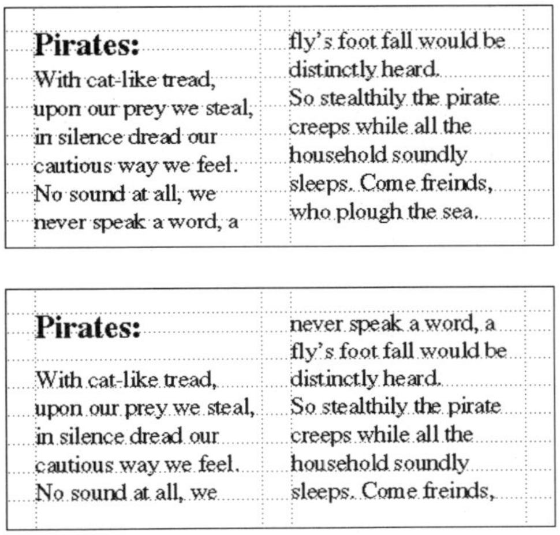

Without "Align to grid," baselines of adjacent columns don't align because of the heading at the start of the first text block.

With "Align to grid" turned on, PageMaker adds space after the heading to make the following paragraph fall on the grid.

when you're setting paragraph space before/after attributes and using "Align to grid" in the same text block. Figure 4-25 illustrates the effect of paragraph spacing on the Align to grid option.

In practice, "Align to grid" does not align the baseline of every text element to the leading grid—only those with the same leading as that entered for "Grid size." PageMaker handles all other elements as they're specified, then adds space below to make the next occurrence of the specified leading fall on the grid (Figure 4-26).

Figure 4-25
How the Align to grid option and paragraph spacing interact

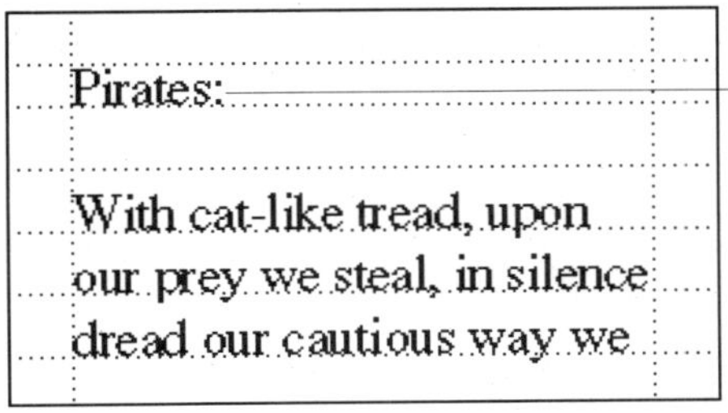

Because this paragraph has a Space after setting of 0p6, the following lines in this 12-point grid are pushed down to the next whole grid increment.

Figure 4-26
Adding space with the Align to grid option

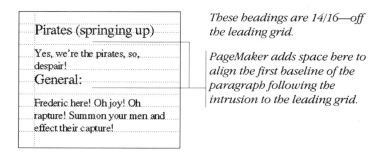

These headings are 14/16—off the leading grid.

PageMaker adds space here to align the first baseline of the paragraph following the intrusion to the leading grid.

Usually, in designing for a leading grid, it's acceptable to specify a leading for multiple-line headings that is off the leading grid. It's very limiting to constrain your choices of type sizes and leadings for headings to those that are completely compatible with the body text. With "Align to grid," it's easy to keep the body text following such a heading on the grid. (You can also create different heading styles with Space before and Space after settings that compensate for the different height of the headings. See the tip "Multiple Styles for Multiple-line Heads" earlier in this chapter.)

Custom Vertical Rulers

To help you align objects on the leading grid, set the vertical ruler increments to the leading value of your body copy (15 points, for instance). The Custom setting of the vertical ruler works perfectly with the proportional leading method, because it displays the value you enter divided into thirds (Figure 4-27). Then set the ruler origin (the 0, 0 point) to the top of the text area, turn on "Snap to rulers," and your moves will snap to the leading grid (Figure 4-28).

Figure 4-27
Custom vertical rulers with the proportional leading method

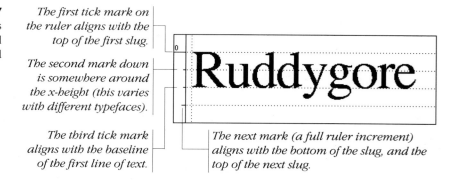

The first tick mark on the ruler aligns with the top of the first slug.

The second mark down is somewhere around the x-height (this varies with different typefaces).

The third tick mark aligns with the baseline of the first line of text.

The next mark (a full ruler increment) aligns with the bottom of the slug, and the top of the next slug.

Figure 4-28
Aligning text blocks using custom rulers and the Snap to rulers option

Combined with "Snap to rulers," the custom vertical ruler makes it easy to get things lined up—try to design your pieces so you snap everything to a grid, to ruler guides, or to both.

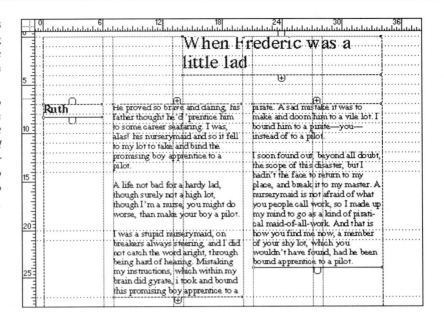

▼ Tip: Placing Illustrations

Positioning illustrations consistently between text blocks can be tricky. When you measure the distance from a text block down to a graphic, you should generally measure from the baseline down. When measuring from a graphic down to a text block, measure down to the top of the slug. In any case, be consistent. If you're using a leading grid, place and size the graphic so that it fits on the grid (Figure 4-29).

Horizontal Spacing and Alignment

So much for all the details of vertical spacing. PageMaker also offers a lot of control over horizontal spacing—type alignment; left, right, and first-line paragraph indents; tabs; and letter and word spacing.

▼ Tip: Keyboard Shortcuts for Type Alignment

Don't use the Alignment submenu to set horizontal type alignment. It's too much work. Use the keyboard shortcuts instead. Select one or

Figure 4-29
Aligning graphics to a leading grid

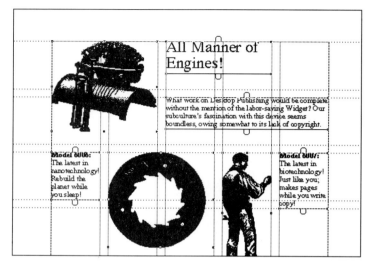

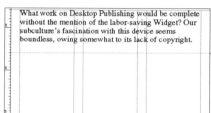

To place a graphic on the leading grid below a block of copy, drag a horizontal ruler guide down to the next even grid increment...

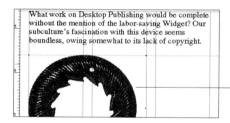

...and place the graphic so that it snaps to the horizontal ruler guide.

more paragraphs and press one of the key combinations shown in Table 4-2 for fast alignment changes.

PageMaker 4's new Force justify option forces the last line of a paragraph to be fully justified to the width of the text block. This is handy when you want a headline spread out across a given distance (Figure 4-30), or when you want to force a line break in the middle of a justified paragraph. Just press return, creating two paragraphs, and change the alignment of the first paragraph to "Force justify."

Table 4-2. Keyboard shortcuts for paragraph alignment

Alignment	Keyboard Shortcut
Align right	Ctrl-Shift-R
	or Alt-T, A, R
Align left	Ctrl-Shift-L
	or Alt-T, A, L
Center	Ctrl-Shift-C
	or Alt-T, A, C
Justify	Ctrl-Shift-J
	or Alt-T, A, J
Force justify	Ctrl-Shift-F
	or Alt-T, A, F

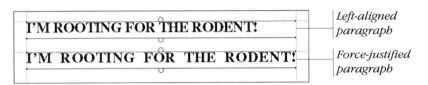

Figure 4-30
Force justifying paragraphs

Left-aligned paragraph

Force-justified paragraph

▼ Tip: Use the New-line Character

There's an even better way to force a line break in justified copy. Use PageMaker 4's "new-line" character—Shift-Enter. This forces a line break, but doesn't force the line flush left in a fully justified paragraph, or create a new paragraph (Figure 4-31).

Figure 4-31
Using the new-line character to break a line in a justified paragraph

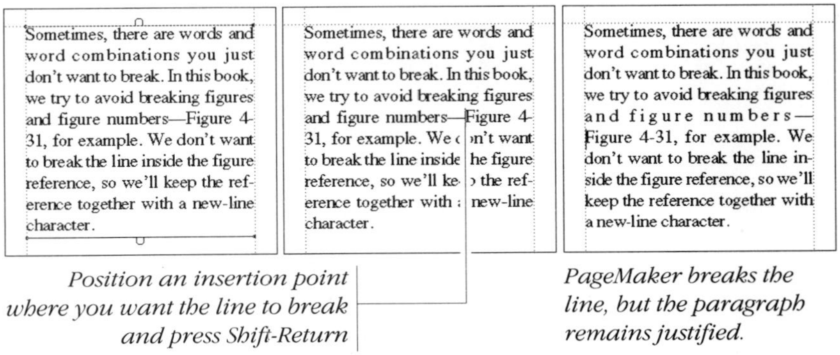

Sometimes, there are words and word combinations you just don't want to break. In this book, we try to avoid breaking figures and figure numbers—Figure 4-31, for example. We don't want to break the line inside the figure reference, so we'll keep the reference together with a new-line character.

Position an insertion point where you want the line to break and press Shift-Return

Sometimes, there are words and word combinations you just don't want to break. In this book, we try to avoid breaking figures and figure numbers—Figure 4-31, for example. We don't want to break the line inside the figure reference, so we'll keep the reference together with a new-line character.

Sometimes, there are words and word combinations you just don't want to break. In this book, we try to avoid breaking figures and figure numbers—Figure 4-31, for example. We don't want to break the line inside the figure reference, so we'll keep the reference together with a new-line character.

PageMaker breaks the line, but the paragraph remains justified.

Working with Tabs

When you set tabs in PageMaker, you're setting them for the paragraph or paragraphs you have selected. You can't have different tab settings for each line in a paragraph. Tabs are measured from the left edge of the text block, and every tab you set must be at a particular point on the tab ruler—there's no way to set, say, a tab at the right edge of a text block, no matter where that boundary falls on the tab ruler. We've seen lots of people expect tabs to move because the right or left indent—or the width of the text block—changed. They don't. They're determined absolutely by the positions you specify on the ruler, no matter how wide a column you're working with.

When you choose "Indents/tabs" from the Type menu (Ctrl-I), the Indents/tabs dialog box appears, aligning its zero point with the left edge of the currently selected text block, if possible (Figure 4-32). This makes setting tabs much easier than in previous versions of PageMaker.

Tab Selection

In PageMaker 3, you could select a particular tab and move it around on the ruler, but, if you wanted to make it into a different type of tab, or change the leader, you were out of luck. In PageMaker 4, you can select a tab that has already been set, then change the tab to any other type of tab by clicking on the tab icon you want. You can also change the tab's leader by selecting the tab and making changes in the Set leader text edit box, or change its position using the Tab action pop-up menu.

Position. Type the numeric position at which you want to add, move, delete, or repeat the tab. After you enter a number in the Tab action text edit box, choose one of the actions on the pop-up menu. If you don't choose an action, nothing will happen.

Add tab. Add a tab of the selected type at the position on the ruler specified in the Tab action text edit box.

Delete tab. Delete the tab at the position specified in the Tab action text edit box.

Move tab. Move the selected tab to the position specified in the Tab action text edit box.

Repeat tab. Repeats the selected tab across the ruler in increments specified by the distance from the selected tab to the previous tab. If the selected tab is the first tab on the tab ruler, "Repeat tab" repeats the tab across the ruler in the increments shown in the Tab action text edit box.

▼ *Tip: Aligning Tabs Quickly*

To set up a table quickly using PageMaker's normal tabbing (as opposed to the Table Editor), first lay down some vertical ruler guides on your page. This lets you see the basic column width. You might include some type to see how it fits in the column widths at different sizes (Figure 4-32).

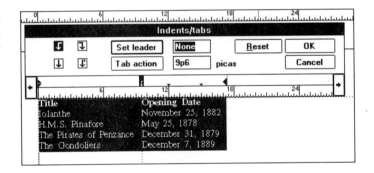

Figure 4-32
Aligning tabs with ruler guides

Once you've got the column widths set up with ruler guides, in Actual view, call up the Indents/tabs dialog box. Finally, set your tabs according to the ruler guides (remember that you first have to select the paragraphs to be affected). There's still trial and error involved, but this method lets you get close pretty quickly.

▼ *Tip: Use the New-line Character Within Tabular Matter*

Use the new-line character when you want to break a line but do not want to start a new paragraph. Often, in complex tables, you need to add a second line to a table item, but don't want to start a new paragraph because you don't want a new first-line indent, space before, space after, or paragraph rule (Figure 4-33).

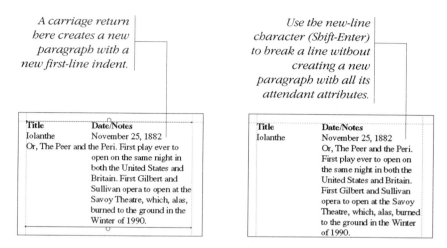

Figure 4-33
Using the new-line character for tables

A carriage return here creates a new paragraph with a new first-line indent.

Use the new-line character (Shift-Enter) to break a line without creating a new paragraph with all its attendant attributes.

The tabs on the new line are the same as on its predecessor, because they're part of the same paragraph. If you want different tab stops on two lines, make them separate paragraphs.

▼ Tip: Use a Tab for Hanging Indents

If you want the first line of a paragraph to hang out to the left, as in a bulleted or numbered list (Ole thinks you should always hang bullets), make sure to use a tab after the bullet or number. Then use "Paragraph specifications" (Ctrl-M) or the Indents/tabs ruler (Ctrl-I) to hang the first line. Make sure to put a left tab stop at the same position as the left indent (Figure 4-34).

Too often, we've seen people create hanging indents using carriage returns and tabs. They'll type the first line, press a carriage return, press Tab, type the second line, press a carriage return, press Tab, and so on. Even worse, they'll keep pressing Tab until the line wraps. You don't need to work that hard to create hanging indents. If you're setting up a style for numbered lists, make sure to leave enough room in your hanging indents for those lists that go beyond 9. Adding that

WORDS 145

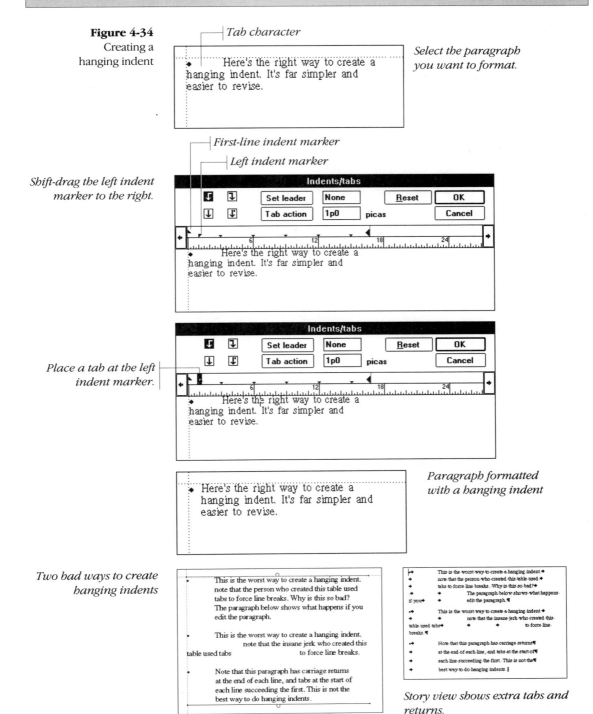

Figure 4-34 Creating a hanging indent

extra digit can blow everything. Remember, though, that no one reads numbered lists that have more than nine items.

In any case, use tabs, not spaces, to create the indent, or things won't line up right. With tabs you can specify exact positions. Spaces are much more equivocal.

▼ Tip: Shift-Dragging the Indent Marker

In previous versions of PageMaker, making a hanging indent in the Indents/tabs dialog box required you to drag the indent marker to the right, then drag the first-line indent marker back to the left. Now it's easier—just hold down Shift while you drag the left indent marker and it will move independently.

▼ Tip: Decimal/Right Aligning Numbered Lists

When you're creating numbered lists, you sometimes want either the decimals in the numbered lists to align, or the last digit of the numbers to right-align. In either case, as you enter the numbered list, press Tab, then type the number and (if you're using one) the period, press Tab again, then type the body of the list item (Figure 4-35). If you're formatting copy someone else has keyed in, be lazy: remember that you can search for carriage returns and tabs in the Story Editor.

Set up your paragraph with a hanging indent that's greater than the width of the largest number you intend to use, then place a decimal or

Figure 4-35
Aligning numbered list items

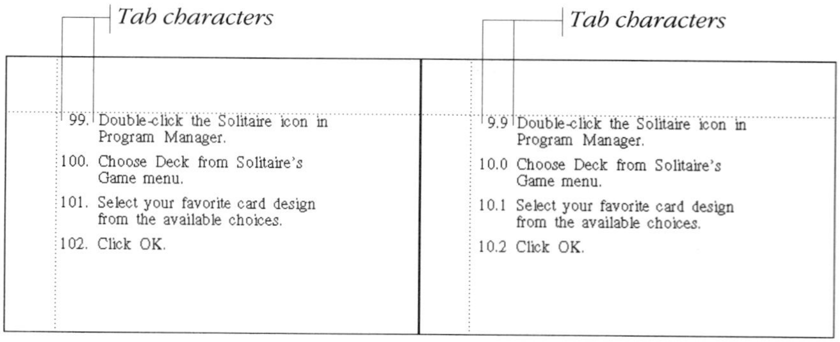

Tab characters

99. Double-click the Solitaire icon in Program Manager.	9.9 Double-click the Solitaire icon in Program Manager.
100. Choose Deck from Solitaire's Game menu.	10.0 Choose Deck from Solitaire's Game menu.
101. Select your favorite card design from the available choices.	10.1 Select your favorite card design from the available choices.
102. Click OK.	10.2 Click OK.

Right alignment   *Decimal alignment*

right tab some distance from the left indent. Finally, place a left tab at the same point as the hanging indent.

▼ Tip: Flush Right/Flush Left

If you have a single-line paragraph and want the words at the beginning of a line to be flush left, and the words at the end flush right, just put a tab in between and spec the paragraph as flush right. PageMaker pushes the stuff after the tab flush right, and leaves the words before the tab flush left (Figure 4-36). This technique is better than setting a flush-right tab at the right edge of the text block, because a flush-right tab doesn't move when you change column widths.

Figure 4-36
Flush right/flush left tabs

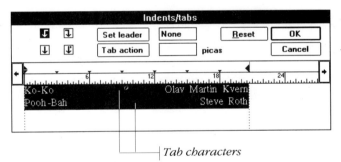

Note that, because of the paragraph's right alignment, the tabs seem to ignore the settings in the Indents/tabs dialog box.

You can also use this technique with text centered between the stuff at the right and left. Just put a center tab stop in the middle of the text block, and use tabs between the center, left, and right text (Figure 4-37). Remember, the center tab won't move if you change the width of the column.

Figure 4-37
Left, right, and centered tabs on the same line

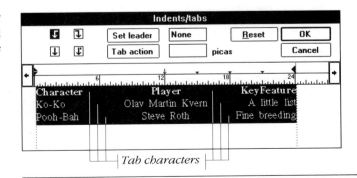

▼ *Tip: Aligning Financial Tabular Matter*

Aligning columns of figures is easy if you use decimal tabs, and PageMaker 4 is even smart enough to align decimal-tabbed figures contained in parentheses properly (unlike version 3). You don't even need decimal points to make this work, as you can see below.

```
   1200
  (900)
15,199³
```

As you can see, though, it gets a bit trickier if some of the figures are followed by footnotes, which push those figures to the left and out of alignment. We've found three solutions, but none of them is pretty.

Method 1. Adjust the tab stops for each line containing a footnoted figure so the figures line up. Take note of how much you have to move the tab, so after you've done one you can just do the arithmetic and type the new position numerically, rather than dragging approximately.

Method 2. Use right rather than decimal tabs. Put a thin space (Ctrl-Shift-T) after every figure that isn't followed by a parenthesis or footnote, select the thin space, and change its type size (which changes its width) until the figure lines up properly. Once you've got a thin space sized so it works correctly, copy and paste it where you need it. Remember to plan ahead for double-digit footnotes.

Method 3. Create an extra left tab for the footnote references to align to, just to the right of each column.

Take Me to Your (Tab) Leader

Tab leaders are strings of characters that run for the length of a tab. They're typically used in tables of contents (between the name of an article and its page number), or in price lists between a description of a product and its price. They're usually dots (periods) or underlines. Their purpose is to lead the eye from one text item to another, much the same as horizontal rules or shaded bars are used in tables.

In PageMaker 4, you can use three default tab leaders (underline, dot, and dotted line), or make up your own leader from any character or two-character combination. To make up your own tab leader, open the Indents/tabs dialog box, select the tab, choose "Custom" in the Set leader pop-up menu, and type the character(s) you want to use for the leader.

▼ *Tip: Changing The Font of Tab Leader Characters*

PageMaker formats leader characters using the font used for the character immediately preceding the tab, but ignores normal spaces. If you want to use fancy characters for the leader dots in tabular matter, or if you just want to use tab leaders for some weird effect, you can use fonts like Symbol or Zapf Dingbats.

1. Place the text insertion point immediately before the tab whose format you want to change.
2. Without moving the insertion point or selecting any text, choose the typeface, size and style you want to use for the tab leader (use the Type specifications dialog box—Ctrl-T).
3. Type a fixed space—a nonbreaking space (Ctrl-Spacebar), an em space (Ctrl-Shift-M), an en space (Ctrl-Shift-N), or a thin space (Ctrl-Shift-T). The tab leader changes to the typeface, size, and style you specified (Figure 4-38).

▼ *Tip: Make These Tabs Like Those*

PageMaker fills in the tabs in the Indents/tabs dialog box based on the tab specifications of the uppermost paragraph in a selected range. So you can format the tabs in one paragraph and then apply them to succeeding paragraphs.

1. Work out the tab settings you want for the first (topmost) paragraph of a group of paragraphs you want to format.

Figure 4-38
Changing the format of tab leaders

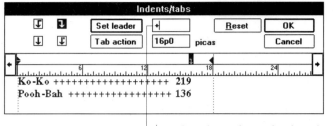

Set the tabs and specify what characters you want used for the tab leaders. In this example, we've typed Alt-Shift-, and a space, for our tab leader.

Place the insertion point just before the tab, then (without moving the insertion point), choose a type style for the leader characters and type a non-breaking space character.

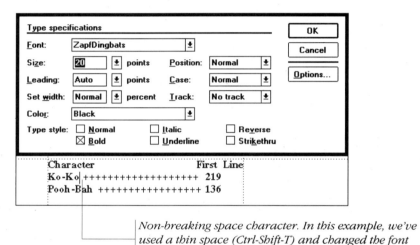

Non-breaking space character. In this example, we've used a thin space (Ctrl-Shift-T) and changed the font from Times to Zapf Dingbats.

After you enter or format the space character, the tab leader takes on the formatting attributes you specified.

2. Drag a selection through that paragraph and any number of following paragraphs.

3. Press Ctrl-I to bring up the Indents/tabs dialog box. The dialog box fills in with the tab values of the uppermost paragraph in your selection.

4. Press Enter (or click OK).

The indent and tab settings of the top paragraph in the selected range are applied to the other selected paragraphs.

Using Table Editor

PageMaker 4 comes with a separate application—Table Editor—for creating tables. If you aren't already committed to the table-making powers of your word processor or spreadsheet, you'll probably find Table Editor a handy application and easy to learn. (Even if you are married to your spreadsheet, chances are Table Editor can import its data.) As Table Editor ships with PageMaker, we have a few tips we'd like to pass on. First, look at the Table Editor screen, as shown in Figure 4-39.

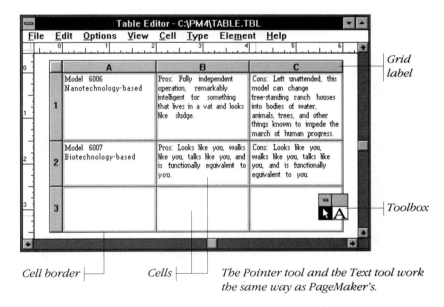

Figure 4-39
Table Editor

▼ *Tip: Changing Borders*

Changing the lines around cells is a pretty simple operation, much improved over the version Macintosh users now deal with. Like many Windows operations, it follows the "select-do" formula. However, there are a few details you should be aware of. When you select a cell, then go to change its line weight from the Element menu, how do you know which of the four lines surrounding the cell will change?

The answer lies in the Borders dialog box. If you need to change specific borders of table cells in Table Editor, as opposed to changing all the borders, follow these steps (as shown in Figure 4-40).

Figure 4-40
Changing borders in Table Editor

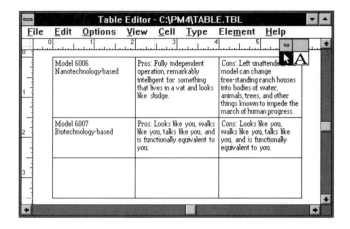

In this example, we want to remove all of the vertical rules in the table without removing the horizontal rules.

Choose "Borders" from the Element menu. The Borders dialog box appears. Select the borders you want to change (or deselect the borders you don't want to change).

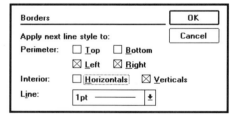

You've got to think backwards. In this case, we want to keep the horizontal rules (including the top and bottom rules), so we select everything else.

After you've closed the Borders dialog box, select the cells you want to change and choose a new line style from the Lines submenu. In this example, we chose "None." The vertical rules in the table disappear.

1. Select the cell(s) you want to change.
2. Choose "Borders" from the Element menu (or press Ctrl-B). The Borders dialog box appears.
3. Choose the lines you want to change and click OK. The selected cells now reflect the new attributes.
4. To change these same lines for other cells, select the cells and choose the line weight you want from the Line submenu.

Any cells you select hereafter will change only the designated lines until you reopen and adjust the Borders dialog.

▼ Tip: Two Fonts in a Single Cell

One problem with Table Editor is that you can't change fonts within a single cell. You can't even change a single word to italics, for crying out loud. Fortunately, we thought of some workarounds for you.

Let's say you want to have more than one item or concept in a cell, and you want to format the items as a list with a Zapf Dingbats bullet. What do you do? In this case, your job is easy. Just create a separate column for the Dingbat items next to the column with the list items. Format the column with the Dingbat font and type in the necessary characters. Then grab the column boundary in the column grid label and drag over to make a narrow column. Finally, set the weight of the intervening cell lines to "None" in the Line submenu (Element menu) so it appears the Dingbat and list are in the same cell (see Figure 4-41). In addition to allowing a font change, this trick has the advantage of creating a hanging indent without resorting to indents or tabs.

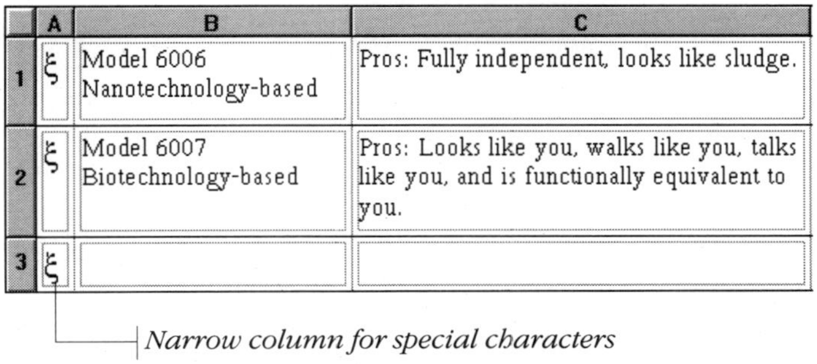

Figure 4-41
An extra column for hanging Dingbats

A	B	C
1 ❖	Model 6006 Nanotechnology-based	Pros: Fully independent, looks like sludge.
2 ❖	Model 6007 Biotechnology-based	Pros: Looks like you, walks like you, talks like you, and is functionally equivalent to you.
3 ❖		

Narrow column for special characters

If you need your font to change from line to line, you can pull a similar trick by adding an extra row instead of an extra column. This won't work, however, if you only need the font variation in one cell or want the font change to wrap to a line with a different font. In those cases, you're better off exporting the table as text and formatting it in PageMaker.

Table Editor can export tables as TBL files, Windows metafile files, or as tab-delimited text. You can export an entire table or a selected range of text (cells, columns, or rows). You can also transfer tables (or a selected range of cells) by copying and pasting to the Clipboard. (Even then, you still have the option of copying it to the Clipboard as text or graphic.) In most cases, the best way to bring tables into PageMaker is as an exported metafile. Not only can you size and crop the table like any graphic, but you can also reopen the table from within PageMaker and make text and format changes.

It's magical. Just hold the Ctrl key and double-click on your imported table in PageMaker. The Table Editor opens to the original TBL file so you can make changes. After you're done editing, save the file as you normally would. Then reactivate PageMaker. If you've set the table to be replaced automatically (in the Link options dialog box), you're given the opportunity to update it. Zowie.

▼ Tip: Export Columnar Text from Table Editor

If for some reason, you decide to export your table as text (so you can edit it on the page, for instance), you might want to select columns, export the columns as text, then place the text columns as separate text blocks in PageMaker. Tables are sometimes easier to set up as separate columns of text, rather than as one wider text block. You end up cutting and pasting a lot less.

▼ Tip: Zooming in Table Editor

Most of PageMaker's zooming shortcuts work the same way in Table Editor. Ctrl-1 for Actual Size, Ctrl-2 for 200%, Ctrl-W for Fit in window, or the right mouse button to toggle between these two. But there's no 400%, and Shift-clicking the right mouse button doesn't get you 200%. The left mouse button is no good for zooming at all.

▼ Tip: New Lines in Table Editor

When you press Enter with a text cursor in a Table Editor cell, you move to the next cell below. If you want to break lines inside the current cell without moving to the next cell, press Shift-Enter to enter a new line, just as in PageMaker.

That Pesky Spacing Dialog Box

One of the most complex and powerful dialog boxes in PageMaker is the Spacing attributes dialog box, which you reach by clicking the Spacing button in the Paragraph specifications dialog box. The Spacing dialog box controls the amount of letter and word spacing in your type. In PageMaker 3.x, spacing settings applied to an entire story; in PageMaker 4, you can have different settings for each paragraph. At first glance, though, the Spacing dialog box is incomprehensible (Figure 4-42). Percentages of what? An em? A space character? The distance from here to Milwaukee?

Figure 4-42
Spacing dialog box

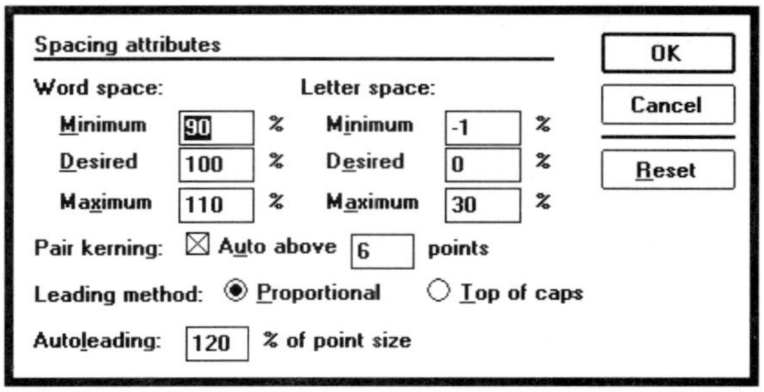

Spacing attributes				
Word space:		Letter space:		
Minimum	90 %	Minimum	-1 %	
Desired	100 %	Desired	0 %	
Maximum	110 %	Maximum	30 %	
Pair kerning: ☒ Auto above 6 points				
Leading method: ● Proportional ○ Top of caps				
Autoleading: 120 % of point size				

[OK] [Cancel] [Reset]

The key thing to understand is that each font has, built into it, values for the width of a space (the thing you get when you press the Spacebar), and for every letter. The percentages given in the Spacing dialog box are percentages of those values. If you type 75 for the desired word spacing value, for instance, PageMaker will do its best to compress the spaces in each line to 75 percent of their normal size. The same is true with desired letter spacing.

If the text being affected is set flush left, you'll get the spacing you entered in the Desired text edit box. If you asked for 75 percent word spacing, PageMaker sets the text with 75 percent word (pretty tight). It's when the text is justified that things get tricky. PageMaker's trying to make every line fill the column width, which is no easy task. If you've ever had to manually hyphenate a column of justified text, you know that words never break in the right places.

In justified copy, the maximum and minimum values come into play. When PageMaker reaches a point where a line should break, it goes through the following steps.

- PageMaker applies word spacing within the range defined by the maximum and minimum word-space settings in the Spacing dialog box. If the line fills the current line width before the word space in the line exceeds that range, PageMaker composes the line and goes on to the next line.

- If PageMaker can't compose the line within the maximum or minimum word-space settings, it applies letter spacing within the maximum and minimum letter-space settings (while also looking at the word following the tentative line break to see if the word could be brought back to the current line while still respecting the minimum letter-space settings). If the line fills the current line width before the letter spacing in the line exceeds the specified range, PageMaker composes the line and goes on to the next line.

- If PageMaker has compressed or expanded the word or letter spacing within the ranges specified in the Spacing dialog box and still cannot compose the line, it applies space to the word spaces in the line until it can compose the line to the required line width and, disgusted, moves on to the next line. If you have turned on the Show loose/tight lines option in the Preferences dialog box, PageMaker highlights the line in gray.

▼ *Tip: See Loose and Tight Lines*

You can see the lines that PageMaker had to set too loose or too tight by checking the Show loose/tight lines box in the Preferences dialog box. PageMaker just goes by the values you entered in the Spacing dialog box, and really has no idea whether the line is tight or loose.

Steve and Ole have this on by default and never turn it off. Scott and Jesse, on the other hand, recommend it for justified copy, but would rather trust their own aesthetic judgement when it comes to ragged (flush right or flush left) text. PageMaker highlights lines that it can't justify within the specified parameters. On a color monitor, it highlights them in gray; on a black-and-white monitor, in a patterned gray.

The only sure way to discover what Spacing settings look best is to experiment and see what happens. And remember that the results will vary from font to font and for different line measures. By the time we get done with this book, we'll have a good idea of what spacing settings work best for Bitstream's ITC Garamond Light, set at 11 points on a 26-pica measure. It always seems to take about 400 pages before you've run into all the possible spacing problems for any particular font. Once you have good numbers figured out for a given font and measure, write them down and put them in a safe.

In PageMaker 3, the Spacing dialog box was almost useless, because it applied to a whole story. Spacing that worked well for Times (a well-spaced font), for example, produced widely spaced text in Adobe's Condensed Bold Helvetica (a very poorly spaced font). If you tried to space the Helvetica well, the Times text would start to collide. The only way out was to either break all of the Helvetica out into a separate story, or to manually kern all of the Helvetica text. Both solutions were ugly.

With PageMaker 4, you can apply different Spacing settings to each paragraph, so you can build them into your styles for fast, automatic, good-looking type—once you've figured out the numbers.

Tracking

When you set type in larger sizes, the apparent space between letters seems to increase. Larger type that's not adjusted tends to look loose. The solution is tracking. This function sets type progressively tighter at progressively larger sizes. How much tracking you need at different sizes depends entirely on the typeface, so in the best of all possible worlds tracking values are built into each typeface.

Unfortunately, there's no facility for designers to specify tracking values in PC fonts. That's why programs generally don't offer tracking; they don't have the information they need.

PageMaker 4 is equipped with tracking values for a number of different fonts, including the standard PostScript "Plus" font set, plus a few others. If you apply tracking to a font that PageMaker does not recognize, PageMaker applies a default tracking setting. To edit PageMaker's tracking information to add your own tracking settings for fonts you use most often, you'll need PM Tracker, the tracking editor for PageMaker from Edco Systems. This product started shipping after this book went to press, so we don't have much to say about it except that it exists. The Macintosh version's pretty good, though.

In PageMaker you can choose from five settings to vary the amount of tracking: Very loose, Loose, Normal, Tight, and Very tight. If you graphed the formula for the Normal setting, you'd see a curve in which PageMaker increases letter spacing for smaller sizes (at one extreme), decreases it for larger sizes (the other extreme), and makes practically no changes for median sizes (the middle of the curve). The other options allow you some design discretion for special effects. You also have a No track option to turn the whole system off. You can specify your choice in the Track submenu (Type menu) or the Type specifications dialog.

Tracking is affected by the settings you specify in the Set width (horizontal scaling) command. So if the Set width submenu shows a value of 80% for your 10-point type (to use a crude example), PageMaker assigns the same tracking as it would for 8-point type.

Note also that tracking values are cumulative with manual kerning and automatic kerning (discussed later in this chapter). If the *tracking tables* (the tables that specify what "Tight," "Loose," and the rest mean) specify tighter spacing, the kern pairs in the font specify a tighter kern for automatic kerning, and you've kerned the type manually, all those adjustments are added together to produce some very tight type.

Paragraph Rules

Being able to specify a rule preceding or following a paragraph as an attribute of that paragraph is one of our favorite new features in PageMaker 4. No more laboriously moving rules when editorial changes force text recomposition! No more careful measuring down from character baselines in 400% view! Paragraph rules make us happy, happy, happy.

Creating, selecting and changing paragraph rules. You can't select paragraph rules with the Pointer tool, or alter their attributes through the Lines submenu, the Define colors dialog box, or the Colors palette. Paragraph rules are linked to their associated paragraph, and can be edited only through the Paragraph rules dialog box and the Paragraph rule options dialog box for that paragraph or style (Figure 4-43).

Vertical positioning of paragraph rules. The position for rules above paragraphs is measured up from the baseline of the first line of text, and the position for rules below paragraphs is measured down

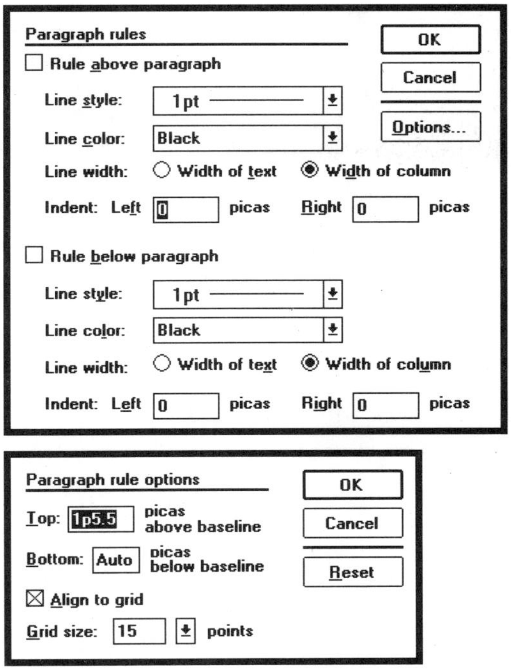

Figure 4-43
Paragraph rules dialog boxes

from the baseline of the last line of text in the paragraph. Make sure to use fixed, proportional leading, so you know where the baselines are (Figure 4-44).

When you set a rule above a paragraph, entering "Auto" in the Position text edit box sets the rule at the top of the line slug (not the paragraph slug—for a discussion of slugs, see "PageMaker Leading" earlier in this chapter). A paragraph rule above specified for Auto position, in a line with a lead of 24 points, will appear 16 points above the baseline of the first line of the paragraph (16 points = ⅔ of 24 points). In this case, if your characters have ascenders of 14 points and you've set the rule width to 4 points, the rule will print over the type (Figure 4-45).

Figure 4-44
Paragraph rule placement

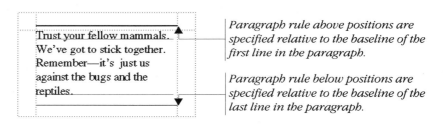

Paragraph rule above positions are specified relative to the baseline of the first line in the paragraph.

Paragraph rule below positions are specified relative to the baseline of the last line in the paragraph.

Figure 4-45
Paragraph rules above set to Auto

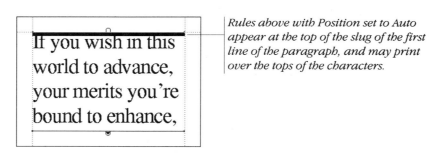

Rules above with Position set to Auto appear at the top of the slug of the first line of the paragraph, and may print over the tops of the characters.

When you set a rule below a paragraph, Auto position sets the rule at the bottom of the slug. In a line with a leading of 24 points, the rule will appear 8 points below the baseline of the last line of text in the paragraph. Watch out for descenders (Figure 4-46).

Horizontal positioning of paragraph rules. You can position paragraph rules relative to the width of the column, or relative to the width of the text. Click "Width of column," and the rule will be the

Figure 4-46
Paragraph rule below set to Auto

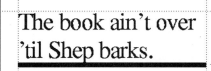

Rules below with Position set to Auto appear at the bottom of the slug of the last line of the paragraph.

width of the text block. It will increase and decrease in width as you resize the text block. Click "Width of text," and the rule will be the width of the top or bottom line of text in the paragraph. It will increase and decrease in width as you lengthen or shorten that line.

Specifying indents based on the width of the column is pretty easy to understand—like paragraph indents, you enter a positive number for the amount the rule is indented from either side of the text block. You can even specify a negative number to force the rule beyond the borders of the text block.

Specifying indents based on the width of the text is a little trickier: you enter a negative value when you want the rule to be wider than the text, and you enter a positive value when you want the rule to be narrower than the text. These simple settings open the door to some powerful formatting capabilities, as shown in Figure 4-47.

Figure 4-47
Setting the width of paragraph rules

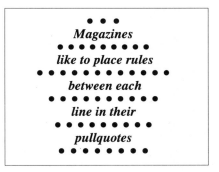

If you enter positive values in the Indent text edit boxes, the rules are indented from the edges of the text.

If you enter negative values in the Indent text edit boxes, the rules extend beyond the edges of the text.

Rules and how they grow. Line weights for rules above are measured down from the point you specify in the Rule options dialog box. Line weights for rules below are measured up from the point you specify, as shown in Figure 4-48.

Figure 4-48
Line weights for paragraph rules

Rules below grow from their position setting up.

Rules above grow from their position setting down.

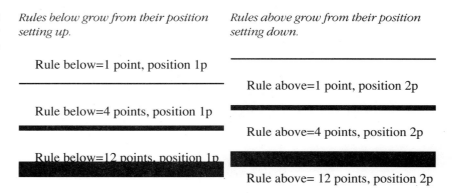

Rules and paragraph spacing. Rules extend the slug of the paragraph. We're sorry, but it's true. Any paragraph space before you've specified is added above and in addition to a rule before. Space after is added below and in addition to a rule after (Figure 4-49).

Figure 4-49
Paragraph spacing and paragraph rules

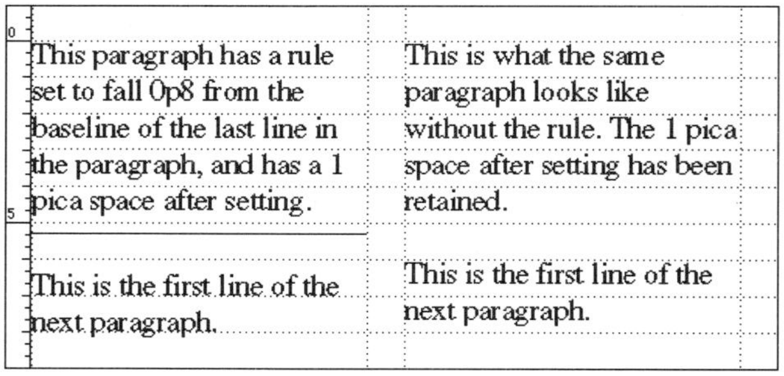

Paragraph rules and drawing order. Paragraph rules are drawn behind text. This lets you put paragraph rules behind type for some wild special effects, as shown in Figure 4-50.

Paragraph rules and text wrap. Paragraph rules act like text when it comes to text wraps. If a paragraph rule encounters a graphic wrap boundary, it obeys the boundary just as text would, altering its

Figure 4-50
Special rule effects

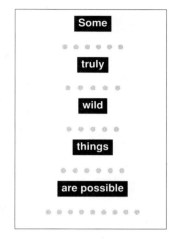

All of these effects were created entirely with paragraph rules. No LBOs were drawn.

width to be either the width of the column outside of the graphic's boundary, or the width of the text in the line, depending on the option you've specified in the Paragraph rules dialog box (Figure 4-51).

Figure 4-51
Paragraph rules and text wrap

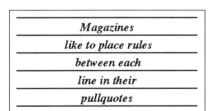
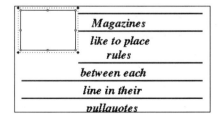

▼ Tip: Slaves to Fashion

These days, you often see headings with two rules above (and sometimes below) them—one that's the width of the column (or page, or whatever), another that's the width of the heading text (Figure 4-52). To create those very fashionable double rules, follow these steps.

Figure 4-52
Double rules for headings

Headline

Marketing and technical comunications documents often use rules above that track to the width of a headline, while a thinner rule fills the width of the column.

Headline

Marketing and technical comunications documents also often use rules below that track to the width of a headline, while a thinner rule fills the width of the column.

1. Create a paragraph with a paragraph rule below that falls to the bottom of its slug. You can get away with a pretty tiny leading increment (like one-tenth of a point). Set it to "Keep with next."
2. Define your heading style as having a rule above (thicker than the rule in the step above), with a Top setting that pushes the rule to the top of the slug (or beyond).

Now, if you use the two paragraphs together, the paragraph rule above in the heading style should touch the paragraph rule of the paragraph above, creating just the effect you're looking for.

Playing for Keeps

PageMaker 4 improves on the paragraph formatting features offered in PageMaker 3 by adding new controls in the Paragraph specifications dialog box over the way your paragraphs relate to each other. "Keep lines together" behaves just as you'd expect it would—keeping the lines of a paragraph from breaking across text blocks. "Keep with next" glues the paragraph to the next 1, 2, or 3 lines of text (whatever you've entered in the text edit box), and is great for keeping heads on the same page or column with following body text.

The controls for widows and orphans, however, are a little different from what you might expect. We always learned that a widow was two or fewer lines of a paragraph isolated at the top or bottom of a column, while orphans referred to single words ending paragraphs. In

PageMaker terminology (based, tragically, on Macintosh Word's definitions), a widow is some number of lines at the beginning of a text block, while an orphan is some number of lines at the end of a text block. You can enter only 1, 2, or 3 in the widow/orphan control text edit boxes.

▼ *Tip: Orphan Killer*

Since PageMaker 4 has no way of preventing one word from appearing on the last line of a paragraph, we thought we'd add one with Recorder. Create a Recorder macro containing the "Literal" keystrokes shown in Table 4-3. They go to the end of a paragraph and insert a nonbreaking space before the last word.

The nonbreaking space guarantees that the last line in the paragraph contains at least two words. Note that this key doesn't work if the last word in the paragraph is a compound number, such as "4.0," or a manually hyphenated pair of words, such as "self-discipline."

This macro should work equally well in layout view or in PageMaker's Story Editor. Of course, depending on your word processor, you might find it faster to execute a similar macro there, so things are fixed before you import them to PageMaker.

Table 4-3 Orphan-killing macros

Literal Keystroke	*What it Does*
Ctrl-Down arrow	Moves the cursor to the start of the next paragraph
Ctrl-Left arrow (three times)	Moves the cursor to the beginning of the last word
Backspace	Deletes the space between the last two words in the paragraph
Ctrl-Spacebar	Adds a nonbreaking space between the last two words in the paragraph
Down arrow	Moves the cursor to the next paragraph so the macro is poised to be executed again

▼ Tip: Setting Widow/Orphan Controls

The widow and orphan controls don't work quite the way you'd expect, at first glance. PageMaker always seems to add one line to the number you specify in the text edit box. In this case, PageMaker's right: when you enter *1* in the text edit box, you really mean that you want PageMaker to break the text block rather than allowing a 1-line widow/orphan, so the smallest widow/orphan you'll see will be 2 lines. When you enter 2, you're really asking PageMaker to outlaw 2-line widows/orphans, and the smallest widow/orphan you'll see will be 3 lines long. And so on.

We refer to all of these paragraph-level controls as "keeps." PageMaker tries to obey the specific keeps settings for each paragraph, but will, in some cases, be forced to break your rules. You can keep an eye on this bad behavior by turning on the Show "Keeps" violations option in the Preferences dialog box. PageMaker highlights places where it's broken your rules using a gray screen over the paragraph (just as it shows loose and tight lines).

Note that there are certain combinations of keep settings and widow and orphan settings that don't make a whole lot of sense. Why would you choose to use both "Keep lines together" and the widow or orphan controls, for instance?

▼ Tip: Keeping Heads with Text

As we mentioned above, you can use the "Keep with next" setting to keep heads and subheads with their accompanying text. If you're using styles—and we urge you to use styles so you get more free time away from the computer—you can set the paragraph formatting for heads to "Keep with next" so that they'll follow their body text across page and column breaks. If you've ever cursed PageMaker 3 for placing your headlines at the bottoms of text blocks, this feature is for you.

Column and Page Breaks

PageMaker 4 also adds two paragraph-control features that are the opposite of the "keeps" discussed above—"Column break before" and "Page break before." When you're autoflowing text, PageMaker will jump to the next column or page when it encounters paragraphs that have these attributes set. With manual or semi-autoflow, it will stop when it reaches one of these items and wait for you to place the next text block.

Note that if you have "Page break before" set for paragraph, Page-Maker won't let you place that paragraph on the same page as the preceding paragraph. In this case, you'll just get a closed-up text block. You won't be able to open it unless you move it to another page or place it on the pasteboard.

▼ *Tip: Use Column break before for Heads in a Companion Column*

If you use heads hanging out in a companion column, as in this book, specify "Column break before" for those heads. PageMaker will stop when it gets to a head, and let you place the head in the companion column. You might also find it helpful to create a style for the first paragraph after a head, and give it a "Column break before" as well. Unfortunately there's no Column break after option, so you end up mucking around with the bottom windowshade handles a bit.

▼ *PageMaker 3 Tip: Forcing Column Breaks*

If you're still working with PageMaker 3, you can force column breaks by specifying a very large space (the height of the column, for example) before a paragraph. This forces the heads to fall at the top of the next column. Remember, PageMaker doesn't apply the space before when the paragraph falls at the top of a text block.

▼ *Tip: Faking "Paragraph break after"*

PageMaker doesn't have a "Paragraph break after" option, but you can fake it by adding a large amount of space after a particular paragraph or style. We've set up the B heads (the hanging side heads) in this book using this technique. When we flow a page, the text stops flowing after the B head and we can then place the next text block.

Character Formatting

Before we get heavily into character formatting, let's get our terminology straight. Computer and software manufacturers have mixed up the terms *fonts* and *faces*, so you never know quite what anyone means anymore. We're stuck with it now, but for those who want to discuss and understand these things, here are some definitions.

Font. A set of characters in a given typeface and size. 10-point Futura Extra Black is a font.

Typeface. In this day and age, a scalable outline from which many sizes of fonts can be made. Janson Text is a typeface. So is Times Italic.

Typeface family. A collection of typefaces. Some families contain a dozen or more typefaces (Futura and Helvetica are examples); others only include four variations (roman, italic, bold, and bold italic).

It gets confusing with groups of typefaces like Stone, which actually includes three typeface families—Stone Serif, Stone Sans, and Stone Informal—each containing several typefaces.

Now that we have that out of the way, let's get on to character formatting, which is probably why you bought this book in the first place.

Type Specs

When you choose "Type specs" from the Type menu (Ctrl-T) or press the Type button in the Edit styles dialog box, the Type specifications dialog box appears. The usual things one associates with specifying type are here—font, size, leading, position relative to the baseline (super- and subscripting), capitalization options, and, in computer jargon, "type styles"—bold, italic, shadow, underline, and so on. PageMaker 4 adds commands for expanding and condensing type and setting tracking values, and gives you control over small caps size and super- and subscript size and position through a new Type options dialog box.

Keyboard Shortcuts for Character Formatting

You can select type and change character formatting quickly with keyboard shortcuts, as shown in Table 4-4 (on the next page).

Keyboard shortcuts are the most direct and immediate method of specifying type in PageMaker. Using the Type specifications dialog box (Ctrl-T) is the next step. It lets you adjust several attributes at once. In either case, though, the results are all local; they only apply to the currently selected text. For more global changes, you'll want to adjust the paragraph styles (see "Working with Styles" later in this chapter).

Set Width

One of the most useful new features in PageMaker 4 is the Set width option. It lets you condense or expand selected type from 5 to 250 percent, in one-tenth of a percent increments. It applies those values to all the characters in the selected text, including word space characters. In previous versions, the only way to condense or expand type was to place type created in a draw program and stretch the graphic type with the Pointer tool.

That technique worked fine for headlines, but if you wanted some condensed or expanded type within a line, or wanted all your subheads condensed by some percentage, there was no good solution. With "Set Width," you can specify a percentage for any selection, or build the percentage into the style for any paragraph.

Note that the percentage you specify for "Set width" works as a multiplier with the settings in the Spacing dialog box. So if you specify 90 for "Set width" and 90 for "Desired word spacing," word spaces will be 81 percent of normal width (in nonjustified text).

Fun with Type options

At first glance, the Type options dialog box (click the Options button in the Type specifications dialog box) doesn't seem to offer much: control over the size of your small capitals and super- and subscript

Table 4-4 Keyboard shortcuts for character formatting

Character Formatting	*Keyboard Shortcut*
Italic	F7 or Ctrl-Shift-I
	or Alt-T, Y, I
Bold	F6 or Ctrl-Shift-B
	or Alt-T, Y, B
Plain text	F5 or Ctrl-Shift-Spacebar
	or Alt-T, Y, N
Underline	F8 or Ctrl-Shift-U
	or Alt-T, Y, U
Strike-through	Ctrl-Shift-S
	or Alt-T, Y, S
Reverse type	Ctrl-Shift-V
	or Alt-T, Y, R
One point size larger	Ctrl-Shift-> (greater than)
Larger	F4 (using these sizes: 6, 8, 9, 10, 11, 12, 14, 18, 24, 30, 36, 48, 60, 72)
	or Ctrl-> (greater than)
One point size smaller	Ctrl-Shift-< (less than)
Smaller	F3 (using these sizes: 6, 8, 9, 10, 11, 12, 14, 18, 24, 30, 36, 48, 60, 72)
	or Ctrl-< (less than)
Small caps	Ctrl-Shift-H
All caps	Ctrl-Shift-K
Subscript	Ctrl-\
Superscript	Ctrl-Shift-\
Square (Set width to normal)	Ctrl-Shift-X
Track very loose	Alt-T, R, V
Track loose	Alt-T, R, L
Track normal	Alt-T, R, N
Track tight	Alt-T, R, I
Track very tight	Alt-T, R, E
Eliminate track kerning	Ctrl-Shift-Q
	or Alt-T, R, T
Autoleading	Ctrl-Shift-A

type, and the position of your super- and subscripts. Ho hum. Great if you need footnote references in the right place, but pretty mundane. On further examination, however, this dialog box can be fun, fun, fun.

Before we start, though, we have to say that this dialog box is almost as confusing, at first glance, as the Spacing attributes dialog box. But you don't have to be a rocket scientist to understand this dialog box: the values in the dialog box are in percentages of the normal height of the characters, and are accurate to one-tenth of a percent. If, for example, you specify 90 for "Small caps size," and the type size of the selected text or paragraph is 24, the small caps will be 21.6 points.

Similarly, if you specify that superscripted type in a line with a leading of 24 is offset from the baseline by 60 percent, the baseline of the superscripted type will appear 14.4 points above the baseline of the rest of the line. With subscripted type, the baseline of the subscripted type would appear 14.4 points below the baseline.

What does all of this mean? Bigger percentages shift super- and subscripts away from the normal baseline by a greater amount, as shown in Figure 4-53.

Figure 4-53
Superscript and subscript

Superscript 20%: Ruddigore

Superscript 40%: Ruddigore

Superscript 60%: Ruddigore

Superscript 80%: Ruddigore

Subscript 20%: Ruddigore

Subscript 40%: Ruddigore

Subscript 60%: Ruddigore

Subscript 80%: Ruddigore

▼ Tip: Type Within Type

We can't think of what this type effect is called, but we've seen it everywhere—particularly in corporate logos and advertising.

1. Create a text block and type a word—words starting with C, S, T, L, or other characters that are open on the right side will work better for this effect than M or N. As usual, make sure you're working with fixed, proportional leading.

2. Select the first character in the word.

3. Bring up the Type specifications dialog box (Ctrl-T) and enlarge the selected character to three or four times the size of the rest of the text in the line.

4. Choose Subscript from the Position pop-up menu.

5. Click the Options button to bring up the Type options dialog box. Type *100* in the Super/Subscript size text edit box, and *25* in the Subscript position text edit box. Press Enter twice to close the dialog boxes.

6. Place the insertion point to the right of the enlarged, subscripted character and kern the rest of the word back until it is nested inside the initial character.

Figure 4-54
Snazzy type

▼ Tip: More Snazzy Type

Once again, we're not sure what this effect is called, and, once again, certain letter combinations are going to work better than others.

1. Type *LoDOWN*

2. Set the type to some point size and some fixed lead (of course you're using proportional leading).

3. Select the "o" and bring up the Type specifications dialog box (Ctrl-T). Choose "Superscript" from the Position menu to superscript the "o," and click the Options button to bring up the Type options dialog box.

4. Enter 95 in the Super/Subscript size text edit box, and 20 in the Superscript position text edit field. Press Enter twice to close the dialog boxes.

5. Place the insertion point immediately to the left of the "o" and kern it back until it is nested above the horizontal stroke of the "L" (Figure 4-55).

Figure 4-55
More snazzy type

Figure 4-56 shows a few other things you can do with superscripting and subscripting combined with kerning (*lots* of kerning).

Figure 4-56
Yet more snazzy type

Each example is a single text block.

Kerning Text

In traditional typesetting, kerning *removes* space between characters (because *kerns*—the portions of characters on a piece of lead type that overhang the edge of the type block—make characters print closer together). In desktop publishing, there's also something called positive kerning that *adds* space between characters. Positive kerning is an oxymoron, but we're stuck with it. And since we're not using lead type, maybe it's not so bad.

There are two types of kerning in PageMaker—automatic and manual. PageMaker does the first for you. You have to do the second.

Automatic kerning (which you can turn on or off in the paragraph's Spacing attributes dialog box) is based on kerning pair values built into the font metrics(the file with the spacing values for the font you're using). PageMaker sees A and W next to each other in Times Roman, checks the kerning pair table in the font metrics, and sees that a certain amount of kerning is specified for that letter pair. If automatic kerning is turned on, PageMaker nudges those two letters together by the specified amount.

Unfortunately, many of the fonts on the market have totally abysmal kerning pair tables. The fonts in the Adobe Plus set are good (bad?) examples. The designers and/or the developers simply didn't bother to put all the kerning pairs in. Others have quite robust kerning pair tables (like the Bitstream version of ITC Garamond used in this book, which has more than 400 kerning pairs per font). There are kerning pair editors on the market (such as LetrTuck Plus for Windows, from Edco Systems), so you can add your own kerning pairs to your fonts. Be warned, however, that defining and editing hundreds of kerning pairs can take forever, even if you know what values to use.

Manual Kerning. Automatic kerning is wonderful, if there are a reasonable number of kerning pairs specified in your screen fonts. There usually aren't, though, and even if there are you always need to fine-tune large type, so you can also kern manually with PageMaker. In layout view, click with the Text tool between two letters and press the appropriate keys to move the letters together or apart (see Table 4-5).

In PageMaker 4, you can apply manual kerning to a range (selection) of text. (Some people call this tracking, but tracking is a more automatic and global function, nudging all letters together more as they get bigger, with tracking values based on the typeface being used.) Select the range of text you want to kern and press any combination of coarse and fine kerning keys. PageMaker applies the kerning amount between each pair of characters in the range of the text. This is really handy if you have a paragraph or block of copy that doesn't quite fit in its allotted space.

Manual and automatic kerning are cumulative in PageMaker 4 (hallelujah! at last!). PageMaker uses the kerning information from the

Table 4-5 Kerning keys

Kerning increment	Key Command
Coarse (+/-.25 of an em)	
Remove space	Ctrl-Backspace
	or Ctrl- -(minus, numeric keypad)
Add space	Ctrl-Shift-Backspace
	or Ctrl-+ (plus, numeric keypad)
Fine (+/-.01 of an em)	
Remove space	Ctrl-Shift- - (minus, numeric keypad)
Add space	Ctrl-Shift-+ (plus, numeric keypad)
Clear manual kerning	Ctrl-Shift-0 (zero, numeric keypad)

font for automatic kerning (unless you've turned off "Pair kerning" in the paragraph's Spacing attributes dialog box), and adds your manual kerning to those values. So if the kerning pairs built into a typeface specify a minus .2-em kern between A and W, and you kern the pair manually minus .3 ems, you'll end up with a minus .5-em kern. Kerning is also cumulative with any tracking applied to the selection.

Kerning in PageMaker 4

The actual operation of PageMaker 4's kerning differs from PageMaker 3's. In the earlier version, kerning increments were stored as invisible characters inserted in the line of text between each kerned letter combination. In PageMaker 4, the kerning increments are stored as an attribute of each character, describing a change to the space after the character.

In PageMaker 3, you could insert kerning characters before the first character of each line that would pull the character beyond the left edge of the text block (that is, beyond the left margin). While this was useful for particular fonts and special effects (especially for drop caps and hanging punctuation), it wouldn't work well with PageMaker 4's range kerning feature. If you selected a whole paragraph and kerned it, the beginning of every line would hang to the left of the margin.

▼ Tip: Kerning Whole Words

If you want to kern all of the letters in a word, but don't want to apply the kerning to the space following the word, don't double-click the word to select it. Double-clicking the word also selects the space following the word. Instead, select all but the last letter of the word. Remember, kerning is an attribute of individual characters, and is applied to the space after each character.

If your text insertion point is immediately before the first character of the word, you could press Ctrl-Shift-Right arrow, then press Shift-Left arrow twice. This selects the word and the space after the word, then shortens the selection by two characters so that you've got all but the last letter of the word selected.

▼ Tip: Lose that Kerning

To clear all manual kerning increments between a pair of characters or within a kerned range, place the text insertion point between the characters or select the range, and press Ctrl-Shift-0.

When you open a PageMaker 3 document with PageMaker 4, manual kerning entered in PageMaker 3 will be rendered as .02-of-an-em increments. PageMaker 3's kerning increment was $\frac{1}{48}$th (.0208) of an em, so kerning will change slightly when you convert publications.

Fractions and Drop Caps

Someday, PageMaker will have some kind of run-in or character-based style that automatically creates drop caps (can you say "Ventura Publisher?"). There will also probably be a keystroke to turn 1/4 into ¼. When that day comes, we'll be able to forget all of the methods for creating drop caps and fractions that we've learned over the years, and use that part of our brains for something else. We don't know what, but something else. Until then, here are the best methods we know.

Drop caps. Gallons of ink have been spilled describing various methods for creating dropped, initial capitals in PageMaker. Here's our puddle. First, do not create drop caps by placing a character within a no-line, no-fill box and setting a text wrap for the box (this one is always turning up in tips columns). That box will trip you up in the future. Instead, use one of the techniques described below.

▼ Tip: Creating Drop Caps as Graphics

Import a graphic for the drop cap and set the Text wrap boundaries for the graphic (Figure 4-57). This is Scott's favorite method.

1. Create the drop cap in a separate drawing program such as Corel Draw, Micrografx Designer, Adobe Illustrator, or Arts & Letters. (If you have Adobe Type Manager, you can even use the

Figure 4-57
Creating a drop cap using text wrap

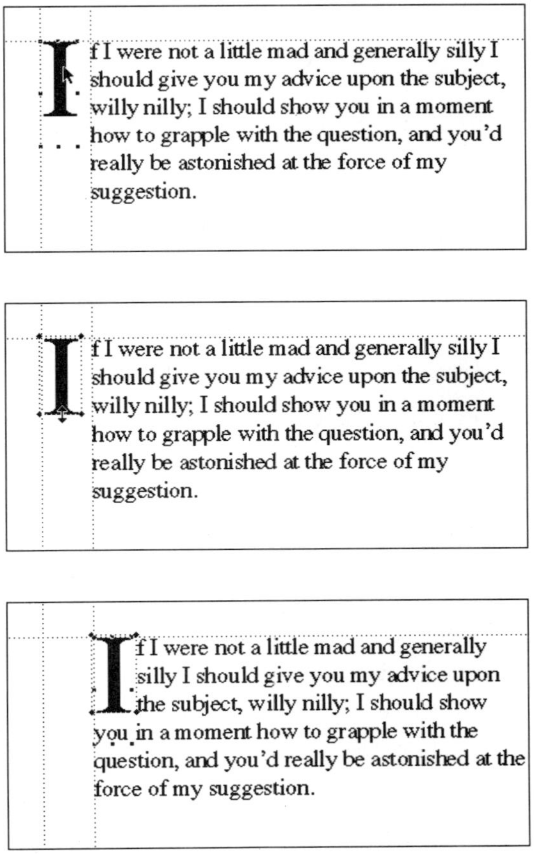

Create the large initial character in a drawing program, then Place the character in PageMaker.

Apply text wrap to the graphic and adjust the wrap boundary.

Initial character in position

Paintbrush application that comes with Windows 3, though we don't recommend it—the characters are still too jaggy and can't be resized without making matters worse.)

2. After you create the letter, select it and copy it to the Clipboard. You don't even need to save it as a file.

3. Return to PageMaker, paste the graphic on the page and resize it to your heart's content (unless you're using a bitmapped graphic from a paint-type program). Ordinarily, the drop cap should be related in size to the size and leading of the body text—two times and three times the base leading of the body text are useful sizes.

4. Select the drop cap and turn "Text wrap" on.

5. Use ruler guides to place the body copy on top of the drop cap.

6. Adjust the text-wrap boundaries for the drop cap.

▼ Tip: The Old, Slow Method of Creating Drop Caps

This method can still be useful. It uses two or more text blocks—one or more to the right of the drop cap, and one below it (Figure 4-58).

1. Place the column of text.
2. Create the drop cap in its own text block (make it a narrow text block so it doesn't get in the way).
3. Position the text block containing the drop cap.
4. Resize the body text block so that it ends at the next leading increment below the drop cap.
5. Click the bottom windowshade handle of the body copy text block. The loaded text place gun appears.
6. Drag-place the remaining body copy so that the it does not touch the drop cap.

If you want to create a nonrectangular wrap—one that follows the contour of the drop cap—you'll have to drag-place each line separately, or use tabs at the beginning of each line and adjust the tab stops.

Figure 4-58
Creating a drop cap by breaking text blocks

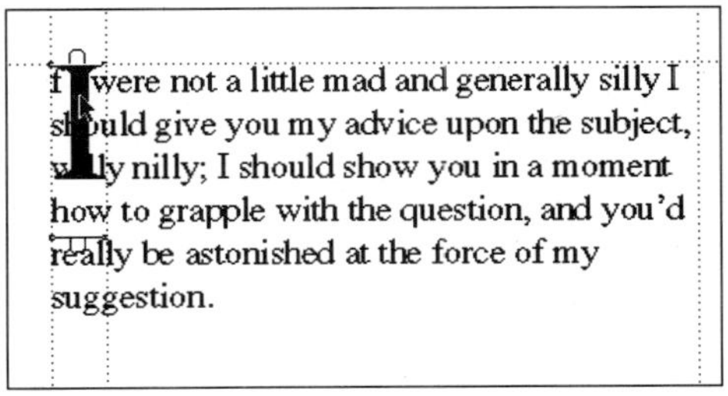

Create the large initial cap as a single text block and drag it into position.

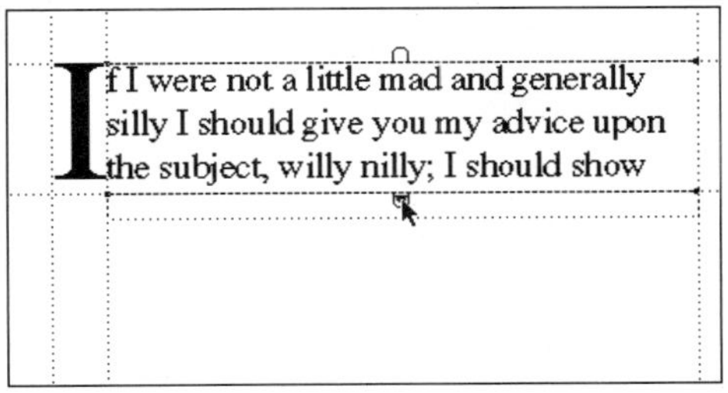

Adjust the body copy so that it's the width you want, then click the bottom windowshade handle to place the rest of the body copy.

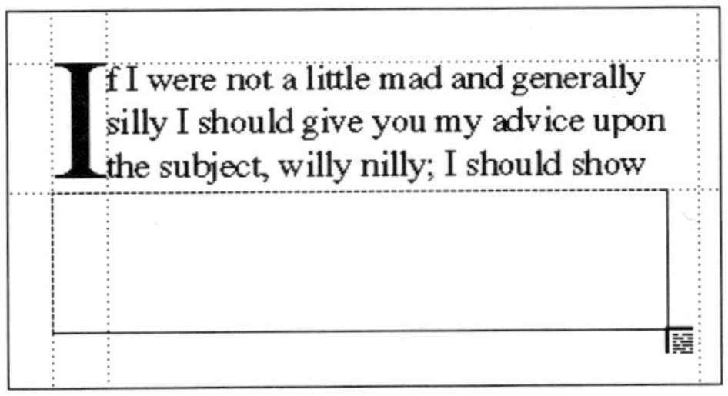

Pull down a ruler guide from the horizontal ruler so that it is exactly in front of the bottom windowshade. Then drag-place the body copy, using the ruler guide to align the top of the text block.

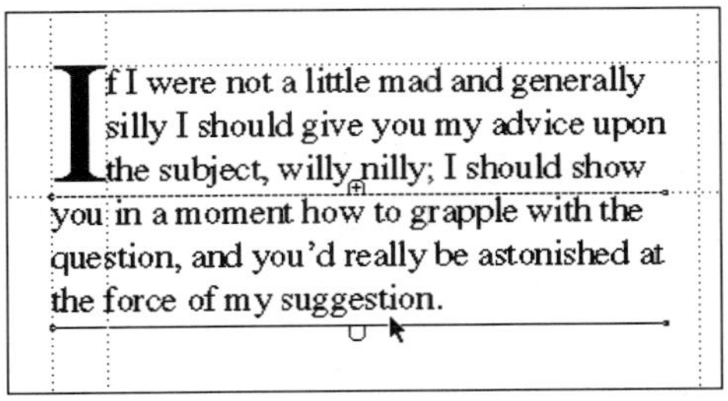

Large initial character in position

▼ *Tip: The New, Nifty Way to Create Drop Caps*

This method uses the variable subscript size and position controls available through the Type options dialog box (Figure 4-59). It works especially well because the drop cap is part of the text block and moves with the paragraph as text reflows. Ole thinks this is the best method for creating drop caps.

Figure 4-59
Creating a drop cap using the subscript position and tabs

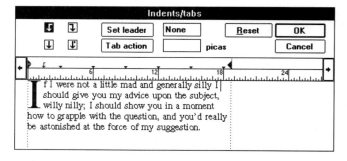

Select the initial cap and increase its size. In this example, we've used 36-point (the body type is 10/12).

Use the Type specifications dialog box to make the character subscript, then click the Options button to display the Type options dialog box.

The baseline of the initial cap drops to the distance you specified.

Use tabs to align the body copy.

1. Select the first character in a paragraph.
2. Increase the size of the character (two, three, and four times the size of the body text are the most common sizes for dropped initial capitals).
3. Bring up the Type specifications dialog box (Ctrl-T). Choose "Subscript" from the Position pop-up list.
4. Press Alt-O (or click the Options button) to bring up the Type options dialog box.

5. Enter *100* in the Super/Subscript size text edit field, and *50* in the Subscript position text edit field (you'll need to adjust these values for the specific typeface and size you're using). Close the dialog boxes.

6. Place the insertion point immediately to the right of the dropped capital (on the first line) and press Tab.

7. Press Ctrl-I to bring up the Indents/tabs dialog box, and adjust the tab settings to position the text following the drop cap. Close the dialog box.

8. Press End to move to the end of the first line and add a new-line character (Shift-Enter) to break the line.

9. Press Tab. Move to the end of the second line of the paragraph and add another line break. Then press Tab.

You can easily make a Recorder macro that does these steps for you for your particular drop cap format.

You can figure out what you should enter in the Subscript position text edit box by dividing the amount of baseline shift you want by the size of the drop cap. If you've got a 36-point drop cap in a paragraph of text with a 12-point lead and you want the baseline of the character to drop 24 points, you'd enter 66, because 24/36=.66, or 66 percent.

Fractions. PageMaker doesn't offer any easy way to create good-looking fractions, and though many PostScript typefaces have a few fractions built into their character sets, there's generally no way to get at them in PageMaker (this side of PostScript programming, anyhow).

You can create decent fractions in PageMaker, but it's a pain. Here's the proper (if troublesome) way to create ¼—the fraction that most people grin and bear with.

1. Set the 1 as a superscript
2. Set the 4 as a subscript.
3. Select all three characters and adjust the values in the Type options dialog box as in Figure 4-60.

Figure 4-60
Creating fractions with the Type options dialog box

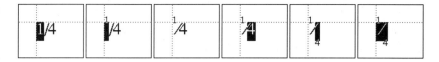

Format the numerator as superscript, format the denominator as subscript, select the fraction, press Ctrl-T to bring up the Type specifications dialog box, press the Options button, and then enter these values.

Type options			OK
Small caps size:	70	% of point size	Cancel
Super/subscript size:	60	% of point size	
Superscript position:	30	% of point size	
Subscript position:	0	% of point size	

Here's what you get.

These values work pretty well with Times, Helvetica, Stone, and Janson, among others. For larger type sizes (above about 14-point), you'll have to adjust with kerning as needed.

▼ *Tip: Fraction-making Macros*

We strongly suggest that you build some kind of macro with Recorder or the like if you plan on using fractions often. A Recorder version of the macro would include the steps shown in Table 4-6. Before beginning, make sure the fraction is on the page and is selected with the Text tool.

Assign a keyboard shortcut to this Recorder macro (maybe Ctrl-Alt-Shift-F), then select a simple fraction. Activate your new macro. Admire your new fraction.

All of this looks like it should take forever to execute, but on a fast 386, it will whiz by at a pretty good clip. Even on a 286, it's a lot faster than doing it all yourself.

Table 4-6 Fraction-making macro

Key	What it Does
Ctrl-T	Displays the Type specifications dialog box
Alt-O	Opens the Type options dialog box
Tab	Tabs to Superscript/subscript size text edit box. Don't type "tab" when you enter the key, just press a Tab.
60 Tab 30 Tab 0	Makes the superscript/subscript size 60 percent, the superscript baseline offset 30 percent, and the subscript baseline offset 0 percent. Change these values if you want your fractions to look different.
Alt-Ctrl-Enter	Closes both dialog boxes
Left arrow, Right arrow	Moves off the selection and moves to the start of the fraction
Ctrl-Shift-Right arrow	Selects the numerator
Ctrl-T, Alt-P, Down arrow, Enter	Makes numerator superscript
Right arrow	Deselects numerator, moves past slash
Ctrl-Shift-Right arrow	Selects denominator
Ctrl-T, Alt-P, Down arrow, Down arrow, Enter	Makes denominator subscript
Right arrow	Deselects denominator, moves to right of fraction

Working with Styles

You've no doubt heard that PageMaker's styles are the key to long-document productivity—tools to automate your design and make pages come together fast. But even that's an understatement. PageMaker styles are the most powerful text-handling tool in PageMaker, especially if you use parallel styles in your word processor to automate your copy processing. We use styles for every piece of type we place on a page. Religiously.

Many people—especially people who first learned PageMaker before version 3—have a hard time understanding styles. Somehow, they've gotten the idea that styles are esoteric, arcane things, understood and used only by gnomes pumping out ten-thousand-page government contracts for aerospace companies. They've also gotten the impression that styles are capable of only the simplest formatting. Both impressions are untrue, and lies of the vilest sort. Styles are not only easy to understand, they're an elegant way of formatting the most complex page layouts.

The main point is this: A style is a name for a collection of formatting attributes—all the specifications you choose using the commands on the Type menu. Whether you know it or not, you are already thinking in styles. When you're working with a page, you think of each kind of paragraph as having certain characteristics—font, type size, leading, indent, color, and so on. You know that subheads have one style, body copy paragraphs have another, and chapter heads have another.

The Hard Way

Without styles, you have to select text and manually format it by choosing commands from the menus—one piece of text at a time. The next time you use that kind of paragraph, you'll have to go through all of those menus and dialog boxes again—one at a time.

None of us (individually or in combination) can count the number of times we've seen people tearing out their hair because a client (or boss, or whatever) has come back to them with a flyer, newsletter, or technical manual and asked them to change every subhead in the publication to another font, type style or size. Because they didn't use styles, they have to go through the publication and manually select each subhead and apply all the formatting changes from the menus.

With styles, you format a sample paragraph once, then create and name a style based on the formatted paragraph ("Subhead," for example). The next time you encounter a paragraph you want to format the same way, place the text cursor in the paragraph, then click on the style name in the Style palette. The paragraph takes on the formatting characteristics you specified for the style.

Further, if you need to change the formatting for a particular kind of paragraph, you just edit its style and then watch all the paragraphs with that style change to the new formatting.

Styles, Tags, and Codes

Think in terms of text *elements*—body copy paragraphs, subheads, heads, bullet list paragraphs, etc.—and you're thinking in styles. You are *tagging* each paragraph, specifying what it *is*. Once it's tagged, you can make it *look like* whatever you want; you just change the style, and the tagged paragraphs change.

Those terms are worth repeating. Tagging specifies what each paragraph is. A style specifies what a tagged paragraph looks like. Tags can be in the form of actual text at the beginning of each paragraph in your word processor—<subhead>, for example—or you can tag paragraphs using style sheets in Microsoft Word, WinWord, or WordPerfect 5.1 (see "Importing Text," later in this chapter).

It's important to distinguish between tags, which specify what different elements are, and codes, which specify what selections of text look like. Many traditional and desktop publishing systems use embedded codes instead of or in addition to tags. You might type <it>italic<ei>, for instance, inserting codes that specify what the word should look like.

PageMaker doesn't read embedded codes in text. You can't insert a code in text to shift to italic, for instance, and expect PageMaker to understand it when you place the file. It only understands tags, and formatting applied with word processors. The exception to that is importing of text in RTF (Rich Text Format), a important new capability of PageMaker 4 which we discuss in "Importing Rich Text Format Files," later in this chapter.

Local Formatting

The difference between tags and codes raises the whole issue of local formatting. We call normal text formatting without style sheets *local* or *hard* formatting. When you apply local formatting, it overrides style sheet formatting. You'll still want to use local formatting to change the type style of individual words or characters in a paragraph—*italics*, for instance. It's the one place where you can't use styles, because PageMaker styles work on the paragraph level.

PageMaker styles can contain the full complement of character formatting (except kerning), but that formatting applies to whole paragraphs. You can't apply a style just to a selection within a paragraph; it's all or nothing. We sure wish there were both paragraph *and* character styles available in PageMaker, like in Microsoft Word and WordPerfect. Character styles are handy for special inline elements, like commands in a computer manual that you always put in Courier Bold, condensed to 80 percent, or run-in heads that are in a different typeface and size.

▼ *Tip: Automate Character Styles with Change*

If you use some combination of local character formatting on a regular basis (10-point Garamond Bold, for instance), you can use PageMaker's ability to search and replace character attributes to save a lot of work (see Figure 4-61).

1. Use some weird character style in your word processor for the special text—underline, for instance—as long as you use it exclusively for the special text. You can invoke these styles in Word, WinWord, or PageMaker with a keystroke.
2. Place the file in PageMaker.
3. Open the story with the Story Editor (triple-click the text block, or click an insertion point with the Text tool and press Ctrl-E or

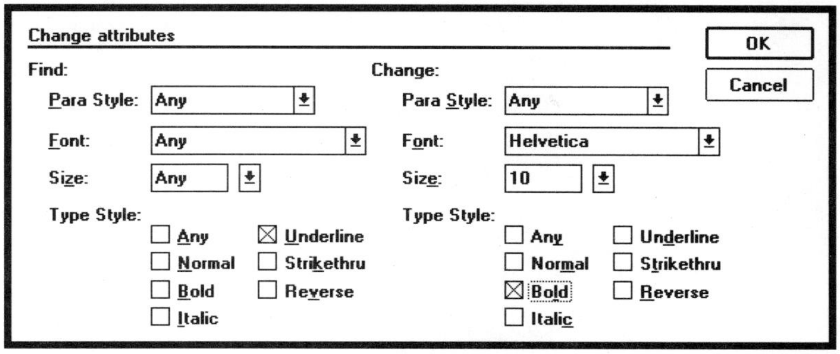

Figure 4-61
Attributes dialog box

Change attributes				OK
Find:		Change:		Cancel
Para Style: Any		Para Style: Any		
Font: Any		Font: Helvetica		
Size: Any		Size: 10		
Type Style:		Type Style:		
☐ Any	☒ Underline	☐ Any	☐ Underline	
☐ Normal	☐ Strikethru	☐ Normal	☐ Strikethru	
☐ Bold	☐ Reverse	☒ Bold	☐ Reverse	
☐ Italic		☐ Italic		

Alt-E, E), and select "Change" from the Edit menu (Ctrl-9 or Alt-E, H).

4. Click the Attributes button and replace any text with underline formatting with 10-point Helvetica Bold. Press Enter to close the Change Attributes dialog box.

5. Click "Change all" in the Change dialog box.

Note that you can't use this technique to change to Garamond Bold condensed to 80 percent, because the Set width attribute isn't in the Change attributes dialog box. Bummer.

When you apply a style to a paragraph, the character formatting defined in the style overrides some of the local character formatting, but not all. It does not override any type "style" attributes on the Type style submenu—italic, bold, underline, etc. ("Reverse" is the exception; applying styles overrides that attribute). All of that local formatting remains, on top of the styled formatting, so to speak. The style formatting does override and remove any other local character formatting—font, size, set width, tracking, kerning, etc.

▼ *Tip: Retaining Local Formatting While Changing Styles*

If you've locally formatted some text in a paragraph—made, for example, individual words a different font—and want to change styles without losing that formatting, hold down Shift as you apply the style. All of your local formatting is retained (see Figure 4-62).

Figure 4-62
Applying styles with Shift held down

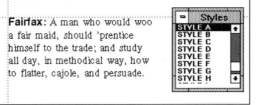
Paragraph with local font change

If you change the style of the paragraph by clicking on another style name in the Styles palette, the new style's formatting overrides the local font change.

If you change the style of the paragraph by holding down Shift while you click on another style name in the Styles palette, the new style's formatting does not override the local font change.

▼ Tip: Getting Rid of Local Formatting

If you have local formatting in a paragraph that's overriding the formatting specified in the style, you can get rid of the hard formatting.

1. Triple-click on the paragraph with the Text tool. Note that the paragraph's style name in the Style palette has a + appended to it, showing that the paragraph contains local formatting.

2. Press Ctrl-Shift-Spacebar (or choose "Normal" from the Type style submenu on the Type menu—Alt-T, Y, N).

3. Reapply the style to the paragraph by clicking on the style name in the Style palette.

Using the Styles Palette

The Style palette is a shortcut; using it is much quicker than using the Define styles dialog box or the Style submenu on the Type menu. The only quicker way to apply styles is to use a Recorder macro (see the tip below). To apply a style to a paragraph, follow these steps.

1. Place a text insertion point in the paragraph (or swipe over several paragraphs that you want to have the same style).
2. Click on the style name you want in the Styles palette.

Ctrl-Y (or Alt-W, S) displays and hides the Style palette. You can resize the Styles palette to display as many style names as you want, and you can drag it anywhere in the publication window. If you resize the Style palette, put it away, and then redisplay it, it reappears at the size and position you specified before you put it away.

▼ Tip: Use Keyboard Shortcuts to Apply Styles

If you're like us, you like to keep your hands on the keyboard when you're working with text. To assign styles without using the mouse, press Alt-T, S; use the arrow keys to select the proper style; press Enter. If each of your styles begins with a different letter of the alphabet, you can save a few keystrokes by just typing Alt-T, S, *X*, where *X* is the first letter of the style name.

Note, however, that if more than one style begins with the same letter, this shortcut will only assign the first style on the list. The solution is to come up with a naming system for your styles in which the first letter of each is unique. For example, you might name first-level heads "1 Head," second-level heads "2 Head," and so on. You might also rename a "Byline" style to "Credit Line" to avoid conflict with the B in your "Body copy" style. By using numbers and letters, you can have up to 36 styles with shortcuts for each. If you use punctuation marks at the beginning of your style names, you can add several more (PageMaker won't let you use the hyphen, however). And you can use the Shift key to start style names with characters like @ or #. But that's getting ridiculous.

▼ Tip: Use Recorder to Apply Styles

If using the Alt-menu shortcuts and naming styles to make that work is too cumbersome, you can always create some Recorder macros to assign the style. Create keys that have some relation to the style you want to apply. In producing this book, for example, we could have used Ctrl-Alt-1 for our first-level heads, and Ctrl-Alt-T for tip heads. Make up some mnemonic crutch that works for you. As always, be careful to avoid keyboard shortcuts that PageMaker already uses, as Recorder will override them. (On the other hand, if you don't use those shortcuts anyway, go ahead.)

▼ Tip: Creating Styles by Example

You can create an example paragraph that's formatted the way you want it, then build a style based on that paragraph.

1. Format a paragraph the way you want it using either the submenus, key commands, or the dialog boxes off the Type menu.
2. Ctrl-click on "No style" in the Style palette. The Edit style dialog box appears.
3. Type a style name in the Name text edit field and click OK or press Enter.

PageMaker creates a style with the attributes of your formatted paragraph. You can now apply that style to any similar paragraphs in your document. Note that creating the style this way does not apply the style to the currently selected paragraph. Usually, you'll want to scroll through the Style palette listing and apply the style before you move on (see Figure 4-63).

▼ Tip: Easy Way to Edit Styles

The quickest way to edit styles is to Ctrl-click on the style name in the Style palette. This takes you directly to the Edit style dialog box. Changes you make to the style are applied to all other paragraphs

WORDS **191**

Figure 4-63
Creating styles by example

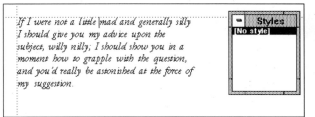

Format a paragraph using the commands on the Type menu, then Ctrl-click "No style" in the Styles palette.

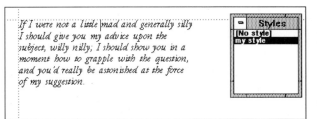

Type a name for the style in the Edit style dialog box and click "OK." The paragraph's formatting appears at the bottom of the dialog box.

The style name you just created appears in the Styles palette. Click on the style name to tag the paragraph with that style.

tagged with the edited style. Editing a style in this fashion does not override local formatting in paragraphs tagged with that style.

Based on and Next style

There are two options in the Edit style dialog box that many people find confusing—Based on and Next style. "Based on" tells PageMaker to base the style you're editing on some other style. We like to format paragraphs that follow heads with no first-line indent, for instance. So we build a "body copy" style with a first-line indent, and a "first para" style based on "body copy," but with one difference—no first-line indent. The description of "first para" in the Edit style dialog box reads "body copy + first indent: 0."

Using the Based on feature, you can really automate changes. Now if you decide that you want a different typeface for the body of the text, you can just change the "body copy" style. The font change ripples through into the "first para" style because it's based on "body copy," but the "+ first indent: 0" doesn't change. With careful planning, you can build hierarchies of styles based on other styles that let you make massive changes to a document with only a few seconds of work.

You can always break the link between styles. Just select "No Style" in the Based on pop-up list.

▼ Tip: Easy Way to Base One Style on Another

If you want to create a new style based on another style:

1. Select a paragraph formatted with the base style.
2. Ctrl-click on "No style" in the Style palette. The Define styles dialog box appears, with the base style's name entered in the Based on pop-up list.
3. Name the new style and make any changes you want. Those changes define the differences between the base style and the new style. Keep clicking OK (or press Ctrl-Alt-Enter) until you've closed all the dialog boxes.

Note that creating the style this way does not apply the style to the currently selected paragraph.

▼ Tip: Merging Two Styles

Sometimes, you need to change all of the text that's been formatted as one style into another style (for instance, if you want to change all the "Normal" paragraphs to the style "body copy"). You could go through the entire document, clicking in the paragraphs and applying the style as you go, but there are two quicker ways. You can use the Story Editor's find and change features, or you can use the Styles palette.

Follow these steps to merge styles with the Story editor. In our example, we'll call the style with the correct formatting the good style, and the style we want to change the bad style.

1. Select the story containing the styles you want to merge and press Ctrl-E to open the story with the Story Editor.
2. Press Ctrl-9 to bring up the Find/Change dialog box.
3. Click the Attributes button to bring up the Attributes dialog box.
4. Choose the name of the bad style from the Para style pop-up menu in the Find section of Attributes dialog box, then choose the name of the good style from the Para style pop-up menu in the Change section.
5. Press Enter to close the Attributes dialog box.
6. Click the Change all button to change every occurrence of the bad style into the good style.
7. Once the search is complete, press Ctrl-3 to display the Define styles dialog box. Select the name of the bad style in the Define styles dialog box and click the Remove button to get rid of the bad style.

If you don't want to open the Story Editor, follow these steps to merge styles using the Styles palette (Figure 4-64).

Figure 4-64
Merging two styles using the Styles palette

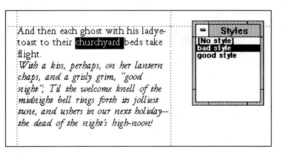

Paragraph tagged as bad style

Paragraph tagged as good style

Figure 4-64
Merging two styles using
the Styles palette
(continued)

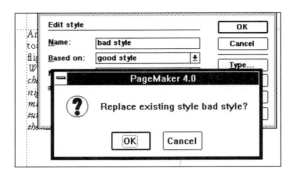

Position a text insertion point in a paragraph tagged with the good style, then Ctrl-click "[No style]" in the Styles palette. Type the name of the bad style in the Name text edit box and press Enter. When the "Replace existing style" alert appears, click "OK."

The bad style takes on the formatting characteristics of the good style. The two styles are now identical in all but name.

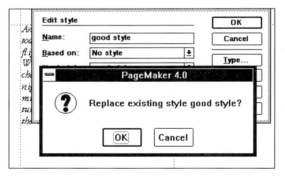

Ctrl-click the bad style's style name in the Styles palette. In the Name text edit box, type the first style's name. Choose "No style" from the Based on pop-up menu and press Enter. When the "Replace existing style" alert appears, click "OK."

You've just merged the two styles—all of the paragraph originally tagged with either style are now tagged with the good style.

1. Click in an example paragraph of the good style.
2. Ctrl-click "[No style]." The Edit style dialog box appears.
3. In the Name text edit box, type the name of the bad style exactly as it appears in the Style palette, and press Enter. A prompt appears, asking if you want to replace the style. Click OK. The bad style now has the same formatting as the good style.
4. Ctrl-click on the bad style.
5. Type the name of the good style. To break the link, make sure "No style" appears in the Based on pop-up list. (It should already be there.) Press Enter. A prompt appears, asking if you want to replace the style. Click OK.

▼ Tip: Copy Styles Between Documents for Formatting Consistency

You can use the Copy button in the Define styles dialog box to bring styles from another PageMaker file into your current publication. The incoming styles appear in the list of styles in the dialog box and override any existing styles that have the same names. This is a great way to keep formatting consistent between publications.

Note that this is different from what happens when you place styled documents from Word or WinWord with styles named identically as existing PageMaker styles. When placing text files, existing PageMaker styles override the formatting in the placed styles.

▼ Tip: Build Specialized Style Sheets

If you have a whole lot of styles that you use often, but don't want to clog up every document with two dozen unused styles, build some specialized style sheets that you can import selectively. For example, we have several specialized style sheets that we use for different kinds of tabular matter.

▼ *Tip: Export Styles for Use in Word*

Using PageMaker's Export command on the File menu, you can export styled text in Word format, with all the styles intact (at least to the extent that Word can understand PageMaker's formatting). Then you can apply the styles in Word, so the text is all styled before it ever hits the page—which is just the way you want it.

You can also edit the styles in Word, to make them easier to work with during writing and editing, if you need to (often, text which looks great in a layout is the hardest to proof and edit). PageMaker's identically named styles will override Word's style formatting when you place the files.

Exporting styles has the added advantage of storing the styles in a separate document (.STY for the DOS version of Word). This lets you create the styles first in PageMaker and then distribute the styles among the writers or editors you work with so they can do a lot of the styling for you. That's actually the way it should work, because the writers and editors know what the different elements are—first-, second-, and third-level heads, bullet lists, etc. When you get to pages, you only have to worry about what the elements look like.

Unfortunately, as of this writing PageMaker can't export styles to either WinWord or WordPerfect format. For more on exporting, see "Getting Text Out of PageMaker" later in this chapter.

▼ *Tip: Printing Your Styles*

To print a copy of your styles, export them to Word for DOS then print them from there. Many of PageMaker's formatting attributes won't be reflected in the printout, but it's better than nothing.

1. Export the formatted text to Microsoft Word for DOS. If you want a record of every style, make sure that every style is used in some part of the text you're exporting. PageMaker doesn't export styles that are not used in the exported text.
2. Open the file in Word.

3. In Word 5.0, open the file and choose "Gallery" from the main menu. From the Gallery menu, choose Print. For Word 5.5, open the file and choose Print from the File menu. Select "Style Sheet" in the Print dialog box and click OK or press Enter.

Word prints a listing of your styles. PageMaker attributes that have no counterpart in Word will not appear, but the formatting information that is there will be correct.

▼ *Tip: Exporting Styles to Word for Windows*

For the time being, PageMaker has no way to export directly to the Word for Windows format. However, you can still export your PageMaker text and styles for use in WinWord by exporting with the Rich Text Format filter.

1. Export the formatted text using the Rich Text Format (RTF). As mentioned above, make sure the text you export has a sample of each style you want to use in WinWord. Don't check the Export tags option unless you want the names of the tags to appear in the text.

2. Open the file in Word for Windows. WinWord will ask whether you want to import the text as RTF. Click OK to accept.

3. You now have a file with all your PageMaker styles, plus the default WinWord styles (Normal, Heading 1, Heading 2, and Heading 3). To print your styles, choose Print from the File menu and select "Styles" from the pop-up list. To share these styles with colleagues, just give them the file and let them merge the styles from that document into their own. (Use the Merge option in the Define Styles dialog box.) If you only want to give away your styles but keep the text confidential, merge your styles to a WinWord template then distribute the template to others.

Editing Text

So far in this chapter, we've been talking about formatting and laying out type. PageMaker also has some impressive features, though, for editing text. You can simply drag and edit, of course, but there are sophisticated tools for search and replace, for spell-checking, and for creating indices and tables of contents.

Using Special Characters

Beyond the normal alphanumeric characters that are so familiar from typing and word processing, there are dozens of special characters available for typesetting and desktop publishing. Most Windows applications, including PageMaker, use a version of the American National Standards Institute, or ANSI, character set, which numbers characters from 0 to 255. Many non-Windows word processors (such as Word), on the other hand, use the IBM PC standard US character set, which differs for characters 128 to 255. In either case, you can enter these characters in your word processor by depressing the Num Lock key, holding down Alt, and typing *0* plus the 3-digit number that corresponds to the character you want.

When it comes to importing, PageMaker is pretty adept at importing either character set just as you typed it, provided the characters in question are supported by Windows. (For some reason, exporting special characters created in PageMaker is only marginally successful.) Most of your problems in this area can be traced to your font and the character set it supports. The HP Roman 8 character set, for example, doesn't follow the ANSI standard. And of course, some fonts, like Zapf Dingbats, have wholly unique character sets. In those cases, you should check out the documentation that comes with your font to find whether you can type the characters you need.

Still another way to enter certain characters is through through special keystroke combinations in PageMaker. Table 4-7 shows both the PageMaker and Windows methods. Unlike characters built into a standard font, you can't type the PageMaker-specific symbols in your word processor. And you'll have a much higher failure rate if you try exporting these characters from PageMaker to a text file.

Table 4-7 Special Characters

Character	PageMaker method	Generic Windows method
Open single quote (')	Ctrl-[	Alt-0145
Close single quote (')	Ctrl-]	Alt-0146
Open double quote (")	Ctrl-Shift-[	Alt-0147
Close double quote (')	Ctrl-Shift-]	Alt-0148
Em space	Ctrl-Shift-M	
En space	Ctrl-Shift-N	
Thin space	Ctrl-Shift-T	
Fixed space	Ctrl-Spacebar	Alt-0160
Discretionary hyphen	Ctrl- - (hyphen)	
Nonbreaking hyphen	Ctrl-Shift- -(hyphen)	
Nonbreaking slash	Ctrl-Shift-/	
Page number marker	Ctrl-Shift-3	
Em dash (—)	Ctrl-Shift-=	
En dash (–)	Ctrl-=	
Bullet (•)	Ctrl-Shift-8	
Paragraph Mark (¶)	Ctrl-Shift-7	Alt-0182
Section marker (§)	Ctrl-Shift-6	Alt-0167
e with acute accent (é)		Alt-0233
e with grave (è)		Alt-0232
o with umlaut (ö)		Alt-0246
o with circumflex (ô)		Alt-0244
n with tilde (ñ)		Alt-0241
c with cedilla (ç)		Alt-0231
LM, RM (Page number)	Ctrl-Shift-3	
Registered trademark (®)	Ctrl-Shift-G	
Copyright (©)	Ctrl-Shift-O	

These special characters can make all the difference between a publication that looks really professional and an obviously amateurish or slapdash job. Remember, this isn't typewriting, it's typesetting. Here's a list of some common special characters, how to get at them, and whether you can get at them from programs other than PageMaker. For other characters, or those that are not PageMaker-specific, consult the documentation that comes with PageMaker, Windows, your word processor, or your fonts.

Quotes. The best way to scream "desktop published!" with your publications is to use straight quotes and apostrophes (" and ') rather than open and close quotes (", ', ', and "). The straight ones are great for feet and inches (or minutes and seconds, if you're a cartographer), but you should use the curved ones everywhere else.

PageMaker converts straight quotes to open and close quotes automatically when you place or import a text file (as long as you've clicked the Convert quotes option in the Place file dialog box). When you're entering text directly into PageMaker, however, be careful to type the true quotes explicitly, and proof carefully for them. We're always seeing these little suckers in captions and headlines. A quick search for straight quotes in the Story Editor can save you from looking foolish.

Em dashes. When you type two hyphens on a typewriter, you're approximating an em dash—like this. Double hyphens are almost as sure a sign as straight quotes for telling people that you're a desktop publisher. Use em dashes instead. An em dash is one em wide—12 points wide in 12-point type.

If you click "Convert quotes" in the Place document dialog box, PageMaker converts double hyphens to em dashes as you place or import a text file. As with quotes, however, you have to be careful when you're typing copy directly into PageMaker, and vigilant when you're proofing.

En dashes. These characters are half as wide as an em dash, and a little wider than a hyphen. You use them in place of "to," for example in "9 am–5 pm" or "the New York–Chicago Express." You can get away with a hyphen here, but, if you want to do it right, use an en dash.

Discretionary hyphens. These are fondly referred to as "dischys" (pronounced dishies). PageMaker will use them "at its discretion" to break a word at the end of a line (unless hyphenation is turned off for that paragraph), but otherwise they remain invisible and don't do anything. Put one of these just before the first character of a word if you don't want PageMaker to hyphenate that word.

Em spaces. A lot of designers specify a one-em indent (as wide as the type size) for the first line of a paragraph. In the old days these were called em quads. You can get a one-em indent by typing an em space at the beginning of a line (though we prefer formatting the paragraph with a first-line indent). There's no way to type em spaces in a word processor, so type some weird character, then replace it in PageMaker.

En spaces. These are half the width of em spaces—half the point size.

Thin spaces. These are half as wide as an en space—one-quarter the point size. They can be useful in aligning tabular matter, or for separating the dots in an ellipsis.

Fixed spaces. The size of these spaces varies from typeface to typeface. A fixed space is generally the width of a normal space, but it doesn't expand or contract within a line of justified type.

Symbols and dingbats. There are quite a few typefaces that don't use the standard English characters. Instead they're full of strange and wonderful beasts. The most familiar are Symbol and Zapf Dingbats. One way to access these characters is to keep a photocopy of the character set at your computer. Or if you're using WinWord, try Dinger (see Chapter 2, *Building PageMaker System*).

Foreign and special-purpose characters. There are dozens of special characters built into most fonts. If you install a font that promises Windows compatibility, you're pretty well assured of getting the Windows ANSI character set (a complete map of which is found in Appendix B of the *Microsoft Windows User's Guide*).

▼ Tip: Use FirstApps for Quick Access to Foreign Characters

If you use a lot of foreign characters and don't want to put up with the pain of looking up and typing in the code for each one, one solution is to shell out for a copy of FirstApps from hDC (see Chapter 2, *Building a PageMaker System*). This program includes a utility called (appropriately) Character Set, which displays the extended ANSI characters and their codes in a window. You select the one you want, click Copy, and paste it into your PageMaker pub.

▼ Tip: Use Recorder for Quick Access to Foreign Characters

If you're really lazy (and you should be), you'll take our second suggestion (which, as stingy Scott points out, is not only easier but cheaper): make a Recorder macro to capture your Alt and keypad keystrokes. There is a trick to this, however. For some reason, Recorder has trouble playing back a single extended character.

The solution is to turn on Num Lock, start the record function, type the Alt-keypad code for your extended character, hit the Spacebar, and then hit backspace to delete this extra space. On playback, you don't even notice these last two steps. Assign some shortcut that resembles the character (like Ctrl-Alt-c for ç or Ctrl-Alt-n for ñ) and you're done. You don't need Num Lock on for playback, only recording.

The Story Editor

The largest single new feature in PageMaker 4 is the Story Editor (Figure 4-65), which provides a second view—the story view—of the text in your publication. The Story Editor is a full-featured word

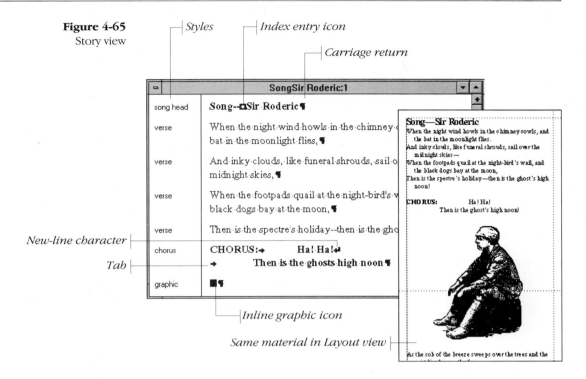

Figure 4-65
Story view

processor you can invoke from layout view using one of several methods.

- Select a text block with the Pointer tool or click an insertion point with the Text tool, and Press Ctrl-E or choose "Edit story" from the Edit menu.
- Triple-click on the text block with the Pointer tool.
- Choose the name of the story you want to edit from the Window menu (if the story is already open in a Story Editor window).

To return to layout view, double-click the control-menu box in the upper-left of the story window, press Ctrl-E or choose "Edit layout" (Alt-E, E) from the Edit menu. (Note that either Ctrl-E or Alt-E, E toggles you between story view and layout view.)

When you open the Story Editor, think "text." Paragraph formatting isn't visible in the Story Editor, and only some character formatting is shown. The Story Editor doesn't show the column widths, tab positions, or first-line indents; it just wraps to the width of the window. This is another reason to use styles instead of local paragraph formatting—you can tell what paragraph formatting is applied to the paragraph from the style bar on the left of the Story Editor window. Try to keep from worrying about the way the text looks until you return to the layout view. You can, however, change the font and type size used by the Story Editor to display your text through the Story Editor settings in the Preferences dialog box.

When you're in the Story Editor, PageMaker's menus change. A new menu, Story, appears in place of the Page menu, and several other menus have commands added to them or deleted from them (Figure 4-66).

Figure 4-66
Story view menus

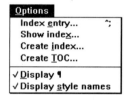

While each Story Editor window contains a single story, you can have several Story Editor windows open at once. Only one Story Editor window can be active at a time, but you can switch between open stories by clicking on that stories' windows to make them active or by choosing between the names of different open stories on the Windows menu.

When you are working on a Story Editor view of a story, the text of the story in the layout view is grayed out (Figure 4-67). PageMaker will not recompose it until you close the Story Editor or return to layout view.

Figure 4-67
Story view and layout view

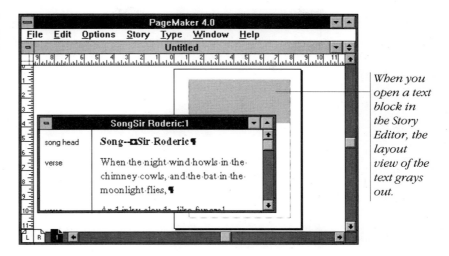

When you open a text block in the Story Editor, the layout view of the text grays out.

▼ Tip: Delete Next Character Right

Use the Delete key to delete the character to the right of the cursor. This only works in the Story Editor.

The Import command on the Story menu provides a way of loading text directly into the open Story Editor. "Import" is basically the same as "Place," except that you won't see a loaded place gun until you leave the Story Editor. For more on importing, see "Importing Text" later in this chapter.

Finding and Changing Text

PageMaker 4's Story Editor includes powerful features for finding and changing text and text attributes hitherto found only in word processors and in PageMaker's competitors. You can use "Find" and "Change" to search through selected text, the current story, or all of the stories in the publication (Figure 4-68).

You can find either a string of characters or formatting attributes, or both. Likewise, you can replace either a string of characters or formatting attributes, or both. In other words, you don't have to specify any string of characters to search for; you can just search for attributes. Nor do you have to specify any characters in the Change to text edit box; you can just change formatting attributes.

Figure 4-68
Find, Change, and Attributes dialog boxes

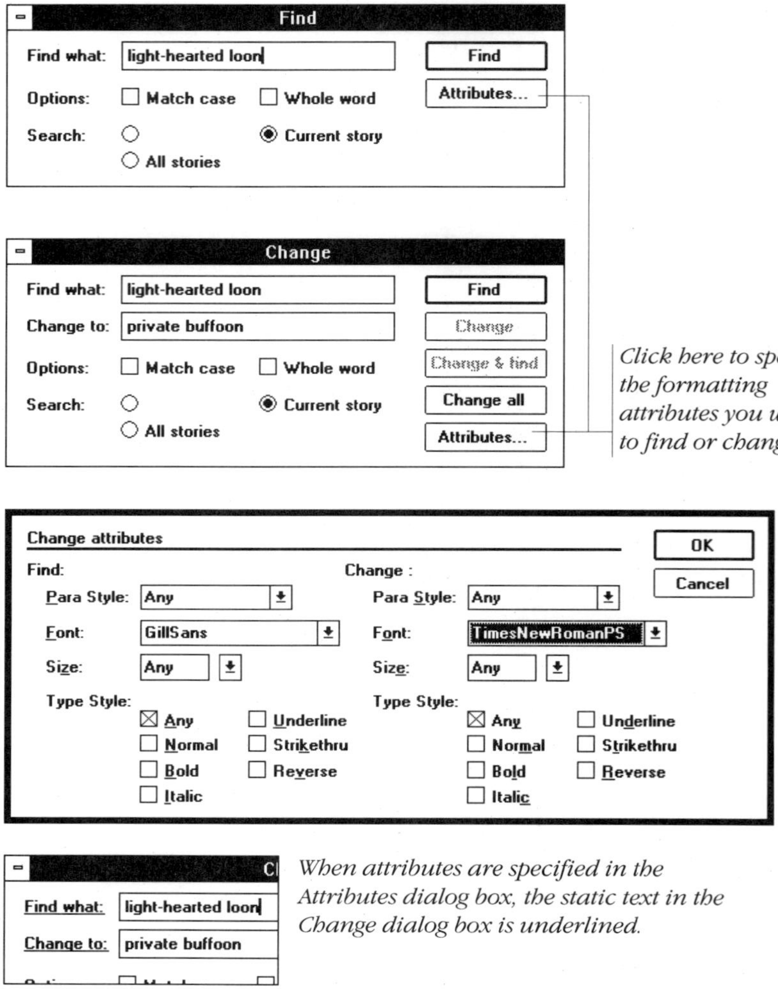

Click here to specify the formatting attributes you want to find or change.

When attributes are specified in the Attributes dialog box, the static text in the Change dialog box is underlined.

To find or change text attributes, click on the Attributes button in the Change dialog box. When you have some attributes selected to find or change, the static text in the Find dialog box and Change dialog box is underlined.

▼ *Tip: Reverting all Change Attributes to Any*

Alt-click on the Attributes button in the Find or Change dialog box to return all the Attribute settings to "Any." This is useful if you've just finished an attribute search, want to start a normal text search, and don't want to go through all the dialog box options.

▼ Tip: Special Characters Used in the Find and Change Dialog Boxes

PageMaker has taken some search-and-replace lessons from Word for Windows. To search and replace special characters, enter the codes shown in Table 4-8 in the Change dialog box. Other characters are entered in dialog boxes by typing them as you ordinarily would.

Table 4-8 Finding and changing special characters

Character	*What You Enter in the Dialog Box*
Paragraph end (Enter)	^P or ^p
New-line (Shift-Enter)	^n
Tab	^T or ^t
Discretionary hyphen	^-
Nonbreaking space	^s
Caret	^^
An unspecified (wildcard) character	^? (This only works in the Find what field; putting it in the Change to field replaces the search string with a question mark, not the wildcard character.)
White space	^w or ^W
Thin space	^<
En space	^>
Em space	^m or ^M
En dash	^=
Em dash	^_
Nonbreaking hyphen	^~
Computer-inserted hyphen	^c or ^C
Nonbreaking slash	^/
Page number token	^3
An inline graphic	^g
An index entry	^;
An index entry sorted by last name	^z

To search for special characters in the Windows ANSI character set, just type them into the Find text box just as you would type them onto a page in any Windows application: turn Num Lock on, hold the Alt key, and type *0* plus the number of the character. The character will appear in the Find what text edit box, and will have no trouble locating its match in your story.

▼ Tip: Using Searches to Enter Index Topics

If you want to search for a particular word or phrase and make it an index entry, type the word or phrase in the Find what text edit box and type ^; in the Change to text edit box. Click "Change all," and PageMaker finds every occurrence of that string in the range you've specified and adds an index entry.

If you're searching for someone's name, type the name in the Find what text edit box and type ^z in the Change to text edit box. This way, when you run the search, PageMaker enters the name in the correct order (Roth, Steve) rather than the way the name appears in the text (Steve Roth).

Checking Spelling

To spell check a story, triple-click on the story to open the Story Editor, and choose "Spelling" from the Edit menu (Ctrl-L or Alt-E, S). The Spelling dialog box appears (Figure 4-69). To check the entire publication, you can triple-click on any story, and then select "All stories" in the Spelling dialog box.

Once you've started a spelling check, PageMaker scans through the range of text you've specified. If PageMaker can't find a word in the user dictionary or selected language dictionary, PageMaker displays the word in the Change to text edit box and selects the word in the story view, always scrolling to make the word visible above the Spelling dialog box.

Note that the Spelling dialog box isn't a modal dialog box; you can reach outside of it to activate other windows, change to other programs, and so on. This can be very handy if you need to sprint to layout view to compare the spelling of someone's name or see the

Figure 4-69
Spelling dialog box

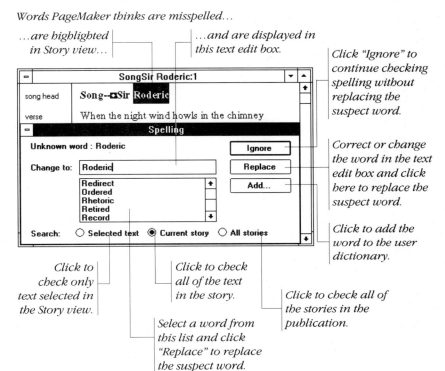

correct street address in another story in the pub. In that case, you might find it helpful to resize or rearrange your windows so that the Spelling dialog box is above or below the story window instead of overlapping it. That way, if you click in the story window, the Spelling dialog box is still visible.

Note also that PageMaker checks for more than spelling. A set of grammar-checking rules is applied to the text in your story—checking for things like "the the," and other common typos.

Although it seems odd to have the suspect word appear in a text edit box titled "Change to," the point is that whatever is displayed in that text edit box replaces the text selected in the story view when you click "Replace."

To retain the suspect word as-is, click "Ignore." PageMaker returns to the hunt. If you want to change the word to one of the words in the suggestion list, select the word in the suggestion list. It will appear in the Change to text edit box and replace the text that's selected in the story view when you click "Replace."

And of course, if all of these automated tools don't correct the problem, you can simply type the correct word in the Change to text edit box and click "Replace."

Adding to the Dictionary

You can add the word in the Change to text edit box to the user dictionary by clicking "Add." The Add word to user dictionary dialog box appears with the suspect word entered in the Word text edit box (Figure 4-70). Most words appear with hyphenation points (PageMaker's best guess) inserted. Edit the hyphenation points as you like: delete them, change their rank (one tilde is the best hyphenation point, three tildes is the worst), or enter new points by entering tildes. Then press Enter to enter the word into the user dictionary. (See "Hyphenation in PageMaker" later in this chapter for more on hyphenation points.)

Figure 4-70
Add word to user dictionary dialog box

Click "Exactly as typed" if you want your capitalization retained in the dictionary.

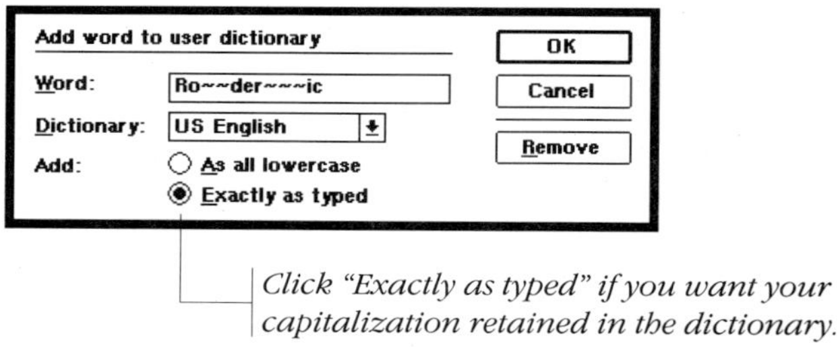

If the word is already in the user dictionary, PageMaker displays "This word is already in user dictionary," which means you'll have to remove the current version of the word from the user dictionary before you enter your new, improved version. If all you've changed is the capitalization or hyphenation, PageMaker gives you the option of overriding the word in the dictionary.

You can also type a new word in the Change to text edit field and click "Add" to add the word to the user dictionary, then click "Replace" when you return to the Spelling dialog box to replace the suspect word in the text file with the word you just added.

▼ Tip: Adding Without Replacing

Sometimes, you want to add words to the user dictionary without replacing any suspect words in your file. Bring up the Spelling dialog box and click "Add." You can add words, one after another, by clicking "Add" over and over again. You can click "Add" while a suspect word is displayed in the Change to text edit box without replacing the suspect word. Just type over it in the Add word to user dictionary dialog box.

You can type lists of words (including hyphenation points) in the Story Editor, then spell check the list. As PageMaker displays each word in the Spelling dialog box, add the word to your dictionary.

▼ Tip: Removing Words

If you add a word to the user dictionary and then find you've made an error (there's no better time for typos than when you're entering words in a spelling dictionary), you can remove the word from the user dictionary by typing the word in the Add word to user dictionary dialog box and clicking the Remove button.

PageMaker displays a Word removed alert if you've typed the word correctly. If, instead, PageMaker displays "Word was not found in user dictionary," you'll have to try typing the word again. It's kind of like playing Battleship.

▼ Tip: Wraparound Spell Checking

When PageMaker's spelling checker reaches the end of the story (or the end of the selected text if you've chosen "Selected text only," or the last story in the publication if you've chosen "All stories"), the message "Spelling check complete" appears in the Spelling dialog box.

If you think you've missed something, or you started the spelling check from somewhere in the middle of the selected range and still need to check the start of the file, or if you just want to re-experience the thrill of whizzing through the text blocks, click "Start" and Page-Maker checks the spelling in the selected range again.

▼ *Tip: Check Selected Word*

Wouldn't it be nice to be able to check the spelling of just the selected word without opening the Story Editor and invoking the Spelling command? It would be very reassuring at the end of a long production edit when everything—including "the," "it," and "dog"—looks misspelled. Why not make a Recorder macro that does it for you?

1. Select a word by double-clicking on it.
2. Open Recorder and start the recording procedure.
3. In PageMaker, press Ctrl-E to open the Story Editor and Ctrl-L to spell check the word.
4. Stop Recorder and assign your shortcut key if you didn't already.

Now, each time you press the key you've assigned to start this macro, PageMaker checks the word you've selected in the story view. Of course, it's not the fastest macro in the world, and when you're done you still have to close the Spelling dialog box and close or switch back from the Story Editor window. But you could make a separate macro that does that. (Ctrl-E closes the spelling checker and the Story Editor window.)

PageMaker's Dictionaries

The dictionaries that make all of this spell checking work (and the hyphenation discussed below) are stored in the PROXIMITY subdirectory in the ALDUS directory on your root directory. When you installed PageMaker, the Installer placed the English dictionary in still another subdirectory called USENGLISH. That's also where you'll find your user dictionary—the one you change when you add or delete words. It's called ALDENG.UDC (the .UDC is what counts—the beginning of the file name depends on what language you're using).

▼ *Tip: Swapping User Dictionaries*

You can have more than one user dictionary, but you won't be able to use both user dictionaries at once. To create and use a new user dictionary, follow these steps (you have to quit PageMaker for this to work).

1. Move your current user dictionary to another directory; open PageMaker.
2. Add entries through the Spelling dialog box to create a new user dictionary. PageMaker uses the new dictionary as long as it's in the directory where it installed the current language dictionary.
3. When you need to use your original user dictionary, verify that PageMaker is closed, move the new user dictionary to another directory, then move your original dictionary into the dictionary directory.

The next time you start PageMaker, you'll be working with your original user dictionary.

▼ *Tip: Using Multiple Language Dictionaries*

You can use more than one language dictionary in a publication: you specify which dictionary to use for a particular paragraph in the Paragraph specifications dialog box (Ctrl-M). The number of language dictionaries you can use at one time seems limited only by the amount of RAM you have available. Additional dictionaries (including special English dictionaries for medical or legal language) are available from Aldus.

Hyphenation in PageMaker

Hyphenation controls in PageMaker 3 were pretty simple. If you wanted to use PageMaker's automatic hyphenation, you checked "Auto hyphenation" in the Paragraph specifications dialog box. If you wanted to hyphenate manually, you entered discretionary hyphens (dischys—entered with Command-Hyphen). If you wanted Page-Maker to show you the likely hyphenation points in a selected range of text, you checked "Prompted" in the Paragraph specifications dialog box. You controlled the hyphenation zone with an entry in the Spacing dialog box. That was it.

The good news is that PageMaker 4 offers more and better control over hyphenation. The bad news is that the way you handle this control is a little tough to learn, at first. The several hyphenation controls interact in interesting ways.

Hyphenation Methods

There are three types of hyphenation in PageMaker—manual, and two automatic methods—dictionary-based and algorithmic.

- Manual hyphenation relies on discretionary hyphens that you enter manually, and that PageMaker uses at its discretion to break lines. If a dischy lands in the middle of a line, PageMaker ignores it. Dischys are only visible when they land at the ends of lines (unlike normal hyphens, which appear no matter what).

- Dictionary-based hyphenation relies on PageMaker's ranked hyphenation dictionaries. The words in these dictionaries contain hyphenation points, ranked according to the quality of hyphenation that results. Hyphenation points are designated with tildes (~); better hyphenation points have fewer tildes (Figure 4-71). You can control which ranks PageMaker uses.

- Algorithmic hyphenation relies on computer logic, which attempts to understand the way words are built in English (or whatever language you're using). By applying rules about prefixes, suffixes, and word construction, PageMaker inserts hyphens even in words not included in its dictionaries.

Figure 4-71
Ranked hyphenation

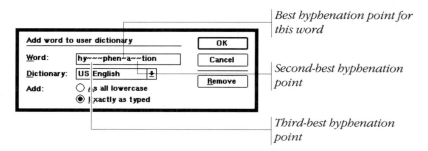

Best hyphenation point for this word

Second-best hyphenation point

Third-best hyphenation point

Manual hyphenation is the most reliable method, assuming that you enter dischys properly. Dictionary hyphenation is also reliable, depending which ranks of hyphens you choose to employ. Algorithmic hyphenation is not very reliable. PageMaker will make mistakes using this method. The more reliable methods result in fewer hyphens, and less consistently justified copy (word and letter spacing will vary more from line to line). The less reliable methods result in more hyphens and more consistently justified copy.

Hyphenation Control

The key to PageMaker 4's hyphenation power is the Hyphenation dialog box (Figure 4-72), which is a paragraph-level control (so hyphenation settings can be built into paragraph styles). Display the Hyphenation dialog box by choosing "Hyphenation" from the Type menu (Command-H).

The first odd thing to get used to is that if hyphenation is turned off, even manual hyphenation won't work. PageMaker breaks words containing hard hyphens (as in "face-melting"), but it will not use manually inserted dischys. We cannot think of any reason you'd want

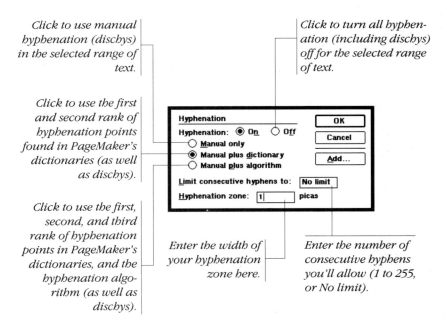

Figure 4-72
Hyphenation dialog box

Click to use manual hyphenation (dischys) in the selected range of text.

Click to use the first and second rank of hyphenation points found in PageMaker's dictionaries (as well as dischys).

Click to use the first, second, and third rank of hyphenation points in PageMaker's dictionaries, and the hyphenation algorithm (as well as dischys).

Click to turn all hyphenation (including dischys) off for the selected range of text.

Enter the width of your hyphenation zone here.

Enter the number of consecutive hyphens you'll allow (1 to 255, or No limit).

to disallow manual hyphenation (if you don't want manual hyphenation, don't enter any dischys), but that's how it works. Steve and Ole strongly feel that dischys should always override settings you've made in the Hyphenation dialog box, including turning hyphenation on and off and number of consecutive hyphens. But Scott and Jesse are glad that PageMaker lets you change your mind about hyphenating without making you search and remove all your dischys.

A great new hyphenation control is "Limit consecutive hyphens to," which lets you control how many consecutive lines can be hyphenated. Stacked hyphens (*ladders*—three or more consecutive, hyphenated lines) are another of the hallmarks of amateur page layout. Ole doesn't like to hyphenate even two lines in a row, though that's another rule that everyone has to break, sooner or later. Keep yourself looking like a pro by entering *1* in the Limit consecutive hyphens to text edit box. Entering *0* for "Limit consecutive hyphens to" does not prevent hyphenation; it allows ladders of unlimited length. Unless you're seeking a route to Nirvana or have hyphenation set to Manual, don't use this setting.

If you're laying out a page and find that one paragraph simply won't justify properly with a limit of one hyphen in a row, you can always override the hyphenation settings for that single paragraph.

Ole still feels that the best hyphenation method is Manual with a Limit consecutive hyphens to setting of No limit. Enter dischys where you want the lines to break. Take charge. If you're serious about getting line breaks right, you'll often spend more time fixing PageMaker-entered hyphens (dictionary or—shudder—algorithmic) than you will entering your own hyphenation points. Lots of the entries in the dictionary allow two-character hyphenations, another of those telltale signs of the inept (or people in a hurry to make a deadline).

In the Hyphenation Zone

The Hyphenation zone text edit box came from PageMaker 3's Spacing dialog box, but, as with spacing, it now applies on the paragraph level. The hyphenation zone might more accurately be called the line-break zone. It's the area where PageMaker looks for a possible line break—be it a word space, hyphen, slash, dischy, or PageMaker-generated hyphenation point.

The best way to understand the hyphenation zone is to think in terms of flexibility. If you specify a large hyphenation (read: line-break) zone, PageMaker has more flexibility in choosing where it should break the line. With a large hyphenation zone, PageMaker's likely to find a space or some other convenient break point within the zone, and won't have to hyphenate. The result is a looser rag (with more variation between line lengths), or less consistent, more variable justification from line to line. With a small hyphenation zone, Page-Maker doesn't have much flexibility. It's less likely to find a break point, so it has to hyphenate more (Figure 4-73). The result is a tighter rag, or more consistent justification.

Figure 4-73
Small and large hyphenation zones

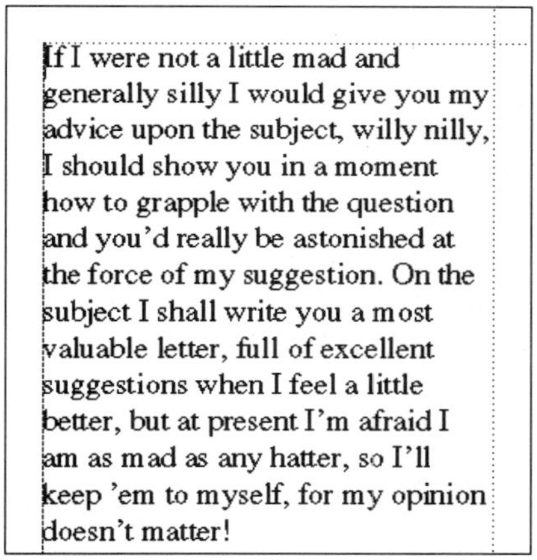

If I were not a little mad and generally silly I would give you my advice upon the subject, willy nilly, I should show you in a moment how to grapple with the question and you'd really be astonished at the force of my suggestion. On the subject I shall write you a most valuable letter, full of excellent suggestions when I feel a little better, but at present I'm afraid I am as mad as any hatter, so I'll keep 'em to myself, for my opinion doesn't matter!

If I were not a little mad and generally silly I would give you my advice upon the subject, willy nilly, I should show you in a moment how to grapple with the question and you'd really be astonished at the force of my suggestion. On the subject I shall write you a most valuable letter, full of excellent suggestions when I feel a little better, but at present I'm afraid I am as mad as any hatter, so I'll keep 'em to myself, for my opinion doesn't matter!

Hyphenation zone set to 6 picas. A large hyphenation zone results in a looser rag, or more variable justification, with fewer hyphens.

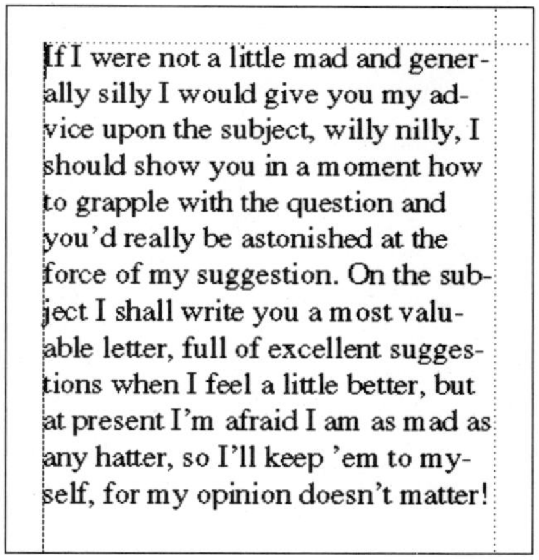

Hyphenation zone set to 0 picas. A small hyphenation zone results in a tighter rag, or more consistent justification, with more hyphens.

You're thinking that there's a loophole, right? Using small hyphenation zone settings with tight hyphenation controls? It doesn't quite work that way. PageMaker will just break your rules more often to compose the line, so you'll see more loose/tight lines highlighted on your screen. Experiment with the hyphenation zone to see what settings work best with your copy and format. To start with, try settings in the 1-pica to 2-pica range.

Dictionary Hyphenation

The Add button in the Hyphenation dialog box works exactly like the Add button in the Spelling dialog box, so refer to "Checking Spelling," above, for a description of working with the Add word to dictionary dialog box. PageMaker uses the same dictionaries for spelling and hyphenation, so you update both at the same time.

▼ *Tip: Keeping Words from Breaking*

You can keep words from breaking by inserting a discretionary hyphen (Ctrl-hyphen, or ^- in the Change dialog box) immediately before the first character of the word (Figure 4-74). This comes in handy when you're fixing tight lines that end with a hyphenated word, or have a perfume product named "Dissolute" that you don't want PageMaker to hyphenate.

Figure 4-74
Keeping words from breaking

If I were not a little mad and generally silly I would give you my advice upon the subject, willy nilly, I should show you in a moment how to grapple with the question and you'd really be astonished at the force of my suggestion. On the subject I shall write you a most valuable letter, full of excellent suggestions when I feel a little better, but at present I'm afraid I am as mad as any hatter, so I'll keep 'em to myself, for my opinion doesn't matter!

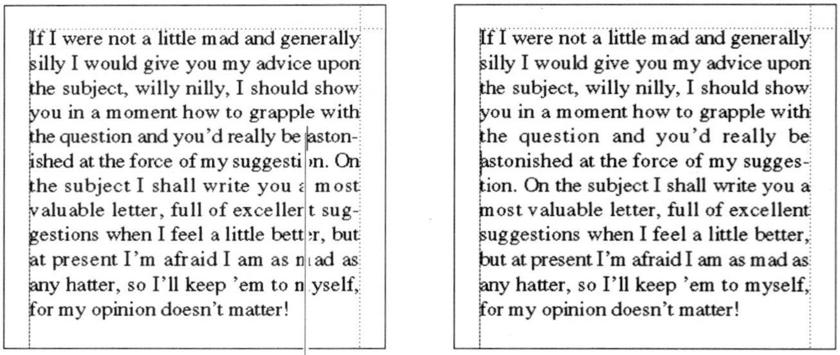

Place the insertion point immediately before the word you want to keep from breaking and press Command--.

If I were not a little mad and generally silly I would give you my advice upon the subject, willy nilly, I should show you in a moment how to grapple with the question and you'd really be astonished at the force of my suggestion. On the subject I shall write you a most valuable letter, full of excellent suggestions when I feel a little better, but at present I'm afraid I am as mad as any hatter, so I'll keep 'em to myself, for my opinion doesn't matter!

The word moves to the next line.

This technique also works when you're adding words to the user dictionary. Put a tilde (~) before the word to keep it from breaking.

▼ *Tip: Keeping Words Together*

You can keep words together by replacing the space between them with a nonbreaking space (Ctrl-Spacebar, entered as ^s or ^S in dialog text edit boxes). This is especially good for fixing the rags of ragged-right paragraphs and for repairing tight or loose lines in justified paragraphs (Figure 4-75).

Figure 4-75
Keeping words together

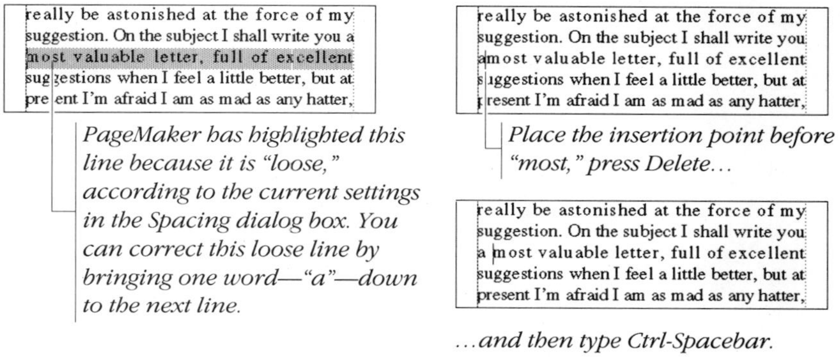

really be astonished at the force of my suggestion. On the subject I shall write you a most valuable letter, full of excellent suggestions when I feel a little better, but at present I'm afraid I am as mad as any hatter,

PageMaker has highlighted this line because it is "loose," according to the current settings in the Spacing dialog box. You can correct this loose line by bringing one word—"a"—down to the next line.

really be astonished at the force of my suggestion. On the subject I shall write you a most valuable letter, full of excellent suggestions when I feel a little better, but at present I'm afraid I am as mad as any hatter,

Place the insertion point before "most," press Delete…

really be astonished at the force of my suggestion. On the subject I shall write you a most valuable letter, full of excellent suggestions when I feel a little better, but at present I'm afraid I am as mad as any hatter,

…and then type Ctrl-Spacebar.

▼ *Tip: Keeping Compound Words from Breaking*

PageMaker 4 has a true nonbreaking hyphen—gone are the days of using en dashes (though we never did) for compound words you don't want to break. Press Ctrl-Shift-hyphen (^ ~ in dialog text edit boxes) to enter the nonbreaking hyphen.

▼ *Tip: Other Nonbreaking Characters*

All of the typographic spaces—em (Ctrl-Shift-m), en (Ctrl-Shift-n), and thin (Ctrl-Shift-t)—are nonbreaking. Em dashes (Ctrl-Shift-=) and en dashes (Ctrl-=) are also nonbreaking characters.

Book Tools

There's one other text-related area where PageMaker 4 has made big improvements—book-related tools for creating indices and tables of contents. By building a "book list" that tells PageMaker what files are in the book and their order (see "PageMaker 4's Book Command" in Chapter 3, *Making PageMaker Mind*), you can build tables of contents and indices based on all those files at once. It also gives you several options for numbering pages consecutively across multiple publications.

Let's TOC

In PageMaker 4 you can tag any paragraph, specifying that the words in that paragraph should appear in a table of contents, by checking "Include in table of contents" in the Paragraph specifications dialog box. Usually, you'll want to set up styles for headings that make each heading an entry in the table of contents.

You can create a *TOC* (table of contents) at any time by choosing "Create TOC" from the Options menu, though you'll probably want to wait until your publication's page breaks are final. After you assign a title to the table of contents and select options in the Create table of contents dialog box (Figure 4-76), PageMaker displays a progress indicator, then a loaded text gun.

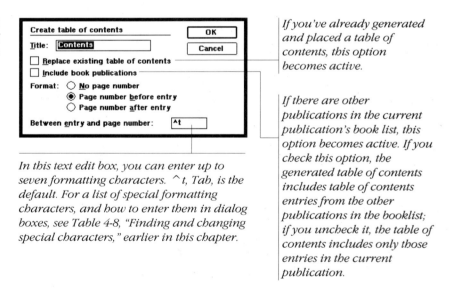

Figure 4-76
Create table of contents dialog box

In this text edit box, you can enter up to seven formatting characters. ^t, Tab, is the default. For a list of special formatting characters, and how to enter them in dialog boxes, see Table 4-8, "Finding and changing special characters," earlier in this chapter.

If you've already generated and placed a table of contents, this option becomes active.

If there are other publications in the current publication's book list, this option becomes active. If you check this option, the generated table of contents includes table of contents entries from the other publications in the booklist; if you uncheck it, the table of contents includes only those entries in the current publication.

When you place the text, you'll see that PageMaker has generated your table of contents, and has assigned TOC styles to each of the paragraphs you specified. The TOC styles are usually the same text format as the paragraph they're derived from. A TOC style derived from a paragraph styled "heading 1," for example, is named "TOC heading 1." You can edit the TOC styles just as you'd edit any other styles, so it's easy to format the table of contents.

Once you've generated and placed a table of contents, subsequent Create table of contents dialog boxes offer you the Replace existing table of contents option. If you choose that option, PageMaker replaces the table of contents you previously placed.

▼ Tip: Where You Can Put Your Table of Contents

For books with three or more chapter files, we recommend that you create a separate publication file just for the table of contents and index, as described in "PageMaker 4's Book Command" in Chapter 3, *Making PageMaker Mind.* That way you don't need to keep track of which file the book list is in, and you only need to keep one book list up to date.

If you keep the table of contents in the publication, place it at the end of the file, rather than trying to leave pages for it at the beginning. If the addition of the table of contents story causes pages to tumble, your table of contents is inaccurate as soon as you place it.

If you're working with a publication that must have the table of contents on the first page, autoflow the text, then generate a table of contents and make room for it on the first page of the publication, then lay out the publication as you normally would. Once you're through with that, you can regenerate the table of contents—the page numbers might change, but the space the table of contents takes up remains about the same and you won't have to reflow pages.

Generating an Index

Many people have gotten the idea that products like PageMaker and WinWord generate indices automatically, without any assistance from a sentient being. If these programs were intelligent enough to understand the meaning and context of the words we typed into them, do you think they'd sit still and let us crank out another memo on corporate culture? No way. They'd be running for public office, kissing babies, and shaking hands (and writing books). Luckily (for us) they're not that smart. They can only do what we tell them, and exactly what we tell them.

The problem with almost every computer indexing system we've seen is that they create concordances—word lists with page numbers—not indices. A good index is conceptually based and carefully thought out, not mechanically generated. A typical computer-generated index will give you two different references to the word "format," even though one page is talking about text formatting, and the other is talking about disk formatting. This type of index is almost worthless.

PageMaker just provides tools that help you create an index. You need to do the thinking, and PageMaker does all of the recordkeeping. PageMaker can't even control capitalization for you (though it provides tools for you to do so, as shown in "Instant Capitalization," later in this chapter), much less the more heady matters of deciding which topics should be indexed under which index headings, and which should be cross-referenced to others.

Given that, we can say that PageMaker 4 provides the best tools we've seen for creating an index on a computer. First and foremost, you can see the existing topics (what you're indexing) in your index at any time, and add a page reference (where a topic *is*) or cross reference to an topic. You don't have to worry about typing the topic exactly as you typed it before, or trying to remember what topics you've already made in that subject area, because the index topic list is constantly updated. You can simply choose an existing topic from a list. That feature alone—we might call it interactive indexing—puts PageMaker's indexing well beyond any other system we've seen.

Creating Index Entries

To create an index entry, select a range of text and choose "Index entry" on the Options menu (Ctrl-; or Alt-O, E) to bring up the Add index entry dialog box (Figure 4-77). The selected range is automatically entered as the first-level topic under which that range will be indexed.

If you've just selected one word, that might be your topic. You will probably need to change the capitalization (first-level entries are

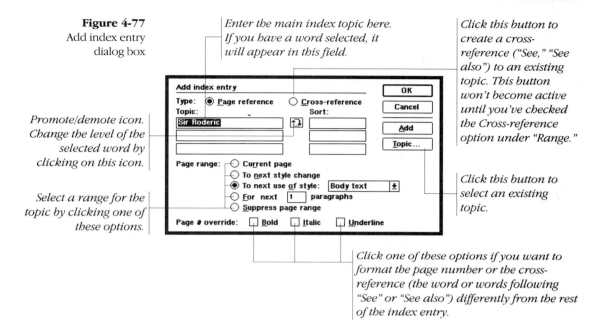

Figure 4-77
Add index entry dialog box

generally capitalized), and maybe the suffix (changing automotive to Automobiles, for example). If you're indexing a range of text larger than a single word, you'll definitely need to edit the index topic, entering some conceptual wording that describes the material in the selected range of text.

Alternatively, press the Topics button to see a list of topics already in the index, and select one. Press Enter or click OK to choose the selected topic. Once you've got the proper topic entered, and all the other options (discussed below) set as you want them, press Enter or click OK to add the entry to the index.

▼ *Tip: The Fast Way to Build a Topic List*

There are two ways to build up a list of topics quickly without spending hours jumping in and out of the Add index entry dialog box. One way is to build the list first in your word processor. An entry from Microsoft Word (formatted as hidden text) might look like this:

.i.Louis XIV;

When you place a file filled with such index entries, PageMaker adds them all to its Topic list. Then you can use those topics for specific index entries, rather than having to create every topic as you go.

The second way is to click the Topic button in the Add index entry dialog box to access the Select topic dialog box. Once there, just keep typing in new entries in the text boxes and press Alt-A (or click Add) after each one. When you are finished, press Enter or click OK to return to the Add index entry dialog box. Only the text listed in this box when you click OK will be added to the index, but all the topics will still be in the topic list for later use. Press Enter and you're done.

▼ Tip: Multiple Topics for a Single Range

You can index a selection under several different topics. Once you have the text selected, press Ctrl-; to bring up the Add index entry dialog box. Click the promote/demote icon (to move the selection down to level 2 or 3. Type in the topic you want as the first-level entry in the top (level 1) text box and press Alt-A (or click Add). Continue typing in topics and clicking Add for as many entries as you want to create.

▼ Tip: Super-Quick Index Entries

When you've found a word that should go into your index as a first level entry, select the word and press Ctrl-Shift-;. The word is instantly entered into the publication's index without bringing up the Add index entry dialog box.

▼ Tip: Quick Index Entries for Names

PageMaker can quickly scoop up proper names and rearrange them with the last name first for proper alphabetizing in your index. Just select the name (for example, Christopher Pike) and press Ctrl-Shift-Z. The next time you view or create your index, you'll see "Pike, Christopher" as a first-level entry. Hyphenated names are treated as a single name (first or last), so you'll have no problems with names like

Jean-Luc Picard. On the other hand, try this shortcut with James T. Kirk, and PageMaker gets confused—the result will be T., James Kirk. To avoid this problem, use a nonbreaking space (Ctrl-Spacebar) between middle names or initials and surnames.

▼ Tip: Instant Capitalization

Chances are many of the words you select from your text to add to your index are not capitalized. But having to open the Add index entry dialog box each time to fix the capitalization renders the Ctrl-Shift-; shortcut useless and returns you to the slow way of doing things. Fortunately, there's a solution. When you're through adding index entries, open the Add index entry dialog box one more time (Ctrl-;) and click on the Topic button. In the Select topic dialog box, Ctrl-click the Next section button. This little move causes all your first-level index entries to begin with a capital letter. If you want the first letter of your second- and third-level entries to be capitalized as well, just Ctrl-Shift-click on the Next section button. The next time you create an index, all the entries will be capitalized. It's magic.

When you're ready to add the index to a publication, choose "Create index" from the Options menu. The Create index dialog box appears (Figure 4-78). Type a title for the index and press Enter. PageMaker generates the index and either replaces the existing index, or loads the new index into a text place gun, depending on what options you've chosen.

Formatting the Index

The Index format dialog box (Figure 4-79) is one of the most terrifying new dialog boxes in PageMaker. It's large, kind of incomprehensible, and features text edit boxes filled with Cuneiform. Don't be scared. The bottom third of the dialog box displays the current index format. If you like it, just click OK.

Otherwise, you'll need to know that " ^ > " is how you enter an en space in a dialog box, and that " ^ = " is how you enter an en dash (–) in a dialog box (see "Using Special Characters" earlier in this chapter).

Figure 4-78
Create index dialog box

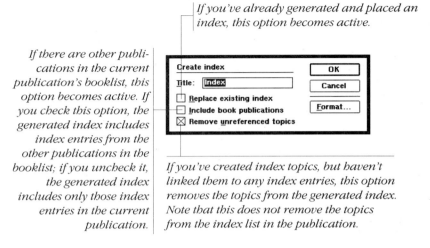

If there are other publications in the current publication's booklist, this option becomes active. If you check this option, the generated index includes index entries from the other publications in the booklist; if you uncheck it, the generated index includes only those index entries in the current publication.

If you've already generated and placed an index, this option becomes active.

If you've created index topics, but haven't linked them to any index entries, this option removes the topics from the generated index. Note that this does not remove the topics from the index list in the publication.

Figure 4-79
Index format dialog box

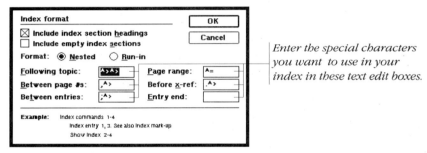

Enter the special characters you want to use in your index in these text edit boxes.

For a list of special formatting characters, and how to enter them in dialog boxes, see Table 4-8, "Finding and changing special characters," earlier in this chapter.

To see the difference between a "Nested" and a "Run-in" index format, click the different option buttons and watch how the index format example at the bottom of the dialog box changes.

Once you've generated and placed an index, you'll see that Page-Maker has assigned index styles to the entries in your index. You can edit these styles as you would any other styles.

▼ *Tip: Viewing Your Index Entries*

One of the hardest parts of creating an index is remembering what entries you've already made. Suppose you come across a brontosaurus in your text, for instance. Should that go under prehistoric reptile, dinosaur, wading animal, or family pet? What entry did you create when you ran across a triceratops forty pages back?

Click the Topic button in the Add index entry dialog box, and you can skim through your already created topics. To navigate through this list, click the Next section button (Alt-N), then type the letter for the appropriate section in the Select section list box or click the arrow button to scroll for the right letter. When you find the right topic, select it and click OK. The topic will appear in the Add index entry dialog box, where you can add it to your index.

If your publication is part of a book list, the import button will be available. Click it to import the index topics from all the publications in your book list into the current list of topics. This won't add any index entries to the current publication; it's only a list of topics from which you can add entries if you choose.

You can also view your index at any point by choosing "Show index" from the Options menu. You can edit the index that's displayed in the Show index dialog box by clicking the Add x-ref, Edit, or Remove buttons. Clicking the Edit button brings up the Edit index entry dialog box for the currently selected index entry, or you can double-click the index entry. The Edit index entry dialog box is functionally identical to the Add index entry dialog box, except that the Add button is dimmed.

Index Levels

Entries in an index are usually grouped under some topic. The brontosaurus and triceratops we mentioned earlier could be indexed as "Plant-eating dinosaurs, brontosaurus" and "Plant-eating dinosaurs, triceratops," though brontosaurus might also be entered under the "Big dinosaurs" topic and triceratops under the "Horny dinosaurs" topic. You decide; you're creating the index. PageMaker can help, though, by taking care of some of the drudge-work.

If you've created index entries for the two dinosaurs using the quick index entry method we outlined earlier in this chapter, your publication's index will contain two first-level index entries—one for brontosaurus, and one for triceratops. If you want to retain these first-level index entries, you can add their second-level references by selecting the word, pressing Ctrl-; to open the Add index entry dialog box, demoting the entry to the second level by clicking the promote/demote icon (see Figure 4-80), and typing "Plant-eating dinosaurs" in the first-level text edit box.

Figure 4-80
Adding a first-level entry

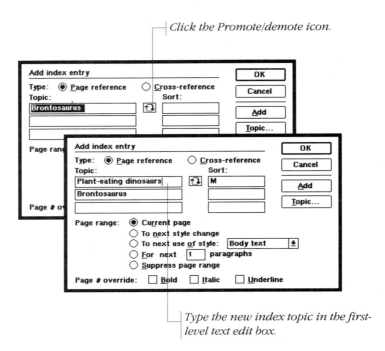

Click the Promote/demote icon.

Type the new index topic in the first-level text edit box.

Sort Entries

Many alphabetical sorting systems have conventional variances. For example, names in the phone book starting with "Mc" usually precede names starting with "Ma." It's not strictly alphabetical order, but many people believe it's the correct way to arrange the entries. In PageMaker, you can control the variance. For example, you enter a sort key of "M" for "Mc" entries to make them appear before "Ma" in the index. Similarly, PageMaker's ASCII sort order ordinarily puts the number 10 before the number 9, so you enter the sort key for "9" as "09" (Figure 4-81).

See and See also

When you're organizing information, you need to keep in mind that not everyone thinks exactly as you do. Often, you need to create cross-references inside an index to help people think the way you do. If, for

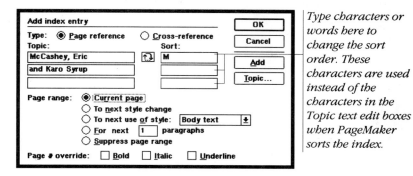

Figure 4-81
Changing the index entry's sort order

Type characters or words here to change the sort order. These characters are used instead of the characters in the Topic text edit boxes when PageMaker sorts the index.

example, you've placed all of your index entries for the author of *Alice in Wonderland* under Dodgson, Charles Lutwidge, you should anticipate that people will search the index for an entry for Lewis Carroll, and enter a cross-reference under Carroll, Lewis.

In this case, if Lewis Carroll occurs in your text, you swipe over his name and press Ctrl-Shift-Z to enter the name in surname-first order. Then press Ctrl-; to bring up the Add index entry dialog box. (If you still have the name selected, it will appear in regular order; click on Topic and fetch the correct version from the Select topic dialog box. Then click OK.) Click the Cross-reference option (Alt-C). Once you've done that, the X-ref button appears and a new list of options, "Denoted by" appears at the bottom of the box. Choose the wording you prefer from this list. The See [also] option gives you the most flexibility, since it inserts the word "also" into the index if Lewis Carroll is a regular entry, but cleverly omits it if he appears only as a cross-reference. Next, click the X-ref button and choose the Dodgson, Charles Lutwidge topic, and press Enter. When you generate an index, the entry for Carroll, Lewis will read something like "Carroll, Lewis 137. *See also* Dodgson, Charles Lutwidge" (Figure 4-82).

If the name Lewis Carroll does not occur in the text, simply press Ctrl-; with no text selected. Then click the Cross-reference option in the Add index entry dialog box. Type "Carroll, Lewis" in the first Topic text box. Click your preferred denotation, then click the X-ref button (Alt-X) to choose the antecedent. Then run to the dictionary and look up "denotation" and "antecedent."

The formatting for the words "See," "See also," etc. is controlled by the mysterious X-ref override options at the bottom of the dialog box:

Figure 4-82
Creating a cross-reference

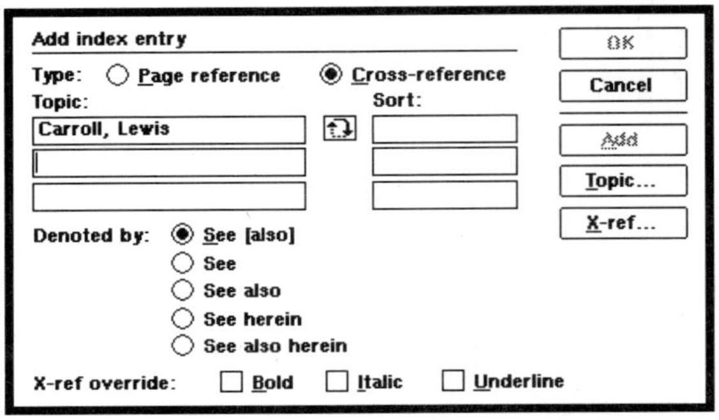

Under "Range," select "Cross-reference (x-ref)." Click the X-ref button to display the Select cross-reference topic dialog box.

Specify the cross-reference's formatting (how "See" will appear).

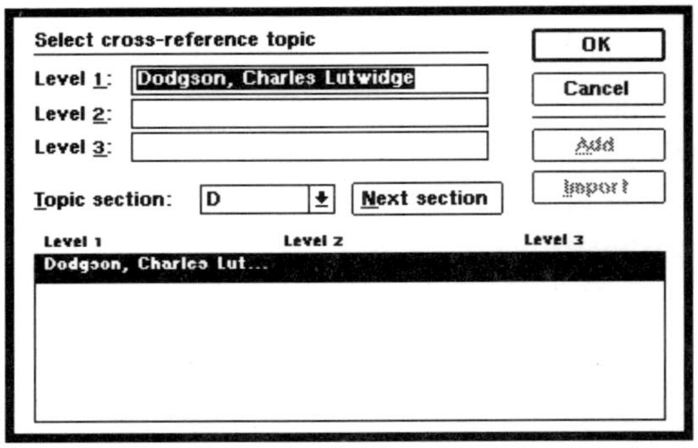

Choose a section from the Topic section pop-up menu, then select a topic in the topic listing under that section.

Carroll, Lewis. *See* Dodgson, Charles Lutwidge

Cross-reference as it appears in the generated index, with "See" formatted as you specified in the Create index entry dialog box

click the Bold check box, and the word "See" will appear in bold in your index. "X-ref override," no matter how dramatic and drastic it sounds, only controls the text format of the page number reference and the words following "See," "See also," "See herein," and "See also herein" (Figure 4-83).

Figure 4-83
See also reference

Liddell, Alice 1. *See also* Alice in Wonderland

Index Ranges

When you're creating an index, you indicate that the discussion of a particular topic runs for several pages by setting the Page range option in the Add index entry dialog box. If the topic continues no further than the current paragraph, choose the Current page option. If the topic will continue to the next time you change styles, choose the To next style change option. If the topic will continue to the next occurrence of some style (notably some heading or subhead style) choose that style in the pop-up menu. You can also enter an explicit number of paragraphs that pertain to the index entry by entering a number in the For next *x* paragraphs text edit box. When you generate the index, the entry shows where the range of text you specified starts and ends in the publication. Finally, you can tell PageMaker not to print any page numbers at all for a given entry. This is useful if you just stuck in an entry as a reminder of things to add and don't want the page numbers to appear on your proofing copy (Figure 4-84).

Figure 4-84
Specifying an index entry's range

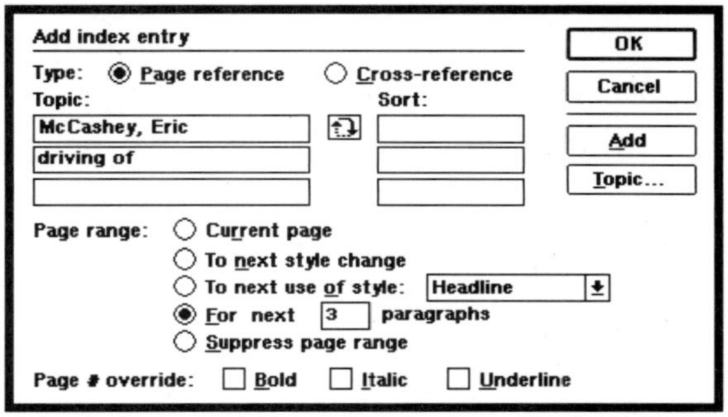

Select one of the range options to specify the range an index entry will cover.

Importing Text

While PageMaker 4's Story Editor covers quite a few word-processing needs, most people who use PageMaker bring most of their text from word processors, databases, and spreadsheets. Story Editor's great for editing the text once it's in PageMaker, but those other programs are better at massaging the text into shape in the first place.

To import text into PageMaker, either use the Place command (Ctrl-D) in layout view, or the Import command when you're in Story Editor. In either case, PageMaker uses a *filter* to interpret the text and bring in any formatting you've applied in the originating program. What formatting it brings in varies depending on the application the text is coming from, and in some cases, the options you select in the Import dialog box.

Text import options

After you press Ctrl-D to place a file, the Place file dialog box appears. Inside the Place file dialog box you'll see several different options controlling how you want to place the file. Choose "Inserting text" to insert text at the current position of the text insertion point, or choose "Replacing entire story" to replace the story containing the text insertion point. If you've got a range of text selected, you'll see the Replacing selected text option instead of "Inserting text." Choose "Replacing selected text" and the text you've selected is replaced with the contents of the file you choose in the Place dialog box. Finally, you can choose "As new story" to place the file as a new story.

Besides the options controlling where you want the file imported, there are three more options in the Place dialog box. Check "Retain format" to keep any local formatting in the file intact as you import it. Check "Convert quotes" if you want PageMaker to convert straight quotes into typographic quotes as you import the file. Check "Read tags" if the text contains PageMaker's paragraph tags and you want to read them. Once you've set up how you want PageMaker to place the file, press Enter. PageMaker places the file.

If the file you're importing uses fonts you don't have installed, PageMaker substitutes a different font and shows the new font on your menus with a question mark in front of it. If you need to have the same fonts, you'll have to install (or load) the fonts, then try placing the file again.

Working with text filters

What follows is a rundown of some of the more significant import filters and how they work. If you want to know little details like whether headers from PC Write import into PageMaker, we refer you to the *Supplement to Aldus PageMaker 4.0 Reference Manual,* which we find to be about the best piece of an already more-than-impressive documentation set.

Importing from Word and WinWord

Microsoft Word (for DOS) and Word for Windows (WinWord) are closely linked to PageMaker. On the Mac, they're almost inseparable, and under Windows, they work very well together. Many of their controls are similar, and they work in similar ways. Besides, Aldus and Microsoft are only about fifteen miles apart.

To be honest, we're still getting used to WinWord. It's a relatively new product, still a toddler, and it shows in places. But its programmable macro language and graphics features make it impossible to ignore. Like Windows itself, we expect WinWord to mature and blossom in the coming years.

In the meantime, we haven't given up on Word for DOS. For one thing, although PageMaker can import table of contents and index entries and styles from both of these word processors, it can only export in DOS Word format (although the Rich Text Format works fine for exporting to WinWord). And since DOS Word can run comfortably under Windows, we'll stick with it until we make the transition.

Word's Own Import Dialog Box

As we've said, PageMaker is very good at importing various formatting elements from DOS Word and WinWord. But that doesn't mean all the work is done. You still need to give some thought to importing and exporting Word files—considering what elements and attributes will move over, and what won't.

PageMaker 4 gives you much more explicit control over that movement than previous versions provided. When you select a DOS Word or WinWord file in the Place dialog box, hold down Shift, and click OK, an import filter dialog box appears (Figure 4-85). With the DOS Word version, you have only two choices: to import style sheets as a "remark field" or a "variant name." Clear as day, right? If you choose "Remark field," PageMaker imports your styles with the same names as they appear in Word. With the Variant name option, PageMaker imports your tags with generic names: Paragraph 1, Paragraph 2, and so on.

The Word for Windows import filter dialog box is more elaborate. In it you can choose from a variety of options that control the way PageMaker formats and places the file. PageMaker does not import any WinWord page-format settings (i.e., page numbering, headers/footers, columns, etc.).

Text formatting. PageMaker imports local text formatting (typefaces, styles, and subscripting, etc.), from both versions of Word with the exceptions on the following page.

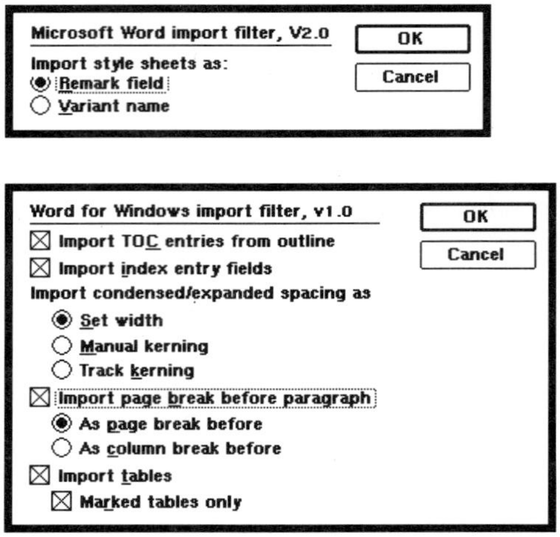

Figure 4-85
Import filter dialog boxes for Microsoft Word for DOS and for Windows

- WinWord's expanded and condensed character spacing are interpreted according to the settings you choose in the Word import filter dialog box. The Set width option changes the appearance of the imported characters, actually condensing and expanding the type. "Manual kerning" provides the most accurate simulation of Word's letter spacing by applying kerning to the range of text. "Track kerning" applies tracks to the expanded/condensed text. The effect is usually somewhat subtler than Word's expanded/condensed settings.

- For both DOS Word and WinWord, hidden text is stripped out of the file on import. PageMaker does import table of contents and index entries, however, which are usually hidden text in these word processors.

Paragraph formatting. PageMaker also imports all of Word's paragraph formatting features, with the exceptions below.

- For both Words, PageMaker will not import vertical bars beside paragraphs. In both cases, PageMaker imports boxes as ruled lines above *and* below. And, as you might guess, PageMaker *will* import both Words' paragraph rules above and below. For DOS Word, PageMaker imports "normal" rules as 1-point lines, "bold" rules as 2-point lines, and "thick" rules as 6-point lines. For

WinWord, PageMaker imports "single" rules as 1-point lines and "thick" rules as 2-point lines. WinWord's "shadow" boxes are imported as 1-point ruled lines above and below the paragraph.

- Word widow and orphan control settings are not imported, which makes sense because widow and orphan controls in Word are document-level, rather than paragraph-level, controls.

Style sheets. For both Words, PageMaker imports all style sheet attributes, excluding the attributes noted above.

Remember that if there's an identically named style in the PageMaker publication when you place or import the Word file, that style's formatting overrides the formatting in the Word style sheet. PageMaker just uses the Word tag specifying what the paragraph is, and ignores the formatting information.

Footnotes. PageMaker also imports WinWord footnotes, complete with their numbering, and puts all of the footnotes at the end of the placed story. DOS Word doesn't fare quite as well: PageMaker imports that Word's footnotes, but omits the numbers.

Index entries. PageMaker imports both DOS Word and WinWord index entries and index levels (up to two subordinate index levels) directly. However the handling of page ranges differs for each.

Unlike WinWord, DOS Word 5 doesn't specify page ranges. If you insert identical index entries on multiple pages, your generated index—in both Word and PageMaker—shows individual page references separated by a comma, rather than a single entry with a page range specified. In other words, a reference for "Kryptonite" might appear as "Kryptonite, 1, 2, 3" instead of "Kryptonite, 1-3." (Fortunately, if two identical entries appear on the same page, both Word and PageMaker list only one page number for both entries.) If you want to show individual entries like this, fine. Otherwise, use only one index entry in Word and enter the page range later using PageMaker's index range options.

With WinWord, on the other hand, you can specify page ranges, but because it does so using its own "bookmarks," PageMaker does not import them. Instead, you get the default range, Current page. Moreover, PageMaker imports the bookmark code as a second-level index topic. To avoid this problem, enter your WinWord index entries without page ranges; you can always add them later in PageMaker.

Tables of contents. For WinWord, PageMaker imports table of contents entries based on the headings in Word's outline mode. PageMaker ignores any table of contents entries created using WinWord's field codes. For DOS Word, PageMaker ignores Word's hidden table of contents entries and instead uses the text following the entry through to the end of the paragraph, as shown in Figure 4-86.

Figure 4-86
Hidden table of contents entries

PageMaker ignores hidden table of contents entries imported from Word. This entry in Word...

.c.Nova Scotia Duck Tolling Retriever;Little River Duck Dog

...results in this entry in the PageMaker table of contents.

Little River Duck Dog   *The best way to handle this is to turn on the Include in table of contents attribute for your heading styles in PageMaker. Don't worry about the settings in Word.*

Inline graphics. PageMaker imports graphics pasted into Word files as inline graphics, which appear in the same position (relative to the text stream) in the PageMaker story as they do in the Word file.

Tables. PageMaker's Word for Windows import filter dialog box provides an option for importing tables or importing only marked tables. If the Import tables check box is unchecked, your tables will be impor ted as regular text, with each cell appearing as a separate paragraph.

To import tables created with WinWord's table features, add a paragraph before the table containing one character—a "t" formatted as hidden text. With this addition, WinWord's tables are imported as tab-delimited text. For an even easier method, just copy the table to the Clipboard and paste it into PageMaker. In either case, however, you lose the table's ruling lines (borders). For this reason, we prefer using PageMaker's table editor.

Equations. PageMaker strips equations out of imported WinWord files. Copying and pasting WinWord equations doesn't work either. Sorry whiz kids: you're out of luck.

Page breaks. Word only has a Page break before attribute for paragraphs. PageMaker has that, and a Column break before setting as well. Depending on your choice in the Word for Windows import filter dialog box, PageMaker converts Word's Page break before attribute to either a Page break before or Column break before on import.

▼ *Tip: Word's Margins and PageMaker's Paragraph Indents*

PageMaker ignores document page margin settings specified in Word, but uses the paragraph indents. When you place the Word file in PageMaker, the paragraph indents push the paragraph in from the edges of the text block (Figure 4-87), just like PageMaker's paragraph indents. In general, PageMaker ignores Word's document, page, and section formatting specifications when you place the Word file.

Figure 4-87
Importing Word's paragraph indents

Text in Word

Text in PageMaker

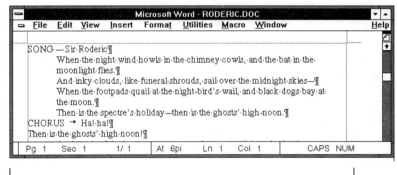

Importing Text from WordPerfect

Unlike previous versions of PageMaker, which only imported the most rudimentary formatting from WordPerfect (bold, italic, and underline, and not much else), PageMaker 4 does a darn good job of importing WordPerfect files. This makes WordPerfect a very workable "front end" for PageMaker.

Styles. The WordPerfect filter is actually ahead of the Word filter this time around when it comes controlling how styles import. If you select a WordPerfect file to place, and hold down Shift while clicking on OK, you get the WordPerfect import dialog box (Figure 4-88), which gives you three options for what you want to do with the Word-Perfect styles.

Figure 4-88
The WordPerfect import dialog box

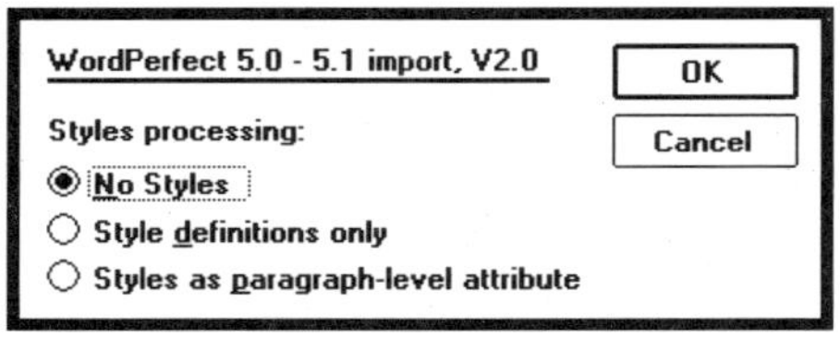

- Choose "No styles," PageMaker to convert all the WordPerfect style formatting into local, hard formatting, retaining all the formatting (with the limitations detailed below). The paragraphs are no longer tagged, nor are the styles added to the Style palette.

- The Style definitions only option imports all the WordPerfect styles, adding them to the Style palette. But it doesn't assign the styles to paragraphs. You're left to do that in PageMaker. This imports all the styles, not just the ones used in the document.

- The Styles as paragraph-level attribute option imports the text, with all styles applied to whole paragraphs (unlike WordPerfect, PageMaker's styles only work on the paragraph level). It also imports those styles into the Style palette (but only those styles used in the WordPerfect document). If you're using this option, try to ensure that the style code is the first character in the paragraph. Otherwise, PageMaker applies the style to the *next* paragraph.

As with all importing of styles (except using the Copy button in the Define styles dialog box), any styles in PageMaker with the same names as the imported styles predominate over those imported styles. If you have a style "subhead" in both PageMaker and WordPerfect, and you import the WordPerfect file into PageMaker, the PageMaker formatting for that style takes control.

Character Formatting. PageMaker's import filter brings in almost all of WordPerfect's character formatting. The notable exceptions are double underline (what is this, a typewriter?) and hidden text. It simply ignores hidden text (except index entries and the like), stripping it out as it imports the file. Text with double underlines imports with a single underline.

Paragraph Formatting. PageMaker does a good job of bringing in WordPerfect's paragraph formatting, as well. Everything comes in except for paragraph numbers, column break settings (it does import page break settings) and borders (it only imports top and bottom rules).

Other Settings. PageMaker imports most other things from WordPerfect, with the exceptions listed below.

- Table of contents codes. PageMaker ignores them. Use the Include in table of contents check box in the Paragraph specifications dialog box to tag a paragraph for inclusion in the TOC. Even better, build that setting into the styles for your heads.
- Graphics and Tables. PageMaker ignores these, as well. You'll have to place your graphics manually in PageMaker, and build your tables in either PageMaker or Table Editor.
- Headers, Footers, and Page Numbers. These elements work differently in PageMaker than in a word processor, so they don't import. Type your headers on the master pages for a publication, and include the page number token (Ctrl-Shift-3).

Importing ASCII Text

The most basic of text files is the straight text, or ASCII, file. These babies have nothing in them except numbers, letters, punctuation marks, and some foreign characters.

An awful lot of the ASCII files we end up with, though, are in pretty rough shape. They've got carriage returns at the end of every line (whether inserted by an ignorant typist or downloaded from an online service, or output from a database), and they've got tables set up with spaces between the columns.

PageMaker addresses these two problems with the Smart ASCII import filter. When you select a text-only file to place (ending with the extension TXT), PageMaker brings up the Smart ASCII import dialog box. This dialog box offers two sets of controls for cleaning up excess carriage returns and spaces.

Remove extra carriage returns. To strip out hard returns while importing a text file, choose one of these options.

- At end of every line. If every line in the file ends in a hard return, choose this check box. PageMaker removes on carriage return in each instance. If there's one carriage return, it removes it; if there are two, PageMaker leaves one; and so on.
- Between Paragraphs. This option causes PageMaker to convert any string of carriage returns to a single return.
- But keep tables, lists and indents as is. This option is only available when one of the two previous options is checked. It causes PageMaker to look for tab characters in a line. If it finds tab characters, it leaves the carriage returns there. Without this option, all your numbered lists, bullet lists, and tables would run together.

Tab Controls. You have two options for dealing with files that use spaces instead of tabs. You can convert any string of spaces with *n* or more spaces in a row to a tab (you'll probably have to massage the table a bit when you're through), or you can use Courier. Since the table was probably created with monospaced fonts (which is the only way that spaces line things up properly), setting it in Courier—a monospaced font—should line things up again.

The only other real control you have over ASCII files is the use of style tags—identifiers at the beginning of paragraphs that specify the type of paragraph—<subhead>, or <caption>. PageMaker's Smart ASCII filter isn't really so smart; it doesn't understand codes like <i> for italic. For that kind of control in text files, you'll have to resort to RTF.

Importing Rich Text Format Files

Microsoft's Rich Text Format (RTF—also known as Interchange format) is an ASCII (or, in Windows-ese, text-only) coding scheme capable of describing everything in a Microsoft Word file, including graphics, style sheets, and local font changes. Also, the Clipboard saves in RTF format when you cut or copy text with the Text tool in PageMaker.

Being able to specify the entire content of a file in ASCII is important because it opens the door to formatting automation. Documents can be written and specified with the text-editing applications found on mainframe computers or workstations, then imported into PageMaker as fully-formatted, styled text. Most database management software, can create ASCII versions of their files, inserting codes and tags for formatting as they go.

Files in RTF must start with the code {\rtf. This lets PageMaker or Word know that this is an RTF file. Immediately following is the font table. If you create your RTF file with PageMaker or Word, the font table and numbering match the fonts on your system. If you create the file with a text editor or by other means, you need only include the fonts you want to use in the document. The application opening the RTF file compares the font names in the font list with the fonts on the current system and reconciles the document's font numbering with the system's font list. This makes RTF a great format for transferring text between different installations.

Following the font table are tables for colors, and style sheets. Take a look at the example RTF document (Figure 4-89) to see how styles are specified. Note that some of the numbers used to specify type size, leading, and paragraph space after look a little different than you'd expect. Type size (fs), for example, is the size you want multiplied by two. Most space settings look like they've been multiplied by 20, because they're in twips—twentieths of a point.

Figure 4-89
How RTF works

{\rtf1\mac\deff2 ⎯⎯ *This line identifies the file as RTF and must be the first text in the file. This file was created using Mac Word.*

{\fonttbl
{\f20\froman Times;}
{\f21\fswiss Helvetica;}
{\f15250\fnil ITC Garamd a;}
{\f15252\fnil ITC Garamd b;}
{\f15253\fnil ITC Garamd d;}
{\f15979\fnil ITC Garamd c;}} ⎯⎯ *Font table*

{\colortbl\red0\green0\blue0;
\red0\green0\blue255;
\red0\green255\blue255;
\red0\green255\blue0;
\red255\green0\blue255;
\red255\green0\blue0;
\red255\green255\blue0;
\red255\green255\blue255;} ⎯⎯ *Color table*

{\stylesheet
{\f20 \sbasedon222\snext0 Normal;}
{\s1\fi-240\li240\sl240\tx2660\tx3420 \f20\fs20
\sbasedon222\snext1 verse;}
{\s2\sb240\sa240\sl240\tqc\tx2160 \f20\fs20
\sbasedon222\snext2 chorus;}
{\s3\qc\tqc\tx2160 \f20\fs20 \sbasedon222
\snext3 graphic;}}

Style sheet

This style ("verse") is Times 10/12, with a negative first line indent of 1 pica

\enddoc\sectd\linemod\cols1 ⎯⎯ *End of definitions*

\pard\plain \sl240\tx2660\tx3420 \f20 ⎯⎯ *Start of text*

⎯⎯ *Bold on* ⎯⎯ *Bold off (back to plain)*
{\b\fs28 Song--Sir Roderic}{\fs20 \par } ⎯⎯ *End of paragraph*

⎯⎯ *verse style tag—defined as s1 in header*
\pard\plain \s1\fi-240\li240\sl240\tx2660\tx3420 \f20\fs20 When the night wind howls in the chimney cowls, and the bat in the moonlight flies.\par
\pard\plain \sl240 \f20 {\fs20 And inky clouds, like funeral shrouds, sail over the midnight skies--\par

Figure 4-89
How RTF works
(continued)

When the footpads quail at the night-bird\'05s wail, and the black dogs bay at the moon,\par

Special character

Then is the spectre\'05s holiday--then is the ghost\'05s high noon!\par
}\pard\plain \s3\qc\tqc\tx2160 \f20\fs20

Start of a graphic

{{\pict\macpict\picw146\pich181
0a390000000000b50092110101000a0000000000b5009

- *We've omitted the body of the graphic. It's about twenty*
- *pages more of this sort of thing. You get the idea.*
-

e00023ffff8f30007fe00010ffff20002ed0002ed
0002ed0002ed0002ed0002ed0002ed00ff}}\par

\pard\plain \s2\sb240\sl240\tqc\tx2160 \f20\fs20 {\b CHORUS\:}\tab Ha! Ha!\line \tab Then is the ghost\'05s high noon!\par
\pard\plain \s3\qc\tqc\tx2160 \f20\fs20 \par
\pard\plain \s1\fi240 \li240\sl240\tx2660\tx3420 \f20\fs20 As the sob of the breeze sweeps over the trees and the mist lies low on the fen,\par
\pard\plain \s1\fi240 \li240\sl240\tx2660\tx3420 \f20\fs20 From grey tomb-stones are gathered the bones that once were women and men,\par
\pard\plain \s1\fi240 \li240\sl240\tx2660\tx3420 \f20\fs20 And away they go, with a mop and a mow, to the revel that ends to soon,\par
\pard\plain \s1\fi240 \li240\sl240\tx2660\tx3420 \f20\fs20 For cockcrow limits our holiday--the dead of the night\'05s high noon!\par }

Song—Sir Roderic
When the night wind howls in the chimney cowls, and the bat in the moonlight flies.
And inky clouds, like funeral shrouds, sail over the midnight skies—
When the footpads quail at the night-bird's wail, and the black dogs bay at the moon,
Then is the spectre's holiday—then is the ghost's high noon!

CHORUS: Ha! Ha!
    Then is the ghost's high noon!

As the sob of the breeze sweeps over the trees and the mist lies low on the fen,
From grey tomb-stones are gathered the bones that once were women and men,
And away they go, with a mop and a mow, to the revel that ends to soon,
For cockcrow limits our holiday—the dead of the night's high noon!

Interpreted RTF file

Note that the ASCII codes for bold and italic make it easy to change character formatting. If you wanted to change all of the bold Times in a document to Helvetica Oblique, you could search for \b and replace with \f21\i (using the font number from the example above). When you interpret the RTF text, the text that had been formatted as bold Times will appear as Helvetica Oblique.

Further, since RTF includes a complete coding scheme for graphics, you can direct a search/replace program to insert a certain graphic every time it locates the string <icon> in the text.

We've only begun to scratch the surface of RTF. With everything in ASCII format, mere mortals can view and edit it, so the possibilities are limitless. Almost any program can generate ASCII, so any program can generate RTF-formatted copy—including inline graphics—for import into PageMaker.

The PageMaker Story Filter

While you can't have more than one PageMaker publication open at a time, PageMaker 4 does have a great method for moving formatted text files between pubs. Choose Place (or Import in the Story Editor), and in the file list dialog box, choose a PageMaker publication. PageMaker brings up the Place PageMaker stories dialog box (Figure 4-90), listing the first 35 characters or so of every story in the pub.

At this point you have several options.

Limiting the length of stories you want to see. You can edit the number in the List only stories over n characters long text edit box, controlling which stories are listed. The default is *20* characters, so you're not bothered with little things like page numbers and headers. If you want to exclude most captions (depending on how long your captions are), you could enter *40* or so. If you want to see every story in the source pub, type *0*. Click the Relist button (Alt-R), and PageMaker updates the list.

Selecting the stories you want to view or import. At this point you can select the stories you want to do something with. Use the standard Windows click-selection techniques—Shift-click to select contiguous items, Ctrl-click to select noncontiguous items.

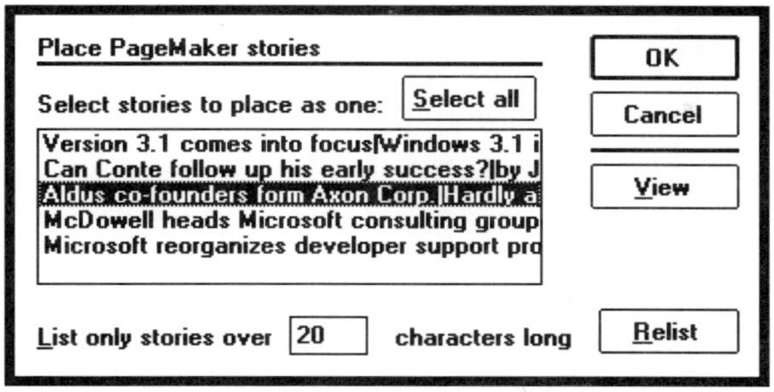

Figure 4-90
Story importer dialog box

Click OK, and PageMaker loads the place gun with all the stories you have selected, combined into a single story. The stories at the top of the list come in first, the stories at the end of the list come in last. This brings in almost all the formatting from the source publication, including styles. Style formatting already in the target pub overrides the formatting of identically named styles as they're imported.

There are some things that the Story importer doesn't import.

- Inline Graphics. The Story import filter simply discards inline graphics. The text comes in without them.

- Rotated text. It imports the text, but it doesn't come in rotated.

- Index entries. It imports simple index entries, but not cross-reference (*See* and *See also*) entries. Also, any entries that specify "To next style change," "To next use of style: *x*," or "Suppress page range" are converted to "Current page" entries.

Viewing Stories. If you click the View button (Alt-V) while you have stories selected in the Place PageMaker stories dialog box, PageMaker opens a little window for each of them (be patient with long stories, it takes a little while to bring them up). You can see an unformatted view of the story, select text, and even copy it to the Clipboard. You can't edit it in any way, however. The view windows are great if you need to see more of the story to figure out if it's the one you want, or if you just want to copy and paste a part of it.

When you use the copy-and-paste method, however, be aware that no formatting comes in—just straight text.

Importing Database Files

Database publishing is, as you'd guess, the process of taking data from a database and massaging it into publishable form. Database publishing is probably the largest single segment of the publishing market today. Think about it. TV Guide is database publishing. Telephone directories are database publishing. Catalogs and price lists are database publishing.

So database publishing is a big deal. You probably have a use for it. How do you start? If you don't care about the appearance of the printed data, you can format it with your database. But if you want fine control over the formatting of your data, you'll probably want to import the data into some page-makeup program.

You can use PageMaker's dBase and spreadsheet filters to do some database publishing, but if you've got a large directory or catalog to lay out, you need to look at two database publishing filters for PageMaker: DataShaper and PageAhead. These two filters aren't really competitors, because they do different things and are in totally different price ranges. Our quick review: if your data's in good shape and you're in control of your database, lean toward DataShaper; if you need to clean up or alter data coming from someone else, or if you need to query SQL databases to get your data, lean toward PageAhead.

Importing dBase Files

PageMaker has a very nice filter for importing dBase files. It lets you choose which fields you want to import, what order you want to import them in, whether you want directory (tabular) or catalog (one line per field) layout, and what styles you want to apply to different parts of the text.

To start, just choose a dBase (or dBase-compatible) file with the extension .DBF in the Place or Import dialog box. PageMaker presents you with the Place dBase file dialog box (Figure 4-91). Select the fields you want to import and their order (select a field on the left and click "Add"), and decide whether you want directory or catalog listing.

Directory. The directory option creates a spreadsheet-like table with tabs between each field (up to forty per line) and carriage returns at

Figure 4-91
The Place dBase file dialog box

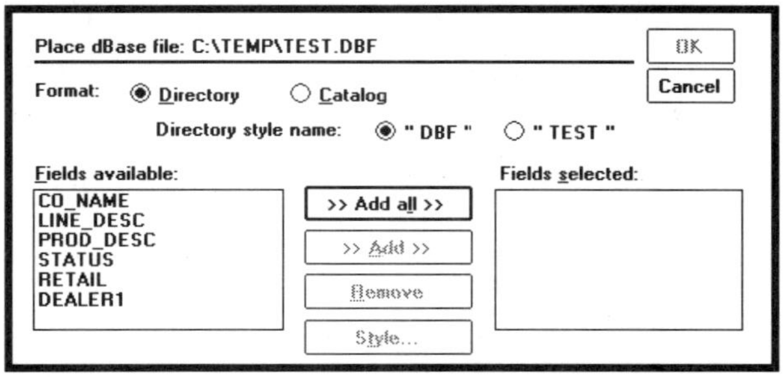

the end of each line. Every line has a style applied to it, either "DBF" or the name of the file you're importing. As usual with style sheets, if you already have a style by that name, PageMaker preferentially uses it.

You can apply basic type styling (bold italic, underline, etc.) and alignment (left, right, centered, decimal) for individual fields in a directory listing by choosing the field in the Fields selected box and clicking on the Style button. The Choose type style dialog box appears (Figure 4-92).

Figure 4-92
The Choose type style dialog box

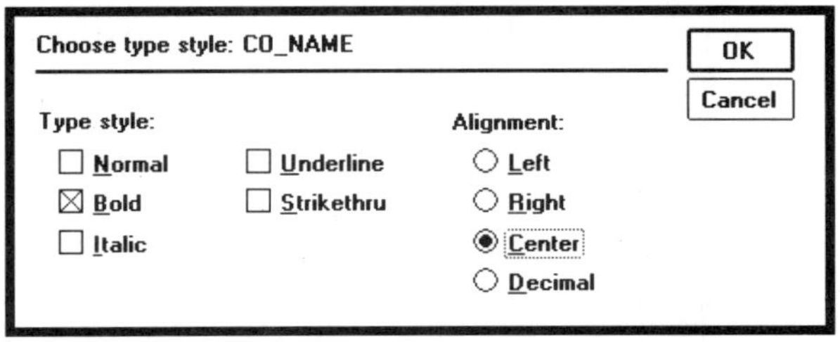

▼ Tip: Applying Interesting Formatting to Database Fields

Type styles aren't very interesting. If you want more sophisticated formatting for certain fields in a directory listing, apply some unique type style (strikethrough, for instance) to that field. Then use "Change" in the Story Editor to search for that type style and apply the formatting you want.

Catalog. The catalog format normally puts each field on a separate line separated from adjacent fields by carriage returns (with two carriage returns between records). You can choose to apply a different style to each field, or to keep it on the same line with the previous field. Select the field you want to modify in the Fields selected list, and click the Styles button. The Choose field position and type style dialog box appears (Figure 4-93), and you can select the style and options for that field.

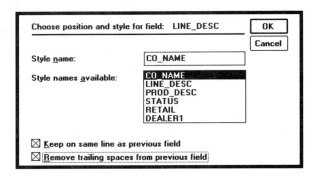

Figure 4-93
The Choose field position and type style dialog box

If you choose to keep a field on the same line as the previous field, PageMaker uses the style of the first field for the whole line. The style name disappears from the Fields selected area of the Place dBase file dialog box, and its name is appended with + in the Fields available area.

▼ *Tip: Importing Date Fields*

When PageMaker imports a date field it doesn't use the format set up in the dBase file. Rather, it uses the date format that you have set in Windows (via the International option in the Control Panel).

DataShaper

DataShaper is a database import filter for PageMaker from Elsewhere, a gang of Aldus refugees. Using DataShaper is about like using any other PageMaker import filter, the main difference being that you first create a PageMaker file that serves as the format template for the filter. Once this template is created, you open or create the publication you want to place your data into, select the format file you created earlier (the template), and then select the database file (which you've saved or exported as a text-only, tab-delimited file) you want to place. The

DataShaper import filter reads the formatting specifications you set up in the format file and applies them to the incoming records and fields.

How do you set up the format file? You format a number of DataShaper-specific codes, as shown in Figure 4-94.

Figure 4-94
What's in a DataShaper format file?

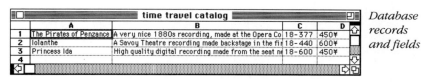

Database records and fields

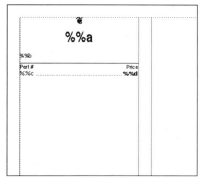

Create a format file using DataShaper codes in PageMaker

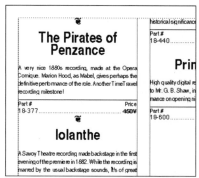

Place your data using the instructions in the format file

You can have many different format files for formatting the same database file.

DataShaper is great for the occasional database publisher ("wonder what my address list would look like in Palatino?"), but it works well for people with larger data formatting tasks, as well ("our catalog contains over 42,000 sprockets and widgets"). In either case, you need to know your database well to get the most out of DataShaper. As a final point, DataShaper costs less than PageAhead.

PageAhead

What if you don't know the database containing the data you need to publish? What if you don't even know how to use it? What if it's all come to you as a gigantic Oracle file? This is where PageAhead comes in. PageAhead is a database-massaging program whose purpose is getting a database ready for import into PageMaker. It translates the data so completely that from PageAhead's point of view, PageMaker's just a great way of driving a printer.

Where PageAhead really shines is in the way that it'll alter, substitute, suppress, or format data from your database. If a particular field in the database has been entered as all capital letters, you can change the field to upper and lowercase (and choose capitalization methods). You can substitute words for codes in your database, or add words and formatting to fields. You can make changes to fields in your database based on the content of other fields ("if this field contains a number greater than 20, then make that field bold").

You can also use PageAhead to sort and filter your data for you. If you need to create a publication containing only address records for a specific state or region, it's a snap with PageAhead.

PageAhead comes in four parts: Work Table, Answer Table, Query Table, and the PageAhead import filter. You use the Query Table to find what's in your database ("give me all of the widgets with a price less than $40 available in Mukilteo, Washington"), the Answer Table to view the data you've extracted using the Query Table, and the Work Table (see Figure 4-95) to format the contents of the Answer Table. Once you've got things the way you want in the Work Table, use the PageAhead import filter to place the formatted data into PageMaker.

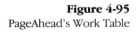
Figure 4-95
PageAhead's Work Table

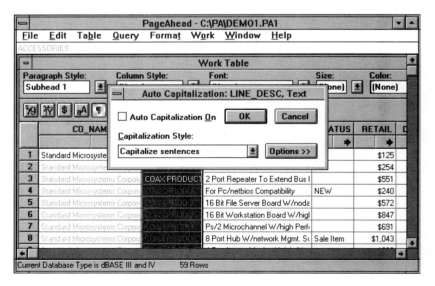

If you want to change the way that PageAhead sorts or replaces data, you can create exception tables using PageAhead's separate TableMaker utility. This way, you can easily tell PageAhead you want "next" capitalized as "NeXT," or "DBASE" capitalized as "dBase," or "Kootenai County" replaced with "Northern Idaho."

Importing Spreadsheets

PageMaker has filters for importing Excel and Lotus 1-2-3 (and compatible) spreadsheets. You can import spreadsheets from both 1-2-3 and Excel as text (tables with tabs between columns and carriage returns separating rows), and you can import Excel spreadsheets as graphics, much like the tables that result from import a Table Editor .TBL file.

When you choose to import a spreadsheet of either type, you get a dialog box to control what portions of the spreadsheet to import, and how (see Figure 4-96). You can either import a named range (this is the easiest to remember) or specify the range of cells in the Range text edit box.

Figure 4-96
Import dialog boxes for 1-2-3 and Excel

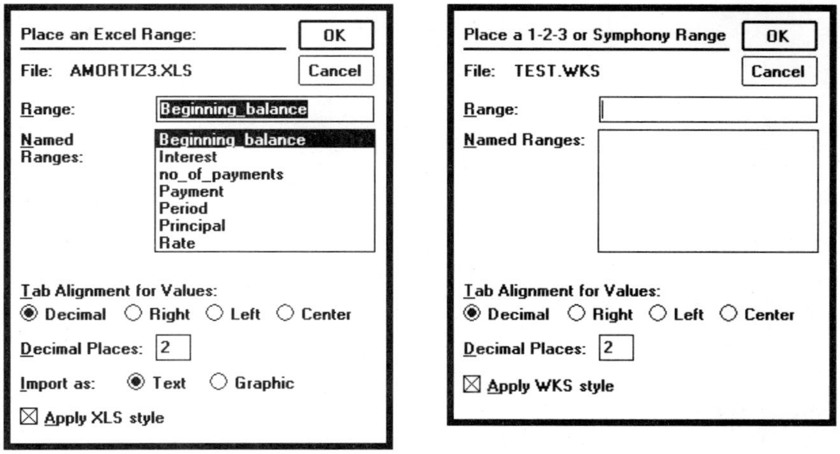

▼ *Tip: Value Formats*

PageMaker doesn't import all its information for value formatting from the spreadsheet file. It positions values, for instance, based on the option you've chosen in the Tab Alignment area. Likewise, currency, date, and time formats don't come in from PageMaker; it uses the settings in Windows (in WIN.INI, set in the Control Panel) on import.

Whether you're importing text from Excel or 1-2-3, PageMaker sets tab stops as it thinks appropriate to match the worksheet, and applies a style to each line (paragraph) of the imported table—WKS for 1-2-3 files, XLS for Excel files. You can edit the style like any other style, and as usual, if you already have a style by that name in your PageMaker pub, the PageMaker style's formatting predominates.

▼ *Tip: Tab stops in the XLS and WKS styles*

If you have XLS or WKS styles set up in your PageMaker pub, and you import new worksheets, PageMaker doesn't adhere to the tab stops defined in the PageMaker styles. It applies hard formatting over the top of that style, setting tabs as it thinks is best to make the columns fit. You can tell the hard formatting's there because when you select one of the lines, the Style palette reads "WKS+" or "XLS+." To convince PageMaker that you really do know where you want your tabs, simply select the imported text and click on XLS or WKS in the Style palette to reapply the style, overriding the imported local tab stop settings.

Importing Excel Spreadsheets as Graphics. All of this style sheet work might be a lot of trouble if you just want the spreadsheet on the page to look exactly like it does in Excel. If that's what you want, click the Graphic button in the Excel import dialog box. PageMaker brings the range in as a graphic, so you can't edit the text, but you can scale, crop, and color the "graphic" on the page like any other graphic.

▼ *Tip: Move Spreadsheets Through the Table Editor*

You can add a lot of nice formatting to a spreadsheet by first importing it into the Table Editor. From there you can import the TBL file into PageMaker.

The Time and Date Filter

One hidden feature of PageMaker 4 is the new Time Stamp import filter. It places a "stamp"—a graphic (at least it's like a graphic in that you can't edit it) on the page that displays a constantly updated date and time. To place a time/date stamp on the page, choose Place (or Import in the Story Editor) and double-click the DATETIME.TYM file (it's in the PM4 directory). PageMaker presents you with the Time Stamp import filter dialog box (Figure 4-97).

Figure 4-97
The Time Stamp import filter dialog box

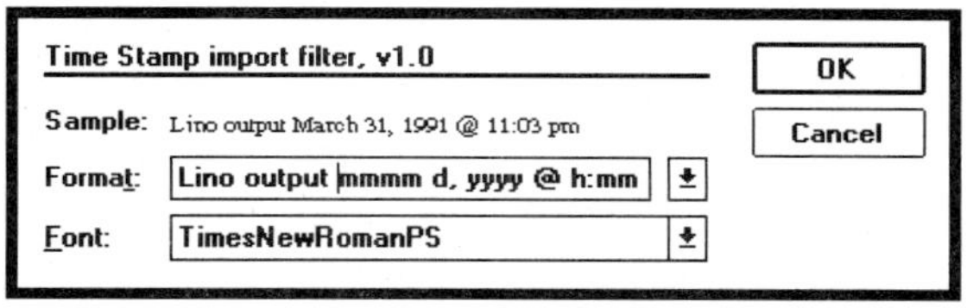

   The Format pop-up menu in this dialog box offers a number of options for how the time and/or date should appear. Choose one, and you can see the results in the Sample area at the top. If those formats don't suit you, you can create your own using the codes shown in Table 4-9.

   Note that with the exception of the AM/PM code, the codes are not case-sensitive. D works the same as d, and H works the same as h. Also remember that the codes are always updated to the time that you display or print the publication. If you want to insert today's date, and you don't want it to change, simply type it out rather than using the Time Stamp import filter.

   You can combine these codes with text, to include a job name or other information in the stamp. If you want to use any of the code letters as text, precede them with a "\" (that's a backslash, not a slash). Table 4-10 shows some example codes and the stamps that result.

   You can set the font for the time and date stamp by selecting from the Font pop-up menu. You don't have a setting for the type size, because you achieve that by dragging the handles on the placed time/date stamp. This graphic is unique, however, because you can't scale it nonproportionally. If you do, it just cuts off some portion of the text.

Table 4-9 Codes used in the Time Stamp import filter dialog box

Code	Result	Examples
Time		
h:	Hour of day (12-hour clock)	3, 4
hh:	Hour of day (12-hour clock, always two digits)	03, 04
h24:	Hour of day (24-hour clock)	3, 16
hh24:	Hour of day (24-hour clock, always two digits)	03, 16
m	Minutes	1, 18, 59
mm	Minutes (always two digits)	01, 18, 59
s	Seconds	3, 30, 59
ss	Seconds (always two digits)	03, 30, 59
am/pm	am or pm	am, pm
AM/PM	AM or PM	AM, PM
Day and Date		
d	Date of the month	3, 13, 31
dd	Date of the month (always two digits)	03, 13, 31
ddd	Abbreviated day of week	Wed, Mon
dddd	Complete day of week	Wednesday, Monday
Month		
m	Numerical month	1, 4, 12
mm	Numerical month (always two digits)	01, 4, 12
mmm	Abbreviated month name	Jan, Apr
mmmm	Complete month name	January, April
Year		
y	Nothing	
yy	Two-digit year	91, 01
yyy	Nothing	
yyyy	Four-digit year	1991, 2001

Table 4-10 Sample time/date stamps

Codes	Resulting stamp
mm/dd/yy, hh:m:ss am/pm	03/23/91, 04:23:18 pm
Ca\mco flier, dddd, mmmm dd	Camco flier, Wednesday, April 13
Printe\d ddd, mmm. dd, yyyy	Printed Wed, Sep. 07, 1994

▼ Tip: Placing a Time/Date Stamp as an Inline Graphic

In addition to including text in your time/date stamp, you can insert the stamp as an inline graphic (either by placing it with a text insertion point or by copying and pasting). This way, you can insert a constantly updated time and date stamp within text. You'll have to drag the stamp up or down to align it with the rest of the text, and make sure to select it and set the leading to match the rest of the paragraph.

You can even include a time/date stamp in a text block that hangs off the page and prints outside the crop marks. See the tip "Printing Outside the Page Area" in Chapter 6, *Printing*.

Getting Text Out of PageMaker

To get text out of PageMaker and into a format readable by a word processor, place a text insertion point in a story or select a range of text and choose "Export" from the File menu (Figure 4-98). PageMaker can only export the text in the currently selected story; there's no Export all stories option. If you need to export text from several stories (unthreaded text blocks), you have to export each story separately (or thread the stories together before exporting (use the Story filter). This is another great reason to keep text threaded in your publications.

▼ Tip: Exporting All Stories

If you want to export all the stories from a publication, create another, blank publication, and import all the stories from the original pub using the Story Import filter. They all come in threaded together, so you can export them all at once.

▼ Tip: Text and Tags

If you need to export text for someone else to work on and don't know what word processor they use, choose the Text only and Export

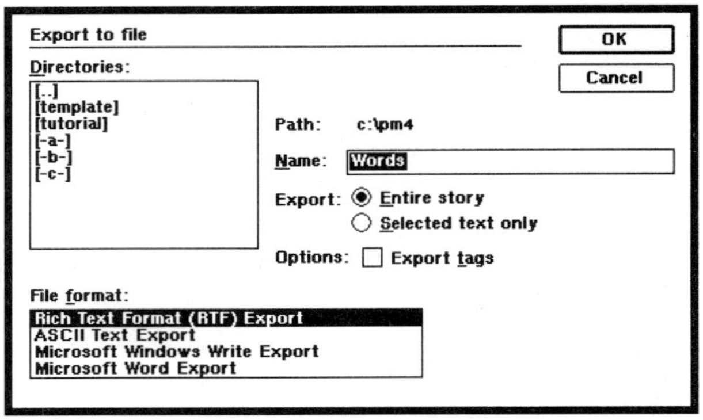

Figure 4-98
Export dialog box

tags options. Virtually every word processor in the world can read this format. And, since you've chosen "Export tags," you've got a reasonable chance of still having a styled document when you get the file back to place in PageMaker.

You lose all your local formatting with this method, however, because PageMaker only knows about embedded style tags. It doesn't know from formatting codes—<I> for italics, for instance.

▼ *Tip: Recompose World*

One last tip for words: You can recompose all the text in a pub by holding down Ctrl as you choose "Hyphenation" from the Type menu. PageMaker recomposes all the text in the publication before bringing up the Hyphenation dialog box. This is especially useful if you switch between different printers and font sets (it's a nice clean-up technique on the Mac, as well).

Even better, if you hold down Ctrl-Shift as you choose "Hyphenation" from the Type menu, PageMaker checks the publication's file structure and makes an attempt to fix any errors it finds. If your publication is clean (or if PageMaker can't find the error), you'll hear one beep. If PageMaker finds and fixes any file structure errors, you'll hear two beeps. If PageMaker finds errors and can't fix them, you'll hear three beeps—and you'll need to start trying some of the other remedies in this book.

Fixing Bad RIX

"Bad record index." Bad RIX for short. It's the touch of Death. It's Matthew Hopkins, Witchefinder General, come to ask you about your two black cats. It's the last thing you want to see two hours before a deadline. It's what PageMaker displays when your publication is hosed, has passed on, is pushing up the daisies.

"Bad record index" is mainly a problem you'll see in publications you've converted from PageMaker 3. We know that you'll never see a "Bad record index" error in a publication created in PageMaker 4, because Aldus engineering will have tracked down all of the imponderabilities in the baroque (and beautiful—tell us about another desktop-publishing program that saves your work when the dog chews through the power cord) maze of PageMaker's file system by the time you get this book. For every possible installation. For every possible file. Well, we're from Missouri (or Steve is, at least). We'll believe it when we see it.

Every "Bad record index" error we've ever seen resulted from PageMaker's style definitions becoming confused. This doesn't mean that every bad RIX error has to do with styles—theoretically, it could mean anything. Still, if you've imported several files from a word processor that supports style sheets, you should probably do a little clean-up work.

When PageMaker imports a document that has styles attached, it first looks to see if the style names match styles already defined in PageMaker. If it finds any such styles, it overrides any style definitions created in the word processor with the PageMaker styles. If it doesn't find a matching PageMaker style name, it imports the style definitions from the word-processing file and displays an asterisk (*) after the imported style's name in the Style palette and the Define styles dialog box. If you edit the style in PageMaker (even if you just Ctrl-click the style name in the Style palette and press Enter), the style becomes a PageMaker style and the asterisk disappears.

What happens, though, when you import a word-processing document containing styles that have no match in PageMaker, then import another word-processing file containing styles with the same style names? Who's on first? Sometimes, in the confusion, duplicate word-processor styles become corrupt—especially the Microsoft Word style "Normal," which you always get when you import a Word file. At this point, you'll start seeing "Bad record index" messages. Bad RIX masquerade as several error messages—notably "Cannot turn the page" when you choose "Define styles" from the Type menu.

To get rid of bad RIX:

1. Locate the afflicted style, if possible, by Ctrl-clicking on suspect style names in the Style palette to bring up the Edit style dialog box, then hitting Enter (or clicking OK). Distrust styles with asterisks first. Once you get the bad RIX message, you've found at least one of the sick styles.

2. Ctrl-click on "No style" and type the name of the bad style in the Edit style dialog box, then press Enter. This replaces the style with a new PageMaker style.

3. Choose Save as from the file menu to compress and clean up your publication. At this point you're probably safe, but we usually move to exterminate the offending style. You can't trust them once they've turned to evil. Bear in mind, however, that removing the style removes the tagging from the styled paragraphs. They'll be styled "No style."

4. Sprint to the Define styles dialog box (Ctrl-3).

5. Select the bad style name and click "Remove."

6. Choose Save as from the file menu to compress and clean up your publication.

Continue through the styles in the Style palette until you can open each one and close the Edit style dialog box without encountering the "Bad record index" message.

You can take steps toward preventing bad RIX by making sure that every style is a PageMaker style before you import a new word-processing file. Ctrl-click each style name followed by an asterisk in the Style palette and press Enter to close the Edit style dialog box. The asterisks disappear, indicating that the styles are now PageMaker styles and override any incoming style with the same style names.

C H A P T E R 5

Pictures

In contrast to the volume of new features, enhancements, bells, and whistles on the text and type side of PageMaker 4, there are only two significant changes when it comes to graphics—inline graphics, and the ability to automatically wrap text around master items. Those two features, though, do as much to affect and improve the way Page-Maker works than half a dozen typographic niceties.

Inline graphics work just like graphics in Word for Windows and Windows Write. An inline graphic is like a character in the text (in most ways), so it moves when the text reflows. A fancy enlarged capital letter, for example, won't be left behind on the page when you make changes to accompanying text. This addition to PageMaker may radically change the way you make pages, especially for longer documents.

The ability to wrap text around master items—items that appear on your document pages because they're on the master pages—means that you can customize your text flow behavior in ways you never could before. You can arrange things so PageMaker does much of your page layout for you as the text lands on the page.

Both of these new features draw on capabilities that have been present in PageMaker for some time. This chapter starts by covering the way PageMaker works with graphics in general—pasting, placing, sizing, cropping, etc. At the end, we cover inline graphics and auto text wrap, drawing on the conceptual underpinnings developed throughout the chapter.

Graphics in PageMaker

To begin with, it's important to understand that there are three ways to get graphics into a PageMaker pub.

- Create them with PageMaker's drawing tools.
- Paste them in from the Clipboard.
- Place them from an external graphics file.

That seems pretty straightforward, but in fact there are a variety of combinations and permutations to these three methods that provide a lot of flexibility.

Working with Layers

Every object on a PageMaker page, wherever it comes from, is on a layer—either in front of or behind other objects. This may not matter if objects don't overlap, but when they do, it definitely does matter. Depending on the type of graphics you're using, underlying objects (graphics or type) may or may not be visible through a graphic that's on top of them. You need to understand what's transparent and what's opaque if you want to build pages without doing a lot of layer shuffling.

Type is easy: the white space around and within characters is always transparent. You're not working with text "frames" as in some other programs, that can have a fill or color applied to them. If you want that effect in PageMaker, you can draw and fill a box behind the type.

PageMaker-created boxes and ovals can be either transparent or opaque. Choose a fill of "None" to create a transparent graphic, any other fill for opaque. Remember that since PostScript uses what's called a "nontransparent ink principle," any fill is opaque. Even if you use only a 10 percent fill or one of the more open patterns, anything behind it will be completely obscured. What you see on screen is what you get on paper (except when you're printing to non-PostScript printers with improperly written drivers).

PageMaker-drawn lines are always opaque. Even if you choose a multiple line or dashed line pattern, the white areas within the line are opaque—even if you reverse the line.

▼ Tip: White-out Boxes

We hesitate to even include this tip because we've been screwed up by it so many times. But sometimes you need it. You can create a paper-colored, no-line box to cover up little glitches on the page or to hide master items.

It works, but as we've said already, don't do it unless there's no alternative. These little monsters hide on the page, waiting to bite your ankles and bury your face in toner. They also slow down display and printing because PageMaker has to draw the underlying items anyway, then draw the box over them.

You control the layer relationships between objects using the Bring to front and Send to back commands on the Element menu (Ctrl-F and Ctrl-B). You can't move items forward or back one layer at a time, however; it's all or nothing.

▼ Tip: Bringing Multiple Objects to Front

You can select several objects using the selection techniques described in Chapter 3, *Making PageMaker Mind*, and bring them all to the front. Their layer relationships to each other remain the same.

For the ultimate in layer control, check out the color pages in this book, which demonstrate ways to get around the nontransparent ink principle—using "Paper" filled boxes to selectively knock out and overprint layers for spot color overlays.

▼ Tip: Selecting Different Layers

You can select objects on different layers without having to use "Bring to front" or "Send to back." If you hold down the Ctrl key while you click the mouse, each click selects objects one layer closer to the page. This is handy for dealing with overlapping text boxes or thin lines drawn on nonprinting guides. The rule of thumb is: when you're having trouble selecting something, try holding down the Ctrl key when you click. You can combine Ctrl with the Shift key to multiple select items that are hidden behind other items.

Aside from basic layer control, and the Snap to rulers and Snap to guides features, we have to say that PageMaker does not offer very robust tools for manipulating objects. There's no elegant way to move an object by a specified amount, for instance, group objects together into a combined object, or align objects automatically. Still, PageMaker provides the basics. And beyond the basics, there are always the workarounds.

PageMaker's Drawing Tools

The simplest way to add graphics to a PageMaker pub is to draw them with the tools in the Toolbox. As we mentioned in Chapter 3, *Making PageMaker Mind,* at Aldus these objects are called LBOs (again, it's pronounced "elbows")—lines, boxes, and ovals. We've seen some amazing logos and graphics that have been created with nothing but LBOs. If you want to see some face-melting examples, check out the images that Ole created for the color pages in this book.

Lines and Fills

You can assign various attributes to PageMaker's LBOs. Lines can have various line weights, patterns, and colors. White boxes and ovals can have both line attributes and fills (None, Paper, Solid, several tint percentages, and some weird fill patterns that some people like, for some reason). LBOs can have any color you've defined applied to them. We do the whole rundown on colors, fills, and patterns in Chapter 7, *Color.* (Remember: grays are colors, too, so that chapter is worth reading even if you're creating black-and-white pubs.)

Bear in mind that you can't control the line style and line weight independently in PageMaker. Either you use a dashed line or a one-point line; you can't specify a one-point dashed line. Also, you're limited to the line weights and fills that are on the menu. You can't get a 50 percent fill, for instance, or a 5-point line. Sorry, no workarounds this side of importing lines and fills from a drawing program.

▼ Tip: Use Recorder to Select Lines and Fills

Set up the Windows Recorder accessory to quickly choose lines and fills. You can create a macro and assign it to a function key to quickly assign both line and fill attributes to the currently selected object (Figure 5-1).

Figure 5-1
Using Recorder to select lines and fills

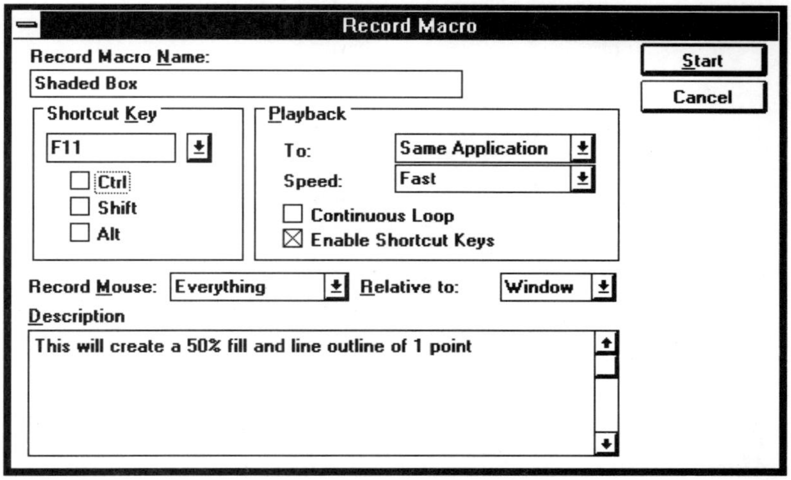

▼ Tip: Custom Gray Fills

You may have noticed that there aren't many choices of tints in PageMaker's Shades menu. It's missing some standard ones, like 25 and 50 percent, not to mention odd ones like 33. If you want to specify a gray percentage explicitly, follow these steps (Figure 5-2).

1. Select "Define colors" from the Element menu and create a new color called Gray33, or something similar.
2. Choose the CMYK color model, and specify 33 percent black, with zero in the other text edit boxes.
3. Use this color with the Solid fill when you want 33 percent gray.

This works great as long as you're producing a one- or four-color pub, but not for spot color overlays. For more on fills, shades, and tints, see Chapter 7, *Color*.

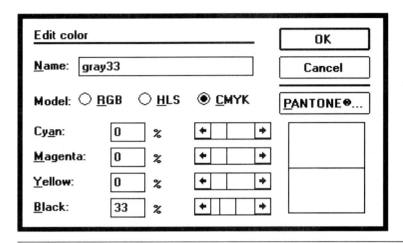

Figure 5-2
Creating new shades of gray with Define colors

Finally, you can't apply colors to an LBO's lines and fills independently. Nor can you specify a percentage for lines unless you apply a color. If you want a box to have a 20 percent fill and a 50 percent line, or a green fill and a blue line, you have to stack two identical objects with different attributes on top of each other (Figure 5-3).

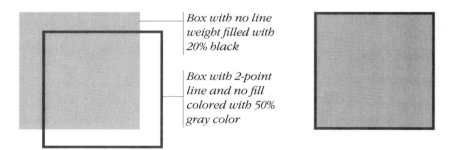

Figure 5-3
Stacking objects with different attributes

Box with no line weight filled with 20% black

Box with 2-point line and no fill colored with 50% gray color

Precise Line Positioning

When you draw a horizontal or vertical line in PageMaker—let's say you use a 4-point line weight—you may wonder whether the 4-point weight goes above or below the line (or to the right or left with vertical lines). The answer? It's your choice. Change your line weight to something heavy—four points or above—and drag out some lines.

Notice how you can pull the weight of the line to either side of the line you are drawing (see Figure 5-4). PageMaker doesn't "stroke" horizontal and vertical lines equally on either side as you might expect if you're familiar with PostScript or most drawing programs. It puts everything on one side or the other. If you've drawn a thin horizontal line, choosing a heavier weight from the Line submenu adds the extra weight below the existing line; vertical lines get thicker to the right.

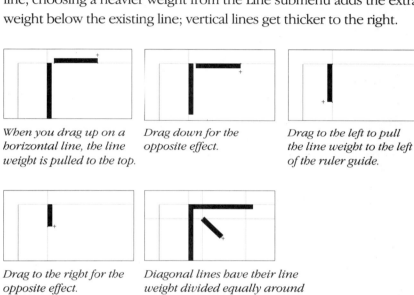

Figure 5-4
Lines positioned relative to ruler guides

When you drag up on a horizontal line, the line weight is pulled to the top.

Drag down for the opposite effect.

Drag to the left to pull the line weight to the left of the ruler guide.

Drag to the right for the opposite effect.

Diagonal lines have their line weight divided equally around an imaginary centerline.

Boxes and ovals are also stroked on one side only. PageMaker always adds the line weight toward the inside, so your box stays the same size even when you make the line heavier. The inside of the box, naturally, gets smaller. With diagonal lines, PageMaker divides the line's weight equally on either side of an imaginary center line.

Line positioning is important when you're aligning objects to grids. With perpendicular lines, PageMaker snaps to either the top or the bottom (or left or right side) of the line. With diagonal lines, PageMaker snaps to the center of the line.

▼ *Tip: Positioning Thick Diagonal Lines*

If you want diagonal lines—especially thick ones—to end at an exact position, you need to decide what part of the line you want to end where. If you want the corner of the line to end at a given point, turn "Snap to guides" (under the Options menu) off and position the line ending visually (use the 400% view). If you want the center of the line to end at a given point, use "Snap to guides."

Constraining LBOs

Using the Shift key, you can draw, move, and scale PageMaker-drawn objects within perpendicular and proportional constraints. Hold down the Shift key to constrain lines to 45-degree angles—whether you're drawing them or moving an end. When you're moving an object, holding down Shift constrains movement to horizontal or vertical. Shift also constrains ovals and rectangles to circles and squares.

One thing that drives us crazy in PageMaker is the way proportional scaling works (or actually, doesn't work) with PageMaker-drawn ovals and rectangles. If you draw a rectangle then grab it by a corner and Shift-drag to size it, it doesn't size proportionally; it turns into a square and then sizes proportionally. It's because PageMaker thinks of its rectangles as nonproportional squares. We're happy to say that it does maintain the line weights you've specified; they aren't scaled along with the graphic.

▼ *Tip: Sizing LBOs proportionally*

If you've drawn an oval or rectangle in the shape you want, and want to size it proportionally, try this. Draw a diagonal line through two corner handles to serve as a guide when you resize the graphic. Then (without holding down Shift) drag the corner of the graphic, positioning it visually on the line you've drawn as a guide (Figure 5-5).

Figure 5-5
Scaling LBOs proportionally

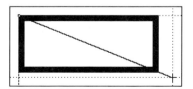

Draw a line between opposite corners.

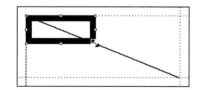

Drag one corner along the line to scale proportionally.

You can also create the rectangle in a draw or paint program, paste or place the rectangle, then size it proportionally. Remember, though, when sizing graphics that aren't LBOs, that line weights scale along with the rest of the graphic.

Pasting Graphics From the Clipboard

At first glance, pasting objects in PageMaker 4 works the same as in previous versions of the program—objects copied or cut to the Clipboard are pasted to the center of the screen. With PageMaker 4, though, you can power paste (Ctrl-Shift-P) objects into exactly the position they were cut or copied from (see "Paste" in Chapter 3, *Making PageMaker Mind*).

You can also change page views and turn pages before you press Ctrl-Shift-P, and the graphic will land in the same position on the page. You can even copy an item, close the publication that you copied it from, open a different pub, and paste the item into exactly the same position in that pub.

Placing Graphics

While creating graphics with PageMaker's LBO tools may be the easiest method, more often than not you'll need graphics that surpass the awe-inspiring powers of these tools. At that point, you'll want to use the Place command to bring in graphics created with other graphics applications.

Placed graphics can be resized, moved, copied, and pasted, just like PageMaker-drawn LBOs. One interesting limitation: PageMaker will not allow you to size any imported graphic so that it is smaller than 3 points in any dimension.

Even if you're placing an EPS line that's one-half point tall in Corel Draw, it will place with two-and-one-half points of extra space around it. LBOs, on the other hand, can be sized down to a quarter point in any dimension.

Bitmaps and Objects

Before we go any farther, we need to explain about the different kinds of graphics and file types that PageMaker can handle. (If you know this already, feel free to skip it.) The first important distinction is between bitmapped and object-oriented graphics.

Bitmapped graphics are matrixes of pixels, or dots. You create bitmapped graphics with paint programs, screen capture programs, and scanners. The dots can be black and white, they can have shades of gray, or they can be in color. The white background of black-and-white bitmaps can be either transparent or opaque, but it's usually transparent. The background of gray and color bitmaps is always opaque. Black-and-white bitmaps are sometimes called *bilevel* or *paint-type* graphics, to distinguish them from gray-scale bitmaps. Since black-and-white bitmaps and gray-scale/color bitmaps behave differently, it's important to know what type of bitmapped graphics file you're working with.

Object-oriented graphics are collections of objects—circles, squares, complex curved paths, and blocks of type. Objects are created with PageMaker's drawing tools, or with object-oriented draw programs like Corel Draw or Micrografx Designer, or business graphics programs like Harvard Graphics. The objects can contain black and white, shades of gray, or color. Bear in mind also that an object-oriented graphic can contain bitmapped graphics as objects. The backgrounds of object-oriented graphics can be either transparent or opaque, depending on the fill specified for the objects.

File Types

DOS-based personal computers run applications that create a bewildering variety of text and graphics formats. Applications, including PageMaker, distinguish between these file formats by the last three letters of a file name—its extension. File extensions tell PageMaker how to place the file (as text, as a graphic, and so on). File types PageMaker knows how to place appear in the file listing in the Place file dialog box, whereas files PageMaker doesn't know how to place are not displayed, so it's a good idea to give your graphics files (and text files, for that matter) the correct file extension when you create them.

Formats and Filters

PageMaker manages to place all the files it can by means of "filters"—actually little miniprograms that it invokes to interpret various kinds of files. If you don't have the proper filter installed, you can't read the corresponding file type. For more on installing filters, see "Installing Import and Export Filters" in Chapter 3, *Making PageMaker Mind*.

▼ *Tip: When You Can't See a File You Know Is There*

If a file that you want to place doesn't appear in the Place file dialog box, it might have a file extension that PageMaker doesn't recognize. Either you don't have the filter installed, or PageMaker doesn't recognize the file extensions. If you named a scanned image scan.xyz, for example, it wouldn't show up. Either rename the file or enter *.* in the Name area of the Place file dialog box and click OK. PageMaker displays all the files in the current directory. Select your file and press Enter.

If the Do not know how to place file dialog box appears at this point, select the correct graphic format from the list. If selecting the correct format doesn't work, try a different one. This shouldn't work, and probably won't, but we've seen it save the day on a couple of occasions. This is called "witch-doctoring."

Bitmapped Graphics

PageMaker knows how to import three different bitmapped graphics formats—PCX, TIFF, and PNT.

PCX. PCX files are bitmapped graphics that may be bilevel, color or, more rarely, gray-scale. PageMaker can import monochrome and bi-level but not gray-scale PCX images. The ability to import color PCX files is new with PageMaker 4; version 3 converted them to monochrome. Many scanners create PCX files, as does Paintbrush, the paint program supplied with Windows.

TIFF. TIFF (extension .TIF) stands for Tagged Image File Format. It's a standard bitmap file format that is supposedly the same for different programs on different computers. In fact, there is a lot of variety in TIFF files; various programs create them slightly differently, so you can't always be sure that another program will be able to read them. PageMaker is about the best program around at reading different programs' TIFF files—not surprisingly, since Aldus was central to promulgating this format.

Bitmaps in TIFF format can be black-and-white, gray-scale, or color (it's the format of choice for color and gray-scale scans). There are also compressed and uncompressed versions of the format, which can often be created by scanners or paint programs. Since PageMaker can place compressed TIFF files, you might as well compress them with your application and reap the reward of more disk space. The trade-off is speed; PageMaker must decompress the files every time you print.

PNT. .PNT is the file extension that PageMaker expects when placing MacPaint-format files created on the Macintosh by bitmap paint programs such as MacPaint. These black-and-white files were created at 72 dpi (dots per inch) and sometimes show up in the form of Macintosh screen shots or clip-art images.

Object-oriented Graphics

Earlier versions of PageMaker ran under Windows 2.x, and placing large object-oriented, or *vector* files, was often frustrated by the limitations of Windows itself. Version 3 of Windows largely eliminates the error messages and hung systems that resulted from working with such files in PageMaker, although really huge object-oriented files may still cause problems. There's not much you can do in this case, except return to the originating application and export the image as a series of smaller files. PageMaker has filters for a wide variety of object-oriented graphics formats.

CGM. The CGM (Computer Graphics Metafile) format is commonly used as a way to move files from Harvard Graphics or Lotus Freelance to PageMaker in non-PostScript environments. The CGM format is rather loosely defined, so different applications produce a wide variety of variations on a theme. Fonts in CGM files often degrade when brought into PageMaker, with curves rendered as polygons.

When you're importing a CGM file, hold down the Shift key while clicking OK in the Place file dialog box to specify import options (Figure 5-6). These stay in effect during a PageMaker session, so you only have to set them once if you're bringing in a number of files.

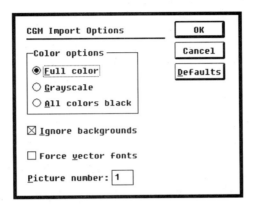

Figure 5-6
The CGM Import Dialog Box

- Color options. Use full color when you're working with color monitors and printers, gray-scale when you're printing to a laser printer or imagesetter. Select the All colors black option when you're importing graphics that have been colored white.
- Ignore backgrounds. As you'd expect, "Ignore backgrounds" ignores the graphic's background on import. This comes in handy when you've created an opaque background behind a graphic, but want the placed CGM file to have a transparent background.
- Force vector fonts. If you check "Force vector fonts," any rotated type is rendered as a bitmap in the imported graphic. If you leave this option unchecked, PageMaker rotates any rotated type in the image back to horizontal.
- Picture number. If the CGM file contains more than one graphic, enter the number of the graphic you want here.

PIC. The .PIC extension is used both by General Parametrics' Video-Show presentation system and by Lotus 1-2-3 (and compatibles) for charts and graphs. Though they have the same extension, the file formats are totally different.

To import Videoshow PIC files, you must have both the CGM and the VideoShow (NAPLPS) filters installed. Holding down Shift when clicking on OK in the Place file dialog box brings up a dialog box similar to the one for CGM imports, except that "Picture number" is replaced with "Text alignment tolerance." Use this setting to accurately align text in imported files. A value of *0* centers text in the bounding box created by the NAPLPS application, while a negative value will keep the original alignment. You'll have to experiment with different values until the text comes in properly aligned.

The Lotus PIC filter must be separately installed (see "Installing Import and Export Filters" in Chapter 3, *Making PageMaker Mind*). Text in these files is given the generic sans serif font in PageMaker, with the graph titles bold and the rest normal. You'll generally obtain better results by setting the text in PageMaker, rather than Lotus. Note that resizing elements containing hatching patterns also resizes the space between the lines of the hatch.

IMA. The .IMA extension is used primarily by Zenographics' Mirage presentation system. It uses a filter that differs only slightly from CGM. If you're using a PostScript printer, PageMaker substitutes Times Roman and Helvetica for the Roman and Swiss fonts it finds in the graphic.

PLT. The .PLT extension denotes graphics printed to disk as HPGL (Hewlett-Packard Graphics Language). You can also import AutoCAD drawings into PageMaker by plotting to an ADI driver, selecting "binary" as the plotter output format. Either all or part of a drawing can then be printed to disk, creating a file with a .PLT extension. Since all elements will consist of straight-line segments, text is usually better created in PageMaker.

WMF. Windows Metafile (or Windows GDI metafile), extension .WMF, is Window's internal format. It can include text, object oriented graphics, and bitmaps as objects. Both Micrografx Designer and Corel Draw can export to this format. Use it if you're using either of those programs, and aren't printing to a PostScript printer (if you're using PostScript, use EPS).

EPS. Encapsulated PostScript (EPS) files come in two basic varieties—with and without screen representations. Straight EPS files are just PostScript code (ASCII text) that follows conventions defined by Adobe. You can place these files on a page, and all you'll see is a gray box with filename, date, and creator (see Figure 5-7), but they'll print correctly when you send them to a PostScript printer. A typical example is an EPS file created by printing a PageMaker publication to disk.

Figure 5-7
A straight PostScript file placed as a graphic

EPS graphics can also contain a bitmapped screen representation, sometimes called a header. Viewable EPS files let you see a graphic on the page, while all the PostScript code is there for printing purposes. The header can add considerably to file size. In Corel Draw, for example, when you export a file you're given the option of creating a header and specifying its display resolution. Lower the resolution or drop the header entirely if the file won't import into PageMaker.

EPS is the format of choice for object-oriented graphics, as long as you don't have to edit the graphics, and as long as you're using PostScript output. Once a file is in EPS format you can count on it to print reliably, but with a couple of exceptions you can't change the contents this side of editing the PostScript code. Don't save bitmaps (particularly those you've created using a scanner) as EPS; EPS-format bitmap files are huge (use TIFF instead). And of course, you can't print the high-resolution PostScript version unless you have a PostScript printer. You'll just get the low-resolution bitmapped screen rendition.

There is one other subclass of EPS—Illustrator-format EPS. It's the format that was used by Adobe Illustrator 1.1 on the Mac. You could call it editable EPS, because several programs, including Illustrator and

Corel Draw, let you open and edit these files. As with normal EPS, there are viewable and nonviewable varieties.

Creating EPS Graphics with PageMaker

If you're using a PostScript printer, you can make use of the ability of Windows 3 to print a page of your publication to an EPS file, which can then be brought back into PageMaker with the Place command.

You can use this technique to turn text into a graphic that can be stretched or resized beyond the built-in limitations of PageMaker's text handling abilities. You can also group objects together, such as collections of LBOs, or create entire pages of text and graphics that can be imported as needed. You can print some text as an EPS file, place it, combine it with graphic elements such as rules and then print the entire group to a file. Instant logo! Figure 5-8 gives an idea of some of the possibilities.

Figure 5-8
Stretching Text

To create an EPS print file, you change the PostScript printer setup. Select Print from the File menu and click on the Setup button. Then click on the Options button, select Encapsulated PostScript File and enter a name for your print file, giving it the extension .EPS (but first see the tip below). In the Margins area, select "None." In the Header section, select "Already Downloaded." This header is the code Page-Maker sends to the printer before sending actual page information:

there's no need to include this in the EPS file, since PageMaker sends it before printing the page on which the EPS file is located.

▼ Tip: Don't Name Your EPS Files—Yet

When making EPS files in the Options dialog box, ignore the text box for the filename. It only allows you nineteen characters for the path and filename. Moreover, if you forget to change the name afterward, your next EPS file will overwrite the first (mainly because the name you type in stays there forever, or at least until the end of your Windows session).

Instead, leave the text edit box blank, click OK, and go ahead as usual. PageMaker prompts you for a filename before printing a file to disk. Not only can you type a longer path and filename in this text edit box, but it also relieves you of the need to change the filename each time. Besides, it's easier.

Click on OK and print the page containing your text or graphics, then import the resulting PostScript file with the Place command. The resulting page-size gray box contains a terse description in the top left corner. It's a movable, resizable graphic that represents not just the elements on the page we printed, but the entire page. It's a weakness of the Windows PostScript printer driver that it can neither create EPS files containing just selected objects on the page, nor a screen preview. A few more steps are necessary to make this process truly useful.

First, print out the original page containing the elements that you want to turn into EPS graphics. Then run the Windows Notepad editor (in the Accessories group) or Write, if the file is too large for Notepad, and open the EPS file you just created. Welcome to the heady realm of PostScript programming. The beginning of the little program, which describes the elements on your page, is composed of comments, indicated by percentage signs.

To make it easier to position our EPS graphic in PageMaker, we need to create a more accurate border, or "bounding box," that more accurately reflects the graphic's true size. This is the tricky part. On the printout of the page, measure the location of the lower-left and top-right corners of the smallest box that could enclose your graphic. Measure in points the distance from the left edge of the page to the left edge of this imaginary box, from the bottom of the page to the bottom of the box, from the left of the page to the right of the box and finally, from the bottom of the page to the top of the box (Figure 5-9).

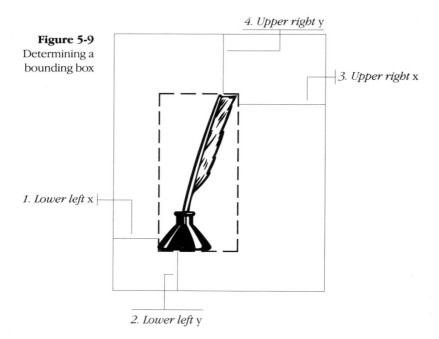

Figure 5-9
Determining a bounding box

This gives you four values, which you should enter in place of the 0 0 612 792 values following %%Bounding Box. Only one step remains. Delete the letters EJ, which will be near the end of the page. Failure to do this will cause the EPS graphic to print on its own page. Now save the changes you've made in Notepad, return to PageMaker and Place the file again. It should be in a bounding box that more accurately reflects its shape. You can move and resize it as you want.

Of course, with a little PostScript programming finesse, you can make changes to EPS files and create fancy type effects, rotations and fills. Before such tools as Corel Draw showed up on the PC, this was the only way to generate these kinds of effects, and programming directly in PostScript still has its uses. There are many books on

PostScript available for those who want to explore this more deeply (we recommend *Learning PostScript: A Visual Approach* by Ross Smith, from Peachpit Press). There are also specialized programs for developing your code, such as PSPlot (Legend Communications), and others that also provide a screen preview, such as GoScript (LaserGo).

▼ Tip: Creating Your Own EPS Graphics

To create your own PostScript code and place it as a graphic, you just need to add a few comment lines to the top of the file, as follows.

```
%!PS-Adobe-2.0
%%Title: My EPS Graphic
%%Creator: Me
%%CreationDate: 6-27-1990, 7:49:27
%%BoundingBox: 0 0 612 792
```

▼ Tip: Extracting EPS Files

If you need to get at an EPS graphic for some reason, but don't have the original EPS file, you can extract it from your publication by printing the page containing the EPS file to disk as a PostScript file, then extracting the EPS files from the PostScript text file with a text editor (Figure 5-10).

1. Print the PageMaker file to disk as discussed in Chapter 6, *Printing*.
2. Open the PostScript file with a text editor (Windows Write is handy for this).
3. Search for %!PS-Adobe to find the first line of the placed EPS file. You can probably identify the graphic by looking at the %%Title: line.
4. Select all of the text from the start of the first line of the EPS file through the last line of that file that begins with %%. To locate the end of the EPS section, search for %%Trailer, or %%EOF, or perhaps %%EndDocument. It varies depending on what program created the EPS file.

Figure 5-10
Extracting an EPS graphic from PageMaker-written PostScript

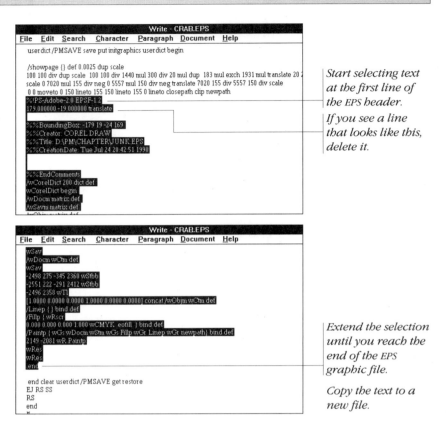

5. Copy the selection, then paste it into another file.

6. Save the file as text-only.

If you notice something like 20.000000 145.000000 translate immediately preceding the line beginning with %%BoundingBox at the start of the file, delete the whole line—the numbers and the word translate. PageMaker adds this line to EPS files when you place them, and you don't need to have them in the extracted file.

Back to Placing

If you've selected a graphic on your page, the Place file dialog box provides you with a number of options (Figure 5-11). Choose the option you want, and click on OK. If you want to bypass all the options and place as an independent graphic, or if no graphic was selected on your page, just double-click on the file name. PageMaker loads the place gun with the selected file. Different graphic file types produce different guns (Figure 5-12).

Figure 5-11
Place options for graphics

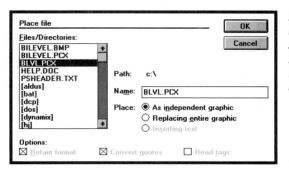

If you have the Pointer tool selected when you select a graphic file in the Place dialog box, the As independent graphic option becomes active.

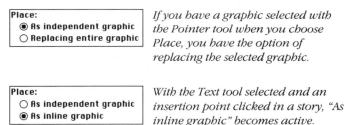

If you have a graphic selected with the Pointer tool when you choose Place, you have the option of replacing the selected graphic.

With the Text tool selected and an insertion point clicked in a story, "As inline graphic" becomes active.

Figure 5-12
Loaded graphic place guns

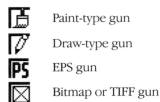

Paint-type gun

Draw-type gun

EPS gun

Bitmap or TIFF gun

Position the pointer where you want the upper-left corner of the graphic to appear, and click the mouse button to place the graphic on the page. You can also drag-place it—hold down the mouse button and drag to the approximate size you want the graphic.

You'd think that holding down the Shift key while drag-placing a graphic would constrain it proportionally, but it doesn't. It doesn't do anything, in fact. Neither does holding down Ctrl when drag-placing cause a magic stretch (discussed later in this chapter). If you try to drag-place an object to a size smaller than 3 points in any dimension, the graphic places at full size.

▼ Tip: Extending your Range of Fills with EPS Graphics

We commented earlier in this chapter that PageMaker has a limited number of percentage fills on the Fill menu. Here's a workaround. You can store a set of EPS, CGM, or WMF files created with a draw program (or with PostScript, coded from scratch), each file containing only a borderless, filled box. Such fills are also sold by a variety of software publishers. The boxes could contain gray tints, graduated fills, radial fills, or PostScript fills. You can size the placed EPS graphics without distorting the fill, and set them to any PageMaker color.

If you need a box with a 25 percent blue tint (you want the 25 percent screen to print on the blue spot color overlay), place an EPS object with a 25 percent screen, size it, and apply the color blue. Use the same placed file to produce a 25 percent black box (that prints on the black spot color overlay) by copying and pasting the box and applying the color black.

Replacing Graphics

Some people like to put graphics onto a page temporarily—in templates, for instance—then replace them with the final graphics when those are ready. If you have a graphic selected when you choose Place (Ctrl-D), the "Replacing entire graphic" option appears in the Place file dialog box.

When you replace the graphic, different things happen depending on the file type of the graphic you're replacing. If you're replacing a placed graphic, the replacing graphic is scaled and cropped to match the original graphic. If you're replacing an LBO, the incoming graphic is scaled to match the LBO, but not cropped.

Sometimes you won't be able to see the new graphic because it's hidden within the scaling and cropping confines of the old. In this case, pan or uncrop the image until you see as much of it as you want. (For more information on panning and cropping, see "Cropping Placed Graphics" later in this chapter).

PageMaker-drawn squares and rectangles replace perfectly, but are rarely the proportions of the art you want to place. You can, at that point, hold down Shift and click on one of the graphic's corner handles to restore the graphic to its original proportions. But if you'd wanted to do that, why would you have chosen to replace the rectangle in the first place?

The bottom line? Use "Replace" when you are replacing graphics with an updated version of the same image (you can also use "Link info"). It works very well. Don't expect it to perfectly scale and crop an imported graphic into the space held by a PageMaker-drawn placeholder, though. You'll have to hold down Shift and drag a corner handle of a replacing graphic to restore it to its original proportions, then crop as needed. Placeholders imported from a graphics program have the same problems—incoming graphics are stretched to fit the dimensions of the placeholder.

Don't bother trying to replace circles, ovals, and diagonal lines (PageMaker-drawn or imported); you'll just get a square or a rectangle. Replacing PageMaker-drawn horizontal and vertical lines is lots of fun, but we've yet to find a use for it (remember, an imported graphic is always at least three points tall, even if it's replacing a hairline rule). Any ideas?

▼ Tip: Replacing LBOs with EPS Shades

Actually, there's a bright side to PageMaker's stretching of imported graphics when you're replacing LBOs. If you want a 50 percent gray box, you can just draw a box the size you want in PageMaker, then replace it with an EPS box that has a fill of 50 percent. It comes in just the size of your PageMaker-drawn box, but with the percentage fill specified in the drawing program. (See "Extending Your Range of Fills with EPS Graphics" earlier in this chapter.)

Aha, you're thinking—you could replace PageMaker-drawn lines with gray patterns and get gray lines of any percentage. Sorry. Lines replaced with EPS graphics always pop out to 3 points—PageMaker's minimum size for imported graphics.

▼ Tip: Replacing Paint-type Graphics

If you're working with lots of paint-type graphics (like the screen shots in this book), select and drag the bitmaps to the upper-left corner of the page in your paint program. This way, each graphic you place and replace will have the same upper-left point of origin, and you won't have to pan or crop graphics as often. Figure 5-13 shows how this can be a problem.

Figure 5-13
Replacing paint-type graphics

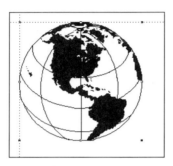 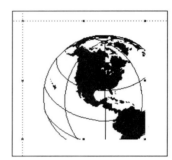

What happens when replacing images aren't in the same location in the bitmap file.

Even better, crop the image to exactly the size you want before you save it.

Working with Bitmaps

As we explained above, there are several different kinds of bitmapped images. Bitmaps can have any resolution, and they can just have black and white dots, or include gray shades or color. There are several tools in PageMaker specifically for working with bitmaps, and the tools work in different ways depending on the type of bitmap you're working with. We've already discussed several methods for scaling bitmaps, but PageMaker also lets you control the appearance of bitmaps, both on screen and on printout.

Image Control

You can adjust the brightness, contrast, screen frequency, screen angle, and halftone cell shape of bitmapped images you place in PageMaker by selecting a bitmapped graphic and choosing "Image control" from the Elements menu (Figure 5-14). Note that you can't select multiple bitmaps and then select "Image control"; you have to select and modify each one individually. Changes you make to the settings in Image control won't show up on screen until you click on OK. Even then, subtle changes won't be evident until you print the page.

Figure 5-14
Image control dialog box

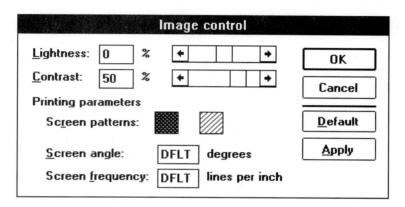

Note that when you replace one bitmapped image with another, the replacing image takes on the "Image control" settings of the original graphic.

▼ Tip: Image Control Settings for Gray-scale Images

Gray-scale images are tricky, and it takes a good deal of experience to predict what will come off a laser printer or imagesetter based on what you see on screen. If you're working with scanned 8-bit images, you'll usually get better results if you set your scanner's brightness and contrast settings to their midpoints and follow your scanner manufacturer's recommendations for the settings in Image control.

▼ Tip: Improving Bitmapped Clip Art

Bitmapped clip art often looks a lot better if you mute it a bit by graying it out (Figure 5-15). Decrease lightness and/or contrast until the black pixels are gray.

Figure 5-15
Remapping grays

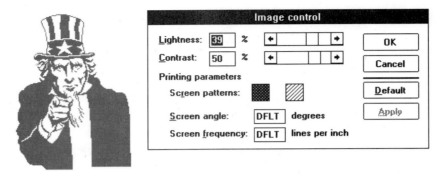

You can use a scanned image or other bitmap as a background for a page or part of a page by dimming it to near invisibility by adjusting its lightness and contrast. Then build your page on top of it.

If you use many screen shots, you can make them look better by giving the white pixels a slight gray tint, and muting the black pixels a little to a dark gray. There are a couple of problems, though.

First, you must have perfectly cropped screen shots, or the gray outside the screens will show up. Fortunately, because the Image control dialog box lets you set lightness and contrast by the numbers, you can create a Recorder macro to consistently apply the same Image control values to any selected bitmap.

▼ *Tip: Making Bitmaps Negative*

To make a bitmap flip from positive to negative, just select the bitmap, bring up the Image control dialog box, and type *-100* in the Contrast text edit box (Figure 5-16). The Macintosh version of PageMaker has a nifty icon to do this, but this works just as well.

Figure 5-16
Making a bitmap negative

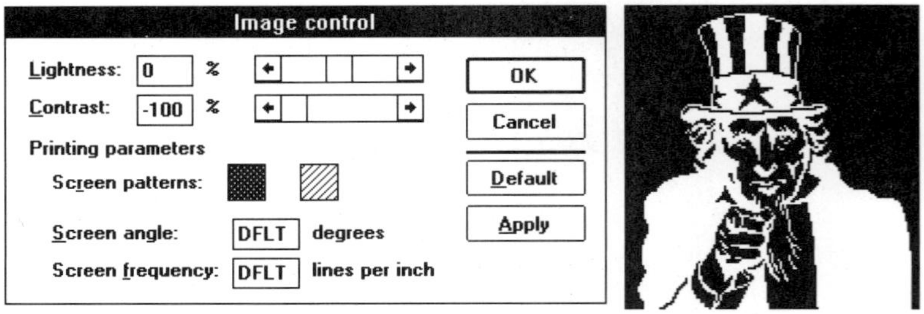

Displaying Bitmapped Graphics

In the Preferences dialog box under "Detailed graphics," you'll see three options for displaying graphics: Gray out, Normal, and High resolution. Here's what these options mean.

Gray out. PageMaker displays gray boxes instead of placed graphics. PageMaker-drawn graphics are displayed normally. Gray out is the fastest display mode.

Normal. Page Maker displays LBOs, EPS files, object-oriented graphics, and bitmaps with small file sizes in a normal manner. For large bitmapped graphics PageMaker creates and displays a lower-resolution screen image, with a pointer to the high-resolution version on disk. (You can control this when you import bitmaps; PageMaker gives you the option of including a copy in the pub, or just keeping a link to the full image file.)

The Normal display mode is basically the same as in previous versions of PageMaker.

High-resolution. PageMaker displays bitmapped images at their full resolution. This can take a long time, so only use it when you want to impress clients (and remember to get it set up before they come in the room, or they'll just stand there tapping their feet).

In High-resolution mode, if PageMaker cannot find the original graphic file, it displays the normal resolution screen image. If a graphic does not seem to be displayed at high resolution, check the Links dialog box to see if PageMaker has lost track of the source file.

PageMaker's Detailed graphics display options have no effect on printing—just display.

▼ *Tip: Switching to High Resolution*

To see a bitmapped graphic at high resolution, hold down Ctrl as it starts to display. PageMaker displays the image at its full resolution, regardless of the setting for Detailed graphics, and continues to display the graphic at full resolution until the screen is redrawn.

Resizing Placed Graphics

The eight handles that appear around the edges of a selected graphic are used for resizing the graphic. The four handles that appear on the corners of the graphic resize the graphic diagonally, while the handles on the sides, top, and bottom resize it horizontally and vertically.

Hold down Shift while dragging a corner handle, and PageMaker retains the graphic's original proportions. PageMaker sizes all of the elements in placed graphics uniformly, including line weights.

▼ Tip: The Vanishing Point

Sometimes, PageMaker's sizing of EPS and draw-type graphics makes very fine lines disappear. Usually this happens if the graphic is very large when imported, then sized down so it is very small. Try to get your draw and EPS graphics fairly close to the size you want them before placing them in PageMaker.

Corel Draw, for example, has an option to retain line width while scaling, so you can scale graphics without approaching the vanishing point. Then save the scaled graphic, and place that in PageMaker.

▼ Tip: Resizing Graphics to a Mathematical Proportion of their Original Size

While we would very much like to see a feature in PageMaker that would resize graphics to a percentage you could enter in a dialog box, the following technique works pretty well.

1. Place the graphic.
2. Choose "Preferences" from the Edit menu, and choose "Inches decimal" for your Measurement system (you could also choose "Millimeters").
3. Drag the zero point to the upper-left corner of the graphic.
4. Measure the width of the graphic.
5. Multiply the width of the graphic by the percentage reduction (or enlargement) you want. If your graphic is 6-inches wide and you've specified an 80 percent reduction, you multiply 6 times .80.

6. Drag out a vertical ruler guide until it reaches the measure on the horizontal ruler you found in the preceding step. In our example, we would place the ruler guide at 4.8 inches.

7. Make sure that "Snap to guides" is on (Ctrl-U toggles it on and off), then hold down Shift, select the handle on the lower-right corner of the graphic, and resize the graphic until it snaps to the ruler guide.

This technique is fairly accurate, especially if you zoom to 400% view (Ctrl-4). In that view on a VGA monitor the ruler increments are every point, .5 millimeters, or 100th of an inch, depending on your Measurement system setting in the Preferences dialog box. In the next section, on "magic stretch," we demonstrate some techniques for scaling bitmapped graphics by percentages.

Magic Stretch

With black-and-white bitmaps, you often have to pay attention to the image resolution vis-a-vis printer resolution to avoid ugly patterns. This is a problem with any bitmap that contains regular, repeating patterns (like the dots in the scroll bars of placed screen shots of Windows applications), but it's especially bad with dithered, black-and-white scanned images. Few things make your publication look as bad as a dithered scan that's plagued by these plaid-like patterns, as shown in Figure 5-17.

Figure 5-17
Avoiding ugly patterns with magic stretch

Magic-stretched graphic. When the printer resolution and bitmap resolution have an integral relationship, you get good quality output.

Non-magic-stretched graphic. When the printer resolution and image resolution do not have an integral relationship, ugly patterns result.

The trick to avoiding these patterns is to make sure that the image resolution is some integral multiple (or divisor) of the printer resolution. That way you end up with one, or four, or nine printer dots for every dot in the image. If you don't have this integral relationship, there may be 6.4 printer dots for every image dot (see Figure 5-18), and a laser printer can't print four tenths of a dot. Something has to give, and what gives is image quality.

Figure 5-18
Integral and nonintegral relationships

An integral relationship between graphic and printer resolution. There's dot-for-dot equivalency.

When there's a nonintegral relationship, image quality degrades.

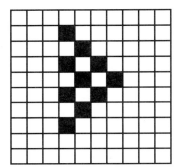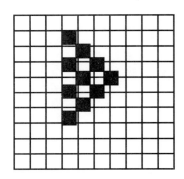

Image resolution is affected, of course, by scaling. If you reduce a 300-dpi image to 50 percent, you have a 600-dpi image. There are the same number of dots in half as much space. Since there's no percentage scaling in PageMaker, it could be tough getting the integral relationship you need—even if you could figure out what the scaling should be.

PageMaker provides an excellent solution, though, that most people call magic stretch. Hold down Ctrl while you size a bitmapped image, and it snaps to sizes that provide an integral relationship between image resolution and printer resolution. Magic stretch works with proportional stretching, so you can hold down Shift and Ctrl and size graphics both proportionally and to the printer's resolution at the same time.

Since there's no problem with patterns when sizing object-oriented graphics, holding down Ctrl has no effect when you're sizing them. Even bitmapped images in object-oriented graphics are not affected by magic stretch, even if the bitmap is the only item in the object-oriented file, because PageMaker thinks of these as object graphics.

▼ Tip: Use the Right Target Printer

PageMaker is able to do this magic stretch arithmetic for you because it knows the printer's resolution; it's defined in the printer driver. So if you want magic stretch to work right, you have to have the right printer selected. Graphics that you've magic stretched based on 300-dpi resolution will give you patterns if you print them at 1270 dpi (they'll work fine at 1200, though). So before you magic stretch, choose your final target printer (or one with the same resolution) by selecting "Print" from the File menu, clicking on "Setup" and choosing your printer from the list.

Note that you have many more choices of magic stretch sizes when you're printing to a high-res device, such as a Linotronic. That factor alone may make it worth printing your final output to an imagesetter.

▼ Tip: Changing Target Printers

Suppose you usually proof your work with an Apple LaserWriter II NT and print your final copies on a Linotronic 300. You could easily go crazy changing to the Linotronic 300 driver every time you want to magic stretch a graphic, and back to the LaserWriter II NT every time you want to print. To avoid this problem, create two macros with Windows Recorder and assign them to function keys to quickly select either device.

Cropping Placed Graphics

Cropping is pretty straightforward, and we don't have much to say about it that you don't probably already know. You probably already know, for instance, that you can't crop PageMaker LBOs—only placed graphics. To crop placed graphics, select the cropping tool, click on the graphic to select it, grab one of the handles (center the handle inside the cropping tool before you press the mouse button), and crop, as shown in Figure 5-19.

Figure 5-19
Cropping a graphic

Center the graphic's selection handle in the Cropping tool, press the mouse button...

...and drag to crop the image.

Once you've cropped a graphic to the size you want, you can move—or pan—the graphic inside the cropped area. To pan a cropped graphic, put the cropping tool right on top of the graphic, press down and drag. The cropping tool turns into a Grabber hand. Push the Grabber hand around without releasing the mouse button, and you'll see that the crop works sort of like a window, and you can move the graphic around behind that window (Figure 5-20). The whole graphic's still there; it's just masked out.

▼ Tip: Cropping a Placed Graphic Proportionally

If you need to proportionally crop a placed graphic, select it and drag vertical and horizontal guides through the midpoint of its handles on all four sides of the graphic (Figure 5-21). Then use the diagonal-line tool to draw a line between two opposing corner handles, using Snap

Figure 5-20
Panning an image

Position the Cropping tool over the image and hold down the mouse button. The Cropping tool changes into a Grabber hand.

Drag to change your view of the cropped image.

to guides to ensure the line is positioned precisely at the corners. Now select the cropping tool and crop the image, using the line as a guide.

Figure 5-21
Croppping an image proportionally

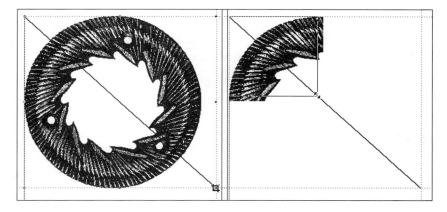

Draw a line from one corner of the image to the other. Position the Cropping tool over one of the image's corner handles and hold down the mouse button.

Drag the cropping tool along the line to crop proportionally.

▼ Tip: Cut, Don't Crop

Ordinarily, avoid cropping graphics. In particular, don't use the cropping tool to pull out just a tiny part of a large scanned image—for example, isolating one face from an enormous class reunion photo. Instead, use an image manipulation or paint program to save just the part of the scanned graphic you want. Or just scan the section you need to begin with, and save the disk space.

We've seen people place a 300-dpi, 256-gray-level TIFF image a dozen times on a page, crop it down and use little parts of it, and then look surprised when it wouldn't print. When you crop, you don't remove any part of the image. That's why you can uncrop it and move the image within the crop. The whole image remains in the publication (or linked to it, at least), and must be processed by the printer, whether you can see it or not.

▼ Tip: Colorizing Placed Graphics

Placed graphics can have PageMaker colors applied to them. If you're printing spot color separations, the graphic prints on the spot color overlay of the color that's been applied to it in PageMaker. If you're separating the publication with a process separation program like Publisher's Prism, the graphic prints using the colors specified in its originating graphics application (and/or according to any changes you make in the separation program).

Inline Graphics

The ability to place a graphic into a text block—to make an inline graphic—is one of PageMaker 4's most powerful new features. Commonplace in Windows word processors, this ability is now available in PageMaker, and it has been very nicely implemented.

Using inline graphics, you can anchor a graphic to a particular position in text so that the graphic moves with the text as the text reflows. The inline graphic acts just like another character in the text (with a few exceptions). The result? No more laborious reflowing of text blocks and repositioning of graphics to keep your graphics in the same position relative to text.

This is very handy for creating check boxes for forms, and creating enlarged initial caps and bullets. (If you want to keep your graphics in the same position on the page, you'll want to place or paste them as independent, or non-inline, graphics.)

There are a few ways to insert inline graphics into a story.

- Paste a graphic into the text as you would paste a text character.
- Place a text file that contains inline graphics.
- Place a graphic as inline at a text insertion point (using the option in the Place file dialog box). This works in either layout or story view (in story view you use "Import" instead of "Place").

Inline graphics that are wider than the width of the text block hang out of the text block to the right (whether they're aligned left, right, center, or justified).

Likewise, if a graphic is bigger than the leading of the line, it may hang off the top of the text block. We'll get to the leading issue below.

▼ Tip: Redraw Your Screen

Any time you're working with elements in a text block that extend beyond the edge of the text block, you need to redraw your screen fairly often. The easiest way to force PageMaker to redraw your screen is to choose the current page view (use the Page menu, or, better, use the keyboard shortcut for the page view—Ctrl-2 if you're at 200%, and so on). Or, click the right mouse button twice (once to change to a different view, and the second time to return to the current view).

Selecting and Modifying Inline Graphics

You can select inline graphics with either the Text tool or the Pointer tool, but the way you select them affects what you can do with them.

Select as text. If you select the inline graphic with the Text tool, you can cut, copy, paste, and apply text formatting commands just as if it were a character of text—with the following limitations.

- You cannot change the font, size, or type style.
- You cannot change the positioning of the graphic using the Superscript or Subscript options.

Choosing "Select all" with a text insertion point selects all of the text in the story—including the inline graphic *qua* text.

Select as object. If you select the graphic with the Pointer tool, the graphic behaves as any other, non-inline graphic—you can change line styles, corner styles, and color for LBOs; you can crop, resize, cut, copy, paste, and replace the inline graphic—with the following limitations.

- You cannot marquee-select or Shift-select an inline graphic using the Pointer tool. If you have other objects selected when you select an inline graphic with the Pointer tool, those objects are deselected and the inline graphic is selected. Choosing "Select all" from the Edit menu (Ctrl-A) while the Pointer tool is selected selects the text block containing the inline graphic, not the inline graphic individually.
- If you click on an inline graphic with the Pointer tool, you select only the inline graphic, not the text block containing the graphic. To select the text block (including the inline graphic), click on the text block or Ctrl-click through the inline graphic.
- You cannot apply text wrap to an inline graphic.
- You cannot use the Bring to front or Send to back commands on an inline graphic independent of the text block containing it.

Commands that affect the entire text block affect any inline graphics contained in the text block. If you cut, copy, or delete a text block, the inline graphics in the text block are cut, copied, or deleted. If you replace an entire story containing inline graphics, the inline graphics are replaced along with the rest of the text in the story. Resizing a text block doesn't resize the graphic, but may change the position of the graphic on the page; it depends on how the text reflows.

You can apply various text formatting commands to inline graphics—leading, leading method, kerning, tracking, word- and letter-spacing, and color. All the paragraph-level attributes (indents, Paragraph space Before and After, Alignment, Keep with next, Column break before, etc.) work with inline graphics.

In story view, inline graphics appear as icons embedded in the text (see Figure 5-22). You can cut, copy, paste, and delete these icons, and you'll see the repositioned graphics when you return to layout view.

Figure 5-22
Inline graphic icons in Story view

Inline graphics appear in Story view as icons which you can cut, copy, paste, and delete.

Layout view

Horizontal Positioning for Inline Graphics

Since inline graphics act like text characters, you can use most of the horizontal text adjustments to position them. You can center them in a text block, position them flush right, kern them to the left or the right relative to other characters, and use tabs to position them exactly.

▼ *Tip: Make Graphics Inline to Center Them*

It can be tough getting an independent graphic centered on a page or across a particular part of the page using the rulers and ruler guides. You measure and measure, and do all sorts of arithmetic, and still seem to come out just a little short on one side or another. If you make the graphic inline, on the other hand, PageMaker centers it for you.

1. Place or paste the graphic inline in a paragraph of its own.
2. Press Ctrl-Shift-C to choose centered alignment for the paragraph (make sure that there are no paragraph indents in effect).
3. Drag the text block out so that it stretches across the area in which you want to center the graphic.

The graphic is perfectly centered.

▼ **Tip: Incredible Horizontal Positioning Accuracy with Inline Graphics**

We've said that one-quarter-point accuracy is the best you can expect using the ruler guides, but there's a way to get finer horizontal positioning accuracy for graphics using tabs.

1. Make an inline graphic by pasting or placing a graphic into a text block. Make sure that the edges of the text block containing the inline graphic snap to the horizontal point you want to measure from.
2. Insert a tab in front of the graphic.
3. Press Ctrl-I to bring up the Indents/tabs dialog box.
4. Click to place a left-aligned tab on the ruler and, with the tab selected, type a value such as *0p6.1* in the text edit box to the right of the Tab action button.
5. Choose "Move tab" from the Tab action pop-up menu. The tab moves to 6.1 points on the tab ruler. Click on OK to close the dialog box.

The left edge of the graphic is now exactly 6.1 points from the left edge of the text block.

PICTURES **297**

▼ Tip: Precise Repeating Graphics

To position repeating graphics at exact positions, select a tab and choose "Repeat tab" from the Indents/tabs Tab action pop-up menu to repeat tabs along the ruler in precise increments (up to PageMaker's limit of forty tabs). Do not touch any of the tabs with the mouse cursor, or they will snap to the nearest full ruler increment. This trick comes in very handy if you're designing for measurement-intensive work such as instrument panel silk-screens, and need centering marks every 1.001 mm (though you might consider investing in FreeHand or a CAD program).

By the way, we wouldn't trust either of the last two tips for increments finer than $\frac{1}{1440}$ of an inch.

Leading for Inline Graphics

While you can place graphics inside a line of text—for symbols, complex dingbats, or company logos—probably the most common use of inline graphics is to create single paragraphs containing only the inline graphic (Figure 5-23). In either case, it's important to understand how the leading works; it's a little tricky.

Figure 5-23
Positioning inline graphics relative to text

Inline graphic within a paragraph

Inline graphic as its own paragraph

We cover leading in detail in Chapter 4, *Words*, but we'll reiterate here that if you want to know what's going on with the leading, you need to use the Proportional leading method, and specify the leading you want rather than relying on autoleading.

That said, here's how leading works with inline graphics: it's basically the same as leading for any text character, except that you can change the position of the baseline. Just grab the graphic with the Pointer tool and drag the graphic up and down. It may feel like you're moving the graphic, and that's essentially the result, but what you're really doing is shifting the position of the graphic's baseline—the graphic's vertical position relative to the rest of the line (Figure 5-24).

Figure 5-24
Adjusting the baseline of an inline graphic

When you drag an inline graphic, you're actually changing its position relative to the text baseline.

It takes a bit of experimentation to get the hang of how this adjustment works. Sometimes the graphic appears to pop back to its original position while the text around it reflows. Try moving the baseline of a few graphics until you develop a feel for what's going on. You cannot drag the baseline of a graphic above the top of the graphic's bounding box.

Since you're using proportional leading (of course), the baseline starts out two-thirds of the way down the graphic. Just as with any text character, one-third of the graphic falls below the baseline; two-thirds of the graphic fall above. When you drag the graphic down, you're actually moving the baseline up. This makes it easy to get small graphics inside a line of text looking right on the line. (You can't do that with text characters; you have to use sub- and superscript.)

▼ Tip: Using Autoleading with Inline Graphics

We know we told you never to use autoleading, and we meant it. But it seems that every time we make a hard-and-fast rule, we end up having to present an exception.

Here it is (Figure 5-25): if you have a paragraph style that will contain only inline graphics, using autoleading is the best way to keep the graphic from hitting lines of text above it or disappearing off the top of the page. PageMaker pushes preceding and succeeding lines out of the way as needed, and, since the paragraph contains only the graphic, you don't have to worry about having one oddly-leaded line.

Figure 5-25
Autoleading with inline graphics

When you place an inline graphic in a paragraph by itself, make the leading for that paragraph "Auto," and PageMaker will make the paragraph slug larger than the graphic. If "Autoleading" is set to the default 120% of type size, though, you'll get an indeterminate amount of space above and below the graphic.

Whoa, you're saying—isn't this going to throw us off our leading grid? How can we know where the baselines of text following the graphic are going to fall if we don't know the height of the graphic?

Simple. In the style you create for the inline graphic paragraph, turn on "Align to grid" in the Paragraph rules options dialog box, and set the grid to your body copy leading. You can count on ensuing lines aligning to the leading grid.

▼ Tip: Slugs the size of graphics

If you want a paragraph containing only a graphic to be exactly the height of the graphic, use autoleading, and set the autoleading percentage to *100* for the entire paragraph (Figure 5-26). The slug is now the same size as the graphic, and you can add space before and after the paragraph to make room for the graphic. You can make this an attribute for paragraph styles that contain only graphics.

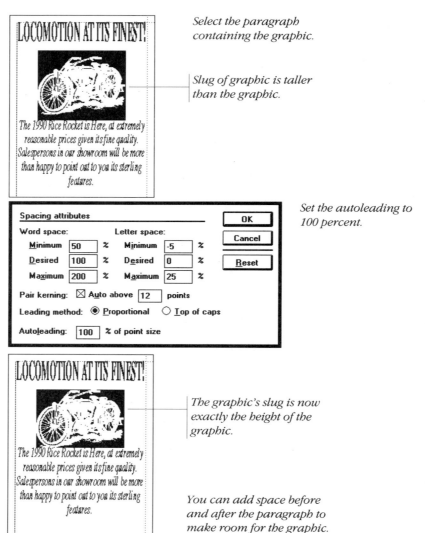

Figure 5-26
Slugs around inline graphics

Select the paragraph containing the graphic.

Slug of graphic is taller than the graphic.

Set the autoleading to 100 percent.

The graphic's slug is now exactly the height of the graphic.

You can add space before and after the paragraph to make room for the graphic.

▼ Tip: Boxed Paragraphs

You can create boxed paragraphs in PageMaker using inline graphics, as shown in Figure 5-27.

Figure 5-27
Creating boxed paragraphs

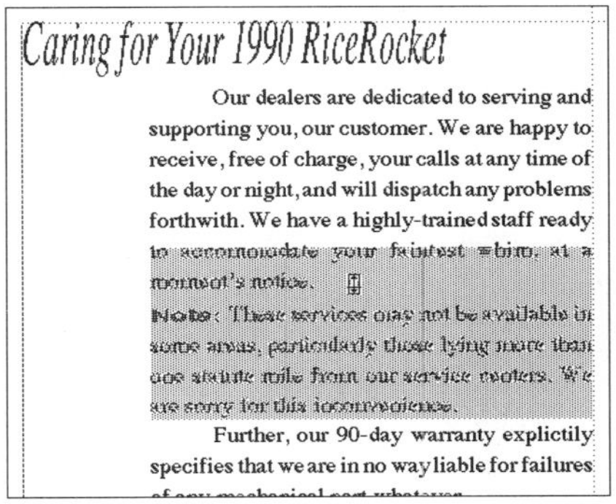

Create a shaded box and paste it in as its own paragraph, preceding the paragraph you want to box. Set the paragraph's leading to 1 (or some other small number) in the Type specifications dialog box.

In the Paragraph specifications dialog box, enter 1, 2, or 3 in the Keep with next text edit box. This glues the paragraph to the following paragraph.

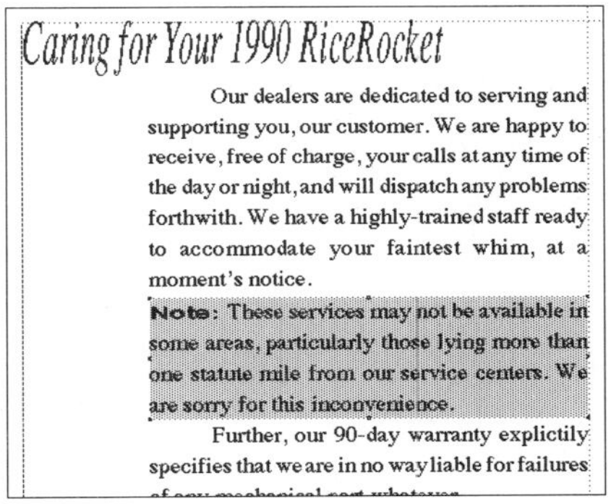

Adjust the baseline and size of the box so that it encompasses the paragraphs you want in the box.

The shaded box and paragraph will now stay together if the text reflows.

1. Create a paragraph immediately before the paragraph (or paragraphs) you want to place the box around.
2. Create a shaded box and paste it as an inline graphic into the paragraph you created in step 1.
3. Triple-click the paragraph containing the box and set its leading to some small leading value. You can use 0-point leading (unless the paragraph containing the inline graphic is at the top of the text block. If this is the case, you'll have to use at least .1 point of lead. Either way, the box falls behind the surrounding text. If you can't see the box, redraw the screen.

4. Adjust the baseline and size of the box so that it covers one or more of the paragraphs following.

5. Set the paragraph's Keep with next option to 3 to glue the paragraph containing the box to the following paragraph.

The box will move with the text as the text recomposes. Build this into a paragraph style, and boxed paragraphs are easy.

▼ *Tip: Hanging Inline Graphics in the Companion Column*

Many books and magazines these days have a design featuring a narrow column to the left of the page that contains headings and small graphics—usually called a companion column. The pages in this book, for example, feature an 8-pica-wide companion column on the left. You can use inline graphics and inline graphic baseline adjustment to hang graphics in the column on the left (Figure 5-28). It works much like normal hanging indents (see the tip "Use a Tab for Hanging Indents" in Chapter 4, *Words*). Make sure that the graphic's leading is the same as that of the text, and once again, refresh your screens often when using techniques of this sort.

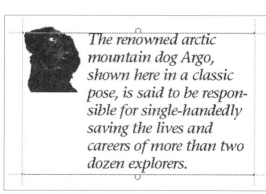

Figure 5-28
Hanging an inline graphic in the companion column

It may not look like it, but that doggie is the first character in the paragraph.

Using Text Wrap

We have serious qualms about using text wrap (it's slow and doesn't let you control the text positioning explicitly), but even we admit that there are a lot of situations when it comes in handy. There are a number of mind-boggling effects you can get with text wrap that you simply cannot get any other way, but purists feel it shouldn't be used for rectangular wraps.

You add text wrap to a graphic by selecting the graphic (or graphics; you can apply text wrap to any number of selected graphics) and choosing "Text wrap" from the Element menu. The Text wrap dialog box appears (Figure 5-29). As is usually the case in PageMaker, if you make changes in this dialog box with no graphic selected, you're changing the text wrap default for all graphics drawn or placed in that publication in the future.

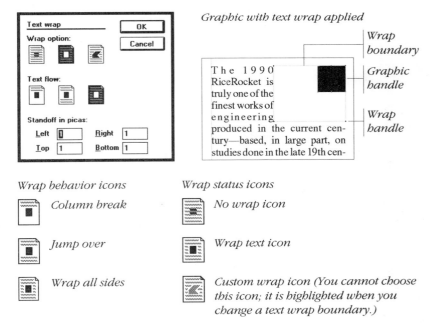

Figure 5-29
Text wrap dialog box

Once you've applied a wrap to a graphic, a text-wrap boundary appears around the selected graphic. You can adjust the boundary by pointing at a handle and dragging the handle to a new position, with Shift constraining the movement to horizontal or vertical. Or you can drag an entire boundary segment to a new position (Figure 5-30); again, Shift constrains the movement.

Figure 5-30
Adjusting a graphic wrap boundary

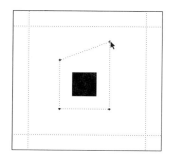

Drag one of the wrap handles to create an irregular wrap.

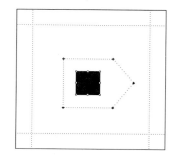

Click on a wrap segment to add a wrap handle.

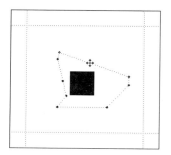

Drag a boundary segment to adjust a wrap.

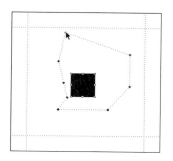
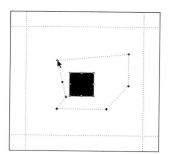

Drag one handle over another to delete a handle.

Finally, you can add wrap handles with a quick click on the wrap boundary. This lets you create very weird irregular wraps. If you end up with too many handles, just drag one on top of another, and they combine into one handle. If the wrap gets too crazy, and you'd like to start over, you can open the Text wrap dialog box, click on the rectangular wrap icon, and click OK to create the default, rectangular wrap.

▼ Tip: A Graphic's Wrap Boundaries Can be Anywhere

The text-wrap boundaries attached to a particular graphic can fall anywhere on a page—they don't have to encompass, or even touch, the graphic (Figure 5-31). If you want, you can even place a graphic off the page and drag the wrap onto the page.

Figure 5-31
Graphic wrap boundaries can be anywhere

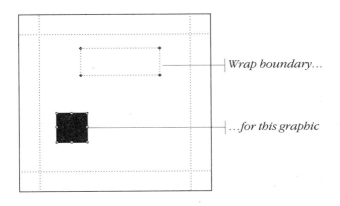

▼ Tip: Delaying Text Reflow When Adjusting Wraps

When you're adjusting a wrap boundary, waiting for the text to recompose every time you move a wrap handle gets pretty tedious—especially if you have a lot of handles to add or adjust. Instead, hold down the Spacebar as you adjust the wrap. PageMaker does not recompose the text as long as the Spacebar is held down, so you can add and adjust as many points as you want without having to wait for the screen to redraw.

▼ Tip: Angled Margins

You can use text wrap to create columns with angled margins. It's pretty easy to do, as you can see in Figure 5-32. Just create a couple of objects, and use their wraps on either side of a text block. You can also use an inside-out wrap for this technique. See the next tip for more on inside-out wrap boundaries.

Figure 5-32
Creating angled column guides

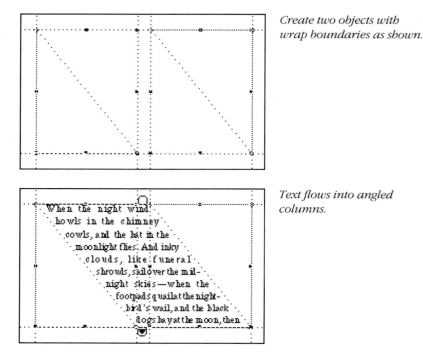

Create two objects with wrap boundaries as shown.

Text flows into angled columns.

▼ Tip: Inside-out Text Wrap

If you really want to amaze your friends and blow away your clients and colleagues, here is probably the coolest tip in the book. It's not the most useful, but it's arguably the coolest. Just watch.

Usually, text wrap repels text outside the graphic's border. But what if you want to wrap text inside the border? Here's how to create inside-out text wraps (Figure 5-33).

1. Select a graphic and choose "Text wrap" from the Element menu.
2. Apply a wrap to the graphic.
3. Select one wrap handle and drag it to near the other side of the wrap boundary.
4. Select the side of the wrap boundary that you have not yet moved, and drag it in the opposite direction, to near the original location of the handle you moved in step 3.

Figure 5-33
Creating an inside-out wrap

Graphic with normal wrap applied

Move the lower-right handle across the graphic.

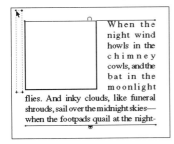

Move the upper-right handle across the graphic.

Move the original left boundary across the graphic.

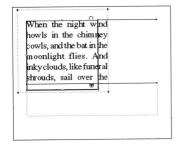

The text now wraps to the inside of the graphic wrap boundary.

5. Place or paste text inside the wrap boundary.

Instead of wrapping to the outside of the boundary, the text wraps to the inside of the boundary. The upper-left corner of the text block must be inside the text-wrap boundary for this to work.

Some very complex inside wraps are possible using this technique, as shown in Figure 5-34.

Figure 5-34
Wild inside wraps

As long as the upper-left corner handle of a text block falls inside an inside-out text wrap, the text will wrap to the inside of the boundary.

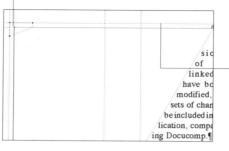

A tiny corridor of the text wrap boundary extends out to the left, connecting to the pocket in the upper-left corner.

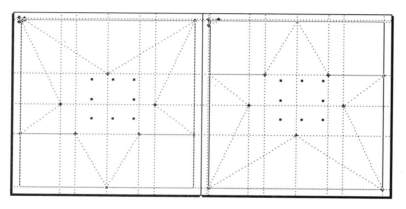

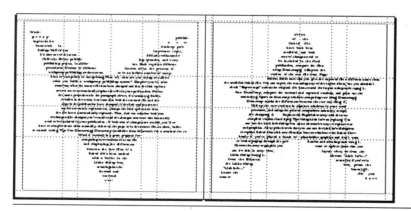

Wrapping Around Master Items

If you have applied a text-wrap setting to graphics on the master pages, text on pages that have "Display master items" turned on will wrap around that boundary. This is especially handy when you're autoflowing text into pages (Figure 5-35).

Figure 5-35
Using text wrap on master pages to control text flow

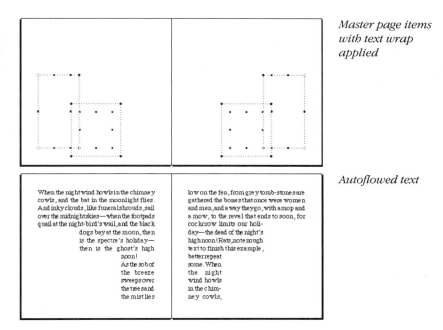

Master page items with text wrap applied

Autoflowed text

You can easily keep text from flowing into a column during autoflow, for instance, yet keep the column open for manual text flow—a good way to produce a book that, like this one, has a companion column on the left for subheads. Just place a line with a weight of "None" and a Text flow setting of "Column break" at the top of the companion column on the master pages (see Figure 5-36). Or you

Figure 5-36
Using text wrap on master pages to control text flow.

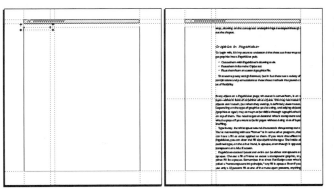

Place a line with text wrap set to "Column break" at the top of companion columns on master pages to keep text from autoflowing into them.

could keep text from colliding with a large page header or an ornamental border by applying text wrap to the item on the master pages.

Getting Graphic

Between the graphics you can create in PageMaker, those you can paste in from the Clipboard, and those you can create in external programs and place on the page, PageMaker lets you put just about any type of graphic on the page. In the next couple of chapters, we'll talk about how to get those graphics out of your PC and onto paper or—for color and other high-quality work—film.

CHAPTER 6

Printing

The ultimate test of any desktop-publishing program is its ability to put images on paper (or film) to produce camera-ready copy. The slickest tools and the best numerical accuracy inside the program mean nothing if the same flexibility and accuracy cannot be repeated outside the program—in printing. Although Aldus has done an admirable job providing for a wide range of options in its Print dialog box, it still falls victim to the limitations of the Windows environment and the quality of the printer driver you use.

In this chapter, we'll tell you everything you need to know about printer fonts and spend some time walking you through the two most popular drivers currently available with Windows, the PCL driver (for the Hewlett-Packard LaserJet family and other printers that support the PCL language) and the driver for PostScript printers.

We'll also give you a peek at the newest alternative to the Windows PostScript driver, available from Micrografx. And you'll find the usual tips and tricks to get the most out of your printing. Finally, we'll look at Publisher's Prism, a supplementary application that can enhance your publication output.

Setting the Target Printer

If you've already laid out your publication and you just turned to this section for the first time to get some tips on printing, you may be in for some bad news—unless you heeded our warning in Chapter 3, *Making PageMaker Mind*.

The Target printer command doesn't actually print anything. And it isn't even necessary for the "target printer" to be connected to your computer. But this command is a vital prerequisite to quality printing. So let's repeat our earlier caution once more for emphasis: *Before building your pages, always use the Target printer command to specify the printer and font cartridges (if any) you will use for your final output.* Do this even if you plan to print proof copies on a different printer before you get to that final print. PageMaker needs this information to optimize your publication for the printer you specify.

Here's an example. Say you're going to get final output from a service bureau that uses a Linotronic 300, but you plan to proofread copies from an Apple LaserWriter. Start by choosing Target printer from the File menu (Alt-F, T). The Target printer dialog box appears (Figure 6-1).

Figure 6-1
The Target printer dialog box

If you installed your LaserWriter driver at the time you installed Windows, but didn't install a driver for the Linotronic, don't worry. The necessary information is already on your hard disk, since they're both PostScript printers. Click the Setup button. This brings you to Windows' specific-printer dialog box (Figure 6-2). Once there, you choose the appropriate Linotronic model from the Printer list box. You can also set paper size and orientation (more on those later).

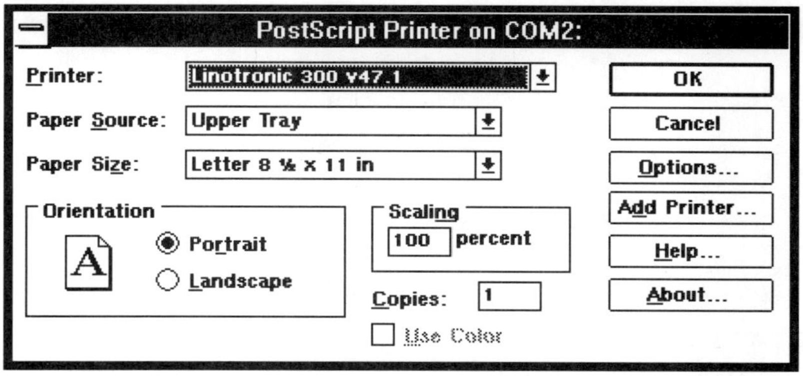

Figure 6-2
Windows' specific-printer dialog box

[Dialog box: PostScript Printer on COM2:
Printer: Linotronic 300 v47.1
Paper Source: Upper Tray
Paper Size: Letter 8 ½ x 11 in
Orientation: ● Portrait ○ Landscape
Scaling: 100 percent
Copies: 1
☐ Use Color
Buttons: OK, Cancel, Options..., Add Printer..., Help..., About...]

If you use an HP LaserJet or some other printer that takes font cartridges, now is the time to specify which cartridges you plan to use in your publication. The list box for these choices is in this same specific-printer dialog box. If you don't see your cartridges listed here, turn to the section "PCL/Hewlett-Packard LaserJet dialog box" later in this chapter to find out how to install new cartridge files. When you're done, click OK.

If you're planning to output to a Linotronic (or some other PostScript imagesetter) but proofing on a non-PostScript printer (such as a LaserJet), you may not have installed a PostScript driver for Windows. In that case, you'll have to open the Windows Control Panel, click Add Printers in the Printer dialog box, choose a printer, then click "Install" to get the right target printer driver. You'll also have to get out your original Windows disks. The dialog boxes will prompt you through the rest. Then return to PageMaker and use the Target printer command to set things aright.

When you've specified the font cartridges and the right printer's name shows in the Target printer dialog box, click OK to return to your publication. If you've followed our advice and done this with a brand new pub, you won't notice any difference. But if you reset the target printer for a publication that's already in progress, watch out. You'll get a message box that asks, "Recompose entire publication for PostScript Printer on LPT1?" (or whatever printer and port you've chosen). Click OK, and PageMaker recomposes the document, substituting fonts and applying the new character widths as necessary. In making adjustments for the new printer, line lengths may be adjusted, and whole stories that once fit perfectly may now be too long or too short. Don't say we didn't warn you.

You are probably wondering how you can print proof copies if your printer driver is set for the final output printer. Good question. For the answer see "Printer" in "The Print Dialog Box" later in this chapter.

PageMaker and Printer Fonts

In desktop publishing, printing inevitably means dealing with printer fonts. Whether your printer uses scalable outlines (as with PostScript printers) or fixed-size bitmaps (as with many older LaserJets and compatibles), you need to understand the distinction between fonts that are *resident* and those that are *downloaded*.

Resident typefaces are in a chip that's either in the printer or in a printer cartridge, and you can use them at any time. Downloadable typefaces, on the other hand (also called *soft fonts*), live on your computer's hard disk. You (or PageMaker) can download them into the printer's memory or hard disk, at which point you (or PageMaker) can use them just like the resident typefaces.

This section will get you up to speed on these and other font handling options. But before we go any farther, you need some background in that holiest of unholies, the WIN.INI file. Knowing how to manipulate the font info in this file is essential to managing typefaces in PageMaker. It's not the push-button world of friendly dialog boxes and simple menus, but it's not a chamber of horrors either. So relax, take a deep breath, and plunge ahead.

▼ *Tip: Back Up That File*

Before you go messing around with WIN.INI, make a backup copy and keep it in a safe place. If you should screw things up, you could have problems printing or even getting Windows to work right. We know it's an obvious bit of advice, but better safe than sorry.

A WIN.INI Primer

WIN.INI is an ASCII (text) file in your Windows subdirectory that stores important information for Windows and many other Windows applications. Among its many listings are information about your printer, the port you specified for that printer, and font information. Sometimes you can modify this information (without realizing it) by choosing different options in the Windows Control Panel.

For example, if you have already installed Windows and later add a new printer, the settings you change in Control Panel are entered in WIN.INI. In addition, some of the software and typefaces you install on your computer also modify WIN.INI for you. Most font manufacturers include an installation program with their downloadable fonts that changes WIN.INI at the time you install your fonts. If you own an HP LaserJet, some of the functions in that driver's Printer Font Installer dialog box also modify WIN.INI.

But there are other times when you must edit WIN.INI yourself—to change your font setup, for example. This is especially true for users of PostScript printers, since Windows PostScript driver lacks dialog box functions that modify WIN.INI for you.

Now let's take a look at a typical WIN.INI printer description.

```
[PostScript,COM1]
feed1=1
feed15=1
orient=1
device=2
softfonts=4
softfont1=c:\psfonts\pfm\hvbl____.pfm
softfont2=c:\psfonts\pfm\hvblo___.pfm
softfont3=c:\psfonts\pfm\hvl_____.pfm
softfont4=c:\psfonts\pfm\hvlo____.pfm
```

You don't need to understand every line of this stuff, but you should be familiar with the basics. As you study the above example, note the following:

- Many of the items in your WIN.INI correspond to settings in your specific-printer dialog box (accessed through the Windows Control Panel or PageMaker). For example, the line orient=1 represents the dialog box's Portrait Orientation option. WIN.INI is the storage place for these settings, and Windows looks here when it needs them.

- WIN.INI is divided into sections, each section beginning with a title. Titles are in brackets and separated by double carriage returns (i.e., there's an empty paragraph between sections). In the above example, [PostScript,COM1] is the heading for a PostScript printer description section—in this case an Apple LaserWriter installed on serial port COM1. If you have installed more than one printer driver for Windows, WIN.INI will have a separate printer description section for each.

- Each [*printer,port*] section must have a list of the fonts you wish to use with that printer (unless they're built into the printer or its cartridges or generated by a rasterizer like ATM). The example above shows listings for Helvetica-Black, Helvetica-Black Oblique, Helvetica-Light, and Helvetica-Light Oblique. The section must contain a line with the total number of fonts (softfonts=4, in the example). If you add to or delete from this list manually, you need to update this total.

- Each font listing begins with softfont*X*=, where *X* stands for the number of the font in the listing. This number must be unique within its own printer section (i.e., you can't have two fonts with the same number on one printer), but it need not be consistent from computer to computer. ITC Garamond might be softfont17 in your computer's WIN.INI, but softfont3 in your colleague's WIN.INI.

- Each font listing must contain the complete path showing where the font's metric file is located on your hard disk. Printer font metric files are not the actual fonts themselves, but are special files that PageMaker uses to give your characters the proper spacing and kerning. You can recognize printer font metric files by the extension .PFM. If you decide to reorganize your disk and move those files to a different directory, you'll have to edit their listings in WIN.INI.

Changing and saving WIN.INI does not automatically change things in Windows and PageMaker. To make your changes take effect, you also need to get Windows and PageMaker to reread the WIN.INI file.

The traditional prescription for this is to exit Windows and start it again. For an easier way, see the tip below.

▼ Tip: Rereading WIN.INI

A number of actions will cause Windows to reread the WIN.INI file, or at least portions of it. To make your changes to WIN.INI's printer sections take effect, you must do two things:

1. If PageMaker is running, close the current publication.
2. Open the Windows Control panel and double-click the Printers icon. Without making any changes in the Printers dialog box, click OK to close it. Then close Control Panel.

Now when you reopen your publication, the changes you made to WIN.INI will be in effect.

There are other actions you can take to replace the second step, including opening and closing other sections of the Windows Control Panel. Opening and closing a DOS application from within Windows also causes it to reread WIN.INI.

▼ Tip: Reorganizing WIN.INI

Many Windows applications deposit information at the end of your WIN.INI file the first time you use or install them. If you install a printer, install some software, and then install another printer, your WIN.INI is likely to reflect this order, and you may be frustrated that all your printer and font information isn't together in one place. Fortunately, the ordering of sections in WIN.INI isn't crucial. To make it easier to edit, cut and paste your various printer and font sections and put them in one place in the WIN.INI file. Just be careful to select and move entire sections, not pieces of them.

Resident Fonts

Resident fonts, the ones that live in your printer or its cartridges, are the most trouble free of all. Your Windows printer driver knows which fonts are built-in and makes them available to PageMaker. If you should change to another printer driver, you'll notice that PageMaker's type menus change, too.

As far as PageMaker is concerned, cartridge fonts are the same as resident fonts. There down there in the printer where PageMaker can ask for them. You just specify your cartridges in your printer driver's dialog box.

For example, if you have a Hewlett-Packard LaserJet, choose Target printer from PageMaker's File menu. In the Target printer dialog box, select your printer and click the Setup button. This opens the specific-printer dialog box for your printer. Because this dialog box is generated by Windows, not PageMaker, it can also be opened from the Printers section of the Windows Control Panel. Scroll through the cartridges in the list box, and select the ones you're going to use.

▼ Tip: Adding Font Metrics for Resident Fonts

Because PageMaker gets the font metrics for resident fonts from the Windows printer driver, these PFM files don't need to be listed in WIN.INI. But like all good rules, this one has an exception: if your target printer doesn't have the same resident fonts as your proof printer, you'll have no way to specify these fonts in PageMaker. That's because PageMaker's Type menu only displays the fonts of the target printer. This can be a problem if you want to use the Palatino or Avant Garde fonts built into your LaserWriter, but have specified the Linotronic as the target printer. How then to select these fonts?

In this case, you'd get the PFM files from your service bureau or from a friend. Because these aren't actually font files, they should have no qualms about giving you copies. Just copy them to your hard disk, then add the path and name of each to a separate softfont line in WIN.INI as you saw before. Update the softfonts total and save WIN.INI. Then follow our earlier tip ("Rereading WIN.INI") to get Windows and PageMaker to reread WIN.INI. Your fonts now show up in the Type specifications dialog box, and PageMaker will be able to space and kern each font properly.

▼ *Tip: Don't Mix Font Metric Files*

Whenever you take your publication to be printed from another computer, make sure the output device uses font metric files that match the ones in your own computer. (This applies to downloaded fonts as well.) A number of font manufacturers make fonts of the same name (Baskerville, Garamond, and so on), but that doesn't mean their PFM files are identical. Subtle differences can make your pages look less than professional. Check with your service bureau to make sure you're using font metrics from the same manufacturer. If you have any doubts, have the service bureau copy their PFM files for you.

Adding and Removing Soft Fonts

Installing new fonts is simple. If you purchase Adobe PostScript fonts, the disks come with their own installation program. If you use Adobe Type Manager, you can install them using the ATM Control Panel. The installer (or ATM) inserts the necessary font listings into your WIN.INI for any PostScript drivers you have installed. To remove fonts, just delete the font files from your hard disk. Then delete the relevant font listings from WIN.INI. Be sure to update the softfonts= total in that section to reflect the changes.

▼ *Tip: Removing Fonts with ATM*

If you're using ATM and you want to remove some fonts, select the fonts and click the Remove button in the ATM control panel. ATM removes the fonts from your WIN.INI file for you. You'll still have to delete the files from your hard disk, though.

To install fonts for a Hewlett-Packard printer, you use the handy-dandy Printer Font Installer dialog box that is part of all Windows HP drivers (Figure 6-3). There are three ways to reach this dialog box:

- Open the Windows Control Panel and double-click the Printers icon to open the Printers dialog box. Click the Configure button to open the Printers - Configure dialog box. Then click the Setup

Figure 6-3
Printer Font Installer dialog box for Hewlett-Packard LaserJets

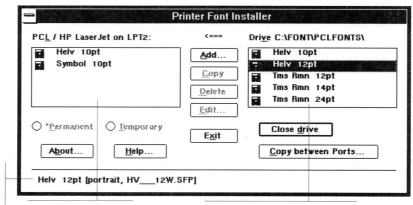

The status line reports the names of selected files.

This box shows fonts already installed.

This box lists fonts available for installation.

button to open the specific-printer dialog box for your printer. Finally, click the Fonts button.

- In PageMaker, choose Print to bring up the Print dialog box. Click the Setup button to open the specific-printer dialog box for your printer. Then click the Fonts button.

- In PageMaker, choose Target printer to bring up the Target printer dialog box. Click the Setup button to open the specific-printer dialog box for your printer. Then click the Fonts button.

If you are making font changes while in a PageMaker publication, it is best to use the last method. When you're all done with the font settings, click OK in the Target printer dialog box so that PageMaker recomposes your publication using the new font information.

As you have probably guessed, you add fonts to your setup by clicking the Add fonts button. A dialog box asks you where to find the new font files. Enter a drive or directory and click OK. You are returned to the Printer Font Installer dialog box, where the new fonts appear in box on the right. (Notice, also, that the Add fonts button has changed to Close drive.)

Select the fonts you want to install and click the Add button near the top of the box to install the fonts. The fonts are added to a directory called PCLFONTS unless you direct otherwise. Click OK and you're done.

If you're adding a font cartridge that isn't listed in the Cartridges section of the PCL/HP LaserJet dialog box, use the above procedure to add the Printer Cartridge Metric (PCM) files that come with your cartridge. After you add the files and exit the Printer Font Installer dialog box, the cartridge appears in the Cartridges list. Select it and click OK.

Deleting fonts is just as easy. The Delete button only becomes active after you select one or more installed fonts. Clicking on delete wipes them out of your printer and your hard drive. If you want to keep them on your disk but not in your printer, click No in the confirmation box.

The Printer Font Installer also includes an Edit button, whose dialog box lets you change the name of the font (in case you purchase two different fonts with the same name), adjust its font ID number (in case you want to change the order of fonts in WIN.INI), set its downloading status (but then you don't need this dialog box just for that), or assign it to a different typeface family (generally unnecessary).

Copying Soft Fonts between Ports

Windows needs font information for every printer driver and port that you intend to use. Normally, you should have your printer driver installed and assigned to the right port before you add fonts. But if you add a new printer to one of your ports after your fonts are already installed, don't worry. You can copy the font information to the port with the new printer.

As with many font-handling procedures in Windows, it's much easier with LaserJets than with PostScript printers.

The LaserJet method. Many Hewlett-Packard LaserJets use the same printer driver (the LaserJet III is the primary exception). You can tell which ones use the same driver by clicking the Add Printer button in the Printers dialog box of the Windows Control Panel. The driver name (PostScript, PCL/ LaserJet, etc.) appears in brackets to the right of each of the printers in the list box.

If the new printer you install uses the same driver, or if you are merely moving your existing printer to a new port, you can copy your soft font info to the new port in the Printer Font Installer dialog box.

1. Open the Printer Font Installer dialog box (choose Target printer from PageMaker's File menu. Click the Setup button and then click the Fonts button).
2. In the list of installed fonts on the left, select the fonts you wish to copy to the other port.
3. Click the Copy between Ports button. A new dialog box prompts you to select the target port.
4. Select the port you want and click OK. You are returned to the Printer Font Installer dialog box, where the Copy button is now active, the Add fonts button is gone, and the Copy between ports has become End between ports.
5. Select the fonts you want to copy and click Copy. At this point, you can also specify downloading options for the fonts on the new port (more on that later).
6. When you're finished, click End between ports (to return the dialog box to its previous condition) or Exit (to leave the box altogether).

If the new printer you added does *not* use the same driver as your other printer, this method won't work. In that case, use the Add fonts procedure described previously. When you are prompted for the drive containing the font files, enter the directory where you have already installed your fonts.

The PostScript method. As usual with the PostScript driver, you have to manually copy fonts by editing WIN.INI. But it's pretty simple.

1. Make a backup copy of WIN.INI for safekeeping. Then open WIN.INI in a text editor like Windows Notepad or Sysedit.
2. Find the printer description section for your old printer. The lines you want begin with softfont$X$= (X is the font number). You also want the softfonts= line giving the total number of fonts.
3. Copy these lines and paste them in the new [*printer,port*] section. It doesn't matter exactly where you paste the copy, as long as it's within the proper section.

4. Finally, save WIN.INI, and make Windows and PageMaker to reread the WIN.INI file (see "Rereading WIN.INI" earlier in this chapter).

In the example below, we have added a Linotronic printer and specified "FILE" as its port so we can make PostScript files for our service bureau. Here's what our printer sections look like after we copy the font information.

```
[PostScript,COM1]
feed1=1
feed15=1
orient=1
device=2
softfonts=4
softfont1=c:\psfonts\pfm\hvbl____.pfm
softfont2=c:\psfonts\pfm\hvblo___.pfm
softfont3=c:\psfonts\pfm\hvl_____.pfm
softfont4=c:\psfonts\pfm\hvlo____.pfm

[PostScript,FILE]
orient=1
feed1=50
feed15=1
device=11
softfonts=4
softfont1=c:\psfonts\pfm\hvbl____.pfm
softfont2=c:\psfonts\pfm\hvblo___.pfm
softfont3=c:\psfonts\pfm\hvl_____.pfm
softfont4=c:\psfonts\pfm\hvlo____.pfm
```

Soft Fonts: Automatic/Temporary Downloading

There are three different ways to handle downloading typefaces to your printer's memory—automatic/temporary, manual/semipermanent, and manual/permanent. In theory, automatic downloading should be the simplest of all: you just print from PageMaker, and PageMaker takes care of everything. When necessary, PageMaker finds the downloadable printer typefaces on your disk and downloads them to the printer. When PageMaker needs to download another typeface and finds that the printer's memory is full, it flushes out the least recently used typeface to make room.

That's the theory anyway. In practice, you might have to make sure your fonts are designated for automatic downloading. Once your fonts are set up for automatic/temporary downloading, you don't even have to think about what gets downloaded when. It just happens.

If you're using this method, you can use many different typefaces, sizes, and variations within your pub. It's also the slowest method of printing with downloadable fonts, though. Wait for PageMaker to download the same typeface 20 or 30 times, and you'll agree. It's not such a big problem if you have 2 or 3 megabytes of memory in your printer, but if you have 1 or 1.5, PageMaker ends up flushing and downloading a lot. It depends on how many typefaces you use in your pub, how often they change (3 times per page, or 20?), and how big they are.

In the worst case, every time PageMaker hits a change in typeface (from Garamond to Garamond Italic, for example, or from Stone to Stone Sans), it has to download that typeface to the printer. Then it flushes it out of the printer's RAM, only to download the typeface again, maybe just a few lines later. No matter what, PageMaker always flushes the typefaces out of the printer's memory when the publication's been printed.

The LaserJet method. If you're using a Hewlett-Packard LaserJet, you can designate downloadable fonts as temporary (automatic) or permanent (manual) in the Printer Font Installer dialog box. Just follow these steps.

1. Open the Printer Font Installer dialog box as usual. (Reminder: Choose Target printer from PageMaker's File menu. Click the Setup button and then the Fonts button.)
2. The fonts you have installed are listed in the box on the left. Select the fonts you want to designate for automatic downloading.
3. Click the Temporary button and click Exit. Keep clicking OK until you back out of all the dialog boxes.

The PostScript method. To make fonts download automatically for a PostScript printer, edit the WIN.INI file. It's pretty simple.

1. Make a backup copy of WIN.INI as usual. Then open WIN.INI with Windows Notepad or some other text editor.
2. Find the softfont lines that designate each of your PFM files.
3. At the end of the line of the font you want automatically downloaded, add a comma (no space), and the filename of the actual font file with its complete path. Remember, the actual font files aren't the same as the PFM files and so may have a different location on your hard disk. PostScript font files can be recognized with the extension .PFB.
4. Save WIN.INI. Then follow our earlier tip to get Windows and PageMaker to reread WIN.INI, putting your changes into effect.

In the example below, the fonts Helvetica-Black and Helvetica-Black Oblique have been set for automatic downloading, but the Helvetica-Light and Helvetica-Light Oblique have not.

```
[PostScript,COM1]
feed1=1
feed15=1
orient=1
device=2
softfonts=4
softfont1=c:\psfonts\pfm\hvbl____.pfm,c:\psfonts\hvbl____.pfb
softfont2=c:\psfonts\pfm\hvblo___.pfm,c:\psfonts\hvbl____.pfb
softfont3=c:\psfonts\pfm\hvl_____.pfm
softfont4=c:\psfonts\pfm\hvlo____.pfm
```

Soft Fonts: Manual/Semipermanent Downloading

You can minimize that repetitive automatic downloading and flushing by manually downloading the typefaces you use most often. Once you've manually downloaded a typeface, it's there until you turn off or reset the printer. That's why we call it semipermanent. PageMaker doesn't have to keep downloading the font, which speeds things up.

How many typefaces you download manually and how many you leave to PageMaker depends on how much printer memory you have, the size of the typefaces, and the number of different typefaces you're using. If you manually download too many and fill up the printer's memory, PageMaker won't be able to do its typeface-shuffling magic, and you may not be able to print your pub. (Some printers, including certain LaserJets, give you an out-of-memory warning on their control panels.) If you don't download enough, you're not getting all the speed you can.

▼ Tip: Download the Most Frequently Used Typefaces

To get the most printing speed, manually download the typefaces that are used most frequently in your pub. It's the best way to avoid repetitive downloading and flushing. Remember, even if your printer has enough memory to hold all the typefaces you're using, with automatic downloading, PageMaker still has to download all those faces each time you print.

If your body copy's in Garamond Light, for example, definitely download that. Then decide which you use more often—the Futura Extra Bold in the subheads, or the Garamond Light Italic that's scattered through your text for emphasis. Or you might choose to download the Futura Light you use for callouts. But you can only download so many typefaces before you run out of printer memory.

The LaserJet method. To download fonts to a H-P LaserJet, use the Printer Font Installer dialog box you saw in Figure 6-3 on page 320.

1. Open the Printer Font Installer dialog box (choose Target printer from PageMaker's File menu. Click the Setup button and then the Fonts button).
2. From the list of fonts on the left, select each font you want manually downloaded and (one at a time), select "Permanent." The first time you do this, an annoying message box appears to remind you that the fonts are only "permanently" in the printer until it is turned off. Click OK to clear the message and continue.

3. Click the Exit button. The Download Options dialog box appears.

4. Make sure only the Download Now box is checked, then click OK.

▼ Tip: Download Selected Fonts on Startup

To avoid having to navigate through several dialog boxes each time you want to download fonts, follow the same steps as above but leave the Download at startup box checked in the Download Now dialog box. This creates a batch file in your PCLFONTS directory (or wherever you keep your fonts) that downloads those fonts each time you execute it. In addition, it adds a line to your AUTOEXEC.BAT file to automatically execute this batch file each time you turn on your computer. This is handy if you plan to use the same fonts every time you turn on your computer. The only catch is you have to remember to turn on your printer *before* you turn on your computer, or the batch file won't be able to download the fonts. If for some reason you restart your printer during the day, you'll have to execute this batch file again.

▼ Tip: Multiple Batch Files for Customized Downloading

Chances are you don't want to download the exact same fonts every day. Solution: Let the dialog box create several different batch files, each with different groups of fonts selected for downloading. Here's how.

Follow the same steps as you did for manual downloading, and check the Download at startup box in the Download Now dialog box. Then open your AUTOEXEC.BAT file with a text editor (like Sysedit, which opens it when it loads) and find the lines added by the Download Now dialog box. They consist of one "remark" line announcing, "rem The Windows PCL / HP LaserJet / DeskJet font installer added the next line," followed by the command that invokes the batch file. Make a note of the batch file's name, then delete the added lines. (If you're afraid of deleting the wrong lines, mak e a backup of your AUTOEXEC.BAT before using the Printer Font Installer dialog box; then just restore that AUTOEXEC.BAT to your root directory.)

Repeat this process for each set of fonts you're likely to use as a group. To run these batch files under Windows, create a program information file (PIF) for each. To simplify the process further, create an icon for each PIF in Program Manager. To dress things up further, create custom icons for each with an icon editor like hDC Icon Designer, or the shareware product Icondraw (see Chapter 2, *Building a PageMaker System*). Then you can download your custom font groups just by double-clicking the icons. For more information on creating PIFs and icons in Program Manager, consult your *Microsoft Windows User's Guide*.

▼ Tip: Speeding Up Font-Downloading Batch Files

If you want your font-downloading batch files to return to Windows as soon as they're finished executing, check the Close Window on Exit box. If you want the DOS window to remain open so you have time to read the screen messages, leave this box unchecked. If you are running Windows in standard mode, your batch file concludes with a prompt to press any key in order to return to Windows.

If you are running in 386 enhanced mode, you have to conclude the process by closing the DOS window yourself (double-click the control menu in the window's upper-left corner). To simplify things, check "Close Window on Exit" in the PIF dialog box and add a line to the end of your batch files that reads:

pause

This keeps the window open and displays the message "Strike a key when ready." Then press any key to close the DOS window and return to Windows.

The PostScript method. Windows doesn't provide this downloading capability with its PostScript printer driver. The good news is you won't have to edit your WIN.INI for manual downloading; most font installers set up WIN.INI for manual downloading anyway. (If you're not certain how your fonts are set up, check your printer section in WIN.INI and make sure only the PFM files are referenced. As explained earlier, if the list also contains the location of PFB files, those fonts are set for automatic/temporary downloading.) The bad news is, you have to resort to a non-Windows downloading utility to get the job done.

All Adobe PostScript fonts come with two utilities, PSDOWN for downloading to printers connected via a serial port, and PSSEND for printers connected to a parallel port. You use these utilities to download selected fonts to your printer's memory or hard drive, display a list of fonts already downloaded or available for downloading, restart your printer to clear out previously downloaded fonts, and send PostScript files and programs to your printer. PSDOWN has the advantage of being menu-driven and therefore easy to use without consulting the manual. PCSEND is a little more arcane, relying on good old DOS-type commands and switches entered at the DOS prompt. In either case, you can run these programs under Windows by creating a PIF file for each. For complete instructions on these utilities, consult the documentation that comes with your fonts, the *Adobe Type Library User Guide IBM PC Version*.

▼ Tip: Batch Files for Customized Downloading

If your PostScript printer is connected to a parallel port, you can use PCSEND to create batch files that download a particular font or group of fonts to your printer. Simply follow the instructions for creating a DOS batch file in the PCSEND documentation. Then create a PIF file for each batch file and, in Program Manager, create an icon for each PIF file. To download a particular font group, just double-click the appropriate icon. Your *Microsoft Windows User's Guide* can guide you in creating PIF files and Program Manager icons. See also our earlier tip, "Speeding Up Font-Downloading Batch Files."

▼ Tip: Downloading Selected Fonts on Startup

If you download the same fonts every day and use a PostScript printer on a parallel port, you can have your computer automatically download these fonts each time you turn it on. Create a batch file to download your fonts with PCSEND as described in its documentation. Then add that batch file's name to the end of your AUTOEXEC.BAT in your root directory. As long as you turn on your printer *before* you start your computer, this batch file will take care of everything. Note, however, that if you turn the printer off and restart it, you'll have to execute the batch file again to download the fonts.

Clearing Downloaded Fonts. If other people are using the laser printer, remember that your manually downloaded typefaces are clogging up their printer memory, too. We won't get into interoffice politics here; suffice it to say that diplomacy and compromise are necessary. If nothing else, reset the printer, flushing the fonts out of the printer's memory, when you're done. If you're using a PostScript printer, you can use Adobe's font downloader to do this from your keyboard. To do this with an HP LaserJet, follow these steps.

1. Open the Printer Font Installer as usual.
2. From the list on the left, select the fonts to clear from the printer and click the Delete button.
3. When prompted whether to delete the files from your disk, click No.

Windows then deletes the fonts from the printer but leaves them on your computer's hard drive. If digging through all those dialog boxes drives you crazy, you can always use the method that works for any laser printer: turn the darn thing off, then back on again.

Soft Fonts: Manual/ Permanent Downloading

Some PostScript devices (the Apple LaserWriter II NTX, for instance, and all imagesetters) let you connect a hard disk that holds downloadable typefaces. It's just as if the fonts were downloaded to memory, but they're on a disk. The font metrics have to be listed in WIN.INI like all downloadable fonts, but your font installer is likely to take care of this for you. To install the fonts to a PostScript printer's hard disk, you can use the same utilities that download to your printer's RAM: PCSEND (for parallel printers) and PSDOWN (for serial printers). Once they're there, you can use them just like ROM-resident typefaces.

Soft Fonts: The Rasterizer Option

Last but not least, you should be aware of a relatively new option in getting your fonts from computer to printer: Rasterizers. Most font rasterizers today use outline fonts on your computer's hard disk to scale type "on the fly"—that is, as soon as you ask for a particular size in PageMaker. Rasterizers such as Adobe Type Manager (ATM), Bitstream FaceLift, and Zenographics' SuperPrint use these outlines to give you accurate screen fonts.

Rasterizers also convert the type on your page to a bitmap image (at your printer's resolution—not your screen's) and send that information to the printer. As a result, you're freed from the need to download fonts (unless you're using ATM on a PostScript printer). You also get out of editing WIN.INI. Like automatic downloading, printing is slower, but not too much. ATM and SuperPrint have the advantage of letting you print Adobe fonts on non-PostScript printers. SuperPrint, in fact, supports a number of font technologies, including Adobe PostScript, Bitstream Fontware, The Company's Nimbus Q (URW typefaces), and Compugraphic Intellifont. However, SuperPrint does not work with PostScript printers. For more on rasterizers, see Chapter 2, *Building a PageMaker System*.

The Blight of the Bloated WIN.INI

Once you get used to the font listings in WIN.INI, it really isn't too difficult to tinker with now and then. But there are a couple of potential pitfalls to be aware of. The biggest is that there is a limit to the number of soft fonts you can list in WIN.INI and (therefore) use with Windows applications like PageMaker. You can also expect problems if your WIN.INI swells to greater than 64K.

Too many fonts. Microsoft hasn't bothered to document this point in its Windows *User's Guide*, but you can expect to encounter problems if your WIN.INI references more than 150 fonts or so. (The actual limit varies somewhat depending on the printer you specify in the Windows Control Panel.) When that happens, you'll get an error message that your printer driver won't load, which basically means you can forget about printing until the problem is resolved.

The best solution is to create several copies of WIN.INI, each listing a different set of fonts. If you run a service bureau or typography business, you may find it helpful to create custom WIN.INIs for specific clients or groups of clients. This is especially practical if your customers tend to use the same fonts from job to job or have font favorites that don't number into the hundreds. You could name these files after your clients (WINNI.TOM, WINNI.DIK, WINNI.HRY, for example) or use a more straightforward numbering system (WIN1.TXT, WIN2.TXT, etc.) or any names that help you remember the contents.

The next step is to create a batch file that replaces the current WIN.INI with the one you need. You can create a quick batch file in any ASCII editor, including Windows Notepad. Just create a new file and save it under a name with the .BAT extension. For convenience, try creating a series of batch files, each having the same name as the backup WIN.INIs (except for the extension)—for example, WIN1.BAT, WIN2.BAT, and so on. Your batch file can include whatever you like, but here's a simple one to serve as an example:

```
echo off
cls
cd\windows
copy winini1.txt win.ini
echo on
```

Finally, create a PIF file for each of your batch files, and create icons for each PIF in Program Manager. Then when you want to change to one of the alternate WIN.INIs, just double-click the appropriate icon in Program Manager. To make your changes take effect, you'll have to close and reopen your PageMaker publication. But you won't have to use our aforementioned gimmick of opening items in Control Panel, since executing the PIF files automatically makes Windows reread WIN.INI when the DOS windows close.

Too much fat. Problems can also arise if your WIN.INI file gets larger than 64K. For most people this is not a problem, especially if you've already parceled up WIN.INI into several versions listing different fonts. But the more applications you install that use WIN.INI, the fatter it can become. When that happens, look for ways to put it on a diet:

- Save a backup copy of WIN.INI for reference. Then, in the WIN.INI (or WIN.INIs) you use, search and delete "comment" lines, which are only there to make the plot more interesting. Any line that begins with a semicolon is a comment line.

- Try relocating your fonts so their path names aren't so long. For example, the line softfont3=d:\windows\fonts\pclfonts\pfm\hv___10w.pfm takes up a lot more space than the line softfont3=d:\hv___10w.pfm. And when you multiply the difference over dozens of fonts, the savings are substantial.

- If you are the type that tries out a lot of shareware, there may be a lot of garbage in your WIN.INI that doesn't need to be there. Most applications add their two cents worth in sections that begin with the application name in brackets [like this]. Skim through WIN.INI looking for these devils, and delete the sections installed by applications you no longer use.

- Similarly, if you've tried out more than one printer or even more than one printer driver, you may have extra printer descriptions in WIN.INI that are just taking up space. Look for sections with the printer name and port in brackets, and delete all sections that don't refer to the printers you actually use.

The Micrografx PostScript Driver

After all that hashing around in WIN.INI, you may find yourself dreaming of greener pastures. Wouldn't it be great, for example, if you could switch between automatic and manual downloading at the click of a button? Wouldn't it be nice if you could download fonts from inside PageMaker instead of running to some non-Windows utility to do the job? Wouldn't it be great if you could adjust the angle and frequency of screen tints without messing around with PostScript commands?

You can. You can have all these things right now with the Micrografx PostScript driver for Windows. This driver comes with the well-known Micrografx drawing program, Designer, but you can purchase the driver separately for $199.

Like all Windows printer drivers, you can reach the Micrografx dialog boxes either from the Windows Control Panel or from inside PageMaker. There you'll find all the goodies Microsoft forgot for its PostScript driver: the ability to install fonts, display fonts currently installed, manually download fonts, and change font status from automatic to manual download, all with a few simple mouse clicks. No more slogging through WIN.INI, where the slightest typo can screw things up.

The newest version of the Micrografx driver also gives you control over the graphic elements of your publications. For example, you can adjust the screen frequency and angle of your gray tint or halftone screens. On a laser printer, this means better-looking gray tones. On an imagesetter, you can adjust the pattern according to your commercial printer's instructions to get the best results from offset printing. The driver also gives you control over the default width of a hairline rule. This comes in handy if the rules you get back from an imagesetter are too fine.

▼ Tip: Dig Out Those Adobe Floppies

Unlike the Windows PostScript driver, which uses only your fonts' PFM and PFB files, the Micrografx PostScript driver uses the Adobe Font Metric files (recognized by the .AFM extension). If you have been using Adobe fonts before you get the Micrografx driver, chances are these AFM files aren't even on your hard drive. To get the Micrografx driver to recognize and use your fonts, dig out your Adobe floppies and copy the AFM files to your PSFONTS directory. Then use the driver's dialog box to install them so you can access all the driver's font features.

▼ *Tip: Skip the Font Print Out*

When you download fonts to your printer manually/semipermanently, the Micrografx PostScript driver gives you the option of printing a sheet confirming the download with a sample of each font. Unless you're having problems with manually downloaded fonts and need this option as a diagnostic tool, don't use it. It's slow, unnecessary, and generally a waste of your printer's valuable time.

The Print Dialog Box

The actual act of printing with PageMaker starts with the Print command on the File menu (Ctrl-P). It brings up the Print dialog box (Figure 6-4). Here's a rundown of the choices in the Print dialog box, and how you should use them for different situations.

Figure 6-4
The Print dialog box

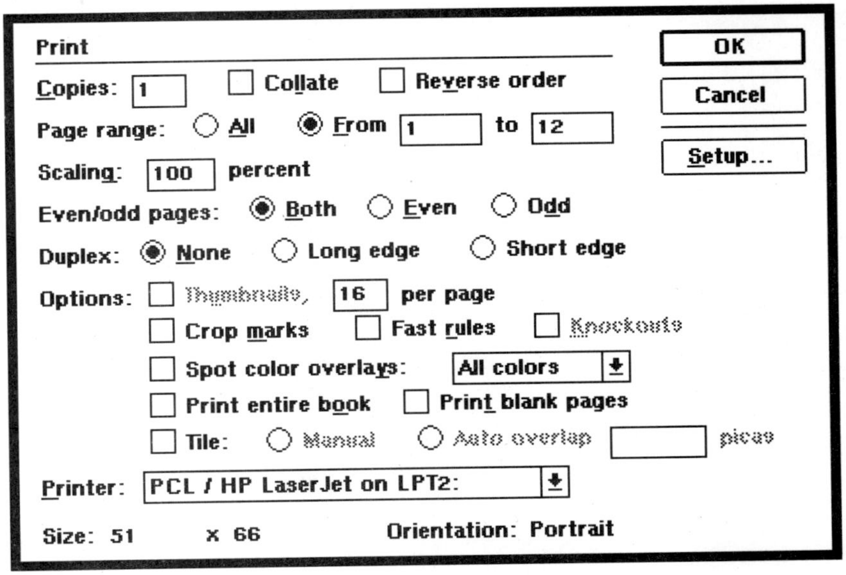

Copies. This is easy. Just type in the number of copies you want. It interacts with the following choice (Collate), however, in ways that can slow you down or speed you up a lot. Also remember that if you're printing spot color overlays, you'll get the number of overlays, times the number of pages, times the number of copies you specify here.

Collate. This option makes the pages in your document come out in the correct order, subject to the paper feed mechanism of your printer and your choice in the next option, Reverse order. If you're printing multiple copies and have "Collate" turned on, PageMaker prints the pub from beginning to end (or the reverse), then goes back and does it again. You don't have to sort pages by hand, but PageMaker and your printer have to rebuild each page from scratch for each copy, which is slow. It's like printing a single copy, then printing another, and so on.

Turning off "Collate" tells PageMaker and your printer to build each page one time and spit out the number of copies you asked for all at once, at the full speed of the laser engine. You'll have to hand-collate the pages, but it's generally much faster than waiting for multiple, collated prints. If you're printing very many copies, just print one and have it copied on a collating photocopier, or invite your friends over for a collating party.

Reverse order. PageMaker is smart about printing pages in the right order. This option is useful for printers that spit out your copies face up. By printing in reverse order, the stack is in correct order when you pick it up from the printer's output tray.

Page range. This is simple, too. Just type in the range of pages you want to print (inclusive), and go. If you click the All button, PageMaker fills in the full page range for you.

▼ Tip: Voodoo Page Ranges

You can enter a page range by Tabbing through the previous options (it takes four Tab presses), *first page #*, Tab, *last page #*, and "Enter." Do this quickly enough and your job starts printing without the Print dialog box appearing. It might not add up to a huge speed improvement, but boy, does it ever feel faster.

Scaling. This option is grayed out for LaserJets and most other printers. If you have a PostScript printer, however, you can use scaling to reduce or enlarge your pages as they print. It's handy for getting large-sized pages to print on smaller sheets for proofing, or enlarging pages that you can reduce photographically to improve printed resolution. Just type in the percentage you want. You can also use this when you're printing a page to disk to size it up or down.

Bear in mind, though, that you can only type integer values here. PageMaker won't accept 100.35, for instance—the value necessary to convert PostScript 72-dpi points to traditional printer's points.

▼ Tip: Fitting Tabloids on Letter and Legal Paper

To fit a single tabloid page on a letter-size sheet, reduce it to 62 percent. If you have a legal paper tray and legal-size sheets, you can fit a tabloid page by reducing to 80 percent.

▼ Tip: Improving Output Resolution

You don't have to buy one of the fancy new high-resolution lasers to improve the look of your printed publications. Just print them enlarged, then have the printer reduce the pages photographically before they make plates. If you print your job enlarged to 125 percent on your 300-dpi printer, for example, and then ask the printer to reduce the output photographically to 80 percent, you end up with an effective printed resolution of 375 dpi.

▼ Tip: Have the Printer Overexpose to Smooth out Jaggies

This doesn't have anything to do with enlargement and reduction, but it works with the previous tip. When you deliver laser-output pages to the printer for offset printing, ask them to overexpose the film negatives a little. The dark area around the type encroaches slightly, smoothing out the jaggies. Have them underexpose if they're making film positives.

Even/odd pages. This option is a real boon if you want to print on both sides of the sheet and your printer doesn't have duplexing capabilities (see below). Just print the odd pages, then put the odd pages back in your laser printer's paper tray and print the even pages. Orientation varies from printer to printer, but for LaserJets, LaserWriters and LaserWriter Pluses (Canon CX engines), put the paper in face up, head in. For LaserJet IIs and LaserWriter IIs (and other printers using the Canon SX engine), put it in face down, head in. You can use the same kind of technique with photocopiers.

Note that if you choose "Even/odd pages," PageMaker prints all of the pages in the range—even if the Print blank pages check box is not checked. That's so you get the correct pages back to back.

▼ Tip: Chill Out Those Pages Before Printing Side Two

If you put the freshly laser-printed pages back in the laser printer immediately, you're likely to get paper jams, and you may even gum up the works with the still-soft toner. Let the pages cool and dry for a few minutes before you print the second side.

Duplex. This option lets you print on both sides of your paper and is only available with certain printers, such as the HP LaserJet IID, IIID, or 2000. The "Long edge" and "Short edge" options control how you want the reader to turn your pages and relate to your page orientation. For example, if you are making a calendar in "Tall" ("Portrait") orientation, click "Short edge" so the pages turn on a horizontal axis. On the other hand, if your calendar prints pages in "Wide" ("Landscape") orientation, you'll still want the pages to turn on a horizontal axis, but this time the "hinge" or binding should be along the "Long edge," so choose that option. For books whose pages turn along a vertical axis (like this one), do just the reverse: choose "Long edge" for a "Tall" book and "Short edge" for a "Wide" book (Figure 6-5).

Thumbnails. Like Scaling, the Thumbnails option is only available to printers with scaling abilities (like PostScript printers). Thumbnails

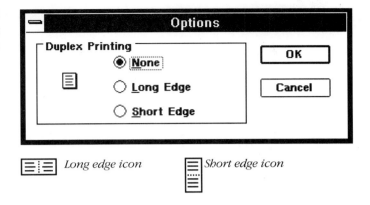

Figure 6-5
Duplex printing options

gives you an overview of a pub by printing multiple reduced pages on a single sheet. The fewer pages per sheet, the larger the thumbnails. PageMaker prints thumbnails of all of the pages in the publication or the selected page range, even if the Print blank pages check box is not checked. Remember that this takes just as long as printing all the pages full-size.

Bitmap smoothing. If your printer allows this option, you can use it to smooth the edges of bitmapped images and fonts. But unless you truly love the look of smoothed bitmaps (it sometimes looks okay with coarse bitmapped clip art), make sure that "Smoothing" is off; it slows down printing. And if you're doing documentation that involves captured screen images, turn "Smoothing" off. The bitmaps aren't smoothed on the screen, so you don't want them smoothed on your printout. Also, jagged bitmaps are rather fashionable right now.

Crop marks. Check this box to print lines outside the page area, showing the boundaries of the page. Note that these are different from registration marks (the little target-like things you see on color separations and overlays). To define your own marks, see the tip "Printing Outside the Page Area" later in this chapter.

Fast Rules. This option, which is only available for PCL (LaserJet- and LaserJet II-compatible) printers, speeds up the printing of horizontal and vertical rules and square boxes. It achieves this trick by sending the printer the dimensions of the line or box instead of transmitting bitmapped information. Don't check this option if you're printing spot color overlays with knockouts.

If you have a HP LaserJet Series III or IIID, you must check the Fast Rules option in order to print reverse type. If you try this and still cannot print reverse type, you may be using the HP LaserJet III printer driver that came with early releases of Windows. Contact Microsoft or your Hewlett-Packard dealer to get the new driver.

Knockouts. This option, which is only enabled when "Spot color overlays" is turned on, lets you decide whether PageMaker should "knock out" underlapping color elements (a portion of a red circle underneath a blue box, for instance). If you're using multipass printing with a laser printer or photocopier to put the color on the page, check this box so red toner doesn't print on top of blue and get all muddy. If you're going to a commercial printer with an offset press, see Chapter 7, *Color*. For a graphic representation of how "Knockouts" works, see the color pages in this book.

Spot color overlays. If you're printing a two- or three-color job (on an offset press or a photocopier, or even with multipass laser printing and color toner cartridges), you can have PageMaker print each color on a separate sheet. Check "Spot color overlays," and the pop-up menu is enabled so you can choose which color overlay to print. Unfortunately, you can't ask PageMaker to print yellow and blue but not black. You either choose one or all. For more on spot color overlays, see Chapter 7, *Color*, and the color pages in this book.

PageMaker prints registration marks automatically if you choose "Spot color overlays." You can even get registration marks on a one-color job if you want them for some reason, by choosing "Spot color overlays" and just printing the one color.

▼ Tip: Printing Outside the Page Area

You can print whatever you want outside the page area, hanging off the page. If you want registration marks someplace other than where

PageMaker puts them, or if you want to print a job name or date or time, here's how (Figure 6-6).

Figure 6-6
Placing printing objects off the page

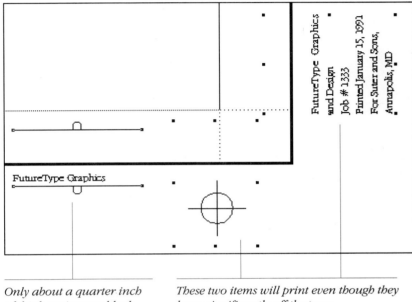

Only about a quarter inch of this hanging text block will print.

These two items will print even though they hang significantly off the page.

Create a white box in a draw program, put the registration mark inside the box, and copy/paste both the box and the registration mark onto the page. As long as the white box is touching the page, the graphic prints (within the limits described in the next tip).

For an even easier method, create only the registration mark in the draw program (forget the white box). Then copy it to the Clipboard (Ctrl-Insert). In PageMaker, create a text block containing nothing but a couple of carriage returns. Place the text block so one end of it hangs off the page. Position the text cursor after the carriage returns and press Shift-Insert. The registration mark is inserted as an inline graphic. As long as one end of the text block touches the page, the graphic prints.

You can also do this for graphics you create with PageMaker's graphic tools. However, you are limited to simple, single-object graphics. If you create a graphic with stacked lines and circles in

PageMaker (like a registration mark) and copy/paste them into a text block as an inline graphic, the objects lose their arrangement and appear side by side as separate inline graphics.

▼ Tip: Hang Rotated Items off the Sides of Pages

Be aware that there's only about a quarter inch strip along the top and bottom of pages that will print hanging graphics. Graphics hanging off the sides of pages, however, seem to print for quite a ways out—at least an inch. To take advantage of this, select the text block you want to hang, rotate it, and hang it off the side of the page.

***

Print entire book. If you've built a book list of multiple publications using the Book command on the File menu, the Print entire book option is enabled in the Print dialog box. If you leave this box unchecked, the printing process proceeds exactly as in PageMaker 3.0—it prints with the options specified. If, however, you choose "Print entire book," PageMaker prints all of the publications listed in the Book publication list dialog box (see "PageMaker 4's Book Command" in Chapter 3, *Making PageMaker Mind*). If you choose "Print entire book," though, "Page range" will be set to "All."

The book feature is mainly for index and table of contents generation. With printing, it's primarily useful for proofs (though it can speed that process tremendously). We recommend preparing your file for its final printing the old-fashioned way: print each file separately (to the printer or to a PostScript disk file) with the print options you want.

Print blank pages. If you have a lot of blank pages in your pub, you can save paper by unchecking this box. It doesn't work if you've chosen "Spot color overlays."

Tile. Use tiling if your page size is larger than your paper size. PageMaker prints multiple sheets that you can paste together to make up the whole page.

Automatic tiling starts at the upper-left corner of your page (leaving room for crop and registration marks), and prints enough tiles to get the whole page out. You choose the overlap, based on how much unprintable area your printer has around the edges of pages. Note that if you use automatic tiling, PageMaker prints all of the tiles—even the blank ones—even if the Print blank pages check box is not checked.

With manual tiling, PageMaker starts the upper-left tile at the ruler origin (the 0, 0 point) and works down to the right. This lets you control the exact positions of the tiles by changing the origin point in the publication window.

When you're tiling, never let the edge of a tile pass through the middle of anything containing a halftone screen (an image or a tinted LBO), because you'll never be able to paste the edges of the screen together so that they match. It's much easier to match solid LBOs or type, even if you have to create more tiles.

▼ Tip: Double Your Pages, Double Your Funds

You can save 50 percent on Lino charges by printing two PageMaker pages side-by-side on a single piece of paper or film. You have to have room for two pages on the roll, of course, so the practical limit for printing across the roll on a Linotronic 300 is 5-1/2-inch-wide pages—about half of the L-300's 11.7-inch width limit. Printing the length of the roll, the only limit is the imagesetter's memory and PageMaker's page size limit. (This also works with laser printers, by the way.)

The trick is to use manual tiling.

1. Set the page size you want in Page setup. Choose "Double-sided" and "Facing pages."
2. Set the zero point to the upper-left corner of the left page. This sets the upper-left corner of your tile.
3. In Print dialog box, click Setup. This takes you to a dialog box for your specific printer.
4. In your printer-specific dialog box, choose "Letter" paper size and "Landscape" orientation. Click OK to return PageMaker's Print dialog box.

5. In the Print dialog box, check the Tile box and select the Manual option. Select any left page to print and press Enter.

PageMaker prints both the left and right pages side by side, within the size limits of the imagesetter. You have to choose each left page to print individually, and service bureaus won't want to baby sit the job that much, so you might want to print each spread to disk as PostScript then send all the PostScript files to your service bureau (see "Printing PostScript to Disk" later in this chapter).

PageMaker won't print automatic crop marks for the right-hand pages using this method, so you'll want to place your own crop marks on the master pages (see the tip "Printing Outside the Page Area" earlier in this chapter).

▼ Tip: Another Way to Get Double Pages

Ole thinks the tip above is ugly and suggests creating a page twice the size of your pages, putting two pages on the single on-screen page.

1. Use the Page setup dialog box to set up a page that is twice the width of your page. Set the Top, Bottom, and Outside settings as you would if you were setting up a single page, then make the Inside setting equal to the Outside setting.
2. Use the Column guides dialog box on the Options menu to set up two columns, then make the space between the columns equal to twice the setting you want for the inside measure of your page.

Now lay out your publication, using the column on the left as your left page, the column on the right as your right page. You can place a vertical ruler guide down the middle of the column to indicate the edge of the pages (Figure 6-7).

The most common use of this technique is laying out 5.5-by-8.5-inch pages to print on 8.5-by-11-inch sheets of paper (run "Wide" or "Landscape"). Steve and Scott think this tip is ugly because you have to number every page manually, rather than having PageMaker do it for you.

Figure 6-7
Two pages on one

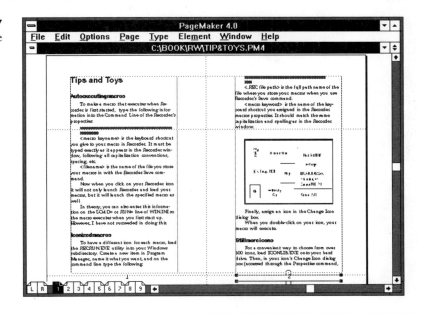

Printer. This pop-up list contains all the active printers you installed for Windows and shows what port each is connected to. As we've noted along the way, the printer selected in this box affects whether other options in the Print dialog box are available.

If you're planning to print final and proofing copies on the same printer (or even printers that speak the same language, like Post-Script), chances are the name of your printer and port are already in this box (You *did* set your target printer earlier, didn't you? If not, go back and read "Setting the Target Printer" at the beginning of this chapter.) If you're printing proofs on an entirely different type of printer—say a dot matrix for proofs and PostScript for final—this is the place to change the printer so you can make your proofs. You'll see an error message telling you that your publication was composed for another printer. Click OK to clear the message and let it print anyway. The proof might not look as good as if it were composed for that printer, but the point is to have a proof that most closely resembles the final copy. When it comes time to print your final copies, remember to change it back to the printer you specified in the Target printer dialog box.

If the printer you want to proof on doesn't appear on the Printer pop-up list, it probably hasn't been installed or isn't active. To check, go to Program Manager, launch the Windows Control Panel, and double-click "Printers." The list box shows which printers have been installed and which are active.

If your printer doesn't appear in Control Panel's Installed Printers window, you'll need to get out your Windows disks and install it. Click "Add Printer," select the one you want, then click "Install." If you have any problems, consult your Windows manual.

If your printer is there but isn't active, select it and click the Active radio button in the Status box. If the Active button is grayed out, you probably need to assign the printer to a specific port. To do this, click the Configure button, and select the proper port from the Ports list (LPT denotes parallel ports; COM denotes serial ports). Then click OK. You should now be able to choose the Active option and click OK.

Setup

As we've already hinted, clicking the Setup button in either the Print dialog box or the Target printer dialog box lets you invisibly tap into the Windows Control Panel and bring up the dialog box for the specific printer driver you have installed. You can find the same dialog box through Control Panel, but it's buried a little deeper. Consequently, this dialog box differs from printer to printer. We'll look at the two most common versions of this box, one for Hewlett-Packard LaserJets, and one for PostScript printers. But first let's cover the options they have in common. Figure 6-8 shows the specific-printer dialog box for PostScript printers.

Printer. This pop-up list shows the specific name of your printer (as opposed to the Printer box in the Print dialog box, which only shows your printer's general category). Here you can choose from among other printers that support the same page-description language as the printer you selected in PageMaker's Print dialog box. So, for example, if you specified Linotronic as your target printer (as described at the

Figure 6-8
PostScript printer
dialog box

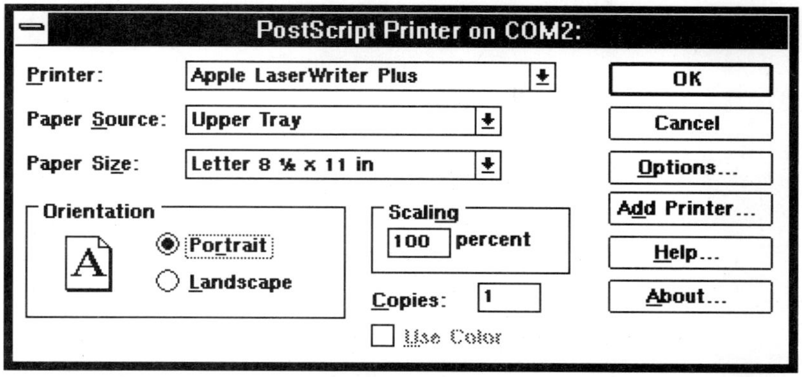

```
┌─────────────────────────────────────────────────────────┐
│  ▭          PostScript Printer on COM2:                 │
│                                                         │
│  Printer:     [ Apple LaserWriter Plus    ↧ ]  ┌──OK──┐ │
│  Paper Source:[ Upper Tray                ↧ ]  │Cancel│ │
│  Paper Size:  [ Letter 8 ½ x 11 in        ↧ ]  │Options...│
│  ┌─Orientation─────────┐  ┌─Scaling──────┐    │Add Printer...│
│  │  ┌─┐  ● Portrait    │  │ [100] percent│    │ Help... │
│  │  │A│  ○ Landscape   │  │              │    │ About...│
│  │  └─┘                │  │ Copies:  [1] │    └────────┘ │
│  └─────────────────────┘  └──────────────┘              │
│                          ☐ Use Color                    │
└─────────────────────────────────────────────────────────┘
```

beginning of the chapter), but for the moment you want to print proofs on your Apple LaserWriter Plus, this is the place to change over to the LaserWriter Plus. Be sure to change back to the Lino when you go to print your final copies.

Paper Source. Use this list box to choose whether to use the printer's paper tray or manual feed option. In the case of LaserJets, you also have an option for printing envelopes.

Paper Size. This is where you tell PageMaker the exact dimensions of your physical paper size (different from the page size you define with "Page setup"). Your choices in this pop-up menu are determined by which printer you have chosen.

▼ *Tip: Use "Extra" Sizes for Imagesetters*

If your specified printer is a Linotronic, you not only have the standard paper sizes (letter, legal, tabloid, etc.) but also a parallel set of "extra" sizes—"Letter Extra," "Legal Extra," "Tabloid Extra," and so on. These are the standard sizes plus about an inch all around to allow room for crop marks. If you're printing to Linotronic anyway, you should use one of these extra sizes plus the crop marks option in PageMaker's Print dialog box. It will be a big help to your commercial printer (or layout artist if you have to do any manual pasteup). If the Print dialog box calls for crop marks, but your specific-printer dialog box specifies letter size, PageMaker assumes there's no room for your crop marks and won't print them.

Orientation. With laser printers and letter or legal-size paper, this option is pretty simple. Choose "Portrait" to print what PageMaker calls "Tall" pages (with the short edge of the paper running horizontally), and "Landscape" to print "Wide" pages. In general, you should choose the orientation that correlates with the one you chose in the Page setup dialog box.

Copies. Because Aldus did not design this dialog box, this option is one of a number of redundancies with PageMaker's Print dialog box. PageMaker overrides this setting, no matter what you enter here. But the number you type in here will appear in PageMaker's Print dialog box the next time you go to print.

Don't ask us why; it's just one of the perversities of the way the two systems (Windows and PageMaker) work together. It's like the tug-of-war you see in marriage: the PageMaker Print dialog box gets its way the first time you print, but the Windows (Setup or printer specific) dialog box gets its way the next time. Save yourself some bother; leave this option at its default setting of *1* and control your copies from the PageMaker Print dialog box.

▼ *Tip: Multiple copies for duplication fanatics*

If you work in an office where you routinely need to print two or more copies every time you use PageMaker (say as proofs to distribute to several proofreaders or administrators), then ignore our advice above and set the number of copies in the printer-specific dialog box. That number is then passed back to PageMaker's Print dialog box as the default (not immediately, but the next time you go to print). It will stay in there until you change it, in fact, even if you exit Windows and start it again.

If you need to override for one or two jobs, you can do that in PageMaker's Print dialog box; your default will return the next time you go to print. But don't come crying to us if somebody else uses your computer and wonders why the Print dialog box always comes up ready to print five copies.

The PostScript Printer dialog box

In addition to settings just discussed, the PostScript printer dialog box also provides options for Scaling. This is another redundancy with PageMaker's Print dialog box. Unlike the Copies option, PageMaker doesn't override this setting; the two scaling settings have a cumulative effect. For example, if you put 50 percent here and 50 percent in PageMaker's Print dialog box, your pages come out scaled to 25 percent. To avoid confusion, leave this setting at 100 percent and control all your scaling from the Print dialog box.

That just leaves the six buttons along the right side. It seems like every time you open a printing dialog box in Windows, it presents you with a set of buttons that leads to another box full of buttons in a series of dialog boxes that goes on forever. For example, what about that Add Printer button? If you get to this dialog box via Control Panel, this is actually the second Add Printer button you come across. Does clicking this button lead to that same path, drawing you into an endless loop of dialog boxes that continually "Add," "Configure," and "Setup" printers? Have you taken a wrong turn somewhere and ended up in Dialog Box Hell!?

Fortunately, the answer is no. This isn't the Twilight Zone, it's just Windows. It may be cheaper than a Macintosh (maybe), but you pay in other ways.

In truth, the Add Printers dialog box is an attempt to look toward the future. As PostScript printers multiply, more companies will bring out their own PostScript drivers. When that happens, you can click this button and put that manufacturer's disk in your floppy drive. Then you'll have to deal with *their* dialog boxes.

The other buttons aren't so intimidating. You already know what OK and Cancel and Help do. That just leaves the Options button. That's next.

PostScript Options

As you might expect, clicking the Options button brings up the Options dialog box (Figure 6-9). Most of the time you can just ignore this box and use the default settings that come with Windows. Of course, there will always be people who insist on pushing every button and poking into every box, and you can learn a lot that way. Even if you're not of that bent, there may be circumstances in which you would want to change these settings. Let's see what they are.

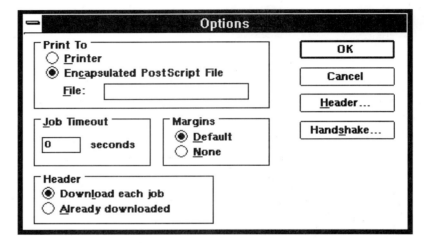

Figure 6-9
PostScript Printer Options dialog box

Print To. These buttons let you divert your output from its normal route (Printer) to an EPS file. This is useful if you want to make one of your PageMaker pages into a picture. Under Print To, click the Encapsulated PostScript File radio button. Under "Header," click the Already downloaded button if you're going to be placing this EPS file back into PageMaker; otherwise, leave it unchecked.

Don't type in the name of the EPS file in this dialog box; leave the text edit box blank and let PageMaker prompt you for the name later. (Unlike this unruly Windows dialog box, PageMaker gives you more room for a path name and removes the name from its text box after the file is printed.) When you're done, you can load your page back into PageMaker as an EPS graphic. For more information on this process, see Chapter 5, *Pictures*.

One little warning: An EPS file is not precisely the same as a PostScript print file. So if you're printing to disk to have your files printed at a service bureau, don't use this method. Follow the instructions in "Printing PostScript to Disk" later in this chapter.

Job Timeout. This text box lets you set how many seconds your printer should wait before receiving data from your computer. As a general rule, leave this setting at 0 to prevent your printer from timing out (giving up and quitting). The 0 setting doesn't mean it won't wait at all; rather, it means it will wait forever.

However, if you want to change the time your printer waits before sending you an error message, you'll need to go to a different dialog box. For that function, go to the Windows Control Panel, choose "Printers," open the Printers-Configure dialog box, and use the Transmission Retry option.

Margins. For most PostScript printers, you can ignore this one. This setting is intended to control the area of the paper on which an application can print. The default setting limits the printing to the area the printer can use; the None option sets the entire page as the printable area.

The settings have no effect on PageMaker, which always prints to the maximum area your printer can handle. Most laser printers can't print any closer to the edge of the paper than about a quarter inch, so you can't "bleed" items off the sides of pages.

Header. The Options dialog box contains two buttons governing the transmission of a PostScript "header" to your printer and another button, labeled Header, which opens the dialog box shown in Figure 6-10. A header is a set of PostScript routines that Windows calls on for various purposes. The printer must receive these instructions before it can print.

By default, the header is sent to the printer every time you print. If you are planning to print to disk for output at a service bureau, use the settings "Download each job" and "Send Header to Printer" so your disk file has the appropriate header information for the service bureau. You should also use these defaults if your printer is connected to a network and shared by others.

Figure 6-10
Header dialog box

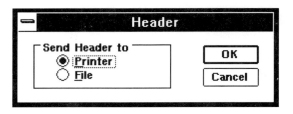

▼ Tip: Download the header semipermanently for faster printing.

If your printer is connected to your computer and you send it lots of print jobs throughout the day, you can save a little time on each by downloading the header only once a day.

In the Header dialog box, click "File." When you click OK, you'll be prompted with a text box. Type in the full path and name of the header file that you want to create. (You have room for 30 characters.) Click OK and Windows creates your header file.

Now you need to download it to your printer the same way you download fonts. If you're using PSDOWN, just answer No when it asks whether to delete the file after downloading. You can even send the file with an ordinary DOS COPY command. For example, let's say your header file is HEADER.TXT, located in the Windows subdirectory, and your printer is hooked up to your LPT1 parallel port. At the DOS prompt, you would type:

copy c:\windows\header.txt lpt1:

You can automate the whole process even further by inserting the above line in your AUTOEXEC.BAT file so that the header goes to your printer each time you start your computer. For this to work, however, you must turn on your printer before you turn on your computer.

Once the header is downloaded, choose "Already downloaded" in the Header section of the Options dialog box. That way, PageMaker won't download the header each time you print. Once you have things set up, you should save about 20 seconds per print job. Okay, that's not a whole lot, but it can add up. You were expecting maybe some miracles?

Handshake dialog box. The Handshake button and its resulting dialog box (Figure 6-11) only affects printers that use a serial port (like COM1 or COM2 or an RS-232 port). Generally, you should leave handshaking set to Hardware. Nevertheless, folks with older Apple LaserWriters or those faced with printing problems might benefit from setting the handshaking to software.

Figure 6-11
Handshake dialog box

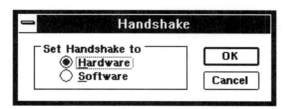

If you decide to go this route, you'll need to make a corresponding adjustment in Control Panel's Ports - Settings dialog box. "Flow Control" should be set to Xon/Xoff for a software handshake and set to Hardware for a hardware handshake. If you still have problems, see section on "Printing Problems" at the end of this chapter.

PCL/Hewlett-Packard LaserJet dialog box

As you can see from Figure 6-12, the PCL/HP LaserJet dialog box is similar to the PostScript dialog box, with only a few differences. Let's go over them.

Memory. Use this pop-up list to tell Windows how much RAM your printer has. If you don't know, you can use the default setting, but you run the risk of unnecessary "Out of memory" messages when trying to print. To find out just how much RAM you have in your printer, run the printer's normal print test (not the font test). The printout contains a report on your printer's memory.

Graphics Resolution. If you do get an out-of-memory message or if only part of your pictures print, you can use this option to free up some memory. Generally, a lower resolution takes less printer

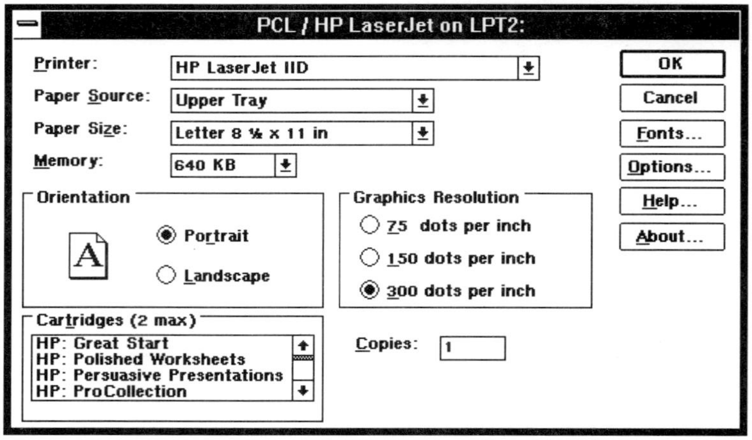
PCL / HP LaserJet on LPT2:
Printer:
HP LaserJet IID
Paper Source:
Upper Tray
Paper Size:
Letter 8 ½ x 11 in
Memory:
640 KB
OK
Cancel
Fonts...
Options...
Help...
About...
Orientation
Portrait
Landscape
Graphics Resolution
75 dots per inch
150 dots per inch
300 dots per inch
Cartridges (2 max)
HP: Great Start
HP: Polished Worksheets
HP: Persuasive Presentations
HP: ProCollection
Copies:
1

Figure 6-12
The PCL/HP LaserJet dialog box

memory. But some graphics, such large ruling boxes, actually require less memory at higher resolutions. Experiment with these options to find out what works best for your publication. If you intend to print the final copy of your memory-hogging work on the same printer, consider investing in a memory upgrade to get the highest print quality possible.

As the name suggests, changing "Graphics Resolution" only affects the resolution of any images (bitmapped graphics) you print, not text. It's also faster, which can speed things along at the proofing stage.

Cartridges. If you followed the pushy and patronizing advice that began this chapter, you will have already used this list box to specify font cartridges for your target printer. Windows will let you select a maximum of one or two cartridges, depending on the printer you selected.

If your cartridges aren't listed here, you can still use them, providing you have the font PCM files, available from your cartridge manufacturer. To find out how to install these files, see the section "Adding and Removing Soft Fonts" earlier in this chapter.

Fonts. Clicking the Fonts button opens the Printer Font Installer dialog box. For a rundown of how to use this dialog box to manage your font chores, turn to the section "PageMaker and Printer Fonts" earlier in this chapter.

Options. If you've selected a printer with duplex capabilities, an Options button also appears in this dialog box. This really only refers to duplex options and brings up a small dialog box with the same (redundant) options as you saw in PageMaker's Print dialog box (None, Long edge, Short edge). Since you can control this from PageMaker's Print dialog, ignore this option.

Printing PostScript to Disk

For many PageMaker users, getting their pages from a laser printer is only the first step in the printing process. Even if you don't do so now, chances are at some point you'll want or need the quality of high-resolution output. That means going to a service bureau with PostScript imagesetting equipment. To get the best results, you need to know what to give them.

Generally you have two choices: (1) handing over your PageMaker publication file or (2) first printing the publication to a PostScript print file and taking that. Most service bureaus we work with give you a discount if you print the pages to disk rather than giving them PageMaker files.

With printed-to-disk PostScript, all the service bureau has to do is download the PostScript file, rather than opening your PageMaker file and worrying about what fonts you've used, whether they have the right printer font metric files, whether you have the same version of PageMaker, what print options you've used, or whether you have special words in your hyphenation exceptions dictionary. What you give them is what you get.

This means that you have to be careful. If your job comes back without crop marks, without spot color overlays, or without knockouts, it's your fault; you won't be able to pin these mistakes on your service bureau. At the same time, you have control over everything this way.

Printing to disk is simple. Open the Windows Control Panel and double-click Printers. In the dialog box, make sure the printer you want is selected and "Active." Then click the Configure button. In the

Printers - Configure dialog box, scroll through the Ports list box and select the word "FILE." If you want to double-check to make sure the correct printer is selected, click "Setup." Click the OK buttons to get out. When you're ready to print, open the Print dialog box in PageMaker and select "PostScript Printer on FILE" from the Printer list box and click OK. PageMaker prints the PostScript file to disk, stopping only to ask you to name the file.

▼ Tip: Install Your Printer Twice

Going into Control Panel every time you need a print file is a pain. You can eliminate that pain by installing your printer twice: once set to the port you normally use, and once set to FILE. You don't even need your Windows' installation disks. Just open Control Panel, click "Printers," and click the Add Printer button. In the list of printers, find and select the same printer you will most often use for print files. Then click "Install." If you've already installed a printer that uses the same printer driver (PostScript, PCL / HP LaserJet, etc.), Windows asks whether you want to use the current driver or a new one (Figure 6-13). Click "Current." Windows installs (or reinstalls) your printer as "Inactive" with "NONE" as the port. Use the Configure button to set the port to "FILE" and the Setup button to make any other adjustments. Now you can change between sending your jobs to your printer or to disk just by selecting a different printer in PageMaker's Print dialog box.

You can use this method to install or double-install as many printers as you think you'll need: an imagesetter configured to FILE, a LaserWriter installed once to COM1 and once to FILE, a LaserJet to LPT1, and so on.

▼ Tip: Selective Downloading of Typefaces to PostScript Files

If you want to download some of the typefaces used in your pub but not all, your job may be easy or hard, depending once again on your printer. If you have a PCL printer, just use the Printer Font Installer dialog box to delete whatever fonts you like from your assigned

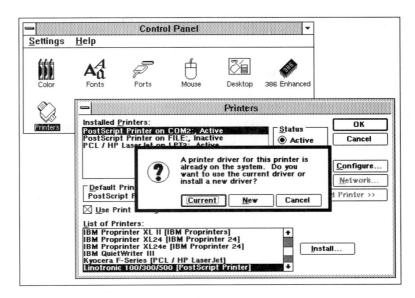

Figure 6-13
Installing one driver for two printers

printer (but not from your disk), as explained in "Adding and Removing Soft Fonts" earlier in this chapter.

If you have a PostScript printer, you are once again faced with the limitations of Windows PostScript driver. You could go back into WIN.INI and edit out all the lines you added to make your fonts download automatically/temporarily (see "Adding and Removing Soft Fonts" earlier in this chapter).

A better solution is to keep two extra copies of WIN.INI, one with fonts marked for temporary downloading and one that assumes the fonts are in the printer (or its hard drive). Then create a batch file that copies the proper replacement over the current WIN.INI. For more on making and running this sort of batch file, see "The Blight of the Bloated WIN.INI" earlier in this chapter.

If your service bureau doesn't own all of your fonts, you could give them your PostScript typefaces to download to their hard disk in advance. But this practice is in violation of your font license agreement (and arguably immoral), and they may not be willing to do it. Instead, download to your print file only the fonts your service bureau doesn't have. This lets them print your words in your fonts without giving them the whole typeface.

If you're preparing an EPS file (to be placed as a graphic, as opposed to a regular PostScript file for printing), you'll have to choose whether to use this method to exclude fonts based on the final destination of the file. You can include the PostScript typefaces, but it makes the file much bigger and may make it difficult to print when placed in a PageMaker pub. If you do include the typefaces, on the other hand, you know they're there no matter what printer it goes to or what computer or program it's being printed from.

Prism: PostScript Without Pain

If you're the adventurous type who likes to experiment a little and get the most out of your applications, then by all means, dive into the world of PostScript programming. You'll gain control over your PageMaker files that PageMaker itself isn't likely to give you for quite a while. You'll inject some professional razzle-dazzle into your pubs and amaze your friends.

But if you're like lots of people, you want those fabulous PostScript effects without the pain of programming. In that case, you might want to look into other programs. The latest Micrografx PostScript Driver, for example, gives you control over line weight and screen frequency and angle. But for more powerful PostScript options, try Publisher's Prism from InSight Systems. This app runs either in DOS (for hardcore PC veterans) or in a simple point-and-click Windows version. Prism does not work within PageMaker directly, but only modifies PostScript files—like the kind you make with PageMaker when printing to disk.

But Publisher's Prism is clearly not for everybody. Its main purpose is to create color separations of PostScript files, a task that can require some expensive experimentation even beyond the program's already hefty $695 price. (For more on the separation process, see Chapter 7, *Color*.) We can't recommend the average user shell out this kind of dough just for a few PostScript effects. But if you run a service bureau and are likely to need a separation program anyway, Publisher's Prism does present some handy features for modifying even single-color print files. Let's look at some of the tricks it can do.

Mirror and Negative

There's not much reason to print mirrored (left for right) or negative (black for white) pages on a laser printer, but if you need either of these options for film output, Prism lets you set up the film the way your commercial printer wants it. Most printers want to get right-reading negatives, emulsion side down. That means when you hold up the film with the emulsion side of the film away from you, you can read it, though you're reading clear type on black film. Prism makes it child's play: if you select Negative, your mirror options are Emulsion Up or Emulsion Down (Figure 6-14). Even if you select the default "Positive" (black type on white), you can choose Right Reading or Wrong Reading.

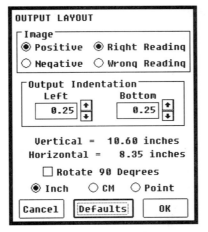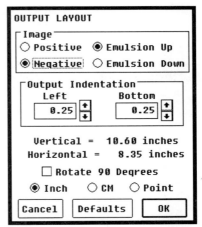

Figure 6-14
Some of Publisher's Prism's output options

Many imagesetting service bureaus prefer to use little PostScript programs or the imagesetter's front-panel controls to control these options (especially inverse), rather than having PageMaker control them, so talk to your service bureau before you set this up.

Rotate Pages

Prism's Rotate 90 Degrees option is also useful for imagesetter output. It prints the pages perpendicular to the roll of film (with lines of type running the length of the roll). Especially if you're printing a lot of pages (or using the side-by-side printing tricks discussed earlier), this saves paper and makes it easy to cut the pages apart because they're side by side on the roll.

Scaling

You already know how to scale your pages from PageMaker's Print dialog box. Unfortunately, neither that dialog box nor Windows' PostScript printer dialog box lets you enter fractional or decimal values. If you need that kind of control, Prism can come to the rescue.

▼ *Tip: Scaling to Match True Printer's Points*

PostScript uses 72 points to the inch, which seems sensible and useful until you consider that traditional printer's points come to a little more than 72 to the inch. If you are set up for traditional printer's points, and don't want to change, scale your pages up to 100.35 percent. With laser printers, for some reason (rounding, most likely), we've had better luck using 100.6 or 100.7 percent.

Halftone Screens

One thing that makes PostScript so powerful is the control it provides over halftone screens—not just for scanned images, but for everything where you use gray. Anything with a gray percentage comes out of a PostScript printer screened. That's the only way to represent gray on a black-and-white device. PostScript lets you control three aspects of the halftone screen—screen frequency (how many halftone cells per inch), screen angle (the orientation of those rows of cells), and cell shape (dots, lines, squares, ovals, etc.).

Even though PostScript gives you all that control over screens, however, PageMaker doesn't—at least not from the menus. To make these changes, you either have to edit PageMaker's PostScript output, or use the handy-dandy Halftones menu in Publisher's Prism.

Screen Frequency. If you're using Prism, choosing Screen Frequency brings up the Halftone Screen Frequency dialog box (Figure 6-15). The frequency you choose depends on how you're going to produce and reproduce the publication. Also remember that the higher the frequency, especially on laser printers, the less possible gray shades you can get. So if you choose a fine screen frequency, you're less likely to get exactly the percentage you ask for. Table 6-1 gives some typical scenarios, and recommended frequencies for each.

Table 6-1 Recommended screen frequencies

Output Device/ Resolution	Output Medium	Reproduction Method	Reproduction Medium	Screen Frequency
Laser/300	Copy paper	Laser	Copy paper	60
Laser/300	Laser paper	Photocopier	Coated paper	60-80
Laser/300	Laser paper	Offset printing	Newsprint	60-70
Imagesetter/1200	Paper	Photocopier	Uncoated paper	70-80
Imagesetter/1200	Paper	Offset printing	Uncoated paper	80-90
Imagesetter/1200	Paper	Offset printing	Coated paper	90-100
Imagesetter/2400	Film	Offset printing	Coated paper	120-150
Imagesetter/1200	Film or paper	Offset printing	Newsprint	75-85

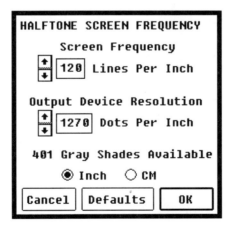

Figure 6-15
Prism's Halftone Screen Frequency dialog box

▼ Tip: Defaults Faults

When Linotype released the version 49.3 ROMs for the L-300, a lot of people were surprised to find that the default screen frequencies had changed. The defaults used to be 90 lines per inch at 1270 dpi, and 120 lines per inch at 2540 dpi. For version 49.3, it's 150 lpi for both.

Linotype has a PostScript file that you can download to change defaults back to what they were. You have to download it each time you restart the machine, or put it in your "Sys/Start" file on the Lino hard disk. If you're anticipating the old defaults, be sure to check with your service bureau to make sure they have this file and will download it before running your job.

Screen angle. For normal gray screens, you'll generally want to use a 45-degree angle. It's the least apparent to the eye, so it gives an impression of a smooth gray fill. For special-effect screens, however (line screens, square dots, ellipses, and the like), you may want to use a 0-degree angle. Once again, Prism reduces this process to a simple dialog box, shown in Figure 6-16. If you're using Prism to do a one-color job, just set the angle value for "Black" and ignore the rest. When you go to print the modified file to disk, choose "Produce Separates" from the File menu and uncheck all but the Black option.

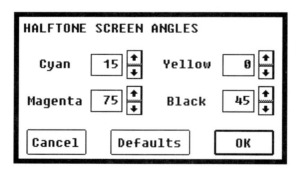

Figure 6-16
Prism's Halftone Screen Angle dialog box

▼ ***Tip: What You Ask for Ain't What You Get***

You might think that when you ask for a given screen frequency and angle on a PostScript device, that's what you're going to get. That just ain't so, although you're more likely to get close if you choose a 0-, 45-, or 90-degree screen angle. It's just a fact of life with digital halftoning. There are only so many frequency/angle combinations available. The lower the resolution, the less available combinations, so the less likely you are to get the frequency and angle you ask for. Table 6-2 shows some standard angles and frequencies requested at 300 and 2,540 dpi, and the angles and frequencies you actually get. PostScript Level 2 is supposed to make the actual values come a lot closer to the requested values, so watch for it. Coming soon to a printer near you.

This is just a sampling to demonstrate the realities. You can see that the variations aren't great with higher resolutions, but if you're doing color separations this will count. If you just want some flat gray tints, especially if you stick to 45-degree increments, you should be fine with whatever spits out.

Table 6-2 Requested versus actual screen frequencies and angles

	Requested		Actual	
	Frequency	Angle	Frequency	Angle
Apple LaserWriter at 300 dpi	60	45	53	45
	50	45	53	45
	60	15	58.8	11
	70	45	67.1	27
	75	45	67.1	27
	65	45	60	37
	65	0	60	0
Linotronic 300 at 2540 dpi	100	0	101.6	0
	100	45	99.8	45
	120	0	121	0
	120	45	119.7	45

Handy PostScript Programs

What if you want to print negatives and don't want to buy Publisher's Prism? Here are several short PostScript utilities that could save you money. Type them using your word processor, save them as text files, and download them to your printer when you need them. Anything on a line following a "%" is a comment and can be omitted.

```
%Mirrorprint on
serverdict begin 0 exitserver
```

```
statusdict begin
/mirrorprint true def %false for normal printing
end

%Negative printing on
serverdict begin 0 exitserver
statusdict begin
/negativeprint true def %false for positive printing
end

%Turn off startup page
serverdict begin 0 exitserver
statusdict begin
false setdostartpage %true to turn startup page back on

%Change RIP name
serverdict begin 0 exitserver
statusdict begin
(printerName) setprintername end quit
```

Send these files to your printer using a downloading program or the Copy command (copy *filename* /b lpt1:).

Changing PageMaker's PostScript

When you print to a PostScript printer, PageMaker uses Windows' PostScript driver to send a stream of PostScript code to the printer. PostScript code is just ASCII text—no special characters, no nonsense. Readable by human eyes.

What happens when these codes reach the printer? They're turned into a large bitmap by the PostScript interpreter in your printer. When you print PostScript to a disk file, PageMaker sends the code to the disk file instead of to the printer. It's about the same code—the only difference in the code that's sent to the file is that PageMaker can't query the printer for fonts or available memory. In this case, PageMaker uses the settings in the printer setup you've specified to make guesses about when the printer would run out of memory, or what fonts are available.

PRINTING 365

PostScript Dictionaries

PostScript relies on dictionaries—collections of procedure definitions that can be used over and over again—to render the text and graphics in a PostScript printing job. On the Macintosh, PageMaker uses a dictionary named Aldus Prep. Under Windows, PageMaker uses Windows' own PostScript dictionary, Win33Dict, also known as the PostScript header. This dictionary contains all of the PostScript procedures PageMaker uses to position and draw text and graphics on your printer.

What's the point of our telling you this? Simple. If you don't like the way that PageMaker or Windows prints something, you can change it. You'll have to learn some PostScript, but it's a pretty easy programming language to learn, as programming languages go. Besides, we'll show you how to do a cool thing.

Making a Copy of Win33Dict

If you want to see what's in Win33Dict, follow these steps to write it to a text file.

1. Choose Target printer from PageMaker's File menu (Alt-F, T). PageMaker displays the Target printer dialog box.
2. Click the Setup button (Alt-S). The Printer setup dialog box appears.
3. Click the Options button (Alt-O). The Options dialog box appears.
4. Click the Header button (Alt-H). The Header dialog box appears.
5. Click the File option, then click the OK button. A dialog box appears, containing a text edit box for you to enter the filename for the file you want to write the dictionary to.
6. Type the file name in the text edit box and press the OK button. PageMaker and Windows write the Windows PostScript dictionary to disk as a text file.
7. Close all of the dialog boxes.

At this point, you can open the text file you've created with PageMaker or any word processor. Go ahead. Do it.

Pretty unreadable, eh? Nothing in here looks like the PostScript you see in the PostScript books. It's all terse little commands like ed or bd where ordinary PostScript would say exch def or lineto. Don't let this worry you, it's just engineers protecting their art. You can make the file more readable, though, by searching for "/" and replacing it with a slash preceded by a carriage return. PostScript won't notice the extra carriage returns, and it'll make Win33Dict easier for you to read.

At this point, you can modify the file. Once you've changed the file, you can download it to your printer by typing copy c:*filename* /b *port* (for example, copy c:\psheader.txt /b lpt1:) to send the file to your printer. Once the file's been downloaded, it's in the printer's memory until you turn the printer off. If you want to download the edited dictionary every time you start your computer, you can put this command line in your AUTOEXEC.BAT file. Note that your printer will have to be turned on before you turn on your system for this to work.

Following is one of our favorite PostScript tricks. It's just a tiny glimpse of what you can do by editing your Win33Dict. To take advantage of this power, though, you're going to have to learn a lot more about PostScript. A great place to start is *Learning PostScript; A Visual Approach* by Ross Smith (Peachpit Press). You'll probably also need the *PostScript Language Reference Manual* from Adobe Systems (Addison-Wesley), a.k.a. "The Red Book."

Apart from books, experimentation is the best teacher. Wonder what a PageMaker-drawn box looks like in PostScript? Draw a box and print it to disk; then look at the text file with your word processor. Make some changes and see what happens when you download the file to your printer. You'll catch on.

Outline text

You've got PageMaker. You've got a PostScript printer. You've got PostScript fonts. Why in the world can't you print outline type? All your friends with Macintoshes, PageMaker, and PostScript printers can print outline type. What's the deal?

We don't know why, but the Type specifications dialog box in Windows PageMaker lacks an option for outline type. What we do know is how to make your PostScript printer produce the outline type you want and need.

This technique modifies your Win33Dict so that it includes a routine for switching to outline text when the type's color is some specific value, in this case 99% Black. Color your type with this color in PageMaker, and you'll get outline type when you print. If you're creating spot color overlays, this method's not going to work—all of your outline type will end up on a separate overlay.

The first thing you need to do is to print your Win33Dict to disk as PostScript, as described earlier in "Making a Copy of Win33Dict." Then, follow these steps.

1. Type the following text in your word processor. The indents and carriage returns don't matter, but the spelling and capitlization definitely do, so take your time and proof the code carefully.

```
/font
    {
    /name ed
    %%the next line is the one that watches for our "outline" color
    bR 2 eq {MakeOutlineFont} if
    /Ascent ed 0 ne
    /fSO ed 0 ne
    /fUL ed
    /Sy ed
    /Sx ed
    10.0 div
    /ori ed
    -10.0 div
    /esc ed
    /BCh ed
    name findfont [Sx 0 0 Sy neg 0 Ascent]
    esc mxE rotate mxF concatmatrix makefont setfont
    fUL
            {
            currentfont
            dup
            /FontInfo get
            /UnderlinePosition known not
                    {
                    pop
                    /Courier findfont
                    }if
            /FontInfo get
```

```
                        /UnderlinePosition get 1000 div 0 exch mxF transform
                        /dyUL ed
                        /dxUL ed
                        } if
            fSO
                        {
                        0 .3 mxF transform
                        /dySO ed
                        /dxSO ed
                        } if
            fUL fSO or
                        {
                        currentfont
                        dup
                        /FontInfo get
                        /UnderlineThickness known not
                                    {
                                    pop
                                    /Courier findfont
                                    } if
                        /FontInfo get
                        /UnderlineThickness get 1000 div Sy mul
                        /cyUL ed
                        }if
            }bd
/MakeOutlineFont
    {
    /basefontdict name findfont def
    /outlineFontName (Yo!OutlineFont) def
    /numentries basefontdict maxlength 1 add def
    basefontdict /UniqueId known not
                {
                numentries numentries 1 add def
                } if
    /outfontdict numentries dict def
    basefontdict
                {
                exch dup /FID ne
                        {
                        exch outfontdict 3 1 roll put
                        }
```

```
                    {
                      pop
                      pop
                    }
                  ifelse
                  }
            forall
            outfontdict /FontName outlineFontName put
            outfontdict /PaintType 2 put
            outfontdict /StrokeWidth 20 put
            outlineFontName outfontdict definefont pop
            /name outlineFontName def
         }
      def
```

2. Open the PostScript header file with your word processor.

3. Search for /font.

4. Select from /font to /min (select /font, don't select /min).

6. Replace the selection with the text you typed in step 1.

7. Save the file.

Now, when you want to use outline type, just select the type you want the effect applied to and color it with a color that's defined (using the CMYK color model) as 99% Black. Download the modified Win33Dict to your PostScript printer and print the file. The text you colored with the outline color prints as outline text.

Printing Problems

While all these nifty tricks are fun and often useful, you probably turned to this chapter because something didn't come out of your printer the way you expected, or didn't come out of your printer at all. This does nothing good for your blood pressure. Despite the wonderful things laser printers have given us in recent years, there are, alas, still things that can go wrong. Here are some favorites, and some favorite solutions.

Most often, PageMaker printing problems have to do with the printer running out of memory. Unfortunately, as you probably know by now, Windows doesn't exactly provide detailed, helpful error messages to tell you stuff like this. "The Print Manager cannot write to [port]. There may be a printer problem; resume the queue when the problem is corrected or cancel the document." Really helpful, huh?

To get any kind of feedback from your printer, you need to turn to other sources. If you have an HP LaserJet, look to the display on the printer's control panel for error messages. A low memory problem will probably read out as "Mem overflow," which basically means you either have to upgrade your printer's memory, or take one of our suggestions below.

If you have a PostScript printer on a serial port, you can get error messages from PSDOWN, the same utility you use to download fonts. Just have PageMaker print the problem publication or pages to disk and use PSDOWN to send the file to your printer. Any messages the printer sends back are displayed on screen. A VM error (for virtual memory), for example, indicates a memory problem. But lack of memory can cause other, even murkier messages. When laser printers run out of memory, they send back whatever their last instruction was as an error message. So you'll often see error messages citing common PostScript commands like def as the offending code. Don't search through the print file looking to eliminate def. You can't have PostScript without def! It's just the last thing that the printer knew before it lost its mind. Instead, try these techniques.

Print fewer pages at a time. Or print pages one at a time. Try to discover what pages don't print and identify what items on them might be difficult to print. RAM-consumptive items include:

- Large, high-resolution PCX and TIFF images (especially if you've done lots of cropping)
- EPS images (especially suspect large and complex Designer, Corel Draw, or PageMaker-generated EPS graphics)
- Text that uses lots of different downloadable fonts

Remove items from a page and print again. Eventually, you'll find the item the printer's getting stuck on. "But wait!" you're saying. "If I didn't need the item on the page, I wouldn't have put it there, and the program's worthless if I can't print the page!" Fine. We only want to establish which item is choking the printer. Then we can work on it. If it's a graphic, think about ways you might be able to simplify it.

Reset the printer to clear its memory. Either use PSDOWN or PCSEND (for PostScript printers), the Printer Font Installer dialog box (for HP LaserJets), or turn the thing off and on (for any printer). (For details, see "Soft Fonts: Manual/Semipermanent Downloading" earlier in this chapter.) This clears out any downloaded fonts you have in the printer's memory, which means you'll have to download fonts temporarily (automatically). If you have a PCL printer, you can do this from the Fonts dialog box (see "Soft Fonts: Automatic/Temporary Downloading" earlier in this chapter.) For PostScript printers, swap out your current WIN.INI with the one you made for auto-downloading (see the tip "Selective Downloading of Typefaces to PostScript Files" earlier in this chapter). This takes longer to print, but it may save the printer from gagging on your publication.

Try using Save as. PageMaker compresses the file, and sometimes it will print afterward.

Print the troublesome pages to disk as PostScript and download them. Sometimes the downloading techniques require less of the printer's RAM than PageMaker's downloading processes. Use PSDOWN, PCSEND, or the DOS copy command to send the print file to your PostScript printer.

Try another driver. If you have a third-party driver (like the one from Micrografx), try printing your publication with whatever one you *didn't* use before.

Have someone else try it. We know it sounds crazy, but sometimes it works.

▼ Tip: If a TIFF Image Prints as a Low-resolution Bitmap

If your TIFF image prints as a low-resolution bitmap, the image is probably not stored in PageMaker, but is linked to the original file. In this case, however, PageMaker can't find the linked file, and so gives you a low-res screen bitmap instead. Choose "Links" from the File menu and update the link. For more information on linking source files, see "Link and Link options" in Chapter 8, *Workgroup Publishing*. When you take your PageMaker files to a service bureau, make sure you take all of the linked files—especially the TIFFs—with you.

▼ Tip: Forever and a Day

If your print job is so complex that the imagesetter or printer gets tired of waiting for data and times out after a while, you need to teach your printer to be more patient. Open the Windows Control Panel, click the Printer icon, and (with your printer selected), click "Configure." In the Timeouts box, increase the number of seconds under "Transmission Retry." Generally the default works best, but if you get error messages when everything else is okay, this might help.

For PostScript printers, you should also go to the Options dialog box (via the specific-printer dialog box accessed from the Print dialog box) and make sure "Job Timeout" is set to 0 (the default). This setting is the number of seconds the printer waits before giving up. With a setting of 0 it should never give up. This is especially useful if you are printing big bitmaps over a network, where communications can get very slow.

▼ Tip: Nested EPS Files

Watch out for EPS files within EPS files within EPS files. Suppose you create an EPS graphic in Corel Draw, for instance, place it in PageMaker and combine it with other graphics, and then save that conglomeration as EPS and place it in PageMaker (again). It's quite possible that the nested EPS files won't print.

As always, the most important trick when you run into problems is to keep poking at it until it works. We've had to go through incredible contortions at times to coax pages out of the printer, but we never (or hardly ever) have to resort to manual pasteup or stripping by the printer. Just keep telling yourself, "it will work."

CHAPTER 7

Color

PageMaker first ventured into the world of color with version 3.0. That version offered the ability to specify up to 256 colors, and to print spot-color overlays. We always thought 256 colors was kind of overkill when all you could do was print spot colors (you couldn't even print in color on color PostScript printers). It's not often that we have a 256-color press to work with, and if we did, we'd need to rent out the Stanford linear accelerator building to house it. Of course, we could do it on a 128-color press with work-and-turn…

Now, with the arrival of version 4, PageMaker has gained several color-related features:

- The ability to place color bitmapped images
- Printing in color on color PostScript printers
- Printing color information to PostScript disk files for separation with other programs
- A color palette that can handle 32,767 colors

This version lets you specify more colors than anyone will ever need, print spot-color overlays directly from the program, and print PostScript to disk that can be separated with other programs like

Publisher's Prism from InSight Systems. In addition, you can print selected spot-color overlays, rather than printing all of them.

In this chapter, we explain the different methods of color production and reproduction (they're intimately connected), and the best ways to use PageMaker to make those methods work—defining colors, applying them to objects on the page, getting output from those pages, and reproducing that output. In addition to this chapter, refer to the color pages in this book for in-depth discussion and illustration of how PageMaker works with color for offset printing.

Color Printing Techniques

The first thing to consider when you're working with color in PageMaker is how you're going to produce and reproduce the pages. There are basically three options, and you'll need to use different techniques in PageMaker depending on which you're using.

Color printing. Print on a color printer or slide recorder. This is for one-off type of work—printed comps for approval, for example, or slides for a presentation. You might use color printers for very short runs (less than 20), but they're mainly good for getting one or two copies to show people.

▼ Tip: Additional Color Printing Options

If Windows doesn't have a driver for your color printer, consider using a third-party driver package, such as Zenographics' SuperPrint.

Spot color printing. Print using multiple passes on a laser printer or photocopier with different colored toners, or on a printing press using one, two, or three PMS inks (PMS stands for Pantone Matching System—a standard, numbered set of colors). Use PageMaker's Spot color overlay feature to print the different color elements on different overlays, and combine the overlays using multiple passes or a multicolor press.

Multiple-pass printing with different color toners is an easy, inexpensive way to get color on your pages for short runs, especially if you combine it with colored paper. One-, two-, and three-color offset printing is less expensive than four-color process printing (the next scenario), and you can ask your printer for PMS inks that are difficult or impossible to reproduce with the process colors—silver, copper, or gold, for example, forest green, or a creamy, rich, slate blue.

Four-color process printing. Print on a printing press using percentages of the four process inks (cyan, magenta, yellow, and black—CMYK). You print the pages to disk as PostScript files, and then use a utility like Publisher's Prism (or Aldus PrePrint on the Mac) to separate the colors into four separations. The printer uses those four pieces of film to make the printing plates, and prints the job using the four process inks. You can create millions of different colors by combining the four inks (even reproducing photographs), but the printing is expensive, and you face the (sometimes formidable) problems of creating process color separations from your color pages.

You can combine the PMS and process methods if you have the budget for a five-or six-color print run. You might use the process inks for most of the work, and use PMS inks for special colors you can't get from the process inks.

Color Models

You can specify colors in PageMaker using any of three different color models. Depending on how you're printing the job, you'll want to use different models. You can use CMYK percentage specs, a Pantone palette, or the HLS/RGB model.

- CMYK is the color model used for four-color process printing. You specify percentages of the four colors, and the four inks combine on press to create your colors.
- Pantone is a standard set of numbered colors that are available in many forms—pens, markers, printing inks, etc.
- RGB is Red/Green/Blue; HLS is Hue/Lightness/Saturation (also called HSB, for Hue/Saturation/Brightness). RGB and HLS are

used for screen displays and most slide recorders. They're different views of the same thing, as you can see with the parallel system found in the Define custom colors dialog box (buried deep within the Windows Control Panel: Click "Color," then "Color palette," then "Define custom color").

Overlays and Separations

Remember that process separations are different from spot-color overlays. Overlays are often called mechanical separations, which adds to the confusion. We'll stick to the two distinct terms—separations (used for process printing) and overlays (used for spot-color printing). But we can't totally alleviate the confusion, because the way you specify color in PageMaker is sort of confused.

You can use CMYK specs, for example, to define a spot color, which basically means a color that will be output on an overlay and printed with PMS inks—with no reference to the CMYK specs. That's weird and confusing (and something different happens if you're using a process separation program), but we'll do our best to comb it out.

To begin with, look at Table 7-1, which shows the different color reproduction methods and how you should spec colors for each. Note for each scenario how you separate the colors, and what you get out of the printer.

Defining Colors

If you need any colors besides PageMaker's canned Red, Green, and Blue (one of the first things we do is delete those from our default Color palette), you'll want to define some colors. Using the Define colors menu item, you can define up to 32,767 colors, all available from the Colors palette.

▼ *Tip The Fast Way to Define Colors;*

Don't go to the Define colors dialog box just to create a new color. Turn on the Colors palette if it's not already on (Ctrl-K), then Ctrl-click

Table 7-1 Color reproduction

Reproduction Method	Recommended Color Model	Number of Overlays/Separations	Separation Method
Color printer or slide recorder	RGB, or HLS	One full-color	No separation required
Multipass printing or photocopying with color toner	Any method	One overlay for each color	Spot color overlays
Offset printing with PMS inks	PMS colors with percentages from the Fill menu	One overlay for each color	Spot color overlays
Four-color process	CMYK percentages with solid fills	Four separations	Process separator
Process plus PMS	CMYK for process colors, PMS for PMS colors	Four separations, plus one overlay for each PMS color	Process separator

on Black or Registration. If you have a colored object selected, the Edit color dialog box fills in with the color values of that object.

The new color you define won't be applied to the selected object (just as new styles aren't applied to selected text), which means you can create any number of colors derived from the color of the selected object by Ctrl-clicking, defining the color, and Ctrl-clicking again. To apply the color, select the object and click on the color name; the object changes to have the color's attributes.

▼ *Tip: The Fast Way to Redefine Colors*

Ctrl-click a color in the Colors palette to bring up the Edit color dialog box where you can edit the color's definition. Unfortunately, you can't change the color name from here as you can when you Ctrl-click a style in the Styles palette. You need to go through the Define colors dialog box.

Applying Colors and Fills

Applying colors in PageMaker comes down to the good old Windows select-then-apply approach, but you'll use different methods for creating overlays and separations. PageMaker has two controls that govern colors and tints for page elements—the Colors palette and the Fill submenu—and they interact with each other. To apply a color, select an object and click the color in the Colors palette. You can apply colors to just about anything on a page, except a graphic that has color specified internally—a color EPS, TIFF, or PCX file, for instance.

When you apply a color to an object, it applies to the whole object. To create a box with a green border and a red fill, for instance, you'll need to create two boxes—one with a green border and no fill, another with a red fill and no border—and align the green-border box on top of the red-fill box. (For more on this, see "Overprinting, Knockouts, and Traps" later in this chapter.)

You apply color to text by selecting it with the Text tool and applying the color. You can also build a color specification into a paragraph style, of course. Selecting a text block with the pointer tool and applying color has no effect.

▼ Tip: Taking Advantage of Being Unable to Apply Color to Text Blocks

Don't worry if you select text blocks when you're trying to color other items. If everything on a spread but the text is to be PMS 274, select everything (press Ctrl-A when the Pointer tool is selected) and click PMS 274 in the Colors palette. The color is applied to everything except the type.

The second method for controlling the color of objects is the Fill submenu. Use this to control tints of spot colors. Just as you can assign a 20 percent fill to a box, you can assign a 20 percent fill and use PMS 286. If you're printing overlays, the box comes out on the PMS 286 overlay with a 20 percent fill.

▼ Tip: Spot Color Tints for Type

Note that you can't apply a fill to type, no matter how you select the type, so you can't have type in a percentage tint of a PMS color using PageMaker's Spot color overlays feature. You just can't.

▼ Tip: Gray Type

If you're working with a one-color publication, you can use the CMYK color model to define shades of gray as colors (50 percent black, for example) and apply them to text to get gray type.

Things get more complicated when you're using CMYK specs and the Fill submenu for process color printing. We don't recommend it, simply because it's confusing and you can do it a better way. Suppose you define a color that's 50 percent magenta, for instance, then apply that color to an object and choose the 10 percent fill for the same object. You'll get a 5 percent tint. You're better off just defining a color that's 5 percent magenta and using that with a solid fill. Table 7-2 shows the results of color/fill combinations when you're creating overlays and separations.

Table 7-2 Color/fill combinations

Color Name	C	M	Y	K	Fill	Results on Spot Color Overlay	Results on Process Separations
C80	80	0	0	0	10%	10 percent	8C
C80	80	0	0	0	Solid	100 percent	80C
PMS 188	0	79	65	47	10%	10 percent	0C/7.9M/6.5Y/4.7K
PMS 188	0	79	65	47	Solid	100 percent	0C/79M/65Y/47K

Notice that the color name has no effect, except that the name prints on the proper overlay when you create spot-color overlays. Also notice that CMYK values don't have any effect when you're using PageMaker's Spot color overlays feature.

The Color Paper

There is one extremely strange color in the PageMaker Colors palette, called Paper. There's also a choice on the Fill submenu by the same name. Both of them are opaque, but they work somewhat differently when you're printing spot-color overlays. If that confuses you, join the club. The setup actually makes sense, though; it lets you obscure items on individual overlays selectively, rather than obscuring items of all colors.

If you apply the *color* Paper to an object, it prints on every color overlay, obscuring any objects that lie behind it, whatever their color. If you apply the *fill* Paper to an object, though, it only obscures objects that lie behind it if they are in the same color. A blue, Paper-filled box, for instance, obscures a blue circle that lies behind it, but doesn't obscure a red circle, regardless of what you see on screen. Wysiwyg (what you see is what you get) is a relative thing.

Another oddly-named color, Registration, works much like Paper, except that it prints black on all overlays.

Paper-colored objects and paper-filled, registration-colored objects print white on all overlays, so use them when you want to obscure something on all overlays. If this all seems confusing to you, see the color pages in this book for a graphic representation of what knocks out of what with different combinations of fills and colors (see "Overprinting, Knockouts, and Traps," later in this chapter).

▼ Tip: PageMaker-drawn Graphics Print on the Wrong Overlay

Watch the Colors palette when drawing LBOs, especially with the Paper and Registration colors, and on monochrome monitors. It's easy to draw in the wrong color so graphics end up on the wrong overlay. Usually, you'll want the Paper-filled objects to end up on the Black overlay, so make sure to choose "Black" in the Colors palette when you fill something with "Paper." Even better, use the color Paper. That way you know it obscures everything behind it, just as it does on screen.

▼ *Tip: To See What it Will Look Like on Colored Paper*

You can redefine the color Paper in PageMaker, so all your on-screen pages are the color you choose. Just Ctrl-click Paper in the Colors palette, and change it to whatever color you want. All your pages on screen are the color of your paper. It doesn't affect output, though; it's just so you can see what your pages will look like on colored paper.

Again, the combinations of colors and fills for separations and overlays result in exceptions to exceptions to exceptions. This is a real mind-bender, especially when you add the choice of printing overlays with or without knockouts. Take a look at the color plates in this book to see the results with various permutations.

Color Specs and Color Correspondence

One piece of advice before we go any farther: what you see on screen, or what comes out of a color printer, will look very different from the final printed output—no matter what your output method. Some colors may be close, but others will be way off. Screen displays, color printers, and printing presses are simply too different to expect good color correspondence. And when you get into overprinting of inks, you can throw wysiwyg right out the window. The screen display is mainly useful to get a general idea of the look, and to make sure you have the correct colors assigned to different page elements.

So how do you know what the colors are going to look like? Use printed color charts, just like always. If you're using an offset press to print your publication, you can get a book full of color swatches printed on coated and uncoated stock. You can get charts of process color combinations (if you're printing CMYK), and charts of PMS inks printed at different percentages. You can even get charts of PMS ink combinations (what does it look like when you combine a 20 percent tint of PMS 206 with a 40 percent tint of PMS 286?). Use these charts. Do not rely on your display. The charts will show you much more accurately what you can expect off the printing press.

Remember, also, that you can't expect to use a color laser printer as a true proofing device for color printing. The colors won't be the same, whether you're using process or PMS inks. You can do a color printout to show to clients or other mucketymucks, but you'll need to get a true color proof (Matchprint, Chromalyn, or the like) from your printer based on the separated film. As they say in the printing trade, "the Chrome is the contract."

▼ Tip Easier-to-Read Composites

When you print composite proofs of your publication to a black-and-white printer, PageMaker renders the colors as shades of gray, making it difficult to proofread color type. Before you print composite proofs, check the Color as black option in the Print dialog box. Now your colored type prints as a readable black, but separates as a spot color.

Color Printer Output

For printing on color printers and slide recorders, you can use any color model you want; you don't need to worry about separations and overlays. You end up with one full-color page or slide. The colors still won't be exactly what you see on screen, but if you use a given output device much, you can create a swatch book for yourself. That way you know how a color you've created will actually come out.

Spot Color Output

For spot color printing—whether on a laser printer or photocopier with color toner, or an offset press with PMS inks—it doesn't really matter what color you see on screen, except to get an idea how your pages look. All that counts is that you have the correct colors assigned to different page elements so they come out on the right overlays.

You can use any color model you want, but the PMS palette is most convenient and the least confusing. You can even modify the CMYK percentages for the PMS colors if you think it gives a better screen representation of what the colors will look like. They'll all come out black on the overlays, anyway; the CMYK percentages have no effect when printing spot-color overlays.

▼ Tip: Use Process Separation for Spot Color Printing

You can get all the percentage tints you want for up to four spot colors by using a process color separation utility such as Publisher's Prism. Use cyan for one spot color, magenta for the second, yellow for a third, and black for the fourth. When the page is separated using a process separation program, you'll get what is effectively four overlays—one for each spot color. If your separation utility lets you do it, change the screen angle for all four process colors to 45 degrees, and make sure it's set up to create knockouts in underlying objects.

What you see on the screen with this method looks nothing like the final output, but it gets around the limitations of the Fill submenu.

▼ Tip: Use PMS Color Names and Numbers

If you're printing using PMS inks, name your colors according to the actual PMS color, chosen from a PMS palette or a printed swatch book. Your commercial printer will be happier with you if the PMS color number you want is specified on the page you give them. Printers have enough to do; they don't need to spend time figuring out color names like "Swamp." There's no reason for you to worry about exactly what CMYK (or HSB, or RGB) values produce that color on screen, except to protect your delicate aesthetic sensibilities.

▼ Tip: Working with Spot Colors on a Monochrome Display

If you're creating a spot color job using a monochrome display, the most important thing is to make sure you have the right colors assigned to the right elements. To that end, choose colors that display very differently in black and white. Don't worry about which color you choose. Just make sure you can distinguish quickly between the different colors on your display. If you're doing a three-color job, for example, choose one color that displays as black, one that displays as dark gray, and one that displays as a dithered pattern. You'll still end up with three black overlays, and you can always change the color names to conform to the previous tip.

This solution is not perfect. If you use percentage fills with the spot colors, for instance, it quickly becomes impossible to distinguish between the different colors on a monochrome monitor. The only really good solution is to buy a color monitor.

▼ Tip: To Replace Every Instance of One Color with a Different Color

If you've ever defined more colors than you want and need to merge two colors (to end up with fewer spot-color overlays, for example), here's what to do. This example shows how to change all the red objects to blue. (This technique is almost identical to the same technique for replacing one paragraph style with another. See the tip "Merging Two Styles" in Chapter 4, *Words*.)

1. Choose "Define colors" from the Element menu (Alt-M, D).
2. Select the color you want to override (Red), and click "Edit."
3. Change the name of the color to the name of the color you intend to merge it with (type "Blue") and click OK. PageMaker displays the prompt: "Change all Red items to Blue?"
4. Click OK. PageMaker merges the two colors.

At this point a peculiar thing sometimes happens (that may or may not be a bug)—the OK button goes gray so it seems you can't leave the dialog box and keep your changes. You can. Just select a color, and you'll be able to click OK or press Enter. Every item that was either color becomes the new, merged color. In our example all the red objects turn into blue objects.

Four-Color Printing

If you're creating a four-color process job, specify your colors by looking at a process color chart, and use the CMYK color model. Do not rely on the screen colors, do not use RGB or HLS and and do not use the Pantone palette. There is no direct relationship between RGB/HLS and CMYK, and there's no such thing as a printed RGB or HLS color chart. You're flying blind with those models. And although most Pantone inks can be simulated using process inks, specifying PMS numbers for CMYK output just puts another layer of uncertainty between you and the printed product.

You're a lot better off specifying the CMYK values yourself rather than letting some separation program do it for you based on mysterious PMS-to-process look-up tables. You may find it easier to remember one number than four numbers, but the paint-by-numbers approach went out with rubber knickers. For some reason even some printers use PMS numbers to spec colors for four-color jobs. We hope they're reading this paragraph. If you're printing CMYK, spec your colors using CMYK.

▼ *Tip: Blacks that are Really Black*

In process printing, you can get richer, more saturated blacks—especially in large black areas—if you add a bit of cyan to the black ink. You can't redefine Black in the PageMaker Colors palette, so create a new color with a name like BlackC or C30K100, and specify 30C/100K. Use this color wherever you have large black areas.

Some people use 30C/30M/30Y/100K, but that's kind of overkill, and it results in a lot of ink on the page, especially if you're printing on uncoated stock. It does have advantages, though; it avoids any problem with trapping (discussed below) when you have black elements on top of another process color.

Overprinting, Knockouts, and Traps

The previous tip—including some of the other colors in your blacks—raises the whole topic of overprinting. This is the area of color work where what you see on the screen differs the most from what comes off the printing press. Using overprinting effectively requires a good deal of visualization, and careful planning. Take a look at the color pages in this book to get an idea of what overprinting does, and why you need to know about it.

The basic question with overprinting is whether colors on top of other colors cause the underlying areas to be "knocked out." Whether you use "Knockouts" in the Options section of the Print dialog box depends on many factors: whether you're printing separations or overlays, whether you want to do the knockouts yourself or let your printer handle them photographically, and whether you want to create *traps* for abutting colors (or again, let your printer do them for you).

First, the bad news: PageMaker doesn't let you specify that a given object on a page should overprint on underlying objects. You can't put two blue circles in front of a yellow box and have one circle overprint while the other is knocked out. (Not without resorting to trickery, at least.) If you want trickery, use the selective knockout techniques demonstrated in the color pages in this book, or print the whole page without knockouts and mark up the overlays telling the printer to knock one out, and leave the other to overprint.

By contrast, both Micrografx Designer and Corel Draw lets you specify overprinting for an object. They even let you specify that the outline of an object—the *stroke*—should overprint, while the fill should not (or vice versa). These controls give you the flexibility to really control your color jobs. In PageMaker, you have to make do with less.

Let's start by discussing overprinting for spot-color overlays, because they're a lot simpler. The basic choice here is whether or not to check the Knockouts option in the Aldus print options dialog box. If you do check "Knockouts," you'll get a hole in overlays where an object of another color is in front. A blue circle in front of a yellow square will result in a circular hole in the yellow overlay. If you don't check "Knockouts," you'll end up with a green circle instead of a blue one off the printing press, because the blue ink will print right on top of the yellow (unless you ask your printer to create the knockouts photographically).

▼ Tip: Knockouts of EPS Graphics

PageMaker can't normally create knockouts underneath placed EPS graphics. Here's how to create knockouts yourself.

1. Maximize PageMaker, maximize the document window, and zoom in to actual size. Then grab a screen shot of the graphic by pressing the Print Screen key.
2. Use a paint program (such as the Paintbrush accessory that comes with Windows) to save the applicable portion of the screen shot as a monochrome bitmap (or bilevel TIFF) file.
3. Place the paint file (you'll notice that nonblack areas are transparent) and align it perfectly with the original graphic.
4. With the paint image selected, click "Paper" in the Colors palette.
5. Select the original image (Ctrl-click through the paint image), and bring it in front of the paint image.

Knockouts sound like just the ticket for printing overlays, but you may not want to use them. Instead, you may want to pass the overlays to the printers without knockouts, marking them up for them so they can create the knockouts using their magical photographic methods. The reason? Trapping.

Getting Trapped

Traps are slight overlaps of abutting colors that ensure the colors meet completely when the printing press is out of register. If you use the Knockouts option, PageMaker creates absolutely perfect holes in underlying areas—just the size and shape of the overlying graphics.

Unfortunately, the real world is not perfect. Printing presses rarely print two colors in perfect register, so you're more than likely to end up with the overlying objects slightly offset from the underlying objects. This results in thin white lines where the colors should abut. It's subtle, but it makes an impression. Think about all those color direct mail pieces you get, for instance. If you look closely, you'll find that a lot of their hokey appearance results from sloppy trapping and registration.

There are a few solutions. You can live with the misregistration; avoid abutting colors; or print with "Knockouts" turned off, mark up the overlays, and ask your printer to knock out the underlying colors, building traps at the same time.

▼ Tip: Trapping LBOs

You can build traps for LBOs and spot color printing by working with power paste (Ctrl-Shift-P) and PageMaker's ruler guides.

1. Pull out ruler guides so that they're 1 point (or whatever distance you feel is appropriate for your trap) inside the selection handles of the LBO you want knocked out.
2. Copy the LBO to the Clipboard.
3. Power paste the copy of the LBO with Ctrl-Shift-P.
4. Snap the upper-left and lower-right selection handles to the ruler guides you positioned in step 1.
5. Fill the LBO with "Paper" and color it the color of the underlying object.
6. Ctrl-click through the Paper-filled LBO to select the original LBO, then press Ctrl-F to bring it to the front.
7. Print the page with the Knockouts option turned off.

For an example of creating traps for spot colors, see the color pages in this book.

▼ Tip: Overprinting Thin Lines

If the only place that your second color overlaps on black is thin lines—for example callout lines pointing to diagrams—you can just skip the knockouts and let the lines overprint on other colors. The eye doesn't notice where they overprint, as it does if the press is out of register and the lines don't land on the knockouts perfectly.

Building traps is a lot easier when you're working with process inks, and there's less chance that you'll need them. If the two abutting colors share any significant percentage of a color (if each of them has at least 30 percent cyan in it, for example), you don't need a trap. If the press is out of register you won't end up with a white line between the two, but a cyan, yellow, or magenta line, which is much less noticeable.

▼ *Tip: Traps for Process Colors*

If two abutting colors don't share a common process color, you can build traps for them pretty easily. Imagine a 50 percent yellow circle on top of a 50 percent magenta square. Here's how to avoid a white line where the two colors abut.

1. Copy and power paste (Ctrl-Shift-P) the yellow circle, so you have two duplicates directly on top of each other.
2. With the front circle selected, change the fill to none, and give it a 2-point line.
3. Define a color with 50Y/50M, and apply it to the new circle.

The line around the circle now has both process colors in it, and it overlaps on the circle, so if the press is out of register you'll get a yellow line or a magenta line between the objects, not a white one. See the color pages in this book for an example of trapping with process colors.

The trapping methods described here are pretty elementary and limited (and they're a pain), but for the time being, at least, they're about the only methods available for creating traps in PageMaker.

CHAPTER 8

Workgroup Publishing

Workgroup publishing is the hot new buzzword in desktop publishing. While it's an important topic, it's also one of the most difficult to discuss definitively. Every publishing operation, and every publishing project, is different. Each requires different procedures. Dozens of factors affect the process of workgroup publishing, so there seems to be an infinite number of exceptions to exceptions to exceptions.

PageMaker 4 addresses the difficulties and opportunities of workgroup publishing with a family of features for controlling links to external source files. These features let you keep track of revisions to the text and graphic files that make up your publication. In this chapter we discuss ways to use those features to achieve the goals of workgroup publishing, and to avoid the pitfalls.

What You're Trying to Achieve

First off, what are you trying to achieve when you build a workgroup publishing system? Simple—you're after seamless, effortless revision control and file transfer. Achieving that goal, however, is not so simple. It involves a complex interplay of people, products, and procedures.

Workgroup publishing systems are not made up of just hardware and software. More than anything, seamless production management results from well thought out procedures for who does what and when. The procedures apply to you (the person making pages), your fellow page makers, and anyone who is supplying you with material—artists, writers, and editors.

On the other hand, your hardware and software system and the capabilities of different components in that system have a direct impact on your procedures. One example: Steve was working on a four-color process publication using QuarkXPress, with illustrations created in Adobe Illustrator 88. Back then, QuarkXPress would color separate placed Illustrator images along with the rest of the elements on a page, so everything looked fine—all you had to do was place the Illustrator EPS files provided by the artists, and separate the whole page into four pieces of film, ready for the printer.

Unfortunately, a tiny technical detail required a complete change in the production cycle. The artists were using Illustrator's Overprint feature to create traps for the color images (see "Getting Trapped" in Chapter 7, *Color*), and that version of QuarkXPress ignored any Illustrator overprint instructions. So the illustrations had to be separated on their own, and stripped into the page film by the printer. Steve had to use dummy versions of the illustrations (provided by the illustrators) for positioning, and type notes to the printer for each.

Four-color process may not be in your future, but this is a good example of how one little technical detail can affect the best-laid plans and publishing procedures. The goal is to set up procedures with all the technical details in mind, so you can just make pages without worrying about those details. Publishing projects have enough details to keep track of without bothering with computers.

What You're Trying to Avoid

Managing the publication process is just as much (or maybe more so) about what you're trying to avoid. The following three scenarios, for instance, are enacted far too often.

- Two or more people making changes to different copies of the same file, so the changes have to be compiled manually
- Using old versions of files, rather than the latest revisions
- Having your only copy of a file destroyed

All of us have had to enter changes manually because two (or more) people made changes to copies of the same file. All of us have had the unpleasant experience of going to imagesetter output only to find that either the pub or one of the source files contained in the pub were not the most up-to-date versions. It's infuriating, and it's well worth setting up procedures to avoid it.

The Fascist Approach Versus the Laissez-Faire Ideal

The kind of procedures we talk about here may sound pretty compulsive. They really stress control rather than the free exchange of material that so often makes a publishing project fun and great. In fact, publishing management procedures are about control. Ole's version of the "who does what and when" line is "who can do what to whom and when." The corporate ideal has always been to set up your group so that they can do whatever they want to whomever they want whenever they want, so every group ends up feeling oppressed by every other group (witness the proliferation of "You want it when?!" cartoons in print shops). We hope that this is not how people want to work in the 1990s, and that networks and cooperation replace hierarchies and competition (we also look forward to Santa Claus visiting every winter).

The goal in any workgroup is to establish procedures that smooth out the normal work flow, while providing back doors that people can dash through when they need to get something done fast. It may be as simple as a writer walking over to the production department and making some changes in a PageMaker file (or looking over a production person's shoulder and telling them what changes to make). Or these exceptions might be procedures in their own right.

When Steve was working for *Publishers Weekly*, everyone had terminals on a big minicomputer-based Atex editorial/production system. Each person had a password and a "queue" of files. Once you sent a file to someone else's queue, you couldn't get at it again unless you had their password.

Of course, everyone knew everybody else's passwords, so they could go into other people's queues and make changes when necessary without having to ask that person to send the file back. That didn't diminish the value of the system, though. Sending a file off to someone else was effectively saying, "I've finished with it for now." People were polite and sensible, and if they had to make changes, they would inform the person whose queue they'd invaded that they'd done so. The production department (editorial had their passwords, too) would often ask an editor to go into the production queue to cut 15 lines in a file, or whatever.

The point is that procedures are necessary, but they can't be cast in stone. People are sick, busy with other things, working on someone else's machine, or (most likely) in meetings, so you're back to the seat of your pants. A big part of workgroup publishing is walking over and talking to the person in the next cubicle, and that will never change (nor would we like it to).

So no matter how up-tight we sound here, remember that we want people to continue doing whatever needs to be done to finish the job. Procedures should help them do that, not hinder them. And once again, the most important procedures in workgroup publishing are also the most important procedures in daily office life: be courteous, thoughtful, understanding, and sensible. Remember that while they're just extras in your movie, you're just an extra in theirs.

Link, Link info, and Link options

PageMaker 4 offers a group of features—Links—that are designed specifically for workgroup publishing. These features provide a lot of flexibility in developing procedures, but they can also open the door to disaster if used injudiciously. With Links, PageMaker keeps track of the external source files that make up your publication. You can direct it to automatically replace the stories and graphics when the source files change, and to notify you before making the replacement.

PageMaker always keeps a copy of a text file in a publication, but graphics are a more complex matter. Graphics over 50K are generally stored outside the publication. PageMaker displays a low-resolution version of the graphic on screen, and sends the linked file to the printer when it's time to print. You can choose to store large graphics inside the publication, but you pay the price in increased file size.

To begin with, you can see where any linked page element came from—its source file—by selecting the object and choosing "Link info" (Alt-M, N) from the Element menu (Figure 8-1).

Figure 8-1
Link info dialog box

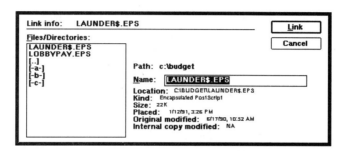

Change your default link options for a specific publication by choosing "Link options" from the Element menu with no objects selected (Figure 8-2). You can set the defaults for all publications by choosing "Link options" with no publication open.

Figure 8-2
Link options:
Defaults dialog box

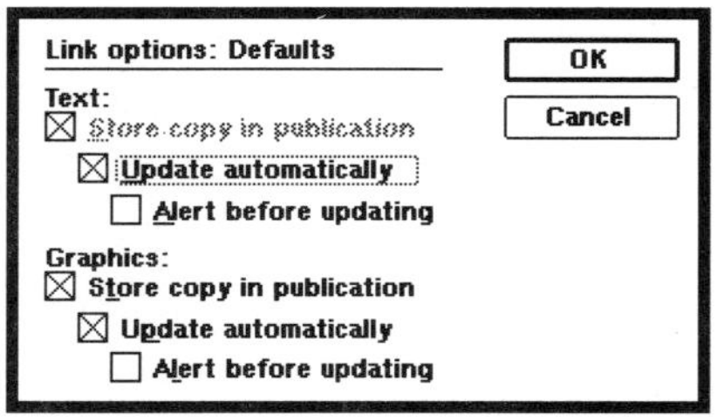

If you check "Update automatically," be sure to check "Alert before updating" or be prepared for some nasty surprises.

You can also set link options for a specific element by selecting the element and then choosing "Link options" from the Element menu. This brings up the Link options dialog box, which varies slightly depending on whether you have a text or graphic object selected (Figure 8-3).

Figure 8-3
Link options dialog boxes for graphic and text objects

```
Link options:    GODZILLA.TIF        [ OK ]
☒ Store copy in publication          [ Cancel ]
  ☐ Update automatically
    ☐ Alert before updating
```

```
Link options:    LIZARDS.RTF         [ OK ]
☒ Store copy in publication          [ Cancel ]
  ☐ Update automatically
    ☐ Alert before updating
```

These options are powerful and useful, but they raise a lot of questions. All of the choices you can make regarding a publication's links affect in a very direct and immediate way who does what and when. If you want PageMaker to automatically replace a file with the latest version every time you open a pub, for instance, you have to make sure that the person working on that source file saves the latest version in the same directory, with the same file name. If they make changes and save the file with a different file name or in a different directory, PageMaker blithely proceeds to use the old version.

You can get an idea of how all the files in a publication are linked, and the status of the files, by choosing "Links" from the File menu (or press Ctrl-Shift-D). The Links dialog box appears (Figure 8-4), showing the file names of all your source files, the pages on which each file appears, the type of file it is, and the file's link status.

The status column (the narrow one on the left) is probably the most important part of the Links dialog box. If it's blank, be happy. That means the external files are the same as the files in the pub (if you're keeping a copy in the pub), and neither has changed since you placed the file (or the item is not linked to an external file).

Question mark. A question mark means that PageMaker can't find the file. If the file's stored externally, locate the file and restore the link.

Plus sign. A plus sign in the status column means the external file has changed (you're not working with the most recent version), and that PageMaker is set to automatically replace the file the next time you

R E A L   W O R L D   C O L O R

Knockouts and Overprinting

The illustrations on these pages demonstrate the use of both spot and process color. To save our publisher money, we're using solid tints of the process colors as spot colors.

The Color Paper and the Fill Paper

When you're printing spot color overlays, Paper-colored objects knock out of everything behind them, whether you have "Knockouts" (in the Print options dialog box) turned on or not. Paper-*filled* objects only knock out of items that are the same color. With "Knockouts" on, everything knocks out of every other color behind it.

What You See

All the colored items you see here are Solid-filled, and colored Cyan, Magenta, or Yellow. The white boxes are a little trickier.

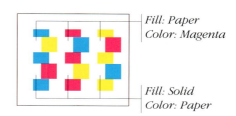

Fill: Paper
Color: Magenta

Fill: Solid
Color: Paper

What You Get

Knockouts off. When you print this illustration with the Knockouts option in the Print dialog box turned off, the overlays look like this (though of course all the overlays would come out of the imagesetter in black). Notice how the colored inks overprint on each other.

Cyan overlay

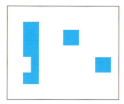

Magenta overlay

Yellow overlay

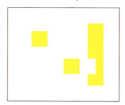

When printed

Knockouts on. Every object knocks out of every different-colored object behind it. None of the colored objects overprints.

Cyan overlay

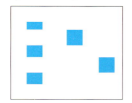

Magenta overlay

Yellow overlay

When printed

R E A L   W O R L D   C O L O R

Selective Knockouts

In this example, we want to knock the colored type out of the background, so it doesn't overprint. The black type, on the other hand, should overprint on the cyan background.

Creating the Knockouts

Copy the text block to the Clipboard, then power-paste (Ctrl-Shift-P) into exactly the same position you copied from. Color the type in the first line "Paper," (or reverse the type—it's the same thing), and then delete the type in the second line.

Send the new text block to the back (Ctrl-B), and then send the black box to the back. The white type beneath the colored type creates a knockout.

What You Get

When you print the overlays, here's what you get (in black, of course).

Cyan overlay

Magenta overlay

Black overlay

If you printed without selective knockouts, it would look like this.

REAL WORLD COLOR

PageMaker and Process Color

You can process separate scanned color images, placed EPS color graphics, and CMYK-specified PageMaker LBOs by transferring your publication to Macintosh PageMaker 4.0 and printing pages to disk as PostScript (use the "for separations" option in the PostScript print options dialog box), and separating the PostScript file with a separation program. Imagesetting service bureaus will often do these steps for you. This page was separated using Aldus PrePrint.

Scanned Images, EPS Graphics, and LBOs

Cyan separation

Magenta separation

Yellow separation

Black separation

Consistent Blacks

If you add a bit of cyan, magenta, and yellow to your blacks, they'll look more consistent where they overprint other colors.

100% Black

100% Black
20% Cyan
20% Magenta
20% Yellow

R E A L W O R L D C O L O R

Building Traps

You can build traps to correct for press misregistration using either spot or process colors. The techniques vary slightly, however, depending on whether you're printing process seps or spot color overlays.

Traps for Spot Colors

To create traps for spot colors, we use selective knockouts, but make the knockouts slightly smaller (a "choke") and the overlapping objects slightly larger (a "spread"). In this example, the cyan and magenta overlays overlap slightly.

Traps for Process Colors

Traps are easier with process colors because you can mix percentages and you don't need traps if abutting colors share some percentage of a process color. The colors here don't have any process color in common, so we had to trap them.

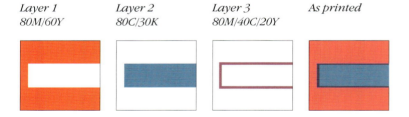

PageMaker Color Tricks

These samples were created entirely in PageMaker and were separated (as spot color overlays) from PageMaker.

WORKGROUP PUBLISHING **399**

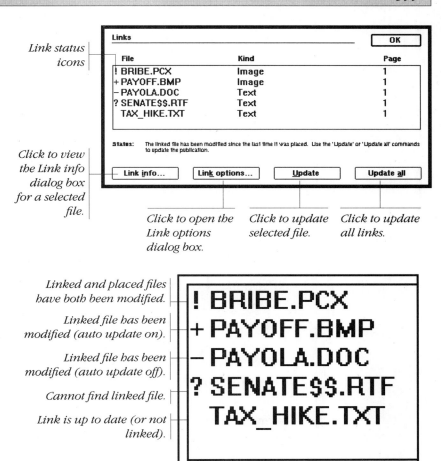

Figure 8-4
Links dialog box

open the publication. You should ask the person responsible for changing the file if their changes need to get into your publication. Sometimes, they've made the changes in error, or they're working on the file for some reason other than inclusion in your publication.

If you haven't made any changes inside the pub, and you know that the external changes are intended for inclusion in your publication, select the file and click "Update" to replace the version of the file in the publication with the most current version of the source file.

Minus sign. A minus sign means that the source file has been changed and that the link options are not set to automatically replace the file in your publication. Follow the procedures shown in the previous paragraph, if necessary.

Exclamation point. An exclamation point is the worst. It means that both the external file and the copy in the publication have changed. Change the link options so that the file is not automatically replaced. Then, find out whether both sets of changes (the changes in the pub and the external changes) need to be included in the publication. If both sets of changes are needed, you'll to have to compile those edits manually. In short, ! = wasted work.

▼ Tip: Use WinWord's Compare Versions

If you use Word for Windows, the Compare Versions command (Utilities menu) provides some help in comparing two versions of a text file and marking areas of change. If a linked file has been marked with an exclamation point, and you want both sets of changes included in the final publication, compare the file using WinWord's Compare Versions command (Figure 8-5). You can open both documents in tiled windows with the areas of changes marked with a revision bar (or some other method that you specify with the Revision Marks command, Utilities menu).

1. Export the version of the text file from PageMaker. Make sure to give the exported file a different name from the modified linked file. If you export the file in Rich Text Format, you'll be able to see more of your format changes. (WinWord won't mark these changes, but its wysiwyg display makes them apparent.) Don't check "Export tags" unless the original file was created for import using style tags.
2. Open both documents and choose "Arrange All" from the Window menu to see both at once.
3. With one window active, choose Compare Versions from the Utilities menu and specify the document in the inactive window. To see changes marked in both windows, repeat this. If you want

Figure 8-5
Comparing document versions with Word for Windows

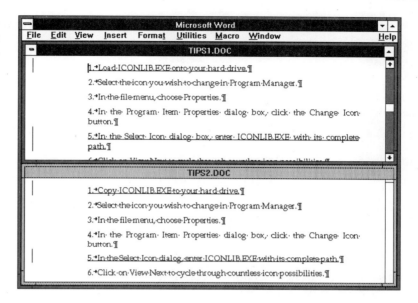

the differences marked in both documents, select the other window and repeat this step.

4. Revision bars mark any paragraphs that have been added or whose text (not formatting) has changed. Unfortunately, there are no markings on moved paragraphs. Merge the changes.

5. Replace the PageMaker story with the new version.

▼ Tip: Using Link info as Replace

You can use the Link info dialog box as an alternate method of replacing text and graphics. The newly linked files need bear no relation to the current file—handy if you've placed a bunch of placeholder graphics and don't want to bother paging through the publication and selecting each one to replace it.

1. Choose the story or graphic you want to replace (you can do this in story view, layout view, or from the Links dialog box).

2. Choose "Link info" from the Element menu (or, if you're in the Links dialog box, press the Link info button).

3. Locate the file you want to replace the currently linked file.
4. Click the Link button. PageMaker replaces the selected file with the file you specified.

▼ *Tip: Link Placeholders for Automatic Replacement*

Because PageMaker links to a filename and filetype, it doesn't matter what's actually in the linked file. You can create an entire dummy publication by placing and linking placeholder files for every graphic and story in the publication, then create the pub automatically once the text and graphics are checked in. This is handy for people doing database publishing of material that changes little in overall shape from publication to publication.

1. Create and name a set of placeholder files. Put them in a directory named PLACHOLD (or anything else that strikes your fancy).
2. Place the placeholder files in PageMaker. Flow the text, and size the graphics as you want. Set the link options for the placeholder files to "Replace automatically." Save the publication. You can save it as a template, so that every time you open it you get an untitled file that you can save under a new filename.
3. Once the actual files you want to use in the publication are ready, give them the same names as the placeholder files, and copy them into PLACHOLD , replacing the originals.
4. Open the publication. PageMaker replaces the original placeholder files with the current files.

Live Files and Dead Files

One important concept with revision control is that of live and dead files. The live files are the current revisions—the ones that will be changed if further revisions are necessary. Dead files are old versions, and electronic versions that you've sent out for review and comments.

The key to workgroup publishing is to make sure there is only one live file for any illustration, story, or pub. That live file might be a story or illustration that's in the pub itself, or it might be an external file that's either linked or has yet to be placed.

You'll often find that when you send out an electronic text file for review or comments, people will insist on editing that dead file with their word processor. Their edits are useless, because there's no automatic way to compile them with other edits into the live file. Talk with them about this, as politely as you can.

▼ Tip: Use Naming System for Source Files

You can simplify the placeholder system even further by developing a standardized shorthand for naming your source files. Code-based naming systems may be hard to learn at first, but quickly become easy to use. The one we use consists of breaking down DOS's eleven-character filenames into segments with a specific function for each:

- Last things first: use the three-letter extension for the file type: .EPS for Encapsulated PostScript, .TIF for Tagged Image File Format, .DOC for Word for Windows (or Microsoft Word). Nothing new here; many applications do this by default.

- Now the beginning. Let the first two characters stand for the project your group is working on: we used RW for this book (*Real World PageMaker*, get it?); your company newsletter could be CN or NL, or whatever. Just be consistent.

- Let the next two characters represent the chapter number for books or issue number for periodicals (01 is January, 12 is December). Use a 0 before the numbers 1 through 9 (you'll see why in a minute).

- Use the next four characters for descriptive purposes.

For example, the source files for chapter one of your soon-to-be best seller, *Handbook for Goldfish Owners*, might be HG01.DOC. The pictures for chapter one might be named as follows: HG01FISH.TIF,

HG01FOOD.EPS, HG01FLOT.PCX, and HG01DEAD.TIF. A newsletter might have file names like NL01LEAD.TXT, NL01NEWS.TXT, NL01MAST.TXT, and so on.

A system likes this lets everyone on the project identify the subject, project, and file format at a single glance. Moreover, it automatically groups files of the same project and issue/chapter for easy copying and directory viewing. For example, to copy all files for your goldfish book into your PLACHOLD directory (see previous tip), you would use a DOS command similar to the following:

copy hg*.* c:\plachold

To only copy the source files for chapter one, you'd enter the following at the DOS prompt:

copy hg01*.* c:\plachold

Now you see why you need leading zeros before the first nine digits: if you tried copying files by typing *HG1*.**, you'd not only copy chapter one, but chapter eleven as well.

Naturally you can use this trick on almost any command from the DOS prompt. Some possibilities: displaying the files for a given project in a directory (*DIR HG*.** in our goldfish example), deleting all project files when a project is finished (*DEL HG*.**, for instance), using a compression utility to archive an entire chapter or project, or "publishing" an entire chapter or project on a peer-to-peer network.

Even point-and-click types (also known as drag-and-droppers) who eschew DOS commands can benefit from this system, since the Windows File Manager displays these files alphabetically, grouped first by project, next by issue or chapter. That makes it easy to shift-click a bunch of files and drag them to the right directory. (For maximum effect, you must have "By Name" selected in File Manager's View menu.)

Of course, this is only one system; you can customize one that's best for your company or publishing group. For example, if you all use the same word processor anyway, you might want to skip the .DOC (or whatever) extension and replace it with something else that's important to your project: author initials, date, number of pages, revision number, just about anything that distinguishes one file from another. What's most important is that everyone uses it consistently.

▼ Tip: Name Publication Files with Version Numbers

Here's another possible naming system. Every time you make a major change to a pub, save it with the same file name, but give each revision a higher version number (MAY01.PM4 for the May newsletter, MAY02.PM4, etc.). You can use letters to indicate subdivisions within a revision level, for example: MAY1A.PM4, and MAY1B.PM4. Then key the primary version numbers to various milestones, like first review, final page proofs, or editorial close. The version you send out for second review might be 2, while 3 might be the final version.

This doesn't work so well in naming source files when you're using PageMaker's links, because PageMaker will still be looking for version 1C when the latest version is 4D. You can use the Link options dialog box and grab the latest version, but it won't happen automatically.

You'll have the same problem if you use this naming convention for your pub files and use the Book command to index several chapters. Your book list may have old files listed, so you'll have to tell PageMaker the names of the latest files (and their order) before you create an index or table of contents.

▼ Tip: Name Publication Files with Dates

Still another system for naming files is to use the date. This is especially helpful for weekly or daily periodicals or publications that change rapidly. To keep files grouped together by date in your directory listings, use the year-month-date-project format: 910917NL.PM4 for the September 17, 1991 newsletter, for example. The numbers are a little hard to read at first, but it keeps everything in chronological order. If you want to group by project or periodical first, move the project code up front: NL911002.PM4 for the newsletter of October 2, 1991.

File Transfer Methods

There are several methods for avoiding the problem of multiple copies—making sure that everyone works on a single, master live file—while having the freedom to move files around between coworkers as needed. The method you use depends on how your workgroup is set up.

Floppy disks. If you're passing around floppies, set up a check-in/check-out system for the floppies, and put each file on a separate floppy. Those are the live files, and only one person can work on them at a time. Nobody can change the file unless they actually have the physical disk in their possession. Nine-tenths of the law and all that. People are free to copy the live files onto their hard disks to make changes (it's actually good practice, because it creates a backup at the same time), but they have to copy it back onto the floppy and return the floppy to get the changes into the production system. Make sure one person is responsible for the floppies, and for copying the revised files onto a hard disk when they come back to Floppy Central.

▼ *Tip: If You've Already Placed It*

If you're working with a floppy check-in system and someone wants to make changes to an already-placed source file, you can just hand them the floppy. If you're using Links, though, it's also a good idea to move the file on your hard disk into a temporary "DEADFILE" directory. That way when you open the pub and look at the Links dialog box, you'll know that a live file is missing.

Alternately, open the source file on your hard disk and make some change (any change) when you hand off the floppy. That way you'll get a plus sign in the Links dialog box, reminding you that something's not right.

Peer-to-Peer Network. If you're using a network like Tops, so people can publish volumes from their machines and mount other people's published volumes, you need a different strategy. Since there's no single, physical object to control the file, copies start to proliferate. Every time someone sends a file to someone else, they're actually copying it. You can get in trouble fast.

One solution is to copy the file to the other person's disk, then move the original into a backup DEADFILE directory. That way it's backed up, but it's also in a place where no one will confuse it with the live file.

The main rule is not to publish your LIVEFILE directory. If a writer or artist wants to make a change to a file you've already received, set it up so they ask you for it, and you send it to them. That way you can delete it from your LIVEFILE directory at the same time, or change it so the Links dialog box shows it's been changed, or whatever. Then when they're done making changes, they can copy it into a temporary transfer directory (call it "INCOMING" or something) that you publish as a volume. You're responsible for moving it into the LIVEFILE directory.

The INCOMING directory works much like the floppy check-in system. People can still make changes to dead files, but they can't get those changes into the production system without the administrator (the person who moves the files) making it happen.

Network with server. If you have a file server on your network, you can have one master live files subdirectory. Anyone can have access to the directory, so everyone works on a single master document. But a problem arises if someone makes changes to a file that you've also changed in PageMaker. The solution, again, is to create an incoming files directory, make sure people inform you when they send an update, and move the update into your live files directory.

Dealing with Text Files

You'll want to use different procedures for managing text and graphics files. Here's an example of a situation where a technical detail affects your procedures: PageMaker always keeps a copy of a placed text file in the pub, and you can change its contents after it's been placed. This is the source of the dreaded exclamation points next to your linked files in the Links dialog box: you've made some edits to a placed story, then a writer comes to you and delivers a revision of that file. You have to replace the story then make all your edits again. And if you've set up any text wraps, corrected for bad line, column, or page breaks, kerned, tracked, or adjusted spacing to make copy fit, you have to start all over.

Once you make edits in a story on the page, you have to consider it as your live file. If writers want to make further changes, you'll have to either give them the pub and let them make the changes in PageMaker, or export the file for them to edit with a word processor—with all the problems of lost formatting. It's hard to say which is worse. Once you've let someone loose in your pub ("But I had to put all those spaces in there to make the line break!"), you can expect to rework the thing quite a bit anyway.

Using Export with Links

When you export a text file created in PageMaker, that exported file becomes the linked file for the story. Any changes made to that source file will be reflected in your pub the next time you open or print it. The Export feature is a wonderful idea, but we find it useful primarily for archiving text files. Because many of the changes you make in PageMaker (kerning, tracking, etc.) aren't included in the exported text file, you're losing a lot of your work when you export and then replace. This problem points out again the importance of getting the copy right before it hits the page. Minor changes are all right, as long as you can make the changes easily in PageMaker and don't have to export or replace the story.

The solution is to get it right in your word processor. You're a lot better off doing the bulk of your copy processing in your word processor and bringing it into PageMaker fully formatted. This is also a nice approach because you can farm a lot of work off on writers and editors. Build style sheets for them (if they're using WordPerfect, Word, or WinWord), and teach them how to use them. They should be specifying what different text elements are, anyway. Styles sheets make it easy for them and you. Otherwise, you may need a production editor to do the copy processing, or if worse comes to worst, you may have to do it yourself. In any case, do your copy processing before the file hits the page.

Dealing with Graphic Files

Controlling versions of graphics files can be tough. You place and link a graphic, then an artist posts a new version. But the new version is larger or smaller, so when you replace (or update the link of) the graphic, it gets resized nonproportionally. You end up having to resize the graphic and sometimes, rebuild your page around it.

The best method to deal with graphic files is to spec the size of illustrations after you've built the pages, and let the artists work to fit. When you can't do that, another alternative is to insist that artists make any changes within the size of the original art. Have them draw a box for the size of the graphic, and work within it.

If at First...

If it seems like we've posed more problems in this chapter than we've suggested solutions, you're right. None of us has ever built a workgroup publishing system that worked flawlessly under the pressures of deadlines, last-minute changes, and workgroups that don't work as groups. We've come close, and the tips here are the best general approaches we've come up with.

When it comes right down to it, the best approaches are those that worked when publishing was done with clay tablets: set up a system for handling the flow of work through the group and adhere to it, and communicate honestly with the other people in the group regarding any problems. Don't build empires. Don't point fingers. Get the job done, figure out where improvements can be made in your process, and refine it. You'll always be refining your process.

CHAPTER 9

How We Made This Book

This chapter comprises a rather lengthy colophon—a bit more than you usually want to know about what went into making a book. In a book about using PageMaker 4 in the real world, though, it seemed appropriate to provide a lengthy, real-world example.

Real World PageMaker 4 was produced, beginning to end, using Aldus PageMaker 4 under Windows and on the Macintosh. We wrote most of the copy in Microsoft Word, again, on both the PC and the Macintosh. Screen shots were made with Tiffany Plus, and cleaned up in PC Paintbrush, Photoshop, and DeskPaint. Other art was created with Corel Draw and Aldus FreeHand. We used TOPS, Batchworks, Recorder, and Launch extensively.

Design

The book was designed by Nancy Sugihara, who sent us a design specification covering most of the text elements and graphic treatments used in the book (but not all; it's almost impossible to create a spec that covers everything for a book that has not yet been finished). We created PageMaker templates and style sheets that conformed to this specification, making slight adjustments here and there to make the design work with PageMaker and conform to a leading grid.

Fonts

We set the book using Bitstream's ITC Garamond family of typefaces (primarily Garamond Light and Bold), with the exception of program listings, which are set in Optima (code listings are generally set in monospaced fonts, but PostScript and other code in this book isn't space-sensitive, so it doesn't matter). Working with the Bitstream fonts was a breeze, and they're gorgeous (though we had to remove almost all the ugly screen fonts and let ATM build them for us on the fly).

Styles

Creating the styles for *Real World PageMaker 4* presented a number of challenges. A-heads, for example, needed to displace an even number of text lines (4 lines, 60 points) to keep ensuing paragraphs on the leading grid—no matter where the A-heads fell on the page. It would be easy to develop separate styles—one to use when the A-head falls at the top of the page, and another for when it falls in the middle of the page—but we wanted to develop one that would work the same way in either case, to prevent problems with last-minute changes. Similarly, the rule above a B head needed to top-align with the top of caps of the body text to its right, though doing that takes the rule off the leading grid. We compensated for this with space above and by specifying invisible rules above the baseline of the paragraph, so that the paragraph would be pushed down a set amount, even if it fell at the top of a text block. (PageMaker ignores space before settings when the paragraph is the first paragraph in a text block.) This way, we could use "Snap to rulers" and "Snap to grid" in production.

Once we'd finished the style sheet, we exported it for use in Microsoft Word, and modified it so it was easy to read and edit on screen and on paper. The one- and two-letter abbreviations at the end of each style name helped us apply styles in Word. We did almost all the styling in Word, then placed the files in PageMaker, where the fully-specified PageMaker styles with the same names took over.

Table 9-1 is a listing of the styles used in this book, with notes on their use. This is the documentation we created at the start of the project for our own use. If you're working on a complex production project, especially with several people involved, you should consider documenting your styles in a similar fashion.

Table 9-1 Styles used in *Real World PageMaker*

Style Name	*Notes*
\<a head,ah\>	Preceded by a \<rule above\> and a \<rule below\> (paragraphs containing a carriage return only). \<rule above\> has a line above set to "None" width to force the \<a head\> down so that succeeding paragraphs align to the grid and observe the 20-point specified baseline-to-baseline from the \<a head\> to the following \<para1\>—even if the \<a head\> falls at the top of the page.
	ITC Garamond Bold Italic, 14/13 (negative lead forces the top of caps to fall the specified 6 points below the preceding \<rule above\>), flush left. The \<rule above\> contains the space above setting (specified as 3-1/2 lines). The baseline of the first line of the \<para1\> following the \<a head\> falls 20 points below the baseline of the last line of the \<a head\>.
\<b head,bh\>	Has a rule above, plus enough space above to force the rule to Top-of-caps-align with the text following. Procedure for working with \<b head\>: flow text down to break just below the \<b head\>, break the text block, then reflow from the grid point just above the \<b head\>'s rule above.
	ITC Garamond Bold 11/13, flush right on an 8-pica width (the companion column), 2p9 space above.

Table 9-1 Styles used in *Real World PageMaker*, continued

Style Name	Notes
<c head>	C heads are local formatting applied to the first sentence of a <para1> (or <para1 plus>). They're preceded by a "plus" style paragraph (<para plus> or <para1 plus>, usually) so that we don't have to make a <para1> style with space above. (local only) ITC Garamond Bold Italic 11/15
<chapter title,ct>	Chapter title. Top of text block aligns to the fifth grid increment. ITC Garamond Light Italic 28/34
<chapter #,cn>	Chapter number. Insert 10 word spaces between each letter (too much to do with the Spacing dialog box, so do it manually or make a key). 11 word spaces between the word "CHAPTER" and the chapter number. Reversed and centered in a black rectangle 1p tall x 26p wide across the text column. ITC Garamond Bold 10/15 (leaded to center vertically in the black rectangle) All caps.
<header left,hl>	Header left. Centered vertically in a 35p3 wide x 1p tall 10% filled, hairline-stroked rectangle. Page number is on a right tab at 2p3, followed by a tab at 2p9, then REAL WORLD PAGEMAKER 4, letterspaced out with 1 word space between each character, two word spaces between words. Spec says "indent r.h. 12pt from folio," but all of the printed samples show 6pt at most. ITC Garamond Light 7/15 (leaded to center vertically in 10% rectangle), on a left tab at 2p9. Page number in 10/15 ITC Garamond Bold, on a right tab at 2p3.

Table 9-1 Styles used in *Real World PageMaker*, continued

Style Name	Notes
\<header right,hr\>	Header right. Centered vertically in a 35p3 wide x 1p tall 10% filled, hairline-stroked rectangle. Page number is on a left tab at 33p, chapter title (letterspaced out with 1 word space between each character, two word spaces between words) on a right tab at 32p6.
	ITC Garamond Light 7/15 (leaded to center vertically in 10% rectangle), on a right-tab at 32p6. Page number in 10/15 ITC Garamond Bold, on a left tab at 33.
\<drop folio,df\>	Drop folio—page numbers for chapter opening pages. These fall 1 grid increment below the bottom of the live area, flush right.
	ITC Garamond Light 10/15, flush right.
\<para,p\>	Paragraph. Has a 1 em (11pt) indent.
	ITC Garamond Light 11/14, justified.
\<para plus,pp\>	Paragraph plus. Same as \<para\>, plus one line space (15pt) below. Use it for paragraphs that fall before \<c head\>s, etc.
\<para1,p1\>	First paragraph. Same as \<para\> but with no first-line indent. Follows \<a head\>s, \<b head\>s, etc.
\<para1 plus,p1p\>	First paragraph plus. Same as \<para1\>, with a line space after. Use it for paragraphs that fall before \<c head\>s, etc.
\<bullet,b\>	Bullet list para. Hanging indent at 22pt from text left margin (which is 9p3—meaning the bullet falls at 10p2, the text at 11p1). Used for l-line bullet list entries, if all or most of the bullet list is made of 1-line entries.
	ITC Garamond Light 11/15, justified.

Table 9-1 Styles used in *Real World PageMaker*, continued

Style Name	Notes
\<bullet plus,bp\>	Bullet list plus. \<bullet\> plus 3pt space after. For use in bullet lists containing multiple-line entries, as dictated by the spec. We'll use this for most of our bullet lists.
\<bullet1,b1\>	Bullet first. First entry in a bullet list. Same as \<bullet\>, with the addition of 7.5pt (½ extra line space above, as specified).
\<bullet1 plus\>	Bullet first plus. Same as \<bullet first\>, plus 3pt space after. Use to begin bullet lists containing multiple-line entries, as in the spec.
\<bullet end,be\>	Bullet end. Same as \<bullet\> or \<bullet plus\> but with "Align to grid" turned on so that the next paragraph will fall back on the grid.
\<list,l\>	Numbered list. All of the \<list\> styles work the same way as the \<bullet\> styles.
\<callout,c\>	Callout. If callouts have a callout rule, a rule goes 3pt right, left, above, or below the callout text, and the callout rule intersects this line (which we'll call a backstop). The callout rule should encounter this line near the horizontal or vertical center of the callout. Callout backstops could be paragraph rules above or below (hairlines) if the callout line comes off the callout horizontally.

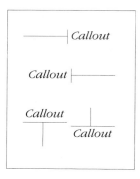
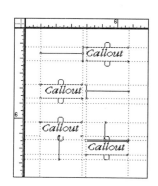

Table 9-1 Styles used in *Real World PageMaker*, continued

Style Name	Notes
<callout,c> (continued)	Callouts sometimes hang out in the companion column with the figure title/number, in which case they're flush right in the companion column (just like the figure number/title). ITC Garamond Light Italic 8/9, flush left
<figure number,fn>	We do figure numbers like this: "Figure 8-4" where "8" is the chapter number and "4" is the number of the figure, counted from the first figure in the chapter. Figure numbers are always followed by the <figure title>, and top aligned with the illustration (1 full grid unit from the last line of text above—which is typically the last line of the paragraph containing the major text reference to the figure). ITC Garamond Bold 9/11, flush right on 8p companion column.
<figure title,ft>	Figure titles are text that describes the figure. Should not be sentences or imperatives, so no period following. If the figure is the Print dialog box, the figure title should be "Print dialog box" but it's fine being creative with figure titles. Figure titles always follow a <figure number>. ITC Garamond Light a 9/11, flush right on 8p companion column.
<rule above,ra>	Rule above. Comes before a <rule below> before an <a head>. Has a "None" weight rule above to force things after the <a head> onto the grid. See <a head> for details.
<rule below,rb>	Comes before an <a head> and just after a <rule above>. See <a head> for details.

Table 9-1 Styles used in *Real World PageMaker*, continued

Style Name	Notes
\<tip,t\>	Starts with an 11-point Zapf Dingbats t (a down arrow). Tips always end with a half-point rule, 7.5 points (one half line space) down from the baseline of the last line of the tip. If a tip end rule style precedes an \<a head\>, drop the rule at the end of the tip to avoid having two rules in a row.
	ITC Garamond Bold Italic 11/15, flush left (hanging indent places text—including second or, god help us, third lines—at 10p—8 points from the dingbat).
\<tip less,tl\>	Same as \<tip\>, but with no space before. Use this when the tip immediately follows another tip (preceding para is \<tip end rule,tr\>), to prevent excessive space in between tips.
\<tip end rule,tr\>	Tip end rule. This para contains only a carriage return, with a paragraph rule attached. Use it at the end of tips, but not when an \<a head\> is immediately following, or at the end of a chapter.
\<table number,tn\>	All tables, like figures, should have table numbers and be treated as if they were illustrations (that is, they can float slightly from their text reference—but, unlike the \<figure number\>, \<table number\> runs across the text column). Tables are numbered "Table 8-1," where "8" is the number of the chapter and "1" is the number of the table, counted from the first table in the chapter. On the same line (in the same style) as the table number, following an en space, there's a table title. Table numbers have 7.5 points space above, per the written spec. The spec also urges that the minimum width of space between columns should be 2p, the maximum, 3p6. There's a paragraph rule below (a hairline), 8 points from the baseline of the table number. 8 points more space below is added, per the written spec.
	ITC Garamond Bold 10/12, flush left.

Table 9-1 Styles used in *Real World PageMaker*, continued

Style Name	Notes
\<table head,th\>	Heads, aligned flush left with each column in the table. \<table head\> has a rule 8 points below its baseline, with an added 4-point space after to push the first table entry down to 12 points below the baseline. ITC Garamond Bold Italic 9/12, flush left with however many columns we need.
\<table,tb\>	Table body. ITC Garamond Light 10/12, flush left in however many columns we need. 12 points of space after each table entry.
\<table end,te\>	Table ends are the same as \<table\>s, but they have a hairline paragraph rule 12 points below their last line's baseline, and they put everything back to align to grid/15 points. ITC Garamond Light 10/12

We tracked all of our styles with the default track "Normal." We used Word space Minimum 95, Desired 100, Maximum 105; and Letter space Minimum 0, Desired 0, and Maximum 20.

Table of Contents

We used PageMaker 4's new TOC features, of course. We had to change the styles for various elements through all the chapters to generate the various lists in the book. First we turned on "Include in table of contents" for the chapter titles, and created the short Contents. Then we turned it on for A-heads and B-heads, and generated the long table of contents. Finally, we turned it off for everything except tips, and generated the tip list.

Index

Once we'd gotten through the production crunch and pages were off to the printer, we went back into the pages to build the index for delivery with bluelines. We created a topic list in Word and imported it into PageMaker. Then we started indexing at the beginning of the book, using the topics we'd imported and adding topics as necessary. We had to take turns working on the same live files, because there's no way to compile two separate topic lists.

Imagesetting

Final page output was at 1270 dpi on Linotronic 300s with RIP IIs and IIIs at Seattle ImageSetting. The color pages were printed to film at 1270 dpi. We printed the files to disk, then took the files to Seattle ImageSetting. There, a capable crew downloaded the files to their imagesetters. While the files were being processed, we drank Pike Place Ale (what else?). We are extremely grateful to Chuck Cantellay, and the staff of SIS for going above and beyond the call of duty, as usual, to help us out.

APPENDIX

Resources

This appendix lists the companies who make products discussed in this book (or at least make them available), sorted alphabetically by company. If you don't know which company made a product, you can either look up the product in the index (you'll find the company name in the text of the book), or scan through this appendix quickly. It's not very long.

An asterisk following a product name indicates that the product is public-domain, freeware, shareware, or whateverware—that it's available through user groups, online services, public-domain software libraries, etc. The addresses and phone numbers for those products and companies are provided merely as a reference. It's generally much easier to go through the underground than it is to get a copy from a harried philanthropist, or revenue-seeking corporation.

Access Softek
Dragnet
Prompt
3204 Adeline Street
Berkeley, CA 94703
415-654-0116

Adobe Systems
Adobe Type Manager
Adobe Illustrator
Font Foundry
Plus Pack
PCSEND
PSDOWN
1585 Charleston Road
PO Box 7900
Mountain View, CA 94039
415-961-4400

Agfa Compugraphic Division
Intellifont for Windows
Type Director
90 Industrial Way
Wilmington, MA 01887
800-873-3668

Anderson Consulting and Software
Tiffany Plus
C-7-3 Cascade Drive
PO Box 40
North Bonneville, WA 98639
509-427-5335
800-733-9633

Bantam Electronic Publishing
Windows 3 Power Tools
666 5th Avenue
New York, NY 10103
800-223-6834

Bitstream
FaceLift
Fontware
215 First Street
Cambridge, MA 02142
617-497-6222
800-522-FONT

Brady Books/Simon & Schuster
Fully Powered Windows
15 Columbus Circle
New York, NY 10023
800-624-0023

Carberry Technology
Express Page
600 Suffolk Street
Lowell, MA 01854
508-970-5358

Computer Support Corporation
Arts & Letters
15926 Midway Road
Dallas, TX 75244
214-661-8960

Corel Systems Corporation
Corel Draw
1600 Carling Ave.
Ottawa, Ontario
Canada K1Z 8R7
613-728-8200

e-Image
Recorder Run*
#106-9830-82 Ave.
Edmonton, AB
Canada T6E 1Y8

Edco Services
Edco Hyphenation Dictionary for Windows
LetrTuck Plus for Windows
PMTracker
12410 North Dale Mabry Highway
Tampa, FL 33618
813-962-7800
800-523-TYPE

Eikon Systems
Scrapbook+
989 East Hillsdale Blvd
Suite 260
Foster City, CA 94404
415-349-4896

Elseware
DataShaper
3201 Fremont
Seattle, WA 98103

Philip B. Eskelin, Jr.
Icondraw*
10007 NE 125th Ln., #4
Kirkland, WA 98034

David Feinleib
RunProg
1430 Mass. Ave. Suite 306-42
Cambridge, MA 02138

Halcyon Software
DoDOT
10297 Cold Harbor Avenue
Cupertino, CA 95014
408-257-0812

hDC Computer Corporation
First Apps
Icon Designer
6742 185th Avenue NE
Redmond, WA 98052
206-885-5550
800-321-4606

Hewlett-Packard Personal Software Division
Type Director
19091 Pruneridge Ave.
Cupertino, CA 95041
800-752-0900

HSC Software
The Graphics Link Plus
1661 Lincoln Blvd
#101
Santa Monica, CA 90404
213-392-8441

InSight Systems
Publisher's Prism
10017 Coach Road
Vienna, VA 22181
703-938-0250

Micrographx
Micrographx Designer
1303 Arapaho
Richardson, TX 75081
214-234-1769

Microsoft Corporation
Microsoft Word
Microsoft Word for Windows
Windows
One Microsoft Way
Redmond, WA 98052-6399
206-882-8080
800-426-9400

Microsoft Press
Windows Companion
Running MS DOS
One Microsoft Way
Redmond, WA 98073-9717
206-882-8080

Peachpit Press
101 Windows Tips
1085 Keith Avenue
Berkeley, CA 94708
415-527-8555

Pinecliffe International (D20)
Dinger*
Woody Leonhard, President
Post Office Drawer 7337
Coal Creek Canyon
Golden, Colorado 80403

Publishing Technologies
BatchWorks
File Organizer
7719 Wood Hollow Drive
Suite 260
Austin, TX 78731
512-346-2835
800-782-8324

QMS
QMS ColorScript
One Magnum Pass
Mobile, AL 36618
205-633-4300 ext. 1253
800-523-2696

Softbridge
Bridge
125 Cambridge Park Drive
Cambrdige, MA 02140
617-576-2257
800-955-9190

David Stafford
Launch*
Kamakura NS Bldg 4-F
Onaricho 4-16
Kamakura, Kanagawa 248
Japan

The Graphics Link Plus
PC Quik-Art
394 South Milledge Ave. #200
Athens, GA 30606
404-543-1779

Wilson WindowWare
Command Post
2701 California Avenue SW
#212
Seattle, WA 98116
206-937-9335

Z-Soft Corporation
SoftType
450 Franklin Road, Suite 100
Marietta, GA 30067
404-428-0008

Zenographics
Superprint
4 Executive Place
#200
Irvine, CA 92715-9976
714-851-6352
800-366-7494

Index

101 Windows Tips, 15
50%, 75%, 200%, 400% views. *See* Page views
About PageMaker, 3, 101, 119
Accenter, 60
Accuracy, 89
Actual size. *See* Page views
Adding pages, 79
Adobe, 19, 22
Adobe Illustrator, 394
Adobe Type Manager (ATM), 19, 22–25, 319, 331, 412
Agfa Compugraphic, 19, 22
Aldus Setup, 3
Algorithmic hyphenation, 214
Alice in Wonderland, 229
Align to grid, 7, 136–137
Alignment, 83, 139–141, 146, 147
Anchored graphics. *See* Inline graphics
Angled margins, 305
ANSI character set, 58, 60, 198, 202
  in Find and Change, 208
Applying colors, 380–382
Asymmetrical layouts, 113
Auto save, 58
Autoflow, 8, 114
Autoleading, 129
  and inline graphics, 299–300
Bad record index, 257–258
Baseline, 127, 129, 131–132
  and paragraph rules, 159
BatchWorks, 51–54
Battleship, 211
Bitmap smoothing, 339
Bitmapped fonts, 17
Bitmapped graphics, 268, 282–285
  importing, 269–270
Bitstream, 19, 157, 331, 412
Blacks, 387
Blank pages, 342
Book printing, 342
Book publication list dialog box, 96
Book tools, 8, 95–98, 219–231
Boxed paragraphs, 301–302
Brightness, 282
Bring to front, 261
Bullets, 135
Cantellay, Chuck, 420
Carberry Technology, 34
Carriage returns
  removing from ASCII text, 240
Cartridges, 354

Centering, 114–115, 139
  inline graphics, 295
Change, 2, 205–208
  automating character styles with, 186–187
  to enter index topics, 208
Character formatting, 4–5, 125, 168–173
  and inline graphics, 295
  importing from WordPerfect, 239
Character sets, 58, 198
Character styles, 186
Cleanup
  recomposition, 256
Clip art, 283
Closing dialog boxes, 68
CMYK, 377
Codes, 185
Collage, 32
Collate, 336
Color, 8
  and placed graphics, 292
  applying, 380–382
  correspondence, 383–384
  defining, 378–379
  display, 383–385
  for custom gray fills, 263
  images, 8
  models, 377
  paper, 382–383
  printers, 8, 376, 383–384
  replacing, 386
  reproduction methods, 376–377
  specifying, 377, 383–384
Color separation, 358
  process separation, 377, 386–387
  spot color overlays, 376, 384–386
Column breaks, 7, 167. *See also* Showing keeps violations
Column guides, 76, 113–116
Combining text blocks, 109–112
Command Post, 38–39
Companion columns, 8, 167, 302
Composites, 384
Compound words, 219
Compressing pub files, 100
Computer Graphics Metafile (CGM), 270–271
Condensing type. *See* Set Width
Consecutive hyphens, 216
Constraining, 70, 83, 121, 266
Contrast, 282

Copies, 335, 348
Corel Draw, 13, 268, 286
Courier, 24
Crashes, 98, 99
Create index, 225
Create TOC, 220
Crop marks, 339
Cropping, 289–292
Cross references, 228–229
Curly quotes, 200
Custom vertical rulers, 132
Database files, 246–250
DataShaper, 248–249
Date, 248
Date and time stamping. *See* Time and date stamping
dBase, 4, 246–248
Decimal tabs, 6, 146–147, 148
Defaults, 66–67
Defining colors, 378–379
Deleting fonts, 20
Diagnostic recomposition, 256
Dictionaries, 2, 6, 212–213
  adding words, 210–211
  and spell checking, 208
  PostScript, 365
  ranked hyphenation, 210
  removing words, 211
Dictionary hyphenation, 214, 218
Dinger, 60, 201
Discretionary hyphen, 201
  before a word, 218
Display master items, 77
DoDOT, 32, 33
Double-page printing, 343–344
Download Now dialog box, 327
Downloadable fonts, 21, 24, 323–330. *See also* Printer fonts
Drop caps, 176–181
Duplex, 338
Edco Systems, 158
Editing text, 1, 198–210
Eikon Systems, 28
Em and en dashes, 200
Em and en spaces, 201
Ems and ens, 105, 201
Encapsulated PostScript (EPS), 273–278
  created by PageMaker, 350
  knockouts of, 388
  nested, and printing problems, 372
Enhanced mode, 15, 16

425

Equations, 237
Errors in PageMaker files, 256
Even/odd pages, 338
Excel, 4, 251–252
Expanding type. *See* Set Width
Exporting text, 255–256
    and Links, 408–409
    special characters, 198
    styles, 196, 197
ExpressPage, 34–35
"Extra" paper sizes, 347
FaceLift, 25–26, 331
Facing pages option, 75
Fast Rules, 339
File formats, 29, 33, 40, 268–273
    and Table editor, 154
File Manager, 36–37
File Organizer, 41–42
File servers, 407
File structure errors, 256
Files
    organization, 96, 394–395, 402–405
    preparation, 64
    transfer methods, 406–407
Fills, 262–265, 380–382
    using EPS graphics, 280
Filters, 3–4, 101, 118–119, 232
    CGM, 270–271
    dBase, 246–248
    graphic, 269–273
    IMA, 272
    Microsoft Word and Word for
      Windows, 232–237
    PageMaker stories, 244–245
    PCX, 269
    PIC, 271–272
    PLT (HPGL), 272
    PNT, 270
    Rich Text Format (RTF), 241–244
    Smart ASCII, 240
    TIFF, 270
    time and date, 253–255
    WordPerfect, 238–239
Financial tabular matter, 148
Find, 2, 205–208
FirstApps, 55, 56–59, 202
Fit in window/world views. *See* Page
  views
Fixed spaces, 201
Floppy disks, 406
FON files, 19
Font Foundry, 19, 24
Font metrics, 318, 334
Font Viewer, 59
Fonts, 17–21, 168
    deleting, 20
    printer, 21, 314–331
    rasterizers, 19–20
    resident, 21
    substitution, 232
    used in this book, 412
Fontware, 19, 27
Footnotes, 148
    importing from Word, 235
Forced justification, 140–141
Foreign language dictionaries, 213
Fractions, 176, 181–182
Fully Powered Windows, 15
Function keys, 71
General Parametrics' VideoShow, 271
Go to page dialog box, 74
Grabber hand, 72
Grammar checking, 208, 209
Graphics, inline, 292–302
Graphics Link Plus, The, 33–34
Graphics resolution, 353
Gray fills, 263
Gray out, 285
Greek text below, 23
Groups, 81, 83, 121, 261
Halcyon Software, 32
Halftone screens, 360–363
    changing with Image Control, 282
Handshake, 353
Hanging indents, 144–146
    and inline graphics, 302
Hanging objects off the page, 340–342
Hard formatting. *See* Local formatting
Harvard Graphics, 268, 270
hDC, 55
hDC Icon Designer, 328
Header, 351–352
Help, 10, 101
Hewlett-Packard, 19
Hewlett-Packard LaserJet, 23, 319,
  321, 324, 353–354
Hidden text, 234, 239
High-resolution, 285
Hopkins, Matthew, 257
Horizontal positioning, 295
Horizontal scaling. *See* Set width
Hyphenation, 2, 201, 213–219
    algorithmic, 214
    and recomposition, 256
    controls, 6
    hyphenation points, 210
    in PageMaker 3, 213
    manual, 214
    preventing, 218–219
Hyphenation dialog box, 215
Hyphenation zone, 216–217
Hyphens, consecutive, 216
Icon Designer, 56
Icondraw, 56, 328
Illustrations, 139
Image Control, 282–284
Image-In, 13
Imagesetting, 347, 420

Importing index entries
    from Word, 227
    from WordPerfect, 239
Importing spreadsheets, 251–252
Importing text, 205, 231–255
    ASCII, 240
    database files, 205, 246–250
    from Microsoft Word and Word for
      Windows, 232–237
    from PageMaker pubs, 244–245
    from WordPerfect, 238–239
    Rich Text Format (RTF), 241–244
    special characters, 198
    spreadsheets, 251–252
    unknown fonts, 232
Include in table of contents, 220
Indents, 139
    hanging, 144–146
    ruler, 146
Indents/tabs dialog box, 6, 142
Indexing, 9, 10, 221–230
    adding a selection quickly, 224
    adding topics, 224
    adding topics with Change, 208
    and styles, 226
    capitalizing entries, 225
    creating entries, 222–224
    creating the index, 225
    editing the index, 227
    formatting the index, 225–226
    importing from Word, 3, 227, 235
    importing topic lists, 223–224
    in this book, 420
    levels, 227
    names, 224
    page ranges, 230
    sorting, 228
    viewing entries, 226
    vs. concordances, 222
    where to keep index, 96
Initial caps, 176–181
Inline graphics, 7, 259, 292–302
    importing from Word, 236
    with time and date stamping, 255
Inner Media, 32
Inside out text wrap, 306–307
InSight Systems, 358, 376
Intellifont, 27, 331
Job Timeout, 351
Justification, 6, 141, 155–157
Keeping paragraphs together, 7,
  164–166
Kerning, 5, 173–176
    and tracking, 158
    approach in PageMaker 4, 175–176
    range, 5
Key-click combinations, 124, 206
Keyboard shortcuts, 45, 64, 67–
  68, 71, 123–124

INDEX 427

for character formatting, 169
in Story editor, 205
kerning, 175
paragraph alignment, 139
selecting tools with, 71
to apply styles, 189–190
turning pages, 74
Knockouts, 340, 387–389
Ladders (of hyphens), 216
LaserJet. *See* Hewlett-Packard LaserJet
Launch, 53–54
Launching PageMaker, 65
Layers, 82, 260–261
and inline graphics, 294
and paragraph rules, 162
Layout view, 68
LBOs, 262
constraining, 266
Leaders. *See* Tab leaders
Leading, 4, 126–129
and inline graphics, 297–302
Leading grids, 7, 131–139
and inline graphics, 299–300
in this book, 412
Left alignment, 139
Letterspacing, 155–157
Lewis Carroll, 229
Line break. *See* New-line character
Lines, 262–265
precise positioning, 264–265
weights and styles, 262
Links, 10, 396–402
Linotype, 22
Lists, 144. *See also* Hanging indents
Live area, 76
Local formatting, 2, 184–188
and exported text, 256
Lotus 1-2-3, 4, 251–252, 271
Lotus Freelance, 270
Macros, 43–53. *See also* Recorder macros
autoexecuting, 47
loading automatically, 45
Magic stretch, 287–289
Manual hyphenation, 214
Margins, 76
and Word, 237
angled, 305
irregular, 114
printer, 351
Master pages, 8, 76, 77–78, 86, 92
and text wrap, 77
Measurement increments, 86, 105
Memory, 15, 59, 70
printer, 353
Memory Viewer, 59
Micrografx, 311, 333
Micrografx Designer, 13, 268

Microsoft Word, 2–3. *See also* Word for Windows
importing from, 232–237
Mini-revert, 100
Mini-save, 99
Mirror, 359, 363
Monochrome display, 385
Monotype, 22
Moving
page elements, 82–84
through text, 122–124
through the publication, 74–75
Multitasking, 16
Negative, 284, 359, 364
Networks, 406–407
New-line character, 6, 141
in Table Editor, 155
in tabular matter, 143–144
Next style, 6
Nimbus Q, 27, 331
Nonbreaking characters, 219
Nonbreaking space, 218
Normal, 285
Numbering pages. *See* Page numbering
Numbers button, 77
Object-oriented graphics, 268, 270–286
Orphans. *See* Widows and orphans
OS/2, 22
Other people's pages, 100
Outline fonts, 18
Outline text, 366
Overlays and separations, 378
Overprinting, 387–389, 390
with Illustrator and QuarkXPress, 394
Overset text, 3
Page breaks, 3, 7, 167. *See also* Showing keeps violations
from Word, 237
Page Down, 68
Page icons, 72
Page numbering, 10, 77–79, 97–98
automatic, 8
prefix, 78
renumbering book publications, 97–98
Page orientation, 76, 348
Page range, 336
Page setup dialog box, 75–77
Page size, 76
Page Up, 68
Page views, 72–75
and rulers, 132
PageAhead, 249–250
PageMaker 3, 257
PageMaker archaeology, 101
Paintbrush, 30, 269
Pantone Matching System (PMS), 8,

376, 377, 383, 385
Paper (color vs. fill), 382–383
Paper fill, 262
Paper size, 347
Paper source, 347
Paragraph and character formatting, 125–126
and styles, 186
Paragraph formatting, 5–7
and inline graphics, 295
importing from Word, 234
importing from WordPerfect, 239
spacing, 155
Paragraph indents, 139
Paragraph rules, 5, 159–164
importing from Word, 234
used in this book, 412
Paragraph specifications dialog box, 125
Paste, 9–10, 90, 267
Patterns, 262
PC magazine, 14
PCSEND, 371
PCX filter, 269
Percentage scaling, 286–287
Personal Publishing, 14
PFM files, 318
PIC files, 271–272
Pike Place Ale, 420
Place, 92
Place guns, 79, 93, 118
Placeholders, 402
Placing graphics, 267, 278–280
Placing text. *See* Importing text
PLT (HPGL), importing, 272
Plus Pack, 24
PM Tracker, 158
PNT filter, 270
Pointer tool, 72
PostScript, 322, 325, 333, 349–353, 363–367. *See also* Encapsulated PostScript (EPS)
header, 351–352
printing to disk, 355
PostScript Type 1, 27
Power paste, 10, 267
and master page items, 77
Preferences, 66–67, 156
dialog box, 23
Preventing word breaks and hyphenation, 218–219
Print blank pages, 342
Print entire book, 8, 96, 342
Print Manager, 26
Print Screen, 30
Print spooler, 26
Printer fonts, 21, 59, 314–331. *See also* Downloadable fonts

Printer's points, 360
Printing
   outside the page area, 255, 340–342
   problems, 369–372
   two pages on one sheet, 343–344
Procedures, 395–396
Program Item Properties dialog box, 55
Program Manager, 3
Prompt, 39–40
Proportional leading, 127, 129–131
Proportional scaling, 266, 286–287
PSDOWN, 329, 370
PSSEND, 329
Publication window, 68–69
Publisher's Paintbrush, 13
Publisher's Prism, 358–363, 376
QMS ColorScript, 8
Quotation marks, 200
QwikSymbol, 60
RAM. *See* Memory
RAM disks, 99
Range kerning, 174
Raster fonts. *See* Bitmapped fonts
Rasterizers, 19–20, 331. *See also*
   Adobe Type Manager (ATM), FaceLift,
   SuperPrint
Recompose, 256, 313
Recorder macros, 44–48, 67–68
   orphan-killing, 165
   to apply styles, 190
   to create fractions, 182
   to select lines and fills, 263
   to spell check selected words, 212
   to store special characters, 202
Recorder Run, 48–50
Red, Green, Blue (RGB), 377
Redrawing the screen, 293
Registration marks, 341
Removing pages, 79
Repeating graphics, 297
Replacing, 95
   automatic, 10
   graphics, 280–282
   tables of contents, 221
   text, 120
   with Link Info, 401–402
Replacing colors, 386
Rereading WIN.INI, 317
Resident fonts, 21
Resolution, and magic stretch, 287–288
Reverse order printing, 336
Revert, 99–100
Rich Text Format (RTF), 3, 185
   for export to Word for Windows, 233
   importing, 241–244
Right alignment, 139, 146
RIX, 257–258
Roman 8 character set, 198
Rotation. *See also* Text rotation

and hanging objects, 342
of pages with Prism, 359
RTF. *See* Rich Text Format (RTF)
Ruler guides, 83, 85, 89
   front and back, 67
Rulers, 84
   custom vertical, 132, 138
Rules. *See* Paragraph rules
Running heads, 76
Running MS-DOS, 14
RunProg, 55–56
Save as, 100, 371
Saving, 98–100
Scaling pages, 337, 360
Scaling graphics, 286–289
   line weights, 267
   proportionally, 266
ScrapBook+, 28–30
Screen angle and frequency, 282, 360
Screen capture, 30–33
Screen fonts, 19–23, 59
   and tracking values, 158
Screen shots, 284
Scrolling, 72
Search. *See* Find; Change
Seattle ImageSetting, 420
See and see also, 228–229
Select all, 79, 124
Selecting, 79–82
   extending with Shift key, 81
   inline graphics, 293–295
   paragraphs, 126
   text, 122–125
   through layers, 82, 261
   words, 126
Send to back, 261
Set width, 4, 158, 169
   importing from Word, 234
Setup. *See* Aldus Setup
Setup (printer), 346
Shaded paragraphs, 301–302
Showing keeps violations, 7, 166
Showing loose/tight lines, 7, 156
Side-by-side page printing, 343–344
Sizing graphics. *See* Scaling graphics
Slugs, 127
   and inline graphics, 299–300
Small caps, 4, 169
Snap to Guides and Snap to
   Rulers, 88, 132, 138
Soft fonts. *See* Downloadable
   fonts; Printer fonts
SoftType, 19
Space Before and Space
   After, 128, 412
Spacing dialog box, 6, 155–157
Special characters, 2, 59, 60, 198–202
   in dialog boxes, 207
   in indexes, 225

nonbreaking, 219
Specific-printer dialog box, 315
Speedo fonts, 25
Spell checking, 2, 208–213
   grammar checking, 209
   selected word, 212
Spot color tints, 381
Spot colors. *See* Color separation: spot
   color overlays
Spreadsheets, 251–252
   and Table Editor, 252
Stacked hyphens, 216
Standard mode, 16
Start page # text edit box, 77
Startup directory, 65
Startup page, 364
Step-and-repeat duplication, 10, 91
Stories, 106–112
   exporting all, 255
   importing, 244–245
Story editor, 1–2, 69, 103, 202–213
   and rotated text blocks, 122
Styles, 184–198
   and bad record index, 257
   and indexes, 226
   and local formatting, 187–188
   and tags in ASCII text, 241
   applying, 189
   based on and next, 191–192
   copying between pubs, 195
   creating and editing, 190
   defined, 184
   exporting, 196, 197
   importing from Word, 233, 235
   importing from word processors, 195
   importing from WordPerfect, 238
   in tables of contents, 220
   merging, 192–195
   next style, 6
   paragraph and character formatting, 186
   printing, 196–197
   removing default, 67
   story view style bar, 2
   used in this book, 412–419
Styles palette, 189–190
Sub- and superscript, 4, 169
   and drop caps, 179–181
SuperPrint, 26–27, 331, 376
SuperQueue, 27
Swiss grids, 113
Symbol, 201
Sysedit, 25, 42
System requirements, 15
Tab action pop-up menu, 142–143
Tab leaders, 6, 148–149
Table Editor, 11, 151–155
   and spreadsheets, 252
Tables from Microsoft Word, 236

Tables of contents, 9, 10, 220–221
 from Microsoft Word, 3, 236
 and page numbers, 78
 and styles, 220
 from WordPerfect, 239
 in this book, 419–420
Tabs, 6, 142–150
 and hanging indents, 144
 and imported worksheets, 252
 and spaces in ASCII files, 240
 decimal. *See* Decimal tabs
 selecting, 142
Tags, 185
 and exported text, 255
 in ASCII text files, 241
Target printer, 64, 312
 and magic stretch, 289
Temporary files, 99
Text blocks, 2, 106
 and paragraph rules, 161
 creating, 116–118
 moving and resizing, 120–121
 moving through, 122–124
 rotating, 122
 threaded, 80
 vanishing, 119–120
Text filters. *See* Filters
Text flow. *See* Autoflow
Text import. *See* Importing text
Text rotation, 2, 122
Text wrap, 302–307
 and drop caps, 177
 and inline graphics, 294
 and paragraph rules, 162
 around master items, 8, 77, 259
Thin spaces, 201
 aligning footnotes in tabular
 matter, 148
Thumbnails, 338

TIFF images, 32
 and printing problems, 372
 color, 8
 importing, 270
Tiffany Plus, 32–33
Tiling, 342
Time and date stamping, 4, 253–255
Timeout, 351, 372
Tints, 280
TOC and index prefix text edit box, 78
Toolbox, 70–72
Top of caps leading, 127, 129–131
Tracking, 5, 157–158, 175
Transparency, 260–261, 268
Traps, 387–391
 with Illustrator and QuarkXPress, 394
Troubleshooting, 101
 printing, 369–372
TrueType, 21
Turning pages, 74–75
Two-up printing, 343–344
Type 1 and Type 3 typefaces, 22
Type Director, 19
Type formatting. *See* Character
 Formatting; Paragraph formatting
Type options, 4, 169–173
 and drop caps, 179
Type size, 4
Type specifications dialog box, 125, 168
URW, 27
US character set, 198
Values, importing from spread-
 sheets, 251
Vanishing point, 286
Vector fonts in CGM files, 271
Vector text above, 23
Vertical bars (importing from
 Word), 234

VGA, 31
VideoShow, 271
Viewing index entries, 226
Views. *See* Page views
Virtual memory, 15
VM error, 370
White-out boxes, 261
Widows and orphans, 7, 164–166
WIN.INI, 314–316
 and downloaded fonts, 24–25
 and value formats, 252
 load= lines, 46, 65
 reorganizing, 317
 run= lines, 65
Windows Companion, 15
Windows Control Panel, 19, 317
Windows metafiles, 272
 and Table Editor, 11, 154
Windows Power Tools, 15
Windowshades, 2
WinWord. *See* Word for Windows
Witchefinder General, 257
Word breaks, preventing, 218–219
Word for Windows, 2, 3, 60, 127
 comparing file versions with, 400
 importing from, 232–237
Word spacing, 155–157. *See also*
 Spacing dialog box
WordPerfect, 3, 238–239
Work Sets, 55, 59
Workgroup publishing, 393
Wrap. *See* Text Wrap
X-ref override options, 229
Zapf Dingbats, 198, 201
Zenographics, 376
Zero point, 88
Zooming, 72–74. *See also* Page views
ZSoft, 19

Calling All Monsters

Just nailed a stack of pages and need to bellow in triumph? Want to share your latest face-melting PageMaker tips and tricks? Got a PageMaker-related product you'd like us to know (and talk) about? Enraged because something in this book didn't work? We'd love to hear from you. Just drop us a line at one of the following addresses.

Open House
4021 Aurora Avenue North
Seattle, WA 98103

Steve
MCI Mail: 252-2575
CompuServe: 72260,3100
America Online: Sroth

Ole
CompuServe: Visit Dr. Kvern's Office in the Aldus forum. Send messages and files to 76702,446 (Aldus account), messages only to 76636,2535 (personal)
America Online: olav kvern

Jesse and Scott
CompuServe: 71337,2052
MCI Mail: computhink